"A SPELLBINDER . . .

Starting with the excitement of his early Colorado days during the gold rush, when his Sunday School teacher was Texas Guinan, he charms and chills the reader with his adventures: in Palestine with Allenby; as the first newsman in post-war Revolutionary Germany; in the desert with T. E. Lawrence, Lawrence of Arabia . . ."
Publishers Weekly

"To read this memoir is to skim the highpoints of 20th century history as seen by a questing American always straining to discover what lay beyond the mountain. World figures pass through these pages from Presidents and Prime Ministers to dictators and explorers."
John Barkham Reviews

"The number of things Thomas did first is staggering. . . . Thomas' story is seductive, charmingly told, and his enthusiasm for life is catching."
United Press International

Good Evening Everybody

From Cripple Creek to Samarkand

by LOWELL THOMAS

AVON
PUBLISHERS OF BARD, CAMELOT AND DISCUS BOOKS

AVON BOOKS
A division of
The Hearst Corporation
959 Eighth Avenue
New York, New York 10019

First Avon Printing, December, 1977

to Anne and David

Contents

Sweet to ride forth at evening from the wells,
When shadows pass gigantic on the sand,
And softly through the silence beat the bells
Along the golden road to Samarkand.

—JAMES ELROY FLECKER, 1884–1915

Foreword:

How I Started All This Reminiscing

> When I look over and see Lowell Thomas sitting
> there, I have to believe in eternity.
>
> —AL CAPP

ALTHOUGH I have never brooded about "time's winged
chariot hurrying near," I am philosophical enough
to be aware that it's back there somewhere, gaining, and
still so many things to do! As I sit down finally to tackle
this project, I wonder if it isn't too late. Do I really want
to squander these precious days—when I could be *living*
my life—in the static business of writing about it?

And what about the mystery of memory, all those years
that have slipped through the present now streaming
away into a darkening past? Can I really be sure of the
things I remember? Can any man sort out his personal
history—the kaleidoscopic parade of faces, the shifting
settings, the tangled skein of episode—and hope to restage
it in the precise patterns of his life as it really happened?

Not I. The best I can promise is that nothing here will
be invented, that what appears is what, at this moment,
I best remember as yesterday's truth.

And finally, among these cautionary notes to the
reader—and perhaps you have already perceived that
"notes" is exactly what these preliminary musings are—
I must warn that this book will be neither a confession of
dark secrets nor the personal philosophy of an aging
oracle. I am not an oracle; age has given me only enough
wisdom to reserve exposure of my inner soul to God and

my wife. Anyone hoping for a peek at it in these pages is going to be disappointed.

Allenby in Palestine near the end of World War I, having brought true the West's thousand-year-old dream by wresting Jerusalem from the Turks, received a delegation of quarreling Greek Orthodox monks, Catholics, Copts and Nestorians. Each was convinced it should have sole charge of the Shrine of the Holy Sepulcher. Each sought Allenby's support. But he, a soldier, not a magistrate, sent them away with a penetrating question: "Who am I to set the world aright?"

Nor do I have any deep thoughts on the meaning of life to offer, or cures for the world's ills. No prescriptions, preachings or panaceas here, only some recollections of the excitement and fun I've been lucky enough to have had over the years, and stories about people I've known, most of them interesting, some merely famous. Anyway, as an old Turkish proverb says, books impart knowledge; only travel imparts wisdom.

And now we come down to it, the fact that my only real claim to the reader's attention may be as a traveler. Once, standing near the top of the Spanish Steps in Rome, I was approached by three elderly ladies, clearly American tourists. One of them recognized me and immediately exclaimed, "Lowell Thomas, don't you ever go home?"

I do. But it is also true that I've long lost track of the number of times I've been around the world or crossed the equator or flown over the North and South poles. Those who worry about such things calculate that since my first flight in 1917 I have logged more passenger miles than any man who ever lived. My epigraph, I suppose, could be the words of Xenophon, disciple of Socrates, describing himself as he leads a Greek mercenary army wandering hither and yon across Asia Minor: *"Enteuthen Exelaunei"* —"From here he proceeded to . . ."

Why, why this endless prowling of the earth's farthest reaches, this urge to see what lies beyond the horizon, and beyond that? It tugs at me still. I can't say for sure, but growing up on a mountaintop may have had a lot to do with it.

Cripple Creek, at the heart of the Colorado Rockies goldfields, was a marvelously appealing place to be a boy at the turn of the century—there were wild burros to break, abandoned mine shafts and tunnels to crawl through, rollicking celebrations of gold strikes, periodic shootings and even runaway trains. But best of all, to live at an elevation above ten thousand feet is to gain some special awareness of the world's breadth, and to be lured by its distances. From our mountain we could see the distant snowy peaks of the Sangre de Cristo range, and I don't remember a time when I wasn't yearning to find out what lay beyond their farther slopes.

Growing up, I worked at nearly every job to be had in a booming mining camp and came to know men who had panned and dug and prayed for gold from the Klondike to the Transvaal. They were a special breed, those men, part dreamer, part cynic, ready to follow their shining vision anywhere, but drawn as much by the quest itself as by any real hope of striking it rich. They held me spellbound with their tales of other lands, other gold camps.

Finally there was my father, a mining surgeon whose thirst for knowledge was unlimited and never appeased. He was intrigued by every aspect of human behavior and achievement—those were his horizons—and in *his* endless studies he followed along trails blazed by the great historians, archaeologists, scientists and poets. In 1951, when he was in his mid-eighties, he was still at it, sending us a little note from England to the effect that he had just signed up for some graduate courses at Oxford. Well, his influence was deep and lasting. He roused in me an abiding curiosity about this planet we live on, and I have spent a lifetime trying to see as much of it as I could.

And so I became a traveler—*Enteuthen Exelaunei*—to places like Afghanistan and New Guinea, to the Andes, the Himalayas, the Arctic and the Antarctic. Those are not the usual tourist haunts, you will agree. I have never gone anywhere as a tourist. My travels have turned out to be a continuous search for the raw materials of a good yarn, the films and books and talks that have enabled me to invite armchair travelers along on the journey. If you're bound to travel the Golden Road to Samarkand, no matter what, that's a happy way to make a living.

I remember a sign in the Tokyo railroad station of many years ago. No doubt intended to reassure foreign visitors, it proclaimed in proud English: "Baggage sent in all directions." So far I seem to be approaching these rambling reminiscences in the same way. I began by trying to explain

—perhaps to myself—how, having long resisted some misguided urgings to write something about my life, I now find myself doing it. Then I, too, went off in all directions.

Now, to get back to the starting point, I wonder whether all this self-communing didn't begin with my longtime radio colleague, Hans von Kaltenborn. "Lowell," he said to me not long before he died, "when the ladies quit taking an interest in me, I decided I'd reached the age of reflection and began writing my memoirs. Now you're in the same predicament. Quit gallivanting around the world! Settle in somewhere and write yours."

I thought about that. I particularly thought about it in the context of something Lowell, Jr., said near the end of our expedition to Tibet in 1949. It had been a magnificent adventure. We were only the seventh and eighth Americans ever to visit that all but inaccessible land in the high Himalayas, the first to make films of the Dalai Lama, its young ruler, and of the faces and landscapes of his mysterious kingdom. Lowell, Jr., has told the whole story, the good part and the bad, in his book, *Out of This World, A Journey to Tibet*.

The bad part began on the journey out. As motorized transport, and even bicycles and carts, were forbidden in Tibet, we were departing as we had come, our caravan crossing the Himalayas on a string of plodding horses, mules and yaks. Then I made the mistake of asking to ride one of the high-spirited, half-broken horses being led out by one of our Tibetan guides for sale in India. For a day and a half my riding experience as a young man in the Colorado Rockies stood me in good stead. Then, in late afternoon, I noticed some intriguing colored rock strata and dismounted to take a few samples. Foolishly, I neglected to have anyone hold my horse's head, which was necessary, while I climbed back on.

I can still see the wicked gleam in his eye as he wheeled and caught me, one foot in the stirrup, then reared. I went flying through the air and out over the trail's edge, landing on a distant boulder, on the loose rocks I had stuffed into the pocket of my windbreaker. I felt all that, then lost consciousness.

Young Lowell was bending over me when I came to. We learned later that my hip was broken in eight places. And there we were at an altitude of seventeen thousand feet, so that it grew bitterly cold as darkness came on, and hundreds of miles from the nearest doctor. As Lowell wrapped me in blankets, then held me in his arms to keep me from breaking apart still more as my bones shook with cold and a fever that came on swiftly with shock and exposure, I had some reason to believe that, at age fifty-seven, I was embarked on my final adventure.

Lowell took charge. A folding army cot was converted to a litter and the Tibetans grabbed hold. We covered four arduous miles that first night, to the shelter of a tiny village, then moved on. For the next twenty days those rugged men, peasants, monks, and nuns, too, carried me across the Himalayas, across unbridged streams and over narrow trails that fell away to eternity, toward medical help and safety on the far side of those gaunt, giant mountains that surrounded us. I don't remember all of it. I seemed to be either fainting with pain or delirious with fever. But I do remember young Lowell's determination to get me out alive.

And it was near the end of that harrowing journey, after we had finally reached an airfield and were flying to Calcutta, that he asked me to consider setting down my life story. "I'd like to read it," he said simply. "I'd want any children I have to read it." And I promised that if I got back to civilization in one piece I would do it.

Well, get back we did. And though one doctor said I might never walk again without crutches, I fooled them, too, and nine months later was glacier skiing in Alaska.

And, in fact, something strange began happening to me. Until then, adventure and movement—some new excitement every day—had not only been an indispensable part of my life, it had been my *entire* life. Now that drive seemed tempered by some first subtle stirrings of reflective memory, something I hadn't conceived possible. "Myself when young," sang Omar Khayyám, and I came to understand its deeper meaning as I was drawn back into my past, as I looked back over the years with nostalgia, humor and, occasionally, surprise.

But still the years slipped by and I hadn't begun the writing. I had long-standing commitments and, out of long habit, fell into new ones. My nightly news program, the longest continuous run in the history of broadcasting, took hours of preparation. I offered myself all kinds of excuses. Then, not long ago, at a Dutch Treat luncheon, speaker Al Capp turned my way and said, "When I look over and see Lowell Thomas sitting there, I have to believe in eternity." The audience laughed appreciatively, as did I.

But a few days later I began working on these memoirs. To save time I taped everything of importance I could recollect and, of course, at my age, almost every memory inspires another. Eventually I needed the help of my friend, Lawrence Elliott, who edited a manuscript of 700,000 words to a publishable length. He rewrote in a few words many of the episodes that were difficult to condense. So, Larry Elliott deserves much credit, and I want to express my gratitude in this inadequate way.

L.T.

Quaker Hill,
Pawling, N.Y.

1.
Gold in the Streets

Well, boys, this sure is some cripple creek.
—LEVI WELTY

THE first time it ever occurred to me that I might have gained a certain modest prominence was in the 1920s when someone sent me a snapshot of a large road sign that said:

Greenville
Home of
ANNIE OAKLEY
and
LOWELL THOMAS

Greenville is the seat of Darke County, Ohio, and Annie and I were actually born nearby, I at the village, Woodington. By the time I arrived on the scene, April 6, 1892, Annie had shaken the dust of frontier Ohio from her petite boots and become the sharpshooting star of Buffalo Bill's Wild West Show. At just about that time, in fact, Buffalo Bill Cody had taken his troupe to London, where another visitor, the Grand Duke Michael of Imperial Russia, had come to choose a bride from among Queen Victoria's granddaughters. The Grand Duke was a man who prided himself on his skill with a rifle and, doubtless thinking to have some sport with the rustic little American girl, challenged Annie to a match. It was a bad mistake. While

Michael was missing fourteen of his fifty shots, Annie plunked forty-seven bull's-eyes, and it is said the consequent humiliation drove Michael all the way back to St. Petersburg—still single.

So, as you can see, I bask in reflected glory on that Greenville road sign. While Annie Oakley may have changed the course of history, it's a claim no one can make for me.

My parents were both country schoolteachers, working to put by enough money so my father could go on to a medical college. Our house was a two-family affair, and many years later, after I'd begun my regular evening broadcasts, I heard from the lady who had lived in the other half. She wrote to explain how she'd always known I would wind up on the stage or making speeches or something of that sort, because I created such a yowling uproar after I was born.

The Thomases, and the Waggoners, who were my mother's people, were both of English and Dutch descent and came to this new world in the 1600s. None seems to have attained either fame or great fortune, but they were all part of the authentic American experience—pioneers and homesteaders. At least one great-great-grandfather served with Washington, and another was ambushed by Indians. Samuel Thomas, born in 1690, and an early settler in Montgomery Township, Pennsylvania, is the earliest ancestor whom I can fix in history. He also appears to have come closest to glory—but only through marriage. His wife's sister, Sarah Morgan, married one Squire Boone and became the mother of the great trailblazer, Daniel Boone. It was Samuel Thomas's son, Daniel, who moved our branch of the family down the Ohio River to Darke County.

The Waggoners, meanwhile, having received a grant of land from William Penn, remained in Pennsylvania until 1795, then traveled west to Cincinnati, a frontier outpost at that time. Jonathon Waggoner moved on from there, staking out a section of land, six hundred and forty acres, in Darke County. The deed of ownership, now among my most precious possessions, was signed by President John Quincy Adams and turned over to Jonathon in 1825. Not long afterward, meaning to dispose of some land he still owned in Pennsylvania, he set out on foot for the old homestead, near Reading. And somewhere along that dark and forested route he was beset by an Indian band and killed. His widow lived to be eighty-eight, running the farm and raising ten fine children.

It is said that all the Darke County Waggoners were good solid farming people, proud of their land and their horses, and that Jonathon's eldest son, William, was the best farmer of all. His son, also named Jonathon, was born in 1833 and lived on into my own lifetime, and I remember him vividly. He had married Emmeline Throp, and of their eight children the sixth was my mother, Harriet Wagner, as the name had come to be spelled, born January 19, 1869.

A few years earlier, a union soldier from Darke County named David Thomas, recently released from the dread Confederate prisoner-of-war camp at Andersonville, Georgia, married an Indiana girl, Pheriba Jackson. Their son, Harry George, was born on May 30, 1869, and became a schoolmate of Harriet Wagner. Harry was a natural student, hungry to learn, and when he had learned all he could in the country schools of Darke County, he went on to the National Normal School of Lebanon.

Absorbed though young Harry Thomas was in his studies, Harriet Wagner remained much on his mind. Almost immediately after he had received his degree—the first of many—he proposed marriage to her and was accepted. The wedding took place on July 30, 1890, and the couple moved into a little house at Woodington where, two years later, I was born.

Harrison was President at the time, and Grover Cleveland was elected for his second term six months later. There were forty-four states in the Union and the population stood at fewer than sixty-seven million. Except for its handful of cities, the United States was a scattered community of farmlands with vast expanses of open land between and still plenty of unexplored territory west of the Mississippi.

But that last decade of the nineteenth century marked the end of an age. America was losing her frontier innocence. As the railroads crossed and crisscrossed the continent, reaching ever farther into the hinterlands, as the magnates of steel and manufacturing forged their great

3

enterprises, the United States began changing, irrevocably, from a self-centered, self-contained agrarian nation to an industrial world power. Indeed, the war with Spain in 1898 was a clear signal that America was moving to take her place in the forefront of nations.

Other changes were in the wind. In 1893, the Duryea brothers drove the first successful gasoline-powered automobile in the United States. (Not long after, the Chicago *Tribune* told how a pedestrian had been knocked down by an "auto cab," the first such accident on record.) In 1896, Samuel Langley flew a steam-driven, heavier-than-air machine with a wingspan of fourteen feet, and immediately set about building one large enough to carry a man. Soon, two bicycle mechanics, Orville and Wilbur Wright, were tinkering with the same idea in their shop in Dayton, Ohio. And on an April evening in 1896, a New York audience sat spellbound as Thomas Edison's "vitascope" projected moving figures on a silver screen.

I suspect none of these epochal events made any immediate impression on my parents at Woodington, Ohio. The school year had ended a few weeks after I was born, and we moved to Cincinnati. There my father enrolled in the State University's medical department, remaining a second year or so, until his money was gone and he had to drop out. But as it was not then necessary to have a license in order to practice medicine, or even surgery, and as some relatives in western Iowa had written telling of a serious shortage of doctors in their section of the state, we moved on again, settling in Kirkman, a little town on the Rock Island Railroad. And my first memories, shadowy and jumbled, are of that time and place.

It is summer, but the day is dark and oppressive with heat. There is tension in our house, some nameless threat. My father is away. My mother stands at the open door and looks out into the distance, over the rows of corn that cover the hills and roll away to the horizon. Suddenly, in midafternoon, the threat is given a name: "Cyclone!" A man goes running down the street shouting that single word over and over. My mother grabs my hand and pulls me out the back door, across the yard, down into the dank vegetable smell of the storm cellar. But I have seen it—that twisting black plume whipping through the sky—

4

and I wish it would come even closer and that I could be outside to watch.

I am sitting on a fence with some other children and the street is crowded with people. A band is playing, too far away for me to see, but the sound has charged our placid little village with excitement: the circus is here! Then— oh, endless wait!—it comes parading by, the tubas and their tantalizing oompa-pa, oompa-pa; the horse-drawn wagon cages full of monkeys and lions; and then the clowns, cavorting in the street, juggling, somersaulting. I am left breathless. Even after they have all disappeared, I gaze down the empty street after them, tingling. But that is the end of it. The circus doesn't stop in Kirkman—we're too small. It is passing through on the way to Harlan, the county seat, and Harlan is ten miles away, so far, and over such a bad road, that the only time we ever went there the buggy got bogged in mud and the horses reared and my father said never again.

The railroad whistle floats on the summer night, calling. I lie in bed fighting sleep. Everything is still but that whistle, and then the rush of the train as it shoots through the junction. Another day, sitting in the buggy with my father, I watch as the train plunges by, all black roar and billowing smoke. When it has passed and my father clucks the horses forward, I ask how far the train goes, whether it goes all the way to Harlan, and he says yes, and beyond that.

In autumn the corn is everywhere, all I can see wherever I look. The men go from farm to farm to harvest, husking by hand, lightening the chore by making a game of it, each one racing to husk the most ears. At my uncle Sam Slates's farm, Aunt Sally and Aunt Ayner bustle about in the kitchen, overseeing roasting chickens and endless pumpkin pies. In the parlor, the other ladies are sewing a mountain of colored patches into a quilt. Someone gives me a piece of pie and I go out to watch the husking bee. My uncle—he is really my father's uncle—is huge and whiteheaded, with a full white beard, and he hoists me high so I can see the men rush through the browning rows, slashing at the stalks with hooked husking gloves and throwing the yellow ears up into the wagons. Then somewhere out on the prairie, beyond the last row of corn, I hear the train whistle and am lost in its sound, and at last my uncle jostles me and says, "Well, boy, cat got your tongue?"

In the cold dark of a winter night, the grain elevator goes up in flames and my mother wakes me and bundles me warmly so we can all go and watch. Everyone is there, and the firelight reaches to the edge of town and throws frantic dancing shadows on the snow beyond. But I do not find it as exciting as the time the circus came.

We are in a place called Omaha and I am wearing my first pair of short pants. Till then they'd had me in skirts! Now the occasion is my father's graduation from the University of Nebraska's medical school: after more years of intermittent study and correspondence courses he has finally earned his doctorate in medicine. He takes me walking. The city astonishes me, for I have never dreamed that there could be so many people in one place or such grand buildings. We come to the long bridge spanning the Missouri River and start across from Omaha to Council Bluffs. We see rafts of logs drift downstream, guided by crews so far below as to seem unreal to me. My father stops to watch them and, idly, I pry a loose red brick from the roadbed. Then I drop it over the side. As soon at it leaves my hand I am overcome with horror at what I have done—surely my brick will hit one of those men below! I want to look away. I want to run. But I am condemned to watch, trembling with remorse, as the brick loses its red color and grows tinier and finally makes a barely discernible splash as it strikes the water. My father has never noticed, and all alone, age five, I have learned something about right and wrong.

At five I began school in Kirkman and, that winter, learned how to ice-skate. My friends and I would follow the frozen country streams as far as we could, for every turn promised an adventure. I'm not so sure my parents enjoyed winter that much, for it turned bitterly cold and the unobstructed wind swept off the prairie and battered our small frame house—my mother tacked heavy wrapping paper around the foundation to keep it from whipping up through the floor. My father, who drove an open buggy

6

to make his calls on rural patients, would be blue with cold by the time he returned.

Still, life was pleasant enough in Kirkman. We were hardly well off, as a good many people paid their medical bills in produce, but then we certainly had plenty to eat. I believe I have eaten corn in every one of its known and suspected guises—soup, mush, hominy, fritters, popcorn, parched—and sometimes, it seemed, all on the same day. But I was perfectly content and couldn't even imagine what it might be like to live in some other place.

Would we have stayed if it hadn't been for Uncle Cory? Who knows? Would my life have turned out differently? I suppose so. Everyone's life, all history, turns on those seemingly small and sometime accidental "ifs." Yet now, looking back across the years from the vantage point of the present, there seems to be a certain inevitability about the way things happened.

Cory, a mining engineer, was my father's older brother. For years he had sought his fortune in the gold camps of the far West. Even before the big rush to the Klondike in 1898 he had made his way to Alaska, where he worked as an engineer on the then famous Treadwell gold mine in Juneau, reputedly the richest of its day. Then he heard about a silver strike in the Colorado Rockies and promptly packed his gear to head there. He had even written and lured my father to the mining camp at Leadville for one summer, not because Dad had been smitten with gold fever, but because, as an ardent amateur geologist, Dad was eager to collect more specimens, in the high Rockies.

And now, all at once, there was another letter from Uncle Cory. He had moved on again, this time to a place called Cripple Creek. It, too, was in the Rockies, a jerry-built town started from scratch less than ten years before and perched, helter-skelter, atop the greatest concentration of gold ever mined by men. The opportunities were fantastic, wrote Uncle Cory. There were hundreds of working mines—he was chief engineer at one of the largest—and a crying need for doctors and mining engineers. Come! the letter virtually shouted to my father, and it didn't take him long to say yes.

Almost at once, it seemed, he was gone, traveling on ahead to find us a place to live, while my mother and I went back to Darke County, Ohio, to await word. It came before the end of summer, and then we, too, were climbing aboard the Rock Island and on our way to Cripple Creek.

It was a trip filled with lasting memories. When we arrived in Chicago to change trains, there was Uncle Ira to make sure we were properly looked after until our departure the next day. He took us to see a new play, *Quo Vadis?* at the Studebaker Theater on Michigan Avenue. It was a revelation to me. So entranced that I'd forgotten the rest of the audience, I felt myself the center of a living dream in which dozens of grown-ups were play-acting for my pleasure. And when Nero put Rome to the torch and the city went up in vividly realistic flames, I was appalled for the doomed Christian martyrs and delighted by the spectacle and became, in that moment, a dedicated votary of the theater.

Then we were off again, the city's friendly lights falling away behind us, twinkling out, until there was only darkness outside my window. I remember the hypnotic sound of those iron wheels clattering westward and the nights of sitting up in the coach chair—there were sleepers, of course, but only people who were rich rode them. I remember dozing in the chair and being jolted awake by some train sound or motion—or by a prickle of anticipation—and realizing in a flash of wakefulness that I was bound for some strange and faraway place. I remember the look of the land as it rose from endless flat prairie to foothills and their wooded valleys. And when the train made a long turn, I saw the magical peaks far ahead. The year was 1900 and I was eight years old.

> The summit of the Grand Peak, which was entirely bare of vegetation and covered with snow, now appeared at the distance of fifteen or sixteen miles from us, and as high again as what we had ascended . . . I believe no human being could have ascended to its summit.

So wrote Zebulon M. Pike, a young army officer and explorer, of the mountain he discovered in November, 1806, and that eventually was to bear his name. It was a reasonable judgment considering the season of the year and the distance Pike had already covered in becoming the first man ever to map this remote region of the Rockies. But though Pikes Peak commands the surrounding plain from an eminence of more than fourteen thousand feet, it is not really a difficult climb. A lady wearing bloomers and the requisite number of petticoats reached the summit in 1858. I did it before I was fourteen. And nowadays half a million tourists a year, visiting the Cripple Creek gold district which lies along Pikes Peak's southwestern slope, make it to the top on foot, by auto or on the cog railway that is older than I am.

No, the enduring American fascination with Lieutenant Pike's mountain is not its lofty inaccessibility but—just the opposite—the simple fact that for a hundred years it has been so unmistakably *there*, a reachable star. It has also provided an appropriate setting for some of the more flamboyant moments in our national past. The Pikes Peak gold rush—which, in fact, began sixty miles away—sent thousands of dreamers and drifters swarming into the Rockies, the call, "Pikes Peak or bust!" emblazoned on their Conestoga wagons and in their hearts. Few of them found riches, but they established the city of Denver.

Twenty-five years later a Leadville mine salter named Bradley started another boom by sprinkling some imported gold dust into a hole on Mount Pisgah, in the shadow of Pikes Peak. When the bubble burst, when Bradley fled with the few hundred dollars he had conned from others for his "discovery," some of the disillusioned prospectors moved on and some others went back to the mundane business of grazing their cattle along the grassy slopes south of the Peak.

Among them was a family named Welty. Levi Welty had come up from Ohio looking for gold, but soon decided that ranching was a saner, if less spectacular, way to earn a livelihood. He found a high valley with a creek running through it north of Mount Pisgah and, with his three sons, built a log house and set his cattle out to feed. One day, while the Weltys were putting in a fence to border the creek, a log got away from one of the boys and struck another, who responded with a bawling obscenity. Startled, old Levi wheeled around to see what had happened—and accidentally fired off his gun, peppering his hand with buckshot. Whereupon a calf, agitated by the discharge, tried to jump the fence, caught both hind legs and broke one.

It took some little time to restore calm to the Welty homestead, but when it was done, Levi muttered ruefully,

"Well, boys, this sure is some cripple creek." The name stuck, so beginning its short and showy moment in history.

Bob Womack was an old friend of the Weltys. He often stayed with them when he was prowling around Cripple Creek looking for gold. Actually, he was supposed to be tending cattle, but if ever a man had the gold fever it was Bob Womack. He was sure infinite riches lay beneath the ground somewhere along Cripple Creek and hoped an outcropping would tell him where to dig. So he kept looking, assuaging occasional bouts of discouragement with liberal applications of whiskey. And one October afternoon in 1890, in Poverty Gulch, where he had built himself a shack, Bob found what he was looking for—a chunk of telluride-streaked rock that assayed out at two hundred and fifty dollars a ton. Elated, he staked his claim, named it the El Paso Lode, ordered drinks all around and set about raising development money.

There were too many people in Cripple who had been skinned by one-shot bonanzas. The memory of the nearby Mount Pisgah hoax was still fresh. As for Bob Womack—well, everyone liked big, shambling Bob, but they knew he was a souse, and a little strange to boot. So there was no development money forthcoming, and eventually Womack sold his El Paso Lode for a few hundred bucks and died broke.

His discovery was the start of it. Two years would pass before the boom really gathered steam—the Buena Vista jackpot, not two miles from the El Paso, was what got it going—and then it took off with a rush and a roar. Before it was over, half a million gold-crazed men and women had come stampeding into Cripple Creek. All told, the district included less than ten thousand acres, the shallow bowl of an extinct volcano about the size of a single cattle ranch—a small one at that. Suddenly a dozen towns sprang up in the area and three railroads came snaking their way up the craggy mountainsides. There seemed to be a new bonanza every day. The West had never seen anything like it, nor ever would again.

This time the gold was there. When Cripple Creek's golden era ended in 1918, more than three hundred million dollars' worth of ore had been taken from the ground; another two hundred million would come out after things quieted down. (Right up to the 1960s, Cripple Creek production averaged two million a year.) That's more gold

10

than California's forty-niners got from the mother lode, more than came out of the Klondike. One mine alone, the Portland, where I worked, yielded sixty million, and Bob Womack's El Paso—which he let go for a mere three hundred dollars—paid out three million. At least thirty men, not one of them prospectors, became millionaires within a few years of Discovery Day, and by the time our Thomases arrived in "the world's greatest gold camp" in September, 1900, four hundred and seventy-five mines were going full blast, shipping a million and a half dollars' worth of gold each and every month. Geologists say there is another billion remaining to be mined, and today I'm a director of the Golden Cycle Corporation, which now controls more than half of the ancient crater.

Our first home was a three-room frame house on Sixth Street in Victor, the city on the slope of Battle Mountain where most of the richest mines were. Cripple Creek, a few miles around the mountain, had a population of twenty-five thousand by 1900 and over the years remained the gold camp's social and financial center. Victor was where the miners lived, and Victor was where the gold came from. The year before we came it had burned to the ground and a thousand men had pitched in to rebuild the entire place in a matter of months, this time with an ornate city hall, many brick buildings and even a handsome opera house.

But no one would ever mistake it for anything but a mining town. Wherever you looked, shaft houses rose up from the mountainsides. The Gold Coin mine dominated the downtown business district, and a lot of the rich ore it sent to the surface came from a vein that ran right under our main street, Victor Avenue. All of our streets were, quite literally, paved with gold. In those early years, when mine operators were interested only in high-grade ore, the rock of lesser value was crushed and some of it became a part of our roads and rocky streets.

It was hard for me to take it all in at first. Kirkman, Iowa, quickly faded in memory, and I came to believe that every town had more saloons and gambling halls than stores, with a red-light district—a tenderloin—only a few blocks away. At the Garfield School, where the third grade was full, I was shunted into fourth and thereafter was always the youngest in my class. This no doubt made for

11

some social problems but never, in the slightest way, cooled my enthusiasm for the gold camp where I spent my youth.

My first friend in Victor was my cousin Carl, Uncle Cory's boy. He was a year older and introduced me to games and pastimes that made the days fly. We played marbles with steel ball bearings picked up around mine-shaft houses, always for "keeps" and always in the street, the only semi-level place in town. We threw rocks at every target in sight because rocks were everywhere. And when I couldn't find Carl I would trudge uphill to Seventh Street, to a spot where one had a clear view of the Sangre de Cristo range. There I'd stand gazing in awe at the spectacular array of snow-covered mountains stretching all the way from New Mexico to Wyoming.

I soon learned that when I couldn't find Carl it was because he was burrowing into his backyard, building his own miniature gold mine. Eventually he let me join him, and under his sure-handed direction—he later became a Puget Sound bridge builder and railroad engineer—we dug an underground shaft and stopes, then set a gallows frame on top with a double-deck cage to hoist the rock. Our mine had everything but the gold, and of course we expected to hit that any day.

From there, our inevitable next step was to go exploring the abandoned mines and mills of the district. And when that palled, we took to dropping down into a canyon a few miles below town where there were limestone caves with endless twists and turnings. That was great fun—until one overcast day when we heard a tremendous roar and came running out to see a wall of water, perhaps three hundred yards away, churning toward us. A cloudburst somewhere in the Pikes Peak area had sent its roaring water into our narrow canyon, and Carl and I had only seconds to scramble up the wall to be out of the reach of the torrent. We watched, awestruck, as it picked up huge boulders and took them, crashing and tumbling, down the canyon. Then, shaking in our boots, we made our way home, to tell of our close call.

In April, 1901, the Vice-President of the United States, Theodore Roosevelt, came to Victor. The streets were festooned with flags and Fourth of July bunting, and throughout the morning a gay and expectant crowd hung around the depot waiting for his train. It was all a far cry from

Roosevelt's first visit less than a year before, when he had been lucky to escape with his life.

On his previous trip to our booming gold camp he had been campaigning for McKinley and the gold standard, which was to fix the price of gold at $20.67 an ounce. This was a stand not calculated to endear him to miners, who wanted to see William Jennings Bryan in the White House and the free coinage of gold and silver as the law of the land. When T. R. stepped off the train into a sea of waving anti-McKinley posters, he never did get to make his speech. He did get his glasses knocked off, which left him half blind, and except for the quick intervention of the Republican postmaster, Danny O'Sullivan, he would have been crowned with a length of two-by-four. For years afterward, Danny ostentatiously sported an inscribed gold watch that Teddy sent him in gratitude. It was inscribed "To the man who saved my life."

When the election was over, even the diehards were ready to concede the gallantry of the old Rough Rider. At noon he came riding up from Colorado Springs on the newly laid Short Line, with its inspiring panorama of the Sangre de Cristo and the Continental Divide to the west. Said T. R.: "This is the ride that bankrupts the English language." This time he was ceremoniously marched to a luncheon at the Gold Coin Club, a blocklong edifice built by the millionaire Woods brothers and patterned after the New York Athletic Club. And there, shuffling slowly forward with everyone else on that long line waiting to greet the Vice-President, I shook his hand. He spoke to me and handed me a lump of sugar from the bowl on the table beside him. So I went outside and got on the end of the line again. On that second time around he said, "Does this mean you'll be voting twice at election time?"

Five months later, McKinley was shot by an assassin and T.R. became President. He was already the number one hero in my pantheon, remained so, and his own sons became my friends in later years—Ted and Kermit. My father had bought me T.R.'s four-volume account of America's westward surge, *The Winning of the West*, and I read it again and again.

There was something about Cripple Creek, that irresistible combination of a no-questions-asked frontier town and the chance to strike it rich, that lured a gaudy cross section of humanity. Bob Ford, the outlaw who shot Jesse James,

13

brought his guns to town—and was promptly run back down the mountain by Sheriff Hi Wilson. Plenty of tenderfeet strapped on six-shooters when they arrived, either to make an impression or bolster their courage, but were relieved of them the first time they ran into the sheriff or his deputy, Pete Eales. "I'll just take that for the school fund," Pete would say, and the sale of assorted weaponry did pay a portion of the district's educational bill. They say Cripple also had the largest number of college graduates and dropouts of any city in America, as well as erudite remittance men from England—a well-educated, hard-drinking bunch.

And right on the heels of this freewheeling crowd came some freewheeling, soul-saving luminaries. We had a traveling evangelist at least once a year. The church would be packed with repentant sinners night after night, come to hear fiery forebodings of damnation and hellfire. It was stirring entertainment, and my mother, a true fundamentalist, never missed a revival. She took me along when Billy Sunday, the most colorful of them all, came to Cripple to do battle with sin, crying out for the devil to rise up then and there and fight like a man. Nor did Mother hang back when Billy sounded the call to "hit the sawdust trail" for salvation. Up the aisle she went with all the others, pulling me along behind. I must say that I was glad to have my immortal soul saved, although believing until the last that the rush had been started by an offer of free candy.

Carry Nation made the biggest splash of all. The newspapers called her the Kansas Tornado, and with good reason. A skyrocketing, hatchet-swinging temperance agitator, she had ten years of well-publicized saloon-busting behind her when she swept into Cripple Creek vowing to "smash all the beer joints and dives from Poverty Gulch to the Last Chance saloon in Victor." So awesome was her reputation that every saloonkeeper on Bennett Avenue boarded up his place and hunkered down to wait for the storm to pass. That is, every one but Johnny Nolan. Johnny, the proprietor of the velvet-draped Manitou, the lushest drinking and gambling establishment in the district, bravely announced as how he was not about to be buffaloed by Carry Nation. In fact, he invited her to the Manitou "to preach some to the fellows. Haven't I always been on good terms with the lads in the Salvation Army?"

All of which didn't help him ward off disaster. She

14

started off with a sermon at Army Hall. "I knew I was needed here, for," said Carry, "this foul cesspool is the most lawless and wicked spot in the country." Then, followed by the Salvation Army band and a crowd drawn by the suspense in the air and maybe the smell of blood, she marched down to preach at Johnny Nolan's—six feet of scowling sobriety, cape flowing behind and altogether a most imposing figure of a woman.

But there was to be no more preaching that night, just action. For the first thing that caught the fearsome Madame Nation's eye as she stepped into Johnny's place was his pride and joy, a life-size painting above the bar called *Venus Emerging from the Sea*, Venus being amply proportioned and alluringly garbed in the altogether.

"Hang some blankets on that trollop!" Carry Nation commanded in a voice that could be heard out on Bennett Avenue.

"We got no blankets," said genial Johnny. "What kind of a place do you think this is?" Then he went after her, as she suddenly began tearing down his red velvet draperies.

"Take your foul hands off me!" she boomed, elbowing poor Johnny belt-high and sending him sprawling. Whereupon she pulled the famous hatchet out from under her cape and set about hacking away at the offending picture with her well-known Carry Nation fury, stopping only often enough to sweep every bottle of whiskey in reach to the floor.

Until that moment, the clientele had been transfixed by the fireworks. But now, with bottles rolling all over the place, they scrambled to rescue what they could. The Salvation Army fled. Soon the Manitou looked as though it had been hit by a cyclone and left with some casualties, Johnny Nolan on the bottom. By the time the police arrived, Carry was so caught up in her hatchetry that they had to put handcuffs on her before they could lead her off to jail.

There she would have spent the night—as well as the next thirty days, for she didn't have the fifty dollars to cover her fine—had it not been for the intervention of big-hearted Johnny Nolan. Slightly dazed and still bemoaning the loss of his beloved *Venus*, he appeared before the district judge and offered to pay Carry's fine if only she'd, for God's sake, take the midnight train to Denver. And so the story had a happy ending—and Johnny even managed

15

to get the Manitou open for business the following day. In honor of the genial saloonkeeper, although Cripple Creek today is a shadow of its former self, there is still a Johnny Nolan saloon on Bennett Avenue.

The list of those who lived anonymously in the Cripple Creek gold camp and went on from there to catch the public's notice is a long one. Groucho Marx once took a job driving a grocery wagon when the show he was traveling with got as far as Victor and folded. Ford Frick, who became a famous commissioner of baseball, covered the district's bonanzas and bar fights for a Colorado Springs newspaper. Actor Fred Stone, comics Gallagher and Shean, writer Robert Coates, and Ralph Carr, who became governor of Colorado in 1939, all spent formative years in Cripple.

Some of us who used to work out at the gym on the second floor of the Victor city hall took boxing lessons from Morgan Williams, a onetime professional. And here's quite a switch: today the same room is a museum devoted to a mining-camp newsboy whose initials are L.T. Later, when I'd gone off to college, Morgan took a promising young fighter under his wing, a tall, rugged kid named Jack Dempsey who mucked at the Portland mine and even had a couple of bouts at the Gold Coin Club. And Bernard Baruch, with his degree from City College in New York, then a giant of a youngster, worked the mines on Bull Hill. Marshall Sprague, in his book about boom time in Cripple Creek, *Money Mountain*, tells how Baruch was once goaded into a fight with a tough claiming to be the boxing champion of Altman. Baruch, supposedly an eastern dude, flattened the "champion" in two rounds—a fight by candlelight far underground, down on one of the levels of the Los Angeles mine. His genius at anything to do with money evidenced itself one night at the Branch saloon: Bernie Baruch sat down to play roulette and hit the right combination twelve straight times.

But of all the gold camp's then-undiscovered notables, my personal favorite was a vivacious girl from Waco, Texas, named Marie Guinan who taught Sunday School at Anaconda and played the church organ. I wasn't the first twelve-year-old to be smitten with a teacher, but in my case love required hiking, with my pal, Jay Herold, around the mountain from Victor to Anaconda on Sunday to be in Miss Guinan's radiant presence. As I couldn't easily explain this infatuation to my parents, and in view of my lack of enthusiasm for Sunday School in Victor, they no doubt were puzzled at the lively interest I took in the one at Anaconda. But this was as nothing compared to my surprise some years later when my demure Miss Guinan metamorphosed into the famous brassy-blond mistress of Broadway's night life. Yes, it was my dear old Sunday School teacher who turned into the unforgettable Texas Guinan, queen of the speakeasy era, greeting her customers with that marvelous cry, "Hello, sucker," and passing into history in the front rank of all those zany characters who enlivened the prohibition era.

I got my first job when I was in the sixth grade, delivering newspapers along a route that included the Victor business section, the red-light district and the town of Goldfield, two miles around Battle Mountain. Such early entry into the employment market was accepted as the way things were in the gold camp. In the first place, as long as Cripple boomed there were plenty of before- and after-school jobs that needed doing; but more to the point, any boy who wanted money in his pockets had to work for it because nobody's father I ever heard about was doling it out.

I needed fifteen dollars to buy a burro. Actually, there were hundreds of them running wild in the mountains, turned loose by old prospectors who had finally given up and settled down somewhere, or left to wander off when the ones who would never give up went on to the rewards of the afterlife. We saw them often enough when we went wandering in the hills, but I was still some years short of the strength required to lasso and break one. So the thing was to buy a burro from some older boy who was moving up to a horse, and the going rate was fifteen dollars.

They were remarkable little animals. Brought to the new world by the Spanish conquistadores, they hauled silver out of the mines of Central America, stone to build the missions of California and endless supplies for the surveyors and explorers of our American West. The prospector, right up to Cripple Creek days, relied on the sure-footed burro to carry his gear, maybe a hundred and fifty pounds of it, and to sniff out water holes as reliably as a camel. Old-timers used to say, "A mule knows three times as much as a horse, and a burro is smarter than a mule."

Of course it's true that every burro had a mind of its own, and sometimes the only way to get it moving was to bite its ear. But I didn't know a boy in school who didn't have or hanker for one. So one autumn afternoon I presented myself at the office of the Victor *Daily Record*, was assigned a route and began saving my earnings in a tin box labeled "Burro." And it was on that job, at the age of ten, that some schoolyard tales suddenly fell into perspective and I learned about still another aspect of life in a mining town.

In the beginning, anxious to do well, I was awake at three in the morning to hurry over to a back room at the *Record* to fold newspapers. By first daylight I was already hustling through the business district, all pinkish-gray and eerily silent, leaving my papers in locked doorways.

The only people awake at that hour were some weary-looking ladies on First Street Row who came to their doors in wrappers, and sometimes less, and appeared relieved to find only the newsboy. They often chattered with me, and I answered respectfully, as I had been taught to do, and this seemed to please them inordinately. One even invited me inside for a glass of milk, but I politely declined, explaining that I still had to deliver papers in Goldfield and get back to Victor before school started. But I came to look forward to exchanging a word or two with them, maybe because I was still a little uneasy about being abroad at that lonely hour and their friendliness helped. I also sold *The Denver Post* in the saloons and gambling halls on Victor Avenue.

When I first realized that I was in Victor's red-light district and affably passing the time of day with its daughters of joy, I'm not sure. I suppose my larger education had something to do with it—listening to the stories of the older boys; understanding, at last, my father's disquiet on those days when, as the official town physician, he had to make what he called his "inspections." He must have thought that I was too young for a frank talk about sex—that came later—but with only a hint here and there, boys come to understand about such matters and care less.

And then one day, in case there were any uncertainties left in my mind, a matron of the staid Women's Club laid it all out in black and white in a newspaper article about contemporary Victor. After describing the town's growth and five flourishing churches, she wrote:

18

There are a number of brothels and dance halls, and it is indeed a pity to see so many young women and girls make their living in this way. The ladies of the Club have talked to them and sent some of the girls home to their mothers. Others have been sent to a house of correction where they will be taught to be good women.

Perhaps so, but there was no shortage of replacements. As for me, after learning about what went on behind those shuttered windows I remained respectful to the girls, and they were always nice to me. When I finally got my burro I promptly led it over and showed it to them. They seemed proud, too.

Incidentally, Cripple Creek's red-light district—as I found out even later—was more notorious than Victor's. Some of the "parlor houses" on Myers Avenue, like the Old Homestead and Nell McClusky's, were luxuriously furnished and famed throughout the West. And they were always open for business. The rates were steep, but that didn't faze the district's more affluent mining men, who often arrived with a party of cronies to spend the weekend. Even the cribs, the one-girl houses at the end of the street, were substantially built and bore on their front doors the picturesque names of their respective proprietresses—Dizzy Daisy, Tall Rose, Greasy Gert. There were three hundred girls in all during Myers Avenue's heyday, as well as burlesques, dance halls and some thirty saloons between Third and Fifth streets alone, the liveliest of which was a place called Crapper Jack's. Victor had an almost equal number.

Naturally, the solid family folk of the Cripple Creek district deplored the audacious goings-on and occasional violence of their sin streets—although the local coffers swelled from a monthly tax of sixteen dollars on every madam, plus six dollars for each of her girls. Actually, most people seemed to take a perverse pride in the flamboyant reputation of Myers Avenue, as exemplified in this verse, by Rufus L. Porter, the "Hard Rock" poet:

> Sin and lust I ain't defendin';
> But history must be fair;
> And there ain't no use pretendin'
> That the Avenue wasn't there.

Years later, in 1914, when the bloom was off the gold rush and Cripple and its neighbors were declining into tired disarray, there was still activity on Myers Avenue. That year, Julian Street, the widely read author and journalist, visited there and wrote a lurid article for *Collier's Weekly*, concentrating on an aging prostitute, Madame Leo, and the slow disintegration of the gold camp. Whereupon the loyal citizens of Cripple Creek rose up in all their wrath, organizing protest meetings to denounce Julian Street and deluging *Collier's* with hundreds of angry letters. But their revenge—and it was sweet—came out of a resolution passed by the aldermen and sent out on the Associated Press wire to every important newspaper in the United States:

TONIGHT THE CITY COUNCIL OF CRIPPLE CREEK
COLORADO APPROVED UNANIMOUSLY CHANGING
THE NAME OF MEYERS AVENUE TO JULIAN STREET.

A year or so after we arrived in Victor, my mother gave birth to a little girl who, soon after, died of pneumonia. Then, in 1904, my sister Pherbia was born. But there were twelve years between us, and I saw far too little of her. Meanwhile, my parents—who were paragons of rectitude in that bluff and burly mining camp, who didn't drink, smoke or swear, who read books and never played cards— my parents concentrated their attentions on me. And I, younger and perhaps more innocent than some of my class-mates, tried to find my niche among them.

It was not easy. A young bruiser named Stubs Corcelius would fling me to the ground with monotonous regularity and no apparent reason, and perched astride my chest, press the stub of his missing forefinger into my nose. This went on until I helped him through a history test, after which he turned his peculiar torment on someone else.

As we had come from the corn country of Iowa, the boys in my class inevitably dubbed me Rube. Later, when they heard that my father was giving me elocution lessons at home, my nickname became Windy. Not until I was well into high school and had proven myself one of them— at the cost of some wear and tear on the rules of conduct set down by my parents—did they begin calling me Tom-my, a name still used by my closest friends. So what fol-lows is an account of how I proved myself to my peers, the lurid list of misdeeds and transgressions that made me a regular guy.

I began smoking when I was around ten. This was just something you did. You didn't necessarily have to like it, but when everyone else began puffing away at a corn silk, or even a section of buggy whip, why, you joined in. Then I graduated to Bull Durham and Duke's Mixture, pinching just enough tobacco out of the little cloth sack to roll into my own cigarettes. There came a day when I finally learned to perform this intricate feat with one hand, like the men outside Crapper Jack's, and thereafter I hardly minded the nausea that followed the cigarette. On Sundays I would often meet Jay Herold behind the Gold Coin, at the distant mouth of the tunnel that ran all the way through Squaw Mountain to the Economic Mill. There, where we could be sure that no one would surprise us, we'd open a packet of Henry IV cigars and really smoke. In fact I persisted in this until I became the editor of a daily newspaper, a job that didn't allow me enough time to light a cigarette.

Then there was Rosser's poolroom. Old boy Rosser had a fine red walrus moustache, six pool tables and a tempting array of slot machines. In time I became fairly adept with a pool cue, but I am afraid the one-armed bandits gobbled too many of the nickels and dimes I ought to have dropped in the collection plate at church. Nor could I take any comfort from the fact that my parents, who often inveighed against gambling at cards, had never mentioned slot machines.

Now for a few words about the first time I was taken to jail. One winter day, Jay and I were amusing ourselves hiding in an alley off Victor Avenue, throwing snowballs at passersby. When a shiny black derby crossed our field of fire, I heaved a perfect strike, recognizing the hat's wearer only a split second too late. The derby flew one way and I flew the other, for my target was none other than Swift Billy Dingman, owner of a local gambling emporium and former shortstop on a semipro baseball team.

It was no contest. Without even breaking stride, Billy scooped up his hat and collared me before I was out of the alley. Then, scrunching up the back of my coat so tightly that my feet barely touched the ground as we went, he hauled me straight to the police station. And there I stayed, no doubt in a nervous sweat, until my father came to collect me.

I'm sure the only times Dad ever saw the inside of the local jail were on errands of mercy—answering a call perhaps to patch up someone who had been clobbered in a brawl or a minor wound from a bullet. And now the humiliation of having to go there and fetch his delinquent son! I got a lecture, of course, but he had a sense of humor—as did Billy Dingman. Not long after, as I was walking past Dingman's gambling hall, he hailed me and, with a broad grin, asked if I'd really caught it from my father. I told him I had.

"Well," he said jovially, "I guess that squares us. And just to show there's no hard feelings, here's some nickels —come on in and play my slot machines."

Swift Billy was not only fast on his feet, he was smart. From then on I spent most of my collection-plate money at his place.

2.

Some More Facts of Life

Goin' up to Cripple Creek,
Goin' on the run!
Goin' up to Cripple Creek,
To have a little fun!
—A Contemporary Canticle

JUST before dawn this morning, June 6, 1904, an extra edition of the Colorado Springs *Telegraph* was rushed to press. Under an ominous headline, the ghastly details:

The worst heinous and diabolical crime in the history of Colorado was committed this morning at 2:25 o'clock when twenty-five miners on the night shift of the Findley Mine were waiting at the Independence depot for the Florence & Cripple Creek train to take them to their homes when an infernal machine of hundreds of pounds of powder was exploded under the platform of the depot. The explosion hurled men into space and mangled and tore the bodies of many so they could not be recognized.

I remember my father being called in the middle of the night and rushing off to the shattered Independence depot, just around the mountain from our home. But thirteen of the miners were already dead, their dismembered bodies flung a hundred and fifty feet from the platform, arms and legs strewn across the dark hillside. Nearly all the others were badly hurt; six had to undergo emer-

23

gency amputations. So did the bloody ten-month strike of the Western Federation of Miners come to its decisive hour.

It had begun, as too many strikes do, in a power struggle between the leaders of labor and management. The Western Federation of Miners, having won a three-dollar wage for an eight-hour day back in 1894, had come to be dominated by Big Bill Haywood, a one-eyed giant of a man who stomped the West bellowing for the overthrow of the capitalist system at all costs and by any means, bloodshed not excepted. In the summer of 1903, Big Bill was about to test his strength in the Cripple Creek district, a stronghold of the W.F.M. In order to cut off the supply of ore to some nonunion mills in Colorado City, Haywood and his colleague, Moyer, ordered our three thousand five hundred W.F.M. miners out on strike.

The owners, meanwhile, were far from passive. Some were still smarting over the union victory in '94. Now they reorganized the Mine Owners Association and dedicated it to smashing the union. As soon as the strike began they imported scab labor and called on the state militia to drive the W.F.M. out of town.

Feelings ran high. The Cripple Creek district was divided against itself until nearly everyone was drawn into the orbit of one side or the other. My uncle Cory was a member of the union and both he and my father sympathized with the plight of the miners, caught up and helpless in the death struggle between the owners and the W.F.M. leadership. But they could only grieve at the excesses of both. Few others were so dispassionate. Many an old friendship ended in bitterness, and through the long paroxysm of violence that marked the strike it was a brave man who ventured out after dark.

Neither side had anything to be proud of. Trains were wrecked and bombs planted in working mines by W.F.M. hirelings. A shift boss and superintendent at the Vindicator were murdered. The militia, their expenses now paid by the mine owners, struck back by imprisoning hundreds of union men and their partisans in a huge bullpen at Goldfield, two miles from our home. They drove others out of town altogether. In the end, two hundred and twenty-five men were arbitrarily deported from Cripple, the innocent along with the guilty. They were taken in locked boxcars across the state line and dumped on the then endless empty plains of Kansas and New Mexico, many with only the clothes on their back and no money. When the Victor *Daily Record*, which sided with the mining men, protested these cruelties, their office was raided and the presses smashed. And so we came to the night of Bloody Monday, when a professional terrorist named Harry Orchard rigged two cases of dynamite under the Independence depot and blew up twenty-five nonunion miners.

Nobody went to work that day. A sense of crisis touched everyone in the gold camp, a nervous perception that the showdown was now at hand. A mass meeting had been called for 3 P.M. and soon angry men, many of them armed, began heading for the site, a midtown lot at the corner of Fourth Street and Victor Avenue. Militia lined the bluff above, standing with ready rifles in front of the Gold Coin shaft house, and W.F.M. men watched from the second story of Union Hall across the street.

Watching, too, were my cousin Carl and I. We knelt at the side window of my father's office above the Boston store which looked directly out on the meeting place. In the explosive atmosphere hanging over us like a storm cloud, and with Uncle Cory summoned to Union Hall, my father had brought Carl and me to the office with him so he could know just where we were when the storm broke.

At three o'clock, with more than a thousand people pressed into that narrow corner lot, a bantam of a man named Clarence C. Hamlin climbed up on a flat-topped wagon and began addressing the crowd. Almost at once you could see the tension mounting toward frenzy. For Hamlin, a lawyer from Colorado Springs and secretary of the Mine Owners Association, was a fiery orator and had been chosen to speak for just one purpose—to whip the crowd into a mob. Arms outflung, he summoned up the image of the gold camp's orphaned children and beseeched "every man with guts" to get a gun and drive the cursed W.F.M. out of town once and for all. "The time has come for you to take this matter into your own hands!" he shouted.

That did it. A union sympathizer yelled something back at Hamlin and was immediately beaten up by others near him. Then a shot was fired and the wagon horses bolted, tumbling Hamlin to the ground.

Suddenly everything swirled into pandemonium. Shots

rang out from the edge of the crowd and, some said later, from the Union Hall windows across Victor Avenue. I saw a man crouching behind a telephone pole just below us, methodically emptying his rifle into the terrified mass of men, trampling each other now in a mad rush to save themselves.

"You two get down on the floor and stay there!" my father shouted at Carl and me, then bounded down the steps and out into the melee.

But of course we did no such thing. We clung to the windowsill and gaped out at the nightmare scene below, frightened but transfixed. A platoon of militia had swarmed down the bluff and, swinging the butt ends of their rifles like clubs, charged headlong into the crowd and drove it out toward Fourth Street. In two or three chaotic minutes the packed meeting ground was emptied—except for the scattering of men who lay motionless on the ground, two of them dead. My father clutched one wounded miner by the armpits and, with the help of some good samaritan, was dragging him toward the office. Except for an occasional shout, everything was suddenly still.

But the carnage wasn't over yet. The militiamen had turned their attention to Union Hall, surrounding the building while someone went in and ordered the W.F.M. men to come out with their hands up. The answer was no. Carl and I could see a line of soldiers standing in the middle of Fourth Street, their rifles trained on the second-story windows. Then someone barked an order. The rifles puffed smoke and the sledgehammer sound of the volley rattled our windows and echoed up and down the street. Round after round was pumped into the building, and I closed my eyes, not daring to look at Carl, and prayed that Uncle Cory would be spared. When the shooting stopped at last and the men came out, Cory was among them. They were rushed away by the soldiers, Carl flying out after them.

And even as the wounded were being carried down, the enraged mob went storming into the hall, smashing everything in sight. Then they set off down Victor Avenue in a vengeful orgy, wrecking and looting every union store and meeting place in town before their fury was finally sated.

Meanwhile my father had gotten the wounded miner, unconscious now, up to the office and onto his operating

26

table. He said he would have to operate at once and called for me to take the man's gun belt. As I reached for it, I caught sight of the bloody bullet hole in the middle of his stomach. I turned away quickly, threw the holstered .45 behind a bookcase and tried not to be sick. Then I stood staring at the wall as my father cut through tissue and went probing for the bullet, announcing every step of the procedure as though he were addressing a class of medical students. When it was done we took the still-unconscious miner to the hospital—where my father spent the rest of that day and all that night tending the other wounded.

The strike changed the Cripple Creek district for all time. The W.F.M. was driven out, but a certain rancor, a great wound of the spirit, remained. Uncle Cory and his family left, never to return, as did hundreds of other veteran miners. Nobody profited. The mine owners, momentarily triumphant, were soon to see the start of the gold camp's long decline. Big Bill Haywood was to build a gaudy legend for himself in the years just ahead, but he was discredited in the eyes of fair-minded laboring men and turned to even more radical excesses. He did become the motive force behind the militant Industrial Workers of the World, the I.W.W., "the Wobblies," and soon after, along with the hired assassin Harry Orchard, was tried for the murder of Idaho's former governor, Frank Steunenberg. Orchard was convicted, but Haywood went free. And in 1921, awaiting trial for wartime sedition, he fled to Soviet Russia where he was lionized, but died lonely and embittered to be buried at the Kremlin Wall. And Harry Orchard, whose monstrous act of wholesale murder had convulsed the town, went to jail—but not for his crime at the Independence depot. Fleeing Cripple, Orchard wandered the West for a year or so, hiring out as a professional killer, and in December, 1905, planted the bomb that killed Idaho's Governor Frank Steunenberg. When he was finally caught, convicted and sent to prison, he claimed to have undergone a great reformation of soul, confessing all his past crimes and asking God's forgiveness. I wonder if he got it. He lived to be eighty-five but spent all the rest of that long life—forty-five years—growing flowers in the Idaho state penitentiary.

Changes would come for the Thomases, too, but for a while longer things went on much as they always had for us. The wounded miner whose life my father saved recovered, then, typically, neglected to pay his bill. When Dad casually mentioned this some weeks later, I remembered the .45 behind the bookcase in his office. "You could sell that and keep the money," I said, proud to make this indirect contribution to the family finances. But not Dad. He fished out the gun and returned it to the miner—holster, belt, bullets and all.

Cripple Creek was full of surprises. When I was twelve or so, there was a girl we knew as "Red" who always seemed to be standing around while the boys played one-o'-cat or chose sides for a game of football. At first we ignored her—naturally—but as she was so eagerly and everlastingly there, it wasn't long before we began to let her fill in when one side or the other was short a man. And as she could kick a football as far as any of us, and wasn't afraid to get up on the line and go charging after the ball carrier, she soon became a regular among us—and a valued ally when, as not infrequently happened, disagreement over a close play escalated into a free-for-all. In time we agreed that Red, who was toughened by regular work alongside her older brothers in the family mine at the foot of Big Bull Mountain, could hold up her end on field and off, and despite the dress and long hair, we quit thinking of her as a girl.

All of which made for quite a shock when her voice began to change and orange hairs sprouted all over her chin: she wasn't a girl; she was the victim of her parents' bitter disappointment that, after five sons, they'd still failed to produce the daughter they longed for. As soon as the truth was out they sent poor Red off to some distant school where, one hopes, she—he—sorted out his real sex and lived happily ever after. Anyway, we never saw him again.

By this time my own voice was changing and I began to take notice of girls who had no aptitude whatever for football or fist-fighting. One of the first was Lucille McAvoy, whose family lived next door in a handsome three-story house with a barn behind and a fine team of horses. It was not the McAvoys' affluence that attracted me but the fine figure cut by Lucille, who, though only thirteen, could really fill out a middy blouse and was otherwise entirely fetching. Unhappily for me, nearly all the other

28

boys in the neighborhood were similarly smitten, and there never seemed to be room for me on her porch. Then came the birthday party at which I was introduced to the charm of a kissing game called Post Office. Pining to deliver a "letter" to Lucille, I was paired, instead, with a sweet girl, Bessie, whose kiss—it was my very first—persuaded me that life without Lucille McAvoy could be worth living after all.

For a while a girl named Dale Latimer and I were supposed to be an item, maybe because her father was a doctor, too. She lived up the street and had a sister, Valley, and two brothers, Glen and Forest. (This nature-oriented nomenclature was carried through the generations: Dale was to have two sons, one of whom was Lane, and *his* children are Brook, Timothy, Heather, Laurel and Linnet. Some years ago, in San Francisco, when a young man came up and introduced himself to me as Ridge Bass, I knew at once that he was Dale's other son.) Anyway, I don't think Dale and I had any grand passion for each other, but when everyone in our group began to pair off it was convenient to pretend. Once, in the McAvoys' barn, the others persuaded me to take Dale up into the haymow. I did, but when we were alone in that seductive, sweet-smelling dimness, we sat a good three feet apart, afraid to so much as hold hands.

Then there was Gertrude Oliver, who came into my life a couple of years later and just bowled me over. She looked and acted older than any of the other girls in school, and when she seemed to respond to my fumbling attentions I was transported with joy. I was at her house as often as I could get away from my own, and stayed until her father, a prosperous mine operator with an antic sense of humor, signaled that I'd better be gone, sometimes by lowering a ringing alarm clock down over the upstairs railing. This went on for a few zesty months until one night, when I'd stayed even later than usual and left breathing hard, thinking that things were going exceptionally well between Gertrude and me, I heard footsteps in the street behind me. I turned and there was Gertrude's father, purposefully closing in. I felt sure he would want to discuss the long good-bye Gertrude and I had just shared in the darkness at their front door, but as it was too late to run I just waited, nervously. But Mr. Oliver didn't seem at all angry. In fact, he put his arm

29

around me in the friendliest way. Then he said, "My boy, do you think you can support my daughter?"

That was the end of the romance! And probably just as well. Her wise father must have foreseen Gertrude was about ready for a husband—and, indeed, got one barely a year later, right after we got our high school diplomas. She married the principal!

As the perceptive reader is now aware, I was not exactly a threat to the local Lotharios. This had nothing to do with any reluctance on my part, not up to that point in my innocent life. But the time was coming—the night of the Port Wine Club ball at the Elks Hall—when my ingenuous male instincts ran head on into some of the sterner facts of life.

Among my friends of those high school years were some who began experimenting with demon rum. Obviously this was not a difficult pastime to pursue in a mining town, but it was one I never fell victim to, perhaps—and for once!—because of my parents' example. So it was that I stuck to root beer, though I was often present when my friends broke open a bottle of whiskey—and sometimes had to lead them home. Maybe that's why they invited me to accompany them to the Port Wine ball.

As this definitely was not the sort of function my father would approve, I sidled out of the house in my good suit that Saturday evening, mumbling something about "going to meet the boys." Indeed, I had second thoughts myself when we arrived, for the smoky clamor of the Elks Hall seemed to fit every ominous description I'd ever heard of a true den of iniquity. But soon enough my interest was piqued by a girl we all knew around town, seemingly unattached this night. She was attractive in a flamboyant way, and squeezed as she was into a shiny black dress, it was breathtakingly easy to believe what my friends were saying about her being "available." Eventually they forsook their leering for some serious drinking, leaving me alone among those at our table still following her with my eyes.

By ten I had worked up the nerve to ask her to dance, and by eleven—the hour I was due home—I was still waltzing her around the floor, inspired by the possibilities into concocting one wild tale after another about my adventures as a young man about town—anything to hide from her the awful truth that I was really only a high school sophomore. And so it went, my breath coming faster and faster as I held her closer and closer, until around midnight some inner sensor picked up a warning from the direction of the entrance and roused me from my reverie. My father was standing in the doorway.

Gone my painfully fabricated poise! Gone my dreams of conquest! Without a word I left my prize where she stood in mid-dance floor and marched out the door in front of my father, out into the night, marveling all the way home at the vast disparity between the two pressing questions on my mind: first, whether my father had recognized my overheated intentions toward that girl; and second, whether there was at least a chance of his now considering me too old for a licking.

He didn't say a word until we were inside. Then he quickly made it clear that the answer to both questions was yes. For the next two hours I listened raptly as he gave me the dark side of the facts of life. He didn't use any street words—I never heard my father say anything stronger than "Hmph!"—but he made the hazards of casual sex in that time and place graphically clear. As city physician, with responsibility for regularly examining the girls of the red-light district, and for treating them—and their victims—he was uniquely qualified to deliver such a lecture with authority. And as, in his quiet, scholarly way, he spared me no grisly detail, I took the lesson to heart, you may be sure. Especially as it was so vividly punctuated by one of my pals of the Port Wine ball: he eventually told me that later on that same fateful night he had tangled with the girl in the shiny black dress—and wound up taking a long series of distressing treatments at my father's office.

My father was the most persistent scholar I ever knew and remained so all his life. His mind was engaged by the whole broad range of human knowledge, from music to mathematics. He probably knew almost as much about geology as any mining engineer in Cripple Creek, and he was also a dedicated student of the great philosophers, of literature, astronomy, botany and comparative religion.

He never quit trying to learn more. When most of the people in our town had an extra dollar they bought a drink; when my father had an extra dollar he took a course or bought a book. The result was that eventually we had a library of three thousand volumes crowded against the walls of our small house. Later, when Dad had an opportunity to travel, he spent endless hours visiting the museums and galleries of the world and came to know not only where the great treasures of art and science were exhibited but in what room and along which wall.

I was the lucky beneficiary of this insatiable quest for knowledge, as was my sister Pherbia later. Hardly a day passed without Dad reading aloud to us from Shakespeare and the English poets, from the Bible, Kipling and Mark Twain. As both he and Mother had been teachers, they had me reading by the time I was three, and thereafter, and for as long as I lived at home, my father coaxed and drilled me in the art of elocution. He had this good old-fashioned idea that life in all its aspects was enhanced for anyone who could speak clearly and explicitly. "Your voice is the expression of your personality," he would say. "Don't cringe behind it."

At ten I had memorized and could declaim from the classics to James Whitcomb Riley, and was not infrequently called on to do so at church and club affairs. Once, when I happened to meet my father in front of our church, he ushered me inside, stood me up in the pulpit and had me recite "Paul Revere's Ride." And sitting in the farthermost pew he kept calling out, "Aspirate your *h*'s! Louder! And put more fire into it—the British are coming!"

I leave the results for history to judge. It is true that my voice has enabled me to earn a livelihood. But it is also true that it is always with me: I don't know how many times my wife has had to shush me in a restaurant, reminding me that even when I whisper I can be heard clearly on the far side of the room.

Every spring and summer of those early Cripple Creek-Victor years, my father would take me on long hiking tours during which we gathered flower and rock specimens for his collections. And oh! the tingling thrill when we came across a fossil, or a geode to crack open, revealing the hollow lined with glittering crystals. In time, Dad bought a three-inch telescope, and often on a winter night, when the heavens shone with particular brilliance in the rarefied atmosphere at ten thousand feet, he would wake Pherbia and me from sound sleep to come and gaze at the stars, which he then proceeed to identify for us with

32

the proprietary affection of a local guide directing the visitor's attention to the places of note in his hometown.

He was of two minds about religion. Whereas my mother could hardly be kept out of church—she sang in the choir, went to revivals, Wednesday night prayer meetings, and never missed Sunday service—Dad usually came late and invariably took a seat in the back, the easier to slip away when the sermon began to pall. I think now that he is probably best described as an openminded agnostic, willing to be convinced but unable to accept the hard-line fundamentalism then so prevalent in hinterland America. His inquiring mind balked at any absolutist doctrine, and the fire-and-brimstone gospel of most of our Methodist preachers was no exception, nor was the contentious piety of what the saloon crowd called the "come-to-Jesus folks."

On the other hand, he was a devoted student of the Bible and could quote from it with the easy confidence of a politician. And when, as sometimes happened, we got a minister tolerant enough to agree that not every line in the Good Book need be taken as literal fact, why, Dad would promptly invite him to join the Century Club, a literary circle he had organized soon after we came to Cripple. A few of those became his close friends. One was Father Downey, the Catholic priest, who enjoyed a good glass of Irish whiskey, a frailty Dad could regard with equanimity in the light of Father Downey's keen mind and charming wit.

Other doctors came to Cripple Creek, salted away goodly sums and eventually moved on to the amenities of Colorado Springs or Denver, but not Dad. For one thing, the business side of his practice found him inept and left him indifferent. He seemed constitutionally incapable of pressing anyone for payment of a bill and had devised a calming strategy for dealing with delinquent accounts: he simply forgot about them. And of course when he did come by some extra money, it went for books or graduate study. (The two leading medical schools in the United States at the time were Johns Hopkins in Baltimore and Rush Medical in Chicago; by 1914 Dad had degrees from both.)

And so the Thomases of Cripple Creek were never affluent, although my father was one of the busiest men in town. He often said that between mine accidents and shoot-

33

ing scrapes he practiced more surgery in a year than most doctors did in a lifetime. As an enthusiast of the music hall and theater, he was further rewarded by being called on to tend visiting performers who, having been abruptly transported up and over the Continental Divide, often found themselves altitude-sick and frightened by shortness of breath. One of his patients was the gorgeous Lillian Russell. So grateful was she for his ministrations that, in the midst of her performance, she threw him a rose. Then, like so many others, she left town without paying her bill.

I suppose my father would have liked me to follow in his footsteps. He never actually said so, but that was the time-honored tradition, and he did once undertake to stimulate my enthusiasm for the practice of medicine by inviting me to observe him at surgery. I expressed polite interest, we agreed to await a suitable case and then I forgot all about it. But that very Saturday he summoned me to the hospital; a miner, struck by a falling rock, was to undergo a trepanning operation to relieve the pressure on his brain.

I remember being properly scrubbed and garbed by a nurse and feeling, suddenly, that everything was going too quickly. I remember being ushered into the operating room where a group of white-shrouded figures—I couldn't even tell which was my father—was clustered around a shaven and shining skull belonging to a shapeless mass on the table, also shrouded. Somebody urged me to move closer so I could see better. One of the mysterious figures—my father, I suppose—was cutting a neat hole in the exposed skull with what looked like a hacksaw. I remember all that, and I remember the bloody mass of brain that was exposed when they lifted out the bone. And that's all I remember because at that point I interrupted the operation by keeling over. Not long after, my father suggested that perhaps I would be interested in pursuing a career in the law.

Cripple may have been in a decline, but I didn't know it. It remained for me—and remains to this day—alive and tantalizing. It lived up to every promise. I looked forward to holidays like the Fourth of July and Labor Day as though they were my birthday, for then all the barely constrained excitement of the gold camp burst into dawn-to-dawn celebration—fireworks, prizefights, hard-

34

rock drilling contests and rodeos, each with its favorites and heroes. One of the greatest was a horse named Steamboat, who became famous throughout the West and put the Cripple Creek rodeo on the map.

Steamboat had gotten his name by throwing a local cowhand, who then vented his frustration by whacking the horse across the snout. Thereafter Steamboat breathed with an audible whistle, but his bucking power was unimpaired: he threw every man who ever got a leg over him, and as his reputation spread, cowboys from all over the cattle country, and many a rodeo champion among them, came to try a hand at taming him. The lucky ones were thrown quickly. A goodly number of others suffered broken ribs when Steamboat exploded into a murderous arching leap and came down, legs stiff as steel, in a jolting landing. None hung on very long, and whenever one hit the dust the Cripple Creek crowd cheered lustily. Steamboat, after all, was one of us.

Another of the district's celebrated characters was Professor Hans Albert, a violinist of such prodigious talent that he'd once been ranked with Fritz Kreisler and Mischa Elman. A Viennese, a protégé of Emperor Franz Joseph, Albert was *Konzertmeister* of the Imperial Opera by the time he was sixteen and, three years later, was invited to America to become first violinist with the Chicago Symphony. He had even played for President Cleveland in the White House.

But it was mosly all downhill for Hans Albert after that. Plagued with crippling asthma, he had come to Victor seeking relief in the lofty altitudes and clear air, letting it be known that he would "consider taking a limited number of pupils." It was soon obvious that he was relying less on fresh air than on whiskey and morphine. He became a familiar figure at the Silver Dollar and Diamond saloons, playing Viennese waltzes in exchange for drinks. No serious student came to his studio, so he went from camp to camp, offering cut-rate lessons to reluctant and untalented miners' children. I remember seeing him trudging down the street, a sad, shambling figure barely five feet tall, hair down to his shoulders, the violin case clutched in his right hand, wearing a cutaway coat greening with age and so big on his slight frame that the tails all but dragged on the ground.

But Professor Albert was due one final hour of glory.

35

A light opera company starring the world-famous Fritzi Scheff had come to the Victor Opera House to do Victor Herbert's *Mlle. Modiste*. When the conductor was laid low with altitude sickness and demanded that he be rushed back to Denver, the Professor was hurriedly pressed into service. All his faded genius returned. The evening, right up to Fritzi Scheff's stirring finale, was an unqualified triumph.

And then every light in the theater went out.

For a little while everyone waited expectantly. But as the house remained pitch-dark, as the ever-present fear of fire spread like a silent alarm, there were nervous whispers and a few people began to push toward the aisles. Another moment, no more, and panic would have had hold of the entire audience and there would be a desperate, trampling struggle for the exit.

Then, suddenly, the heartening strains of a violin playing the finale, "Kiss Me Again," seemed to light the darkness. A few brave souls began to hum. And as it seemed inconceivable that anything really bad could happen while there was such music playing, the audience—still a little nervous—sat down again. When the lights finally came on, there was Professor Albert in the orchestra pit, playing away as though he were oblivious of where he was or what had happened.

There was tremendous applause for him, and the show went on. When it was over Miss Scheff gave special thanks to "your maestro, whose great presence of mind prevented a disaster." Then she reached down to take the Professor's hand and said, "You are a true artist."

For a while he became a celebrity in Cripple. People who had scorned him before now came up to shake his hand and clap him on the back. And it seemed as though he might even have conquered his dependency on drugs and drink. But it was not to be. Another choking bout of asthma drove him back to morphine and, in the end, he had to be taken away to an asylum in Nebraska. No one in Cripple ever saw him again.

Both Victor and Cripple Creek had handsome new opera houses and, given my father's devotion to the theater, the Thomases had a chance to see some of the most gifted performers of the time as they toured from Denver through the mining camps of Cripple and Leadville before going on to Salt Lake City and San Francisco. We saw

Lillian Russell, John Drew, Anna Held, Lew Dockstader and his minstrel band and—greatest night of all!—the incomparable John Philip Sousa. Hard-rock miners, who wouldn't have paid ten cents to see the Statue of Liberty play the fiddle, lined up to buy dollar tickets when the March King came to town, and we were lucky to get in. The actress Blanche Walsh played Cripple once, but she may not even have made expenses. She ventured into the Last Chance saloon after her performance and put a thousand dollars on the roulette wheel, on the black. It came up red and she walked out broke.

Obviously not all the excitement in Cripple was scheduled. One afternoon, working at something in our backyard, I heard a tumultuous clanging behind me and looked up to see a whole string of boxcars tumbling down Squaw Mountain. They had broken away from a locomotive and, gathering speed plunging down the steep incline, jumped the tracks at the first sharp turn.

That sort of thing happened often enough in our mountainous terrain, and not always to empty boxcars. One summer night a coach loaded with Fourth of July celebrants returning from Colorado Springs broke loose and, after a terrifying runaway ride, crashed into an embankment near Cameron. Miraculously, only three were killed. I still have a yellowed newspaper clipping that tells the grim story:

> The scene in the car was one of great excitement as the occupants realized they were facing a disaster that might bring death to many of them. But notwithstanding the awful outlook, not a scream or a cry came from one of the many women and children in the car. On the contrary, they listened to the advice of the men occupants, and endeavored to prepare themselves for the crash they were expecting.
>
> The injured were at once placed upon the special train brought by Conductor Wood and taken to Cameron, where a number of surgeons who had been rushed from Victor on a special were ready to attend to their injuries. The surgeons were Drs. Thomas, Latimer, and Cohen of Victor, and Driscoll and Hays of Goldfield.

It was nearly midnight when they brought the special into Cripple Creek. The crowd, waiting in silence, then walking fearfully among the dead and injured in search of loved ones, made it the most mournful arrival in the history of the Short Line.

As for me, I continued to generate my own excitement—mischief may be a better word—mostly, I suppose, because I was still the youngest in my class and felt obliged to somehow emphasize my presence. The particular schoolroom shenanigans in which I regularly engaged mercifully elude me now, but I do remember that I was in hot water often enough so that a certain sinking sensation in the pit of the stomach seemed to be my natural state.

Some teachers reacted by giving me the stony-faced silent treatment. I didn't like that; I didn't want anyone mad at me. I preferred the more direct response, painful as it might be. When it was over, you had the feeling that accounts were squared and you could be friends again. In the eighth grade, Miss Elistine O'Connor, a teacher of substantial muscular proportions, with red hair and an Irish temper to match, obliged me by knocking me down and pummeling me black and blue while I apologized for whatever outrage I had perpetrated. I never resented it, and in fact we corresponded for years afterward.

In high school, my mathematics teacher was unhappily named Mr. Lady, and I suppose some sophomoric remark I made in that regard led to further mayhem. Mr. Lady, who definitely wasn't, worked me over in front of the class, then sent me to the principal's office for more. But as the principal was then otherwise engaged, he suggested I return the following afternoon and, in the meantime, that I go home and confess my villainy to my father. Honorably I did so, and got a second licking, with the third delivered, as promised, in the principal's office next day. I would like to believe this established a Victor High record for corporal punishment for a single offense.

My favorite teacher was Mabel Barbee. She captivated me first—along with every other boy in class—with her cool good looks. Then, having fallen head over heels in love with her, I followed willingly as she led me into the magic of ancient and modern history, and through the complexities of Spanish grammar. Mabel Barbee Lee was to become to the Cripple Creek gold camp what Bret Harte was to the California of the forty-niners and what Jack London and Robert Service were to the Klondike gold rush, unofficial historian of an epic era.

She lived many of its most dramatic moments, her life full of tragedy and triumph. She had come to Cripple Creek as a child in 1892, the stagecoach in which she and her mother traveled having been held up by bandits en route. Her father, known as Honest John, discovered the El Paso mine but was so hard up for cash that he had to sell out before it began producing. Eventually the El Paso paid out some thirteen million dollars in gold, but Honest John died without a penny to his name. When he died, a coffee can appeared on the counter of Griff's drugstore. "For Honest John's girl," read the label pasted on it, and with the dollars and dimes tossed in, Mabel Barbee paid for her college education.

While teaching at Victor, she met a young mining engineer, Howe Lee, and married him. They went off to live in a remote mining camp in Oregon and there, only a few years later, Lee died, leaving Mabel with a small daughter and no money. She promptly packed up and went back to Colorado College, her alma mater, and became dean of women. Then she moved east to Radcliffe and eventually helped launch Bennington College in Vermont. Although we corresponded all through those years, I didn't see her again until after she'd retired. Then, when I pointed out that she had a superb story to tell and, at last, the time to write it, she set to work. The result was *Cripple Creek Days,* a best seller, with two fine sequels.

Like nearly every other boy my age I worked after school and all summer. I did not necessarily distinguish myself at first and learned only slowly, as Shakespeare so eagerly wrote, that "If all the years were playing holidays/To sport would be as tedious as to work."

In the beginning I worked for a cattle rancher named Kennedy whose scraggly spread wound around the rocks at the base of Nipple Mountain south of Victor. Every meal there consisted of stacks of pancakes, and my particular job involved following a tired old horse and plow and clearing a boulder-strewn field that seemed to me to stretch away into eternity. At the end of a week, when the very sight of pancakes was enough to stifle my appetite, when I had tilled a strip about four feet wide and my back ached and my brain felt scrambled from the plow's constant collisions with huge and malevolently hidden rocks, I stopped in mid-field and evaluated my situation. True,

I had not yet been paid. True that at this late date I had no prospect of another job for the summer. But, on the other hand, if I left quickly and quietly the poor horse would have a few hours of rest before anyone realized I was gone, and as for me—well, what could be worse than interminable pancakes and endless boulders?

So I turned up the trail for home—and found out.

My father listened respectfully to my tale of woe, then put his arm around my shoulder and walked me outside. I knew he was vastly displeased that I'd quit on a job I had promised to do, but he made no mention of this. Instead, in the backyard, he pointed to a load of freshly cut pinion pine, brought in by some rancher in lieu of the cash due on his medical bill. "I was planning on hiring this cut into firewood," my father said, "but as you now seem to be unoccupied this summer, it will provide something to keep you busy."

It did. Pinion pine oozes pitch, which makes it burn well even when green, but sawing through its three-foot diameter, with that gooey tar grabbing at the saw blade and clogging its teeth, was sheer hell. Once in a while through that everlasting summer I could cajole a friend into getting on the other end of the huge crosscut saw, which helped, but mostly I was out there alone, day after day, hacking away and sometimes groaning with fatigue and frustration. But at last our mountainous pile disappeared and the work was finished, and though my father never paid me a cent for doing it, I came to realize that I had been otherwise rewarded: all the physical labor I have ever done since has seemed easier by comparison. Long after, when I mentioned this to my father, he responded with a line from the Book of Common Prayer: "And that thou, Lord, art merciful: for thou rewardest every man according to his work."

The following summer I went to work in the mines as a mucker. My job was swinging a pick and shovel, also pushing ore cars out to the shaft from the Buena vein of the Empire State mine, this vein at the time the richest single streak of ore ever discovered, $36,000 in gold to every ton of rock. A vein of such high-grade was an irresistible temptation to the miners: each day they chipped out rich bits for themselves and smuggled them out of the mine in boot tops and secret body belts. This practice was appropriately known as high-grading, and the driller for whom I worked, a boisterous bull of a man named Ed Cody, was getting rich at it. Before long he was able to realize a long-time ambition. He rounded up his pals, chartered a private train and took them all out to Los Angeles for a month-long celebration.

Both the government and the mine operators tried hard to put an end to high-grading. But it was so widespread, so much a part of the life in Cripple—high-grade was often dropped in the church collection plate—that even the local law winked at it. In one celebrated case in which a miner was caught red-handed with a load of rich ore taken from the Independence, the judge ruled that ore was real estate and how could anyone "steal" real estate? Not guilty.

But even convictions didn't always help. A Denver man named Sullivan was charged with perjury—the prosecution couldn't prove that his gold was high-grade from Cripple, but it did prove, by color comparisons, that it couldn't have come from Sullivan's mine in Boulder County, as he claimed. So Mr. Sullivan was sent off to serve a year at the federal penitentiary at Leavenworth—whereupon he returned to Denver to report to one and all that he knew of no better way to make $50,000 than to take the penalty. High-grading at Cripple eventually ended, it's true, but not by edict or the threat of punishment; it ended because the mines had less and less high-grade.

For a time I worked at the Tornado, in a stope—a huge underground cavern—notorious for the number of miners injured by falling rock. Accidents of all sorts were common enough in the mines—cave-ins, fire, falls, premature explosions—and people tended to become hardened to them. But that summer Cripple suffered a disaster of such tragic magnitude, the worst mining accident in its history, that nobody in the district was unaffected. Somehow, something went wrong with the hoist at the Independence mine. At dawn, loaded with men coming off the "graveyard shift," it shot to the top of the gallows frame with a terrific speed, then, completely out of control, dropped even faster, thirteen hundred feet to the bottom of the shaft. The bodies of twenty-two miners were brought to Hunt's Mortuary in Victor that morning, and people watched in stupefied silence as the big Clydesdale horses pulled wagon after wagon through the street.

In time I held nearly every job there was to be had in a mining camp—mucker, trammer, driller, ore sorter.

Sorting ore was one of my favorite jobs because the ore house was on the surface, and as you routinely sifted the various grades of rock you could listen to the gaudy tales of men who had been on the trail of gold in the farthest corners of earth, from the Klondike to South Africa. This experience had a marked effect on me. Only a few years later, when I had a chance to break away from the day-in, day-out routines of life, I too went off looking for adventure, and it was those ore-house stories that sent me on to Alaska. And even later, when I would be called on to speak to black-tie audiences, I could always break the ice by telling them that I had gotten my start in an *ore house*.

I suppose the peak of my mining career was riding assay for the great Portland mine. It was located on Battle Mountain, named for the epic labor war that raged there in '94, and its assay office also serviced innumerable smaller mines and "prospect holes" in the mountain all around. For two summers, nine hours a day, I rode horseback over those mountains, my saddlebags filled with ore samples and the high hopes of prospectors and small, independent operators. The ore was then roasted in the assay office furnace and the residue of pure gold weighed. Next day, on my rounds, I would report the results to the miners. They were nearly always disappointed, for there is a certain harsh and eternally unequal equation in the quest for gold: dreams are boundless, but gold is still a rare metal.

Sometimes, in the long afternoon, when the sun was hot and the snow-covered peaks shimmered hypnotically in the distance, the seductive rhythm of my horse would lull me, nodding, dozing in my saddle. And one day, following a late night of dancing, I fell into a sound sleep. All might have gone well, for the trail was familiar and the horse surefooted, but as we crossed the railroad tunnel near the Ajax mine, a train entering the far end let loose a blast from its steam whistle that set the horse into a bolting leap across the tracks. That woke me, but unfortunately I hadn't made the leap as gracefully and, in fact found myself hanging from the horse's underside and tangled in the girth and saddle straps. Luckily the horse stopped—I suppose he was as unsettled as I was by this unorthodox alignment of steed and rider—and I was finally able to crawl free and remount.

As it happened, I was reporting some good news to the next miner on my rounds, and he broke out a bottle of bourbon to celebrate. But when he offered me a drink I refused politely, remarking that I had already fallen off my horse once that day.

Even now, when I return to Cripple Creek, I manage to find a moment for a visit to the mountain above. My favorite place is a height called Windy Point, where I'd sit in the saddle and marvel at the great arc of peaks, the spine of our continent, reaching from New Mexico to Wyoming. Now there is a metal marker there, noting the names of the 14,000-foot mountains of the Sangre de Cristo and the Collegiate Range, visible from the spot. Unmarked are the other places I remember best, mines like the Bluebird, the Wild Horse, the American Eagle, Ramona, Joe Dandy, the Lost King, the Doctor Jack Pot, trails now overgrown and forgotten, and forgotten with them the dreams of thousands of eager and hard-working men and women, all now gone from that place. Cripple Creek and Victor, Anaconda and Altman, all are a curiosity. But whenever I go back and stand a moment at Windy Point, they all come to life again.

In the summer of 1907, my father concluded that boom times were over in "the World's Greatest Gold Camp." He sent Mother, Pherbia and me back to Darke County to stay with relatives while he set off to look for a new opportunity somewhere in the Northwest. It was a strange year. Ohio seemed a foreign place to me, and in my western clothes—boots, flannel shirt and broad-brimmed Stetson—I felt much the young barbarian. Here the local heroes were the high school football and baseball players, and while I had always managed to win a berth on school teams —mostly, I suspect, because there were so few eligibles— I was far from the shining light on any of them. And, as always, I was the youngest.

After a summer of poaching on the hospitality of a series of aunts and uncles, my mother rented a house in Greenville, the county seat, and there, in September, I was enrolled in the high school, in the junior class. For a few miserable days I tried to make myself invisible among those effete Easterners who wore cotton shirts and red ties to school, and they obliged by treating me accordingly. Then an unusual thing happened, abruptly changing the tenor of that entire year and making it one of the most important of my life.

Along about the third week, our English teacher, red-haired Ada Bowman, with a taste for the classics, decreed that each of us was to memorize a famous oration or part of one and deliver it before the school assembly. For the others in class the assignment had the ring of doom—make a speech in the assembly—and the husky football players quivered perceptibly as the fateful hour drew near. But as my father had been coaching me in public speaking from the time I could walk, I never gave it a thought beyond brushing up on the piece I'd decided to do, Wendell Phillips's famous tribute to the Haitian patriot, Toussaint L'Ouverture.

On the appointed day, a parade of unhappy young men stumbled up to the platform, mumbled into their neckties, forgot their lines, perspired and finally fled back to the oblivion of their seats. I deserve no particular credit for doing better—I had, after all, been doing this sort of thing for years. But the reaction was astonishing. There was a burst of applause when I finished, and all the rest of that week boys and girls with whom I'd never exchanged a word crossed the classroom, the hall and the street to greet me as though I were a lifelong friend. The following Monday they elected me captain of the football team. Actually I won the election by default—because the team was evenly split on two other chaps, one of whom should have had the honor.

From then on, life in Greenville was fine. I belonged. I was somebody. Cripple, for all its romance, was a place where I had constantly to strive to keep up with the rough and tough sons of miners, gamblers, saloonkeepers. Not only was I younger, but all the things that came so naturally to them—their casual profanity, their card-playing, and drinking—were strictly forbidden in our house. And though I sometimes broke the rules in an adolescent effort to be one of them, I could never manage it with their easy grace. Now, in Greenville, the success of my oracle effort plus, I suppose, the aura of my western background stood me in good stead. The local newspaper, reporting the line-up of our first football game, listed the captain and quarterback as Lowell "Two-Gun" Thomas. All at once I was cast into a position of leadership, and it was all heady and gave me more confidence in myself than I had ever had.

I had my first ride in an automobile that year, a splendid new Reo belonging to Noah Markee, a distant relative, and

44

I even attained a certain celebrity in the neighborhood pool hall. With my experience at Rosser's and Swift Billy Dingman's gambling places on Victor Avenue, I could out-shoot most of my contemporaries. They were impressed but vastly overestimated my talent when they matched me with the local pool shark, Jelly Burns. Jelly, a onetime ball-player who had pitched in the high minor leagues and now spent all his days shooting pool, was quite simply the best player I ever saw in action. In short order he won all the money my friends and I had bet on me.

Years later, when I returned to Greenville to speak on some special occasion, the townspeople gave me a parade and asked if there was anyone in particular from the old days that I'd like to see again. I told them yes, I wanted to see Jelly Burns and take him on in another game of pool. And so it was arranged, complete with a full crowd, as well as press and photographers from Dayton. And old Jelly, now well along in years then, hadn't lost a thing. I have a copy of one of the newspaper photos of the great event, with a caption beneath. "Lowell Thomas," it said, "scratched the cue ball in the side pocket, whereupon Jelly Burns cleared the table."

That year in Greenville went swiftly, and the following summer we returned to Colorado. My father hadn't found anyplace that suited him as well as Victor did, and so I spent my last year in high school back in the gold camp. I organized and edited our first school paper, *The Sylvanite*, and spent a lot of time sending letters of inquiry to various colleges and universities. There had never been any question but that I would continue my education, not in my father's house. And when I was called upon to deliver the com-mencement address, I loftily, if naïvely, exhorted my class-mates to do the same: "Those who cannot cope with what they consider the faults of college might as well make fools of themselves there as anywhere," I declaimed. "Young men and women of Victor High! Consider well before giving up your opportunity to acquire a higher education!"

I had had a letter of acceptance from a place called the University of Northern Indiana. Suddenly there was a flurry of packing, last-minute reminders and advice, hur-ried kisses. Then I was climbing aboard the train at the Victor depot, waving good-bye to my parents and, age seventeen, off on my own.

3.

Adventures in Journalism

Hello, Lowell. Are you still in bed? Well, listen,
you'd better stay there. The mayor is out looking
for you, and he's got a gun.

—HONEST JOHN WHITE

OFFICIALLY, it was the University of Northern Indiana
at Valparaiso. There were some who called it the poor
man's Harvard, but to those of us who were students
there during its golden era, the years before World War I,
it was plain old Valpo. Its strength was a straightforward
and uncomplicated attention to the matter at hand—education. There was no football team, no athletic program, not
even a gymnasium; there were no accommodating courses
in knot-tying, ballet dancing or leisure-time management.
There was no leisure time. The student body was about
equally divided between those young men who, scholasti-
cally, would have been eligible for a Big Ten or Ivy League
school but couldn't afford it and those who had already
been out in the world and belatedly discovered the value
of a college education. And they worked!

This doggedly industrious attitude must have impressed
me when I appeared in that late summer of 1909. Without
consulting anyone, I signed up for both the freshman and
sophomore years. By the time this monumental arrogance
was discovered, the semester was half over; Vice-President
Kinsey, who had sent for me with every intention of dressing me down and throwing me out of the sophomore class,
could only stare at the record and, his big red moustaches

twitching, mutter, "Well—harrumph—you seem to be—harrumph—managing."

"Yes, sir," replied Two-Gun Thomas, straining to hide self-satisfaction.

"But look here, young man," Professor Kinsey exclaimed, moustaches dancing with agitation at this affront to tradition and experience, "at this rate you'll have your bachelor's degree in little more than a year!"

"Then I'll stay two and take a master's," I replied. Perhaps one of my many weaknesses has been an oversupply of confidence.

And so it was to be. Meanwhile, though, I had to provide for myself, as did so many others at Valpo. My first job was as a janitor in Stiles Hall, where I roomed with a stiff, poker-faced Spanish-American War veteran named George Washington Vilain. My job included tending the furnace, sweeping the halls daily and scrubbing them weekly, and milking the cantankerous old cow that the widow Stiles kept in the backyard. A nonglamorous occupation? Yes, but it paid for room and board.

As I was intent on maintaining my double class load, I could not have been luckier in the roommates that fate chose to send my way. Vilain—nobody ever called him George—a law student in his thirties, could have been a character in an O. Henry story. The scion of a modestly well-to-do New York City family, he had, years before, broken his parents' hearts by spurning a university education and running off to join the army. But unlike other young men who yield to some rash impulse and are never heard from again, Vilain made a distinguished career with the Corps of Engineers in the Philippines, rising to the rank of major. Then came the moment of truth: Vilain realizing his parents had been right in the first place, that he needed and wanted an education; George Washington Vilain deciding that he would return to the States, study, earn a law degree, all without a word to his parents; Vilain planning the letter he would write inviting them to his graduation, knowing their joy at such an unexpected surprise. And so it all went—until, only a few months before he was to be awarded the coveted degree, both his mother and father died, never to know of the dramatic turn in their son's life.

But now Vilain was firmly fixed on his course, nor was he to be distracted by the attentions paid him by Mrs.

Stiles's Amazon daughter, Jessica. To escape her ardor, he would flee to the library or an unoccupied classroom to study, leaving me alone to do the same without distraction. When he graduated, I moved over to Mead Hall and was assigned a roommate who was equally considerate—for the opposite reason—and shall therefore be nameless here. He was a genial student in engineering who had discovered the charms of a lady living nearby known as Mabel the Campus Widow and some less kind appellations. Except for exam time, he was at her place day and night, so again I had a room to myself.

By this time, having discovered that there were easier ways of paying for my keep than sweeping floors and serving as valet to a spavined cow, I was working as waiter and cook in a short-order restaurant. Then my horizons expanded again. Although Valpo tolerated no fraternities —like intercollegiate sports, they were considered diversionary to the goal of learning—one, Alpha Epsilon, had flourished sub rosa and attracted some of the most gregarious students and even a few of the faculty. I was invited to join and made some of my most prized and lasting friendships.

One of the earliest was with a handsome and persuasive young man from Kansas, Preston Burtis, known by everyone as Cap. Now Cap, as the cliché goes, could sell refrigerators to Eskimos, and he soon sold me on a new way to make some money. The national census of 1910 had left nearly all town and county maps out of date; we would take a month or two off that summer and tour the countryside selling revised maps. "Tommy," he assured me, we'll clean up." Well, we didn't, but we had a lot of fun and, clip-clopping along in the leisurely manner dictated by a horse and buggy, we met some interesting people.

As we seemed to have our best success in the farm country of northern Illinois, we made our headquarters in the city of Elgin. It was a place with a special aura in those days, home of the Elgin Road Race. Automobile racing was just coming into its own—the Indianapolis Speedway had recently been built and, the following year, would get its famous brick surface for the first running of the Indianapolis "500"—and a new kind of hero, the racing driver, was taking his place in the American pantheon. Given my unabashed Colorado mining camp background

48

and Cap's silver tongue, it is hardly surprising that we got to know three of the top racers.

The first was a starchy litle man with icicles for nerves named Ralph DePalma. In the next four years Ralph won the national racing championship twice, then capped his career by taking the Indianapolis "500" with an average speed just under ninety miles an hour, a record that stood until 1922. One evening DePalma introduced us to Barney Oldfield, a cigar-chomping daredevil, whose name had become synonymous with speed. As gregarious as DePalma was terse, Oldfield bewitched us with endless stories about his early days in racing.

It had all begun for him in 1902 when a man named Henry Ford, trying to get started in the motorcar business, hired him to race against a well-established competitor, Alexander Winton. "I had never even been behind the wheel of an automobile then," Oldfield said, grinning around the ever-present cigar—which, incidentally, he bit into while speeding over the jarring tracks of the day to keep from breaking his teeth—"but I guess Ford had heard that I'd try anything once." With only a few weeks' practice, Oldfield climbed into Ford's "999'" and beat Winton's record-setting car with room to spare. His long and illustrious career as a racing driver was launched—and Henry Ford didn't do badly either.

The third member of that daring trio was the most remarkable of all. His name was Eddie Rickenbacker, and though he was only a year or so older than Cap and I were, he had already thrown himself into the maelstrom of life, dreaming big dreams, unafraid to test himself against the roughest and toughest. History has recorded how well he succeeded—America's greatest air ace of World War I, builder of a major airline, survivor of devastating crashes, one of which cast him adrift in the Pacific for twenty-two days, one of the towering figures of the twentieth century. He remained my close friend and companion over many of those long years from 1911 to 1974, when his wife and sons asked me to deliver the eulogy at his funeral.

For all the fame of the professionals listed to participate in the road race that Cap and I were in Elgin to see, most of the publicity went to a wealthy young amateur from Philadelphia. His name was Spencer Wishart and, like the sons of the ultra-rich before and after, he sought to gratify his own sense of himself by staking the only thing that was truly his—his life—in a wild race. It wan't even winning that mattered; surviving was enough.

It was clear that young Wishart was popular with the other drivers, but as laconic Ralph DePalma put it, "He's out to prove something, and that's no way to drive a race." Some other drivers were more direct. "If I had your money," one told Wishart before the race, "the last thing I'd do is risk getting killed before I had a chance to enjoy it all." The words were prophetic. Early in the race, watching with horror and disbelief, we saw Wishart fail to hold the road on a turn, his sleek car peeling off into the field and demolishing itself against a tree. He was killed on impact.

The time at Valpo went swiftly after that summer. I remember the gathering sense of exhilaration as I realized that I was being drawn onward into unsuspected realms of knowledge, as I was challenged to imagine the unimaginable, to let my mind wander freely, beyond what was written in the books. Much of this full, rich sense of discovery was obviously attributable to Valpo's star-studded faculty, none of whose members was hired only for his solid—and sometimes brilliant—grounding in his subject. Cofounders Kinsey and Brown sought and found teachers who could *teach*, who could convey not only the lesson but their enthusiasm for it, who could goad, inspire and uplift. I was lucky to have been there in their time.

America's foremost man of eloquence in those days was the "Silver-tongued Orator of the Platte," William Jennings Bryan. I was lucky enough to hear him deliver his second most famous oration, "The Prince of Peace." I may have been the only member of the student body to have a chat with him. After his address, when I went around to interview him, he invited me to get in his carriage. All I remember of our conversation was his saying that he invariably made his best speech when on the way to the railway station. Later we again met at T.R.'s Bull Moose convention in Chicago.

Another who appeared for a lecture at Valpo was the handsome British Antarctic explorer, Sir Ernest Shackleton, with whom I was to have a brief encounter many years later in London.

In June, 1911, now all of nineteen years old, I returned to Colorado with a Bachelor of Science and a Master of Arts. My mother and father may have been pleased with me, but neither had a specific suggestion as to how I could convert my newly acquired wisdom into suitable and remunerative work; there were no more Cripple Creek employers out beating the woods for young scholars now than there had been before I left. And so I did what young scholars in mining camps have always done: I took a job swinging a pick and shovel in the mines.

But fate was preparing to smile at me. Before I'd even had a chance to work out the aches and pains from exertions I was no longer used to, the telephone rang and George Khyner, the fast-talking owner of both the Victor *Daily Record* and the Cripple Creek *Times* was on the line:

"I hear you've got a job mucking at the Portland. Is that what you went to college for? Are you interested in mining as a career or something? How much do they pay you?"

"Yes," I mumbled, trying to thread my way through the maze of questions. "I mean, no, no—I'm not interested in mining, but—well, they pay me three dollars a day."

"Oh, yeah? Well, I'll give you ninety-five a month to come to work for me on the *Record* as a reporter. Room for advancement. Take it or leave it."

"Why, yes, sure, Mr. Khyner." My hands had grown wet on the telephone and my heart leaped into double time. I wanted to be absolutely sure he understood I was taking it: "I'll take it, Mr. Khyner, and thank you. When should I come to work?"

"Right now," he said, and hung up.

That was George Khyner. He had turned up shorthanded that night. Employees didn't always stay long with George— and when someone reminded him that I was home from college he got me on the phone. Thereafter he went around telling everyone how he had saved me from throwing my life away in the mines, never mentioning that for ninety-five dollars a month he expected me to turn out the *Record* almost single-handedly. Reporter? It turned out that I was to be reporter, editor, legman, rewrite man and front man for reader complaints.

George always got his money's worth. He had gone into the bitter strike of 1904 supporting the Western Federation of Miners, but when the militia smashed up the *Record*'s offices and press, he abruptly took an editorial stand in favor of the owners. People naturally assumed that a healthy

51

fear for his own skin was responsible, but the fact was that George wasn't afraid of anything. Once I'd gone to work for the *Record,* I found out how the owners had compensated him for the ruined press. Then they threw in another three thousand as an argument in favor of a change in the *Record*'s editorial policy, and the argument proved persuasive.

But I don't want to carp. George Khyner gave me a chance to get started in journalism in a time and place of zesty news stories breaking outside your front door or just down the street. In any given ten-day period, you could count on a shooting spree in a gambling hall or one of the red-light districts, a holdup, a fire, a mine accident and an indignant reader proposing to horsewhip the editor. There were also rodeos, prizefights, evangelists heralding imminent doom for sinners—duly reported also were fraternal-order marching competitions with the winner sometimes decided by a general brawl that extended the length of Victor Avenue and drew the biggest crowds of all. It was an opportunity to intrigue any young man with a taste for the great human drama, and at the time this just suited me.

But I was still a few months short of my twentieth birthday and made a fair number of mistakes. One was to use a type size for headlines that more accurately reflected my enthusiasm than the importance of the story. Once, after a fire, I pulled out a wooden type face three inches high, the kind usually reserved for posters and handbills, and the *Record* proclaimed, "BLAZE SWEEPS LOCAL BUILDINGS!" That afternoon, one of my predecessors, Frank Arkens, who had moved on to a job with a New York newspaper, returned for a visit to his old haunts. He glanced at the headline.

"Do you think it's too big?" I asked.

"How many local buildings were swept by this blaze?"

"Three."

"Well, I tell you what, kid," he said, "I'd try to hold something back for the Second Coming."

One mistake I didn't make was to stay too long running a one-man operation in that pressure cooker of a frontier newspaper. If I had, all the journalistic juices would have been boiled out of me. I had some distinguished predecessors—among them, Ralph Carr, later governor of Colorado; Charlie Ross, press secretary to President Truman—and all left the *Record* before losing their sense of wonder at man's frailties and foibles, a newspaperman's greatest asset.

My chance came about six months after I went to work for Khyner. A group from Denver was starting a second newspaper in Victor, the *News*, and offered me the job as editor. Since they suggested a salary of a hundred thirty-five dollars a month—Khyner was still paying me ninety-five, still talking about "room for advancement"—and promised a qualified staff to help get out the paper, I didn't take too long to make my decision.

I never regretted moving on, but the fact is that nothing much changed at first. Victor was still a boomtown and I was still covering all the action. As for the staff, it consisted of mining editor Sam Vidler, a general manager with a game leg, Honest John White—he was always called that, Honest John, I don't know why—who looked after circulation, advertising and paying the bills, and a series of itinerant linotype operators.

Linotypers were a special breed in those days; they all seemed to be midway in a headlong flight from something or someone—debts, the law, a woman—and the only lasting friendships they made were with a bottle of whiskey. We had one, Honest John insisted, who spilled more whiskey in a day than any man at Crapper Jack's could drink down. Another, a decent-looking young chap, told me he had taken to the road when his marriage broke up.

"That's too bad," I said sympathetically. "How long were you married?"

"Three days," he said, and suddenly sat up straight. "Say, I'm still carrying around the tails and striped pants I was hitched in—you want to buy 'em?"

"Uh, no. I don't think I can spare the money."

"Maybe you've got something to trade for 'em—I keep remembering things whenever I open my bag and see 'em, know what I mean?"

"Well, I don't know . . ."

We were pretty much of a size and I didn't mind imagining myself dressed in formal clothes at some grand banquet to which no one had yet invited me, but I couldn't think of anything I owned that might interest him. He kept pressing me and hesitantly, I mentioned a pair of roller skates I no longer used.

"Sold!" he exclaimed, slamming his hand on the table. The following week, roller skates slung over his shoulder, he rode out of town and I had to start looking for another linotyper. But I had my first set of tails.

Mining editor Sam Vidler had woman trouble, too. He was English and had served as an officer in India, where he won the broadsword fencing championship of the world. But Sam had a weakness for the ladies, a failing his wife viewed with some heat, and as Honest John farsightedly put it, "This could lead to quite a misunderstanding."

It did. One day Sam's little boy misbehaved at school and was given a whipping. Mrs. Vidler thought this unjust and went out to find her husband and have him do something about it. The trouble is she found him in Room 213 in the National Hotel and, approaching the door, heard the sighs and banterings of her Sam and a girl named Nellie Smith. Whereupon Mrs. Vidler marched forthwith to a nearby store, purchased a revolver, had the accommodating clerk load it for her and give her a quick lesson in its operation. Back up to the hotel she went, still marching, turmoil in her breast and righteousness on her side, flung open the door of Sam's room and shot the undraped Nellie dead. She would have finished Sam off, too—she emptied the gun in his direction—but he went diving under the bed and the mattress got the worst of it. It took a jury only ten minutes to acquit Mrs. Vidler—Cripple took a broad view: it tolerated philandering but always deferred to outraged womanhood—and she and Sam went home together. Nor did anyone ever hear of him trespassing again, not after he found out his wife was serious.

A story like that could really sell papers, as William Randolph Hearst had recently discovered. And following in his tumultuous wake, newspapers large and small were trying to nourish their circulation with a daily dose of sex, sensationalism or, at the very least, the picture of a pretty girl on the front page. The Victor *Daily News* was no exception and, as its editor, I was constantly made aware that we were in a no-holds-barred battle for readers with the *Record*. Mostly, the Cripple Creek district worked valiantly to provide the proper grist for the paper's melodramatic mill, but every now and then an unfortunate peacefulness settled on the gold camp and I had to go casting about for some far-flung sensation. And that's how I got in trouble.

It was a gallingly quiet Saturday night, nothing happening in Victor, not a word from Cripple, Goldfield, Independence, Elkton, Anaconda or Altman. There was a possibility from Denver—man shot by paramour—but no pictures of either. Then a vague similarity in names suddenly crystallized for me into what seemed like a piece of good luck—the victim was the nephew of our mayor! In no time at all I had the story written—"MAYOR'S NEPHEW SHOT IN LOVE NEST!"—and prominently placed on page one. Naturally, a picture of the mayor accompanied it, grinning as he received the returns from the last election. Then, feeling the honest exhaustion that comes after a hard job well done, I went home to bed.

In the morning, before breakfast, the telephone rang. It was Honest John White. "Hello Lowell?" he said. "Are you still in bed? Well, listen, you'd better stay there. The mayor is out looking for you, and he's got a gun."

Having digested this along with my coffee, I concluded the mayor had cause to be angry and, since I was in no position to leave town, I'd better exercise my other option and apologize. So I dressed and went directly to his home, where I first explained my mission to his wife. Bless her, she agreed to serve as intermediary and, when the mayor returned, calmed him sufficiently so he would suffer me to come out of the kitchen and enter his presence. Whereupon I expressed my contrition, mentioned the possibility of doing an interview with him for next Sunday's paper, extolling the promise and progress he had brought to our fair town, until, finally, he put away the gun.

In the fall of 1912, a yen for more schooling, inherited, I suppose, from my father, overtook me. I quit the paper and, with my savings, went down to Denver and enrolled for a year of graduate study at the University. Chancellor Buchtel suggested that as I was still quite young and had gotten both my degrees in only two years, it might be wise to take some of the Denver University senior courses as well as doing graduate work. So again I was enrolled in two classes, and when the year ended I had another bachelor's degree and a second M.A.

It was a full fruitful year. Denver was the state capital, a young and vigorous city, financial headquarters of the Rocky Mountain region, crossroads for miners and ranchers heading hopefully into the wide open spaces of the West, and the shining metropolis to which, if they reached the end of their rainbow, they returned to sometimes lavish retirement.

I had no trouble finding a job, two jobs, in fact; when I wasn't at classes, I worked as part-time reporter for the Rocky Mountain *News* and Denver *Times,* and at night I was the clerk at a small downtown hotel, where I did my studying and even managed to get in a little sleep. Until then, everything I knew about journalism was learned on the firing line, and as I've confessed, I was shot down more than once. Now, though, I began to find out how little I really understood about my calling.

My first mentor was city editor William L. Chenery, who was soon to head east to edit the New York *Globe* and eventually become the distinguished publisher of *Collier's Weekly.* This paragraph from his autobiography suggests some of the subtle truisms of the craft he conveyed to me:

Children of six and men in their sixties are often impelled to tell any who will listen the strange, interesting, or exciting happenings that have come to their individual attention. The teller of the tale is not always the best judge of its interest or significance, as every young reporter should learn.

I learned a good deal from other reporters I met on assignments, and particularly from a tall and striking whirlwind of talent named Gene Fowler. Ahead of him were the glory days as a Hearst editor, top Hollywood script writer and biographer of such cronies as Charlie Chaplin, John Barrymore, Jimmy Walker and Jimmy Durante. When I first met him that autumn of 1911, he was working for the opposition Denver *Post,* but that didn't keep him from sharing his lore—and sometimes his scoops—with an inexperienced kid reporter from the gold camp.

Although none of his colleagues knew it, Gene was also well on his way to becoming America's most widely quoted author of unprintable poetry and its number one practical joker. He only improved with the years. Once, just before World War II, he was staying at the Savoy in London and heard that Fran and I would be checking in the day after his departure. With earnest mien, he told the manager that the Thomases must have his suite, the best in the house, and that of course they would settle his bill. A week at the Savoy is not for bargain hunters at best, but Fowler's bills for meals, liquor, laundry and valet service would have done credit to an Arabian caliph.

I was prepared to chalk it up against my long-ago lessons in journalism, but Fowler wasn't quite finished with me. Not long after, there came a letter from him with check enclosed. Going through his old uncle Dewey's papers, Gene wrote, he had come across an unpaid bill from my father, Dr. H. G. Thomas, for setting Dewey's broken leg. The bill was now some thirty years old, true, but a debt was a debt, he said piously, and if one Fowler couldn't pay, another would. The check was for $3.98. Today, framed, it's on my studio wall.

When Gene was editor of Hearst's New York *Examiner*, he occasionally jousted with another Hearst favorite, Arthur Brisbane. Brisbane was probably the best-known newsman of the time, a crusty, pompous sort who dictated his widely syndicated column, "Today," into a recording device as he drove into the city from Long Island in a Rolls-Royce. Each day he would deliver the column to the *Examiner*, and each day Gene was required to run it on page one, regardless of what other news might be breaking, an edict that rubbed my freewheeling friend the wrong way. That he would strike back could hardly surprise anyone who knew Gene Fowler, but his modus operandi was sheer, staggering bravura.

The inspiration came to him on an otherwise quiet afternoon as he looked down from his office window and saw Brisbane's empty Rolls parked at the curb. Without ado, he went down, turned on the recording machine and dictated into it one of his wildly obscene poems. Upstairs, he substituted this record for the one Brisbane had done and had it set in type. Then he waited. Around midnight, just as the paper was about to go to press, he telephoned Brisbane on Long Island and woke him from a sound sleep.

"Listen, Arthur," he said, "I think you'd better come down here. There seems to be something wrong with your column."

"What," demanded Brisbane haughtily, "is the matter with my column?"

"Well, there's a lot of dirty words in it."

Brisbane dove into his Rolls and raced to New York to beat the deadline. He read his "column," first with stupefaction, then with exploding wrath as he realized what

Fowler had done, and he swore vengeance. Indeed, soon after Gene was sent off to exile in the green fields of Hollywood. But around the *Examiner*, there was no question about who had had the last laugh.

In the last crowded months before I left D.U., several rather important things happened, the least of which caused me to decide not to become an impresario of the boxing ring. A classmate, a rugged redhead from Wyoming named Art Shauer, had a few amateur bouts, and somehow we both took it into our heads that he might have what it would take to beat the champ, Jack Johnson. I managed to locate a well-known, unranked heavyweight, Farmer Smith, and even arranged to stage the bout secretly in the university gym. The only thing I couldn't manage was to keep poor Art on his feet. Smith knocked him cold early in the first round, and we both continued searching for conquerable worlds.

For a while Paul Chamberlin, a lighthearted, curly-haired playboy from Colorado Springs, was my roommate. Paul and I became good friends, in spite of the fact that I obviously didn't share his penchant for the bottle. His favorite recreation seemed ironic since his father, a doctor, was a leader of the Prohibition movement and had, in fact, run for governor on the Prohibition ticket. Today's parents, alienated from children who have turned to marijuana or worse, may take some small comfort from the fact that such phenomena aren't new. Anyway, Paul was to play a decisive if unwitting role in the course my life was soon to take.

And there was a girl, a freshman named Fran Ryan. Although I had never taken her out and we hadn't spent ten minutes alone—we met at parties and occasionally saw each other at school—there was something about her, a certain look, a kind of heightened sensitivity to life's promises, that must have kept sending messages to my brain. I didn't do anything about it. Maybe I didn't clearly understand the messages. But surely something was happening to me.

Meanwhile, I was coming face to face with my future and still had no clear idea of the direction I wanted it to take. For all my four degrees, I had nothing but a general education in the liberal arts, essential for the enrichment of soul and spirit, but only a bare foundation on which to build a career. Did I want to be a newspaperman? Or was I still heading for the law? And one of my father's favorite theologians, Dr. Wilbur Daniel Steele, who taught on the D.U. campus, had recently honored me by urging that I consider the ministry.

"A good many of the young men I see who want to enter the clergy think they have had the call," this wise, white-bearded old gentleman said to me one day. "They think the Almighty has spoken directly to them. But you know, I don't think they make exceptional ministers; they become so involved in their private dialogue with God that they tend to neglect their congregations. Do you think you have the call, Lowell?"

"No, sir."

"Good, because I think you have other qualities that would make for a rewarding career in the ministry. Will you think about it?"

"Yes, I will," I said, confused by the unexpected addition to the possibilities before me. "Thank you, sir."

And I did think about it. I thought about the ministry, the law, journalism and half a dozen other callings that popped into my head, trying each on for size, imagining myself engaged in that one profession and no other for all the rest of my life. And when school ended and I had my degrees, I packed up and went off to a ranch my father had acquired in the southwest corner of Colorado, near "The Four Corners," and I thought some more.

Once my father said to me. "Son, when it comes to land, the easiest marks are doctors, lawyers and preachers."

He was no exception. When an old friend who owned a profitless spread in the San Juan country ran into stormy financial weather, Dad bailed him out by taking the ranch off his hands. He had to use all his savings and borrowed money to do it, and then of course was too busy with his practice ever to spend any time there. But it did serve as a temporary haven for his brother, Ira, who had retired from the railroad and been advised to get out of Chicago to cure a persistent cough. So Uncle Ira, Aunt Rose and my cousin Ruth were running the ranch when I turned up there that summer.

The San Juan was spectacular country, much of it open range then and still roamed by bands of Ute Indians led by Chief Buckskin Charlie. Our place was in the valley of the Los Pinos River, at an altitude of seven thousand feet. Uncle Ira raised some alfalfa but depended, like the other ranchers, on the state-owned rangeland to graze his cattle. This meant I spent most of the summer in the saddle, helping with brandings and roundups, sleeping on my saddle blanket under the stars that seemed almost within reach over that high valley. And sometimes, riding along in chaps and spurs, the clear, cool breeze in my face, I wondered why the life of a cowboy wouldn't suit me.

And then, suddenly, for reasons that remain a mystery to me to this day, I decided that I would go to Chicago and study law. And before July was out I was on my way.

Chicago. It was then the center of our midwestern universe, big, bustling, important, but still rooted in the bedrock of America's heartland. It was our big city—imaginable, attainable, understandable—not like those Gomorrahs at the extremities of the continent, New York and San Francisco, which—everyone knew!—were awash with alien philosophies and bizarre notions of morality. How absolutely certain we can be, how unwavering our pronouncements, when we are twenty!

When I arrived in Chicago, the Republicans, having renominated William Howard Taft for President against the wishes of everyone but the bosses, had slunk out of town and left it to Teddy Roosevelt's Progressives. Unable to buck the machine, T.R., "feeling like a bull moose," had formed his own party and, announcing to his enraptured followers at the convention that "We stand at Armageddon and we battle for the Lord," prepared to take on Democrats and Republicans alike. The streets were festooned with banners, Bull Moose posters and pictures of T.R., just as though no one knew that by splitting the party he had assured Woodrow Wilson's victory in November. It was a heady, exciting time, especially for a young fellow just in from the Ute country.

As soon as I arrived, even before I found a place to live or began looking into law schools, I went down to newspaper row in search of a job. There were four papers located on Market Street, near the Chicago River, in those days, the *Evening Journal*, the *Post* and Hearst's *Examiner* and *American*. I don't know why I chose to try the *Journal* first—maybe because it was an evening paper, which meant that it was written and put together in the daytime and fitted my plan to attend law school at night; but more likely it was the broad stairs and massive double doors invitingly swung open in the summer heat. Anyway, it seemed a casual enough decision at the time.

There were a dozen reporters at their typewriters, the horseshoe copy desk, and, overseeing it all from his corner looking out on Market Street, the young city editor, cool and decisive, absolutely in command. It was a moment I've never forgotten.

Apparently I was noticed from on high. Or at least that's the way Dick Finnegan, then city editor, told it years afterward when he introduced me as a speaker at a Chicago Press Club banquet. "I looked up," he said, "and saw this young fellow from the West standing outside the bullpen, wearing a Stetson, and I said to the assistant city editor, 'Find out what he wants; if it's a job, he's got it.'"

I could not have had a more effective sponsor. Dick Finnegan, as I was soon to find out, *was* the *Evening Journal*. A dark, handsome man with a law degree and a youthful fling at politics behind him, he now knew everyone in the city, county and state governments, not only those who held the offices but those who pulled strings from the dark corridors of power. Seated at his desk that first day, my head whirling at the speed with which things were happening, I was enthralled by the incisive way he went at things:

Looking for a newspaper job? Any experience? Good. You'll start at fifteen dollars a week. Did I have a place to live? No? Okay, the assistant city editor had an apartment on the South Side and was looking for a roomer. What else?

When I told him I was hoping to attend law school at night, he scrawled a name and address on a piece of paper —Guy Guernsey, Chicago-Kent College of Law, Lakeview Building, Michigan Avenue. "Tell him Dick Finnegan sent you." And so my future in Chicago was all settled in the space of ten minutes.

Fate smiled on. Guy Guernsey turned out to be the dean of Chicago-Kent, a flourishing institution with well over a thousand students. He seemed much interested in my debating and oratorical experience, as much so as in my four degrees. A few days later he called me to his office and introduced me to a distinguished gentleman, one Edmund W. Burke, the president of the Chicago-Kent College of Law. There had been an unexpected vacancy on the faculty, in the department of forensic oratory, which he described as devoted to the techniques of courtroom debate; did I think I could take the place of the departed professor until they found a suitable replacement?

I didn't think at all—I just said yes. That's the sort of thing you do at twenty-one, when the world is young and its challenges all look like gifts. In the end they never did hire another professor of forensic oratory, and I went on studying law, working full time as a reporter on the *Journal*, and giving instruction in public speaking with the entire student body in my classes.

In time I learned to lighten my load by inviting notable figures from the legal profession to address my pupils. "Just talk about your own experiences," I'd tell them. And we had some electrifying performances. One was by a young man named Glenn Frank, who came as a last-minute substitute for his ailing superior, the president of Northwestern University. His address was inspirational—"Two Fisted Men," the theme—and the cynics among my students prepared to doze off. But Glenn Frank held them spellbound with as brilliant an affirmation as I have ever heard of man's inherent ability to take his future in hand and mold it to his soaring dreams. When he was finished, the class gave him a standing ovation, and after he had left, I told them to keep an eye on him—that surely he was going places.

He might have gone all the way. Next I heard, he had moved east to head a widely heralded social-improvement program for the Boston merchant prince, Edward A. Filene. Soon he was named editor of the prestigious *Century Magazine*, head of President Taft's League of Nations Union, and then, still not forty years old, president of the University of Wisconsin. His counsel was sought by the highest political figures. I visited the Franks at Madison one autumn and in the late 1920s went to the Wisconsin-Minnesota game with them. While Bronko Nagurski ripped holes in the Wisconsin line, Mrs. Frank was telling me how she expected her husband to become President of the United States. Then the wheel of fortune turned. On a winter day in 1940, driving with his son on an icy Wisconsin highway, Glenn Frank's car was in a collision and both he and the boy were killed instantly.

A second star I recruited to address my class was Clarence Darrow. This was years before the memorable "monkey" trial in Tennessee at which Darrow defended young John T. Scopes's right to teach his students Darwin's theory of evolution, and in the process reduced the prosecution's veteran William Jennings Bryan to impotent bluster. Even in my time he was a legend, the best-known criminal lawyer in America. It was Darrow who had defended Big Bill Haywood in the case involving the dynamite assassination of Governor Steunenberg, winning a spectacular victory over William E. Borah; Darrow who gave up a lucrative practice to defend society's underdogs; and Darrow who made headlines with a speech to the inmates of the Illinois Cook County jail in which he said, "Not all the best people are in jail."

He was a staunch believer in shocking juries, and audiences, to attention. Opening his talk to my Chicago-Kent law students, he announced, "All lawyers are crooks." From that launching pad he rocketed off into a dazzling examination of the inherent conflict in the legal principle that every defendant has the right to qualified counsel. This meant, he said, that not all lawyers could have virtuous clients all the time. And this meant that any lawyer could find himself using the law for undesirable social and moral ends. And yet the principle was central to our constitutional rights: every accused *was* entitled to be defended in court, and the most agonizing decision a lawyer had to make was to turn away a client because he was antipathetic to his case.

I can still see him standing there, the rumpled clothes, the shaggy, leonine head thrust forward in perpetual challenge, and his eyes shining with the fire of his beliefs. He came back several times, and his wife always came with him, sitting in front, lips apart in adoration, watching his every move. Every time he came the auditorium was packed, with some even sitting in the aisles. There has been only one Clarence Darrow.

I plugged away at my law classes—somehow I couldn't get excited about torts and wills—but I guess my heart sang every morning when I reported to the city room. Sometimes I think that no city, before or since, has been so full of color and life as was Chicago in those years before the First World War, and my press card took me wherever the action was.

What characters! The mayor was William Hale Thompson, a cartoon caricature of a machine politician. While his notorious administration plundered the city, he was returned to office again and again by playing variations on a single theme—corner the Irish and German immigrant vote. One year he did it by proclaiming a one-plank platform: "If the King of England comes to Chicago, I'll punch him in the snoot!" When German militarism plunged all Europe into war, he unabashedly sided with "Kaiser Bill." So thoroughly was the city tucked into his hip pocket that, on election night, he didn't even bother to stay up for the returns. When, early morning, I was the first to bring him word that he'd won, he snorted and said, "You call that news!" And then asked me to join him for breakfast. He said, "I knew that before the polls opened. Now come on in and have some bacon and eggs." That morning I remember because it was my first time to eat grapefruit—a new thing in American stores.

Big Bill's henchmen were the likes of Hinky Dink Kenna and Bathhouse John Coughlan, who, alternating sweet talk and skulduggery, ran the First Ward like a private fief. Hinky Dink operated a saloon on the side that featured jumbo beer tankards and the festooned Latin inscription, *In Vino Veritas,* over the bar. Someone once asked Hinky Dink if he knew what it meant. He cast bloodshot eyes up at the classical phrase and replied, "It means that when a man's crocked he gives his right name."

Bathhouse John—so called because he had risen to eminence as a rubber in a Turkish bath—was even more literary. He fancied himself a poet and could sometimes be persuaded to spout his effusions at meetings of the Chicago aldermen. You had to be careful, though, because once he got started he was hard to stop. One of his better-known works was entitled, "They Buried Her by the Side of the Drainage Canal." It had thirty-eight verses.

My colleagues of the press were an equally rare lot. Some of them made history. Floyd Gibbons was sent off to cover so many foreign invasions, revolutions and sieges that it was said no war was official until Floyd arrived. Richard Henry Little, also a *Tribune* correspondent, had gained a certain immortality by reporting on his expense account the cost of replacing a horse shot out from under him in battle. This became his invariable practice, even once when he did a stint on an American battleship that put to sea for two weeks.

Now and then I ran into some other young Chicago reporters who would make a more lasting work—Carl Sandburg, Harry Hansen, Charlie MacArthur, Bob Casey, Marquis James and a sports columnist named Ring Lardner. In the *Journal* city room, a stubby, pink-cheeked innocent who always wore a Lord Byron tie had the desk next to mine. His name—Ben Hecht, whose first best seller, *1001 Afternoons in Chicago,* a steamy chronicle of harlots, pimps and other purveyors of illicit love, earned him the sobriquet Pagliacci of the Fire Escape, and clearly established that his innocence was only skin deep. Nearly every Thursday I could count on Ben hitting me up for a small loan, but that wasn't what he remembered about me when he wrote a memoir of those newspaper days, "Gaily, Gaily":

Another of the early escapees was the juicy-voiced Lowell Thomas. He, too, wore an extra high collar. I remember that we both vied for the smiles of a girl reporter, Betty Saltgelt, and that I lost out to Lowell's superior diction. He would soon be off to half invent the British hero, Lawrence of Arabia, and to fill the nation's air waves with his Ciceronian tones.

Among the several inaccuracies in the foregoing is his reference to the estimable Miss Saltgelt. In the first place, it was never a girl's smile Ben was after, and in the second his most fervent attentions were then being paid to Marie Armstrong, a voluptuous blonde who graced our corner of the city room as the *Journal's* sob sister. In fact, they were soon married, albeit briefly.

No one ever caught the flavor and rhythms of that raffish journalistic heyday better than did Hecht and Charles MacArthur when they teamed up to write *The Front Page,* a tough classic that still turns up on the stage, television and in the movies. In his book about MacArthur, his collaborator and dear friend, Ben wrote, "We interviewed thieves, swindlers, murderers, lunatics, firebugs, bigamists, gangsters and innumerable sobbing ladies who had taken successful potshots at their married lovers." And they set it all down for uncounted millions of readers every day. "Talk about your fiction!" Carl Sandburg once said. "Man, the first page of today's newspaper has human stuff in it that puts novels in the discard."

I had my own set of memorable moments on that beat

where comedy, tragedy, pathos, inspiration, homicide and mayhem were the daily stuff of life. My first assignment in Chicago was to interview Booker T. Washington, the country's most prominent black leader, in the posh old Palmer House, the one with the silver dollars in the floor; also Jane Addams, the celebrated reformer, in Hull House, her social-service center in the heart of the West Side Halstead Street slums and flophouses. I stood the death watch with the other official witnesses through the long night before Henry Spencer paid the penalty for murdering twenty-eight women; Ben Hecht, assigned to do a feature, was stewing nervously at my side as he tried to conjure up a way to sneak in to see the prisoner—or even to help him break out—in the interest of a better story; and, in the end, Spencer walking to the gallows, his eloquent farewell speech—and then the hood they dropped over his head, the sound of the trap springing. Then silence.

One summer morning I got to work early, and Dick Finnegan, on the city desk telephone, was there alone. When he hung up, he told me to get down to the nearby Chicago River where there had been an accident. It turned out to be one of the worst maritime disasters of American history. The Great Lakes excursion steamer *Eastland,* loaded with two thousand eager voyagers, had capsized at her dock in the Chicago River, throwing the crowds on deck into the water and trapping hundreds in the suffocating depths below.

I was among the first to reach the scene—men and women, some clutching children, flailing for the shore; and the huge hulk of the *Eastland,* like a stranded whale, her starboard side turned up flat, fifteen feet above water. I clambered aboard and joined those trying to haul the living up out of portholes and the drowned and drowning from the river. I suppose I'd have had a real scoop if I'd rushed back to the office with the story, but I stayed on the *Eastland* and finally got back around noon, wet and dirty, my face no doubt reflecting my emotions at having been there when 812 souls met their deaths. Dick Finnegan looked up and said, "Go some place and forget it, Tommy! See you tomorrow."

Another morning, another empty city room. Finnegan handed me a slip of paper with a name written on it: Carlton Hudson. "Dig up what you can," he said. "It may be nothing, but some old people have been uncommonly nice to him in their wills. We'd like to know why."

Hudson had a handsome office in one of the taller buildings on Dearborn, and though I never seemed able to catch him in, it was not hard to flesh out his background from other sources. People in the building volunteered that he was a successful financier and philanthropist. A lawyer I knew told me that he was a pillar of the Moody Temple, an evangelist church founded by one of the first of those celebrated soul-savers, Dwight L. Moody. There I found a good many other people, mainly elderly ladies with solid bank accounts, who vouched for Hudson's integrity; several had made him their financial adviser and channeled their charitable contributions through him. Three had remembered him in their wills.

Now all this was interesting, as Dick Finnegan agreed, but what did it prove? I kept digging. Hudson apparently had first turned up in Chicago in 1892, nobody knew from where, but everyone spoke of his cultured manner and a few mentioned his "Eastern" accent. On a hunch, I wrote to every college president in New England, describing Carlton Hudson and explaining that I was looking for him because he had fallen heir to a gold-mining fortune.

I struck pay dirt. A letter from a college in Vermont told me that my description fitted the writer's former roommate, who had gone to live in New York City. The reason I was having difficulty locating him, the gentleman added, was that I had the name wrong. It was Carlton Hudson *Betts*. Two hours later Finnegan handed me an envelope containing a train ticket to New York and a hundred dollars in expenses; I was off on the kind of story a young reporter dreams about.

In the clipping morgue of the New York *World*, I found two fat folders marked "Carlton H. Betts." Five minutes' reading told me that we had our man. A con artist with the same flair that had endeared him to the ladies of the Moody Temple, Betts had victimized New Yorkers in the years before he went out to Chicago. When arrested he had gotten himself out on bail and then simply vanished. And now I knew where he was! And I was determined not to let this scoop get away.

Noting that the former district attorney, Charles S. Whitman, was now governor, I took the train up to the state capital at Albany and asked for an appointment. "Governor," I said, trying to sound as self-assured as I imagined Dick Finnegan would, "I have something the people of New York State want. In exchange, I want something for my paper, the Chicago *Evening Journal*."

Then I told him the whole story. It was obvious he was pleased, also several steps ahead of me. "Now you want me to give you a little time to write your story before the other papers get it, right?"

"How did you know?"

"Because you're not the first reporter I've ever talked to." He smiled. "I'll give you twenty-four hours, young man; also the thanks of the people of New York."

When I got Finnegan on the phone he switched me to our top rewrite man—Arthur J. Pegler (father of Westbrook). The following afternoon, when Carlton Hudson Betts stepped out of his office building, the police were waiting for him. So were the newsboys, with our extra edition of the *Journal*—the story of the Carlton Hudson exposure all over the front page.

There were postscripts. I got a bonus and a raise. Mark Sullivan, writing in *Printer's Ink*, the trade journal of the newspaper business, called my story the scoop of the year. And Silas Strawn, head of Chicago's largest law firm, asked me to drop by his office.

"Lowell," he said, "when you exposed Hudson as a swindler and sent him back to prison in New York, you saved some clients of mine a lot of grief." The clients, he went on, were the great meat packinghouses of Chicago—Swift, Armour and Wilson. Some time before, they had jointly been involved in a Texas oil venture, where they had inadvertently broken a federal statute. Somehow Hudson had gotten wind of it and was trying to blackmail them.

"So, we're indebted to you," Strawn said. "And my clients have asked me to tell you that if there is ever any way in which they can be helpful to you, you have only to say so." He added that I had perhaps saved his clients some eleven million dollars—the equivalent of sixty or seventy million today.

That was quite a blank check for a young fellow to carry out into the streets of Chicago on that lucky autumn day. I would remember it.

4.

Fooling Around

There's nothing to it. Just grab that cable and
pull yourself across, hand over hand.
— COWBOY CARL at the Grand Canyon

I began to feel a certain restlessness, a sense of having
been too long in the same place. Throughout my life,
it would catch up with me again and again, this urge to *do*
something, to see some other part of the forest. I never
did anything either to cause or accelerate it; I just went
on doing what I was doing. But sure enough, before long
there always came to me a logical and irresistible reason
for taking a trip. And so it was to be this time. But meanwhile I continued working, teaching and studying, waiting
for the unknown catalyst.

I also decided it was time to make a change in my
housing arrangements. All these months I had been room-
ing with the assistant city editor's family which, in most
regards, had been quite satisfactory and, in one way, too
good to be true. It turned out that he had a most attractive daughter and often, when I returned late from classes
and the rest of the family was asleep, I'd find her waiting
up for me in the parlor. Not wanting to be impolite, I'd
sit a while and chat, and as we got friendlier the talk
slipped into some normal boy-girl fooling around. So far
so good. But the time came when this lissome lass turned
all dreamy-eyed and whispered that I brought out her
mother instinct, and I suddenly realized she was eminent-
ly marriageable. I was not. Without ado, I moved out.

My new quarters, a room in the Auditorium Hotel, one

side of which faced the Loop, were notable because they were cheap. This because some of their less desirable rooms directly above the Opera House had windows looking out on "the elevated," and did they rattle! The room shook every few minutes when trains roared by. For additional thrills, you could leave your shade up and be eyeball-to-eyeball with a passing parade of Loop commuters.

But I still had trouble making ends meet. Dick Finnegan, unwilling or unable to raise my salary again, would assign me to cover a banquet nearly every Saturday night, thereby assuring me of at least one square meal a week. As a painful bonus, I also got some valuable insights into why most banquets are a bore.

There is, to begin with, a direct, almost infallible ratio between a speaker's oratorical ineptitude and the length of his speech. President Hoover used to amuse himself at luncheons and banquets by clocking the interval between the time a speaker reached his conclusion and ought to have sat down and the moment when, having restated it four or five more times, he finally did. I had no such reserves of equanimity in those early years; I just suffered.

Another speaker's sin is to read from a prepared script. People who cannot remember what they want to say ought to send letters to the audience, for rare indeed is the speaker who can hold attention with his nose buried in a sheaf of paper. The only man I ever knew who used a manuscript with real effect was Theodore Roosevelt. He didn't read it; he just crumpled it in his fist and waved it dramatically.

The most disastrous banquets were those ten-dollar-a-plate political rallies—on which the price has now gone up to a hundred or more. Self-serving pieties are the almost invariable fare, and by midevening the most loyal party hacks are numb with boredom. One I remember at the LaSalle Hotel was reduced to shambles by a cavalcade of speeches even before the main speaker, a United States senator, who shall here remain nameless, got to his feet and finished us off. Reading from a speech an inch thick, he droned away until those who remained awake took to applauding hopefully every time he paused. Finally they all mounted their chairs and waved their napkins. Unfazed, he went on to the bitter end.

Only the final speaker, our amiable oaf of a mayor, Big Bill Thompson, made friends that memorable night.

70

He at least had the political instinct to know when an audience was glutted with words. Leaving his prepared speech behind, he simply repeated his time-honored threat to commit mayhem on the King of England and bade us good-night. I was so grateful that if there had been an election the next day I might have voted for him.

So, though I paid the price, I learned some things about public speaking that not even my father could have taught me. Mostly they were glaring examples of what not to do; but from an occasional outstanding speaker I also learned how many drops of humor it takes to successfully administer a dose of more serious matter, how to get the audience on your side with a provocative or witty opening, how to keep them there and, finally, how to leave them happy by adroitly putting your message adrift on a sea of humor. Besides, I gained twenty pounds.

That winter I had a visit from Paul Chamberlain, my playboy friend from Denver University. He was in a wheelchair. It seems that back in September, while celebrating, he had walked out of a party and into an open elevator shaft. The result was a near-record collection of broken bones and internal injuries that put him flat on his back for months. Now he was on his way to convalesce with an uncle in the sunnier climes of New Orleans. I was to help him transfer from one station to another in Chicago.

But he had been trapped so long in the chastening presence of his family and seemed so grateful to see an old pal that I invited him to stay overnight with me. I hope the visit cheered him, but the fact is that it had its greatest effect on me; Paul Chamberlin turned out to be the catalyst. Though neither of us then recognized the portents, his unexpected appearance, the fact that I had impulsively asked him to stay over, was to change my life.

That night, to the accompanying thunder of the El, we naturally fell to talking about the old days at D.U. And Paul, whose thoughts seldom drifted far from wine, women and song, was soon regaling me with accounts of his amatory exploits. But suddenly—I think he was actually in mid-sentence—he said, "Tommy, of all the girls we knew at D.U. which one did *you* like best?"

"Fran Ryan," I replied at once.

"Why?"

"Why? Who ever knows why? Because she's pretty and

71

has a brain and—I don't know, but of all the girls I've *ever* known, she's the one who's stuck in my mind."

"Did you ever tell her?"

"Well, no. We just saw each other at parties now and then. I've never even been alone with her."

"It's not too late, you know."

I suppose there was some more talk, but I was no longer really paying attention. It was as though Paul's words watered a seed that had lain dormant in my consciousness and now, in an hour's time, it had bloomed and burgeoned and crowded every other thought from my mind. I put Paul on the southbound Wabash Cannonball the following morning, a Sunday, and spent the afternoon and evening composing a letter to Fran Ryan, a girl I barely knew and had suddenly decided I wanted to marry. I didn't tell her. I just said I wanted to come out to Denver and have a "talk." I hadn't the money for such a trip but managed it by persuading some railroad advertising managers to send me on a longer one—via Denver, of course. Fran was already a factor in my life. She was inspiring me to begin a new career; she was starting me on my travels.

What I did was to get in touch with the heads of railroads running west of Chicago. I reminded them that the Panama-Pacific Exposition in San Francisco was about to open. Citing my newspaper experience, I told them I was prepared to go west and write a series of articles about the scenic wonders people should plan to see on the way or after visiting the fair, a public service sure to boost passenger traffic. Would they be interested in sponsoring me to the extent of rail passage?

They would indeed—building passenger service was important in those days! The Santa Fe agreed to see me to Los Angeles and San Francisco, and the Milwaukee & St. Paul wanted me to visit the Pacific Northwest, where they had just put some electric locomotives into service; and they would get me back to Chicago.

I arranged a leave with the *Evening Journal*, and as soon as the Kent spring semester ended, I was off. And I suppose the euphoric cloud I traveled on swept right into Fran's living room with me. I probably wasn't there fifteen minutes—she had inquired about where I was staying, where I was bound, things like that—when I suddenly came right out and asked her to marry me.

72

There is no question but that she was surprised. In the end, I could take heart from the fact that she wasn't outraged, but at the time her response sounded pretty final. "Why, Tommy," she said, "what do we know about each other? When you were at D.U. you never even asked me out on a date."

There was no arguing with that sort of cold logic. But before I left, I did get her to say that she would give this outlandish idea some further thought and that I could come and see her again. And with that for encouragement—and the lure of the entire Pacific Coast for solace—I set out for the Far West.

My railroad credentials opened all sorts of doors. In Los Angeles, then as now as nondescript a collection of outskirts ever to call itself a city, the president of the chamber of commerce invited me to a luncheon. He was touting an arid little suburb called Hollywood which, he said, would someday be the motion picture capital of the world. To further its cause, he had invited the country's best-known producer, Mack Sennett, to speak at the luncheon.

It was a fiasco. Poor Sennett, who by this time was directing the fortunes of stars like Mable Normand, Gloria Swanson, and Fatty Arbuckle, was tongue-tied before a live audience and stammered from inanity to non sequitur. He finally extricated himself from this mutually mortifying predicament by introducing an English music hall performer whom he had recently signed to do some comedy shorts—Charlie Chaplin.

Going north, I stopped in San Francisco long enough to ride the ferry out into the bay and make some notes about the turmoil of activity on mud flats where the fairgrounds were just taking shape. Then I went on to Seattle and met the man who turned a fairly ordinary trip into an odyssey, thereby also taking a hand in encouraging my future wanderings. He was George W. Hibbard, general agent of the Milwaukee & St. Paul, and the first thing he did was to organize a mountain-climbing expedition on my behalf. In company with Joe Ball, Hibbard's right-hand man, and the editor of the Tacoma *Times*, we did some climbing on Mount Rainier! One of the most impressive peaks in the world, Rainier rises over fourteen thousand feet, almost from sea level, and is laced with glaciers.

Hardly had we returned from this jaunt when Joe Ball hustled me into the cab of one of the Milwaukee's new electric locomotives for a trial trip "over the line," Seattle to Spokane, across the great range of the Cascades and the Columbia Basin, and back. Next we were off on a tour of the Olympic Peninsula by Stanley Steamer. When we reached the coast, Joe arranged with a band of Quiliuit Indians to take us out on a sea lion hunt in a dugout canoe. It's a wonder I ever made it back. Those Pacific rollers had our frail little craft standing on end, and, whether it was my worst encounter with the great waters or just that I've since become acclimated, I know I've never been so seasick. The Indians kept apologizing because we hadn't sighted any sea lions, but as I was contemplating quietly slipping over the side in quest of an end to my misery, sea lions hardly mattered. As the observant reader may have guessed, our return to the beach was the high point of the trip.

But back in Seattle, when Mr. Hibbard asked if I was ready for more, I assured him that I was. "Good," he said crisply, "because I've fixed it for you to go to Alaska."

Alaska! My heart sang at the very word—and still does. Aquiver with anticipation, I heard him say that he'd arranged passage for me on a coastal steamer sailing the Inside Passage; I was leaving the next day.

It was an unforgettable trip. Ships that follow the Inside Passage thread through the wooded islands off the Canadian coast—mountains, glaciers and sparkling fjords to the east, and the vast Pacific, sensed even when unseen, to the west. We stopped at each of the alluring fishing towns of the Alaska panhandle—Ketchikan, Petersburg, Wrangell, Sitka, the old Russian capital, Juneau, the capital since 1900, and finally Skagway, once the tumultuous jumping-off point for the fabulous Klondike goldfields five hundred miles further north.

It was in Skagway, before I even debarked, that I was first introduced to one of those justifiably famous Alaskan characters. She sat in a carriage on the dock, a handsome, well-corseted Amazon of a woman, red hair massed atop her head, holding the reins of a team of horses and waiting to conduct her guests, including me, back to the Pullen House. I soon learned that, except for its beams and clapboard, she was the Pullen House—its originator, proprietor and leading light, though nearly every celebrity who had ever visited southeast Alaska signed the guest register. She was Harriet Smith Pullen, known from the Aleutians to Dawson City as Ma, a Washington State widow who had brought her four toddlers north in 1897 and made a home for them in the midst of that milling horde of ruffians, scoundrels, black sheep and lost sheep who swarmed to Alaska in the year of the gold rush, dreaming of striking it rich.

She told me her story as we sat on the memento-filled sun porch of the Pullen House one afternoon—Ma was no shrinking violet!—and it seemed to me that only a frontier like Alaska could have contained the likes of her. Penniless, she started out by baking apple pies for the hordes of cheechakos (newcomers) bound for the Klondike over murderous White Pass. There was an easier way for a woman to make money in a boomtown with thousands of lonely men, but Harriet Pullen slept alone—and kept a stout chair handy to her bed to be sure she stayed alone.

Soon she had enough money to start running a pack train to the summit of White Pass. As the gold seekers bought her supplies at twenty-five dollars a load, grateful not to have had to haul them on their backs up the steep switchback they called the Heartbreak Trail, her capital mounted. But not everybody loved her. She once came upon a wild-eyed sourdough furiously beating a horse that had broken an ankle on the merciless trail. "That animal is in misery," she said. "It can't go any farther."

"Mind your own damn business," was the reply.

She did. She fetched out the revolver she always carried and shot the suffering horse through the head. When the half-maddened man turned to her, she pointed the gun squarely between his eyes and said, "You look in a misery of sorts, too." He quickly vanished up the trail.

Eventually she saved enough to buy a big white house just off the street they called Broadway. She had a giant sign painted—PULLEN HOUSE—and for the next fifty years it was Alaska's most famous hotel. Robert Service and Jack London stayed there, as did President Harding and Herbert Hoover. But more important in a way were the thousands of ordinary men and women who passed through—and I was one—each of us brushed with Alaska magic by the legend known as Ma Pullen.

They closed down the Pullen House after she died in

1947, age eighty-seven, because nobody could take her place. But to this day there are people from one end of Alaska to the other whose eyes light up when you mention her name, and who are ready to pull up a chair and swap stories about those days when Ma Pullen was Skagway's most colorful and celebrated citizen.

The stampeders who struggled over White Pass from Skagway, or over the Chilkoot from Dyea next door, must have thought the worst of their journey was behind them. It's true the Klondike still lay five hundred miles dead north; but by following the lakes and rivers into the mighty Yukon, they could sail the whole distance. As soon as the ice went out in the spring, the headwaters around Lake Bennett were miraculously filled with a flotilla of disparate craft—huge barges crammed with oxen, one-man rafts, canoes, kayaks and converted packing boxes. There were, as Pierre Berton so aptly put it in *Klondike Fever,* boats that looked like coffins and boats that were coffins. For before this ungainly fleet ever reached the relative safety of the Yukon, it had to run the rapids beyond where the river was pinched tight between the sheer stone walls of Miles Canyon and exploded into a fury of foam and geysers at Whitehorse Rapids. In a monument of understatement, a Seattle outfitter touting the Klondike route advertised: "Of those who have gone to the Whitehorse Rapids not more than half a dozen have lost their lives."

After a few days in Skagway, the lure of the trail of '98 took hold of me; all at once I decided to head north for the fabled Klondike. The first part of the trip was easy enough, for by 1899 some daring railroad engineers had laid a narrow gauge track across the mountains all the way to Whitehorse. That ride in the quaint cars of the White Pass & Yukon, still running today, remains one of the most sensational ever contrived by man. Chugging up over the St. Elias range, crossing from the U.S. into Canada, it teeters on the edge of the roadbed, the wild Yukon stretching beyond—and only a pair of slender rails between you and disaster.

I suppose this ought to have been sufficient in the way of thrills. But when I reached Whitehorse I got the notion that it would be fun to shoot Miles Canyon and the rapids, just the way they did it in '98, and I went around asking if there was anyone in town willing to pilot me. I was directed to a saloonkeeper, an old-timer named Ed Bennett, who had made his stake by running the stampeders from the headwaters of navigation to the Yukon. Bennett seemed doubtful—he hadn't done it in more than fifteen years, and it was no picnic then. But when the requisite amount of money changed hands, and with the barflies needling him on, he finally agreed.

The following morning, with Bennett at the tiller, I stepped into a twelve-foot skiff at Lake Tagish and we cast off. We sailed smoothly into the river, moving toward a distant, insinuating murmur. Then the river turned and, suddenly, unbelievably, the rolling drone of sound burst into thunder and there it was before us, the steep black gorge of Miles Canyon, the water sweeping through at racehorse speed, surging out into the rock-studded rapids and filling the sky with frenzied cataracts of spume and spray.

We slammed through the canyon in seconds and were abruptly flung forward onto the swirl of Squaw Rapids. Soaked, clutching the gunwales, I was too involved trying to keep from being pitched out to be frightened. Then there was a moment's comparative calm before we went crashing into the Whitehorse Rapids, the water churning demoniacally with whirlpools and exploding against great menacing boulders. In a kaleidoscopic flash I saw the riverbank lined with spectators, and dazzling rainbows in the flying foam; and as we sped by dripping black rocks, any one of which would have smashed our craft to kindling, I gave silent thanks that there was a skilled hand on the tiller.

And wanting to show my appreciation and confidence in the tough old man, I managed a smile and turned to show it to him. Ed Bennett sat ashen-faced, his shaking hand slack on the tiller as we plunged, unchecked, uncontrolled, through the torrent. A moment later it was over; we were cast into a friendly eddy of water and the thunder began to recede. I had shot the Whitehorse Rapids—by sheer good luck, the skill of a veteran of the Trail of '98 days, and the grace of God!

And so I went on to Dawson, the city of gold, heart and soul—and breadbasket and cashbox—of the Klondike gold rush. Until the year 1896, it was a muskeg swamp on the east bank of the Yukon River, a mile or so from the mouth of the Klondike. Then in August, a prospector named Robert Henderson, washing gravel on a creek not far away, found that he had about eight cents' worth of gold left in his pan, a good prospect. He told a squaw man, George Washington Carmack, about it and the squaw man—as they called the white men who married Indian women—prospecting on another creek nearby, panned four *dollars*' worth of gold out of each wash, the richest yield taken in the Yukon to that moment.

The gold rush was on. It made the squaw man and some others rich; it broke Henderson's heart—Carmack never bothered to tell *him* of the fabulous discovery—and the hearts of thousands more. Before it was over, a hundred thousand men started for Dawson, and half actually made it. Overnight the mud flat boomed into the glittering metropolis of the North, where the sounds of revelry rang from dark to dawn; where ten miles away, in the Klondike's storied creeks—Bonanza, Eldorado, Hunker, Last Chance—fifty million dollars in gold was sluiced from the frozen ground in five years; and where ten thousand people all but starved to death in one bitter winter; where miners, merchants and the inevitable dance-hall girls fled spring floods and suffered recurrent plagues of scurvy and typhoid fever.

The big boom ended almost as suddenly as it had begun. Out from Alaska in 1899 came word that they'd found gold on the beaches at Nome, and a new stampede was on. Then the big mining companies moved in to consolidate whole blocks of claims; huge dredges took the place of the picks and shovels and homemade sluice boxes. And eventually even they lay still, rotting by the creeks. Now Dawson is a ghost town of perhaps five hundred stubborn souls, and the wind blows down empty streets and rattles the loose boards on long-deserted saloons and outfitters' shops, and some tourists come every summer to take pictures of the wreckage of the gold rush and to ask where Robert Service's cabin is.

There was some life in the place yet when I landed there that summer of 1914, and the smell of gold still hung over it. I walked up the hill to the little log cabin, a pair of moose antlers fixed over the door, where Service had lived. Only a few years before, he had sat here writing poems about the great stampede, a shy Scottish bank clerk who hadn't even arrived until it was all over. The poems made him rich and, in ironic contrast to the men who inspired them, he kept his money. But nobody, not sourdough nor cheechako, ever begrudged it to him because, better than anyone before or since, Robert Service caught the spirit and flavor of the gold rush and set it down forever.

> This is the Law of the Yukon, that only
>   the strong shall thrive;
> That surely the weak shall perish, and
>   only the fit survive.
> Dissolute, damned and despairful, crippled
>   and palsied and slain,
> This is the Will of the Yukon—Lo, how
>   she makes it plain!

In Dawson, I stayed at the home of Joe Boyle, a hulking former prizefighter who had come north in '98 and taken a job as a saloon bouncer. But Joe Boyle had an idea. He talked the Canadian government into granting him dredging rights in the Klondike valley, then started building the biggest gold dredges in the world. Nobody thought they would work, but they did, three stories of floating bucket runs and sluices, digging their own ponds as they went, each one washing out more gravel in an hour than a hundred men could do in a week. Naturally Joe became rich. When I was there he owned the power plant and telephone company, the laundry, sawmill and coal mine.

It was also while I was in Dawson that some momentous news came down the river: war had broken out in Europe, a world war involving Germany, Russia, France and England. Naturally, Canada immediately announced its intention to fight alongside the British. We talked about it at dinner that night; Joe said if the Canadians told him he was too old to serve, he would muster a unit from the Yukon Territory. And he did—and paid for every cent it cost to outfit those two hundred men and ship them overseas, known as Boyle's Rifles.

Joe Boyle had his ups and downs after that. One of his dredges sank and he went off to Europe to raise money to replace it. But he got sidetracked by a British railroad mission to Russia and somehow became a confidant of queens and princes, particularly the glamorous Queen Marie of Rumania. Meanwhile his company went bankrupt. But Joe was now spending so much time in the private company of the beautiful Marie, whose love life had already gained her worldwide notoriety, that he became known as the Uncrowned King of Rumania. He never went back to the Klondike—they say Queen Marie was somewhat demanding—and finally Joe died in 1923 of a heart attack. What a way to go.

I returned from Alaska determined to go back—and that's all I knew for certain about my future. I had little enthusiasm for my law classes that second year, and though my job at the *Evening Journal* provided lots of excitement, I had a restless feeling again, a sense of something waiting for me just beyond the range of my imagination. I continued writing long letters to Fran—with only tepid encouragement—and sent off an application for admission to the new graduate college at Princeton, without much hope of being accepted.

Early in 1915, I got a chance to cover another big story—and this one almost ended my career in journalism for all time. That spring, every paper in the country was headlining the elopement of a Chicago heiress, Helen Morton, with Roger Bailey, her father's jockey. You can see the possibilities, a juicy scandal with everything from pathos to comedy—her father's *jockey?* The fact that the nubile Helen's father and his brother Joy were matter-of-factly referred to as the Salt Kings of America, and that her uncle, Colonel Fabian, could be tabbed the Woolen King, only piqued the natural appetite for every minute detail of this human drama.

Alas! Helen and her horseman were caught in Kentucky —it was around Derby time—and the poor girl brought back in disgrace, and thereafter an iron curtain clamped down on her uncle's Fox River estate. It was suddenly surrounded by a battalion of guards armed with pitchforks, and not a morsel of news trickled out to the hordes of waiting newsmen, of whom I was one; consequently there was no word, either of solace or spite, that we could pass on to the panting public. Day after day we sat around Wheaton, the nearest town, playing cards or shooting craps and waiting for lightning to strike.

When it finally struck, Webb Miller of Hearst's *Evening American* and I were the ones bathed in its light of divine inspiration. Our stories were spread over page one of both our papers. We told how we had walked some miles up the Fox River by a circuitous route, found a flat-bottom scow and, hiding in the bottom, drifted downstream. Undetected, we managed to sneak ashore at the Fabian estate and, since such enterprise could not go unrewarded, we found the pensive Helen in a hammock, happy, at last, to be able to unburden her heavy heart. We were able to tell the world how she felt (melancholy) and what she thought about jockeys in general (not much) and hers in particular (she missed him). Anyway, she said, she believed in romance.

The story was a sensation, as well it should have been. During one of those waiting days, Webb, who didn't enjoy shooting craps any more than I did, had started us speculating on the "what ifs" that led to our farfetched yarn. We had simply invented the whole thing.

We might have gotten away with it, at that, if our papers hadn't insisted on photographs. The Mortons and Colonel Fabian were making no statements, acknowledging or denying nothing. But the morning after our big newsbreak, there was a fresh clutch of press people at the Wheaton railroad station, including the *Journal*'s faithful Japanese photographer, Saito, hoping for a glimpse of anybody named Morton or Fabian. And as luck would have it, the kings—both salt and wool—showed up.

Little Saito scurried forward for a close-up, and the next thing I realized, one of the Mortons had him by the throat and his camera was flying through the air, to come crashing down on the brick platform. As no one else seemed about to intervene, and as poor Saito was, after all, *my* cameraman, I suddenly found myself flying across the station and, with the rage of the righteous, I began flinging Morton salt kings hither and yon. At least that's how Ben Hecht, who by then was with the Chicago *Daily News*, reported it. I only knew that when Saito and I got back to the *Journal*, my watch was smashed and I could otherwise tell that I'd been in a losing fight.

An hour later I was called to the office of John Eastman, owner of the paper. The Morton lawyers had already given him their version of the encounter; now he wanted mine. When I finished, he rather sourly said, "My boy, if we lose this case, we'll have to give them the *Journal* and owe them the rest."

Well, luckily we didn't lose it, or at least we won round one. In the Wheaton justice of the peace court, a few days later, Saito, Miller and I confronted the Mortons—and some of Chicago's most formidable legal talent—and won an assault and battery judgment against them for five dollars plus costs. I suppose you could call it an early test of the freedom of the press, and Webb Miller and I, two vindicated, ink-stained wretches, celebrated our victory. Webb went off to Europe to become a top foreign correspondent and eventually head of the United Press London bureau, and I went back to Alaska. But both of us, for years afterward, heard the rumblings of the Mortons' multi-million-dollar libel suits which, I believe, eventually outlived both our newspapers and all the Mortons.

For my second trip to Alaska, I bought an Ernemann camera. Like all the motion picture equipment of the day, it was cumbersome and barely portable; certainly it left me at a distinct disadvantage should I encounter an angry bear in the bush. But already I had a glimmer of an idea that if I made some really interesting film—I don't mean the ordinary run of sunsets and mountain panoramas and more sunsets that cluttered the travel pictures of the time—I might be able to induce people to pay money to see them. Once again I made some beneficial travel arrangements with the railroads and the Alaska Steamship Company and, early that summer, I was on my way.

This time I was bound for Fairbanks and Nome. The voyage was enlivened by the presence on board of twelve Vassar girls who, shepherded by their geology professor, were headed into the great North to study its natural wonders. Among them was a captivating blonde from Tarrytown, New York, with the unlikely name of Al McIlravey to whom, I'm afraid, I paid considerable attention. In feeble defense, I can only say that she never told me she was already engaged.

Having no fixed itinerary, I arranged one at the start that coincided with the route of the Vassar class, which never did seem to get down to the serious study of geology. From Skagway we crossed the range, and by a river sternwheeler down the mighty Yukon we went to Dawson and on to the mouth of the Tanana, and thence to Fairbanks, then and now the metropolis of interior Alaska. It was a magnificent trip, through a vast, barely touched wilderness, with daily performances by bears, moose and caribou for our amusement.

One morning, chugging along, we were hailed from the shore by a bedraggled young man, and in true Alaskan tradition the captain pulled over to pick him up. And so I came to know still another of those hardly believable north country characters. His name was Jack McCord and, with his ragged beard and torn clothing, he looked that day as though he had been battling the bush for a month and finished up in a hand-to-hard go with a grizzly. But no, he had only been doing some prospecting far up the Koyukuk, a river that crossed the Arctic Circle. I suspect he had a fat pouch of gold dust on him, for Sourdough Jack and I became good friends and I soon learned that he seldom failed at anything.

Raised in the Dakotas, he had taught school in western Canada, then heard the cry of gold from Alaska and traveled on. He had had a hand in the construction of the Copper River railroad over the mountains to Cordova on the coast, an epic feat immortalized by Rex Beach in his novel *The Iron Trail*. Not unexpectedly, one of the principal characters was based on Jack McCord.

He never smoked or drank and was one of the most powerful men I ever met. His favorite trick was to pick up a dance-hall girl, sit her in the palm of one hand and muscle her straight up over his head. But Jack's real gift was promoting outlandish schemes. He became one of Alaska's most energetic lobbyists, heading "outside" each year to talk up the opportunities and wonders of the Big Land. One of the most spectacular was his own. Irritated by Alaska's eternal dependence on food shipped north from Seattle—at exorbitant rates—he bought an island off the Aleutian chain and stocked it with beef cattle.

He was full of surprises. In the 1940s, already well along in years, he went to England, where he met Grace Doering, a lady lawyer from Cleveland—a vice-president of the American Bar Association—and married her at Westminster. Not until statehood came was there such a hullabaloo in Alaska as the day *Life* magazine appeared with a picture of their own Sourdough Jack striding from the church, a new bride on his arm, and wearing spats, striped pants, tailcoat and a silk topper. Jack lived on until his mid-eighties and was in San Francisco when his final illness caught up with him. Somebody sent for an ambulance; when it came Jack insisted on riding up front with the driver.

In Fairbanks, I was detached from the enchanting Miss McIlravey and the Vassar girls by a persistent young man named Bobby Sheldon. Bobby had a Model T Ford and was convinced he could drive it across the Valdez Trail, the dogsled route over which supplies for the interior went north each winter. The fact is that he had already done it —once—banging and battling his way over the Alaska Range to the coast. But Bobby had the idea that if he could do it again, if he could prove that the first trip was no fluke, he'd be entitled to call the Valdez Trail a road. Then, of course, if there was a road between Valdez and Fairbanks, why, they'd have to give the mail contract to the only man in town who owned an automobile—Bobby Sheldon!

As he was not about to venture forth alone in the Model T, he pressed two improbable passengers into service: the Episcopal bishop of Alaska, the Right Reverend P. T. Rowe, and me. Only after we'd started out did Bobby generously announce that he was charging us only a hundred dollars for the trip. Years afterward Bobby became a member of the state legislature and his favorite after-dinner story, if I was in the audience, was an account of that epic journey. "I should have paid them," he'd say, wheezing with laughter, "because they pushed me a lot of the way."

Walking wouldn't have been so bad; the fact is we pushed his mulish Model T much of the way. But the trip had its rewarding moments, thanks mainly to the inimitable Bishop Rowe, already an Alaskan legend. He knew everybody, had visited the remotest native villages by dogsled and was the embodiment of human kindness and generosity. At every roadhouse where we stopped along the way, he made straight for the bar to have a talk with the prospectors and trappers in from the creeks. I listened eagerly, for never had I heard such wildly colorful tales, some of which may even have been true. One, told with heavily accented fervor by an old Scandinavian woodsman they called Whisky Nels, still ranks as my favorite bear story—which is saying something, as every Alaskan appears to have one.

It seems that Nels was out panning for gold one day and somehow let a grizzly get between him and his rifle. He started to run, but the grizzly was gaining. His only hope was a tree just ahead, its lowest branch twenty feet above the ground. "By the time I reached it," he said, panting as though the grizzly were after him again, each of us leaning close to catch every word, "well, cheez, I could smell bear's breath. Boy, did I yump for that branch!"

"Did you catch it?" I asked.

"Not going up," said Whisky Nels coolly, "coming down."

To celebrate our return to Fairbanks—and because he seemed to feel there were gaps in my larger education—Bobby invited me to join him on a visit to the Fairbanks Stockade, the red-light district. The evening was not an unqualified success. The girl Bobby had chosen for me—apparently he knew them all—was appealing enough, and her appeals were all too evident in the filmy thing she wore as she sat in my lap. But I fell into my old habit of behaving toward her as I would to any other lady, and I suppose she didn't know what to make of that. Pretty soon she was weeping and telling me the story of her life, and pretty soon I headed for the hotel. The next I heard of Bobby Sheldon he had gotten that mail contract after all.

From Fairbanks I went on down the Yukon to St. Michael and Nome, boarding the last steamer to sail south before ice closed it down for the year. Also aboard—as I knew they would be—were Al McIlravey and the other geology initiates from Vassar. By the second evening out, Al and I had rekindled our friendship and were up on the hurricane deck watching whales cavorting and the red sun disappear in the sea. Suddenly, with miserable timing, a United States marshal appeared to clap a pair of handcuffs on my wrists and order me below "to hear the charges against you." Stunned, I followed him down to the main salon.

And there the evening's entertainment had already been laid out—a breach-of-promise trial, with me as the culprit and a young male passenger named Wallack, son of the owner of the Deshler Hotel in Columbus, Ohio, painted up to look like some tenderloin floozy, preferring the charges; this, "she" quavered, pointing to her slinky outfit, was the sinful life I had driven her to. The jury consisted of eleven of the Vassar girls, the twelfth, Al McIlravey, of course, being cast as the "other woman." Well, there was some lurid testimony, we all had a lot of laughs and I was sentenced to buy every female passenger aboard a box of candy at the first port of call. One who testified against me was a relative of a former President of the United States, bewhiskered Colonel Webb Hayes—son of Rutherford B. Hayes.

What wasn't such fun was that the fake trial had attracted the geology professor's notice to what he suddenly conceived as a genuine romance between Al and me. Knowing that his lovely blond student was already engaged, aware of his responsibility, he fretted all the way to Cordova. There, as soon as we tied up, he sent a cable to Al's parents in Tarrytown apprising them of this unhappy development and urging them to do something about it at once. Which is too bad, because he put them to a lot of unnecessary worry and expense. When our steamer reached Seattle, not only were Al's parents waiting nervously on the dock, but so was her roiled fiancé!

I was the only one who wasn't there. In Cordova, someone had told me that the final salmon run of the season, a thrilling spectacle, was about to begin, and on the spur of the moment, I decided to stay behind and film it. With shouted good-byes to my friends aboard, I grabbed my bag and the big Ernemann camera and ran ashore. Smartest spur-of-the-moment decision I ever made!

Before I left Cordova, I wrote to Fran and said I would stop off to visit her as I headed east. But on the way, I made a side trip to see the Grand Canyon and came close to adding my bones to the fabulous fossil collection embedded in the five-hundred-million-year-old rock.

The Grand Canyon is America's—indeed the world's—most astounding natural wonder. Vast seas once swept over this land, and the earth buckled and the mountains rose. Perhaps twelve million years ago what we now call the Colorado River began cutting out the mile-deep gorge of the Grand Canyon, laying bare nature's story in layer after layer of geologic history, exposing sharks' teeth from the Devonian period, when the land lay under water, and revealing the remains of life-forms long extinct. Nowhere else on earth is the autobiography of our planet so vividly laid out.

The canyon was discovered and promptly forgotten in 1540 by the conquistadores of the Spanish explorer Francisco Coronado, who were vainly searching for the fabled Seven Cities of Cibola. It finally caught the world's imagination when John Wesley Powell, a daring naturalist, ran the Colorado River through its immense canyon in 1869.

And here I was in the late summer of 1915, eager to see it all. I seemed to have made a good start when, on my first evening there, I met a cowboy from a ranch in the Kaibab Forest on the Utah side of the canyon; he offered to take me across the next day.

"How do we get over the river?" I asked.

"Easy," he said.

That seemed reasonable enough and I didn't press him further. He told me his name was Carl and we shook hands, agreeing to meet at the rim in the morning.

I was full of anticipation as we started into the rocky gorge, its walls that marvelous violet color of early morning and sunset, and the Colorado a white-flecked thread of blue slate. Near the bottom, when the river's roar was already loud in our ears, Carl showed me where a rusty cable, embedded in the rock, ran all the way across the great chasm to some invisible anchor on the far side. The early Mormons had strung it, he told me, and, in a cage suspended below, transferred themselves, their animals and their belongings from Arizona to Utah.

Then Carl said, "That's how we're going across." It was obvious he wasn't kidding, and yet I couldn't believe it. I mean, that inch-thick cable was so old and rusty that broken strands popped out of it like barbed wire.

From his pack, Carl took two pairs of heavy work gloves. In place of the Mormons' cage, now rotting against the canyon wall, he produced two lengths of half-inch wire, threw them over the cable and hooked their separate ends under a couple of narrow boards. Then he installed himself on one, tested its balance and, almost as an after-thought, turned back to me and said, "There's nothing to it. Just grab the cable and pull yourself across, hand over hand." And following him, watching the crashing torrent as we sagged to within thirty feet or so of one of the wildest rivers in the world, then pulling ourselves higher and higher, I crossed the Grand Canyon.

From the Utah side we climbed up Bright Angel Canyon to the Kaibab Forest. On the rim we spent the night in a ranch camp. But there was much to see the following day, and it was late afternoon before I started back, alone this time, over the old Mormon cable.

Night comes rapidly in the desert. After I reached the Arizona side and began the long ascent to the top, darkness overtook me and I knew I'd have to pass the night somewhere on that sloping canyon wall. All too conscious of the rattlers and Gila monsters said to infest the region, I built a fire, starting it with some unexposed film from my pack, and huddled there, shivering with cold and hunger until, finally, I grew too tired to care about anything but sleep. I stretched out on the stony ground and cradled my head in my arm.

The next thing I knew it was morning and a search party was clattering down to my improvised camp—I'd been due back the previous afternoon! I apologized and gratefully accepted the food and water they offered. Before long, to our mutual relief, I was back on my way to Denver.

Arriving there a day or so behind schedule, I found Fran concerned enough to make me hopeful that I was making progress. She seemed intrigued by all I had to tell her about Alaska and when I promised to take her there on a honeymoon her eyes seemed to light. Incidentally, it took me forty years to make good on my promise. A couple of world wars got in the way. Anyway, Fran still had a year to finish at D. U. and, as she put it, she wasn't marrying anyone until then.

Encouraged, I returned to Chicago to find a letter from Princeton that had been gathering dust all summer. I had not only been accepted at the graduate college, but also been awarded a scholarship. I suspected my lawyer friend Silas Strawn of having something to do with this, for I had given him as a reference. In any event, there was no time to lose, and I quickly closed out all my affairs in Chicago and headed east.

Princeton was considerably different from any of the schools I'd ever attended. The aura of its prestige, silent and unseen, was everywhere felt on that lovely campus, like an invisible shield of excellence. Woodrow Wilson, who had been the university president until 1910, was elected governor of New Jersey and had gone on to the White House. The new graduate college, a mile or so from the main campus, seemed in splendid isolation, as required for the most elevated intellectual pursuits. And all of us, even when dining, wore black scholastic gowns.

Classes were small. In one, constitutional law, there was

only myself and one other student. The other man's name—Dulles. He was tweedy, pipe-smoking Allen Dulles, who came from a distinguished family and, with his brother, John Foster, would add to its luster. As far as I was concerned, Allen already was someone special. For one thing, he had come to Princeton from a year on the faculty of the University of Allahabad in India. For another, he was definitely the number one man in our class of two—I never could warm up to constitutional law. And finally, and to me most important, he had, at the age of eight, written a book on the Boer War which his proud grandfather had had published; it sold several thousand copies, whose royalties the young author contributed to the Boer relief fund.

While Foster Dulles was working his way through the diplomatic ranks, eventually to become Secretary of State, Allen went early into foreign intelligence and wound up as the first head of our Central Intelligence Agency. Just a year or so after leaving Princeton, when the U.S. entered World War I, he was off on a spectacular series of cloak-and-dagger assignments in Europe. But he never lost his sense of humor, and later we would often sit around after dinner at my home while he told stories of being caught with his cloak open and his dagger down. Once, based in Switzerland in 1917, a friend arranged a contact for him with a "wild Russian" who lived across the lake and went about condemning the war as the last spasm of capitalism, and calling on the workers to mount a worldwide revolution. But Dulles had his mind on other matters, which in a way was a shame. For soon the "contact" was speeding across Germany in a sealed car, to turn up in Petrograd, where he led the overthrow of the moderate Kerensky regime and established the communist dictatorship of Soviet Russia. His name was Vladimir Ilyich Lenin.

When I had been at Princeton only two or three weeks, the president of the university, John Grier Hibben, called me to his office. Would I, he asked forthrightly, be willing to take over their speech department? I suppose I gulped. I know I didn't reply at once, for President Hibben went on speaking.

There was, he said, a professor in charge, who was elderly and becoming senile. He would retire soon. Meanwhile, the department needed an infusion of vitality, new ideas. My academic background and Kent experience had impressed Dr. Hibben, who said if I were willing to consider a career in education he was prepared to offer me the department on a permanent basis.

I thanked him, but told him I wasn't yet settled on a career, but if he wanted to entrust the speech department to me for a couple of years, I'd give it my best.

And so we shook hands on it and I was off again on another of those frenetic programs—classes and work during the week, with still a third job on weekends. For I had been bombarding nearby colleges, clubs and lecture committees with a brochure telling about an illustrated talk on Alaska—and bookings were coming in. I was busy every Friday and Saturday night and soon realized how, by showing my films and talking about the wonders of Alaska, I was earning more in two days than the average college teacher made in a week. Furthermore, I enjoyed it.

Things got so hectic I had to hire a secretary, Jim Smith—a freshman son of a Denver policeman. An Alaskan gold miner who heard my talk was enthusiastic enough to offer to back me in a try for the big time and for this rented Carnegie Hall, then the largest and best-known auditorium in New York. Unfortunately, it required a lot more advertising and promotion than either of us realized to fill Carnegie Hall for a single night, and I'm afraid my Alaskan angel took a bath. I never heard from him again. All that winter and spring I put on my show for smaller audiences and more modest fees, gaining invaluable experience.

When summer arrived, I invited my mother and sister, Pherbia, to come east. Dad, a devoted Anglophile, had volunteered his services soon after the war broke out and was now on the surgical staff of the London General Hospital. So for this year I took an apartment on Nassau Street, where the three of us lived through the rest of our stay at Princeton.

Mother brought happy news. Fran had ridden the train up to Victor to visit her, and they had taken to each other from the first. Was there a wedding in the offing? Mother inquired. "Ask the lady," I answered. But the fact is that I had been asking her myself. She had won her precious degree by then and, in September, set off to teach all six grades in a one-room schoolhouse at a place called Jackass Ranch near Castle Rock, south of Denver. Would she marry me in June, when school was out? I wrote. Yes, she replied. I must have been an optimist—then as now—for I was broke.

Shortly after the first of the year, I received an unusual speaking invitation. It came from Washington—from the office of Franklin K. Lane, Secretary of the Interior. Lane, a onetime newspaper publisher from the Pacific Northwest, was an ardent booster of America's wonders of the West. Now, with Europe at war and closed to tourism, he decided the time was right to launch a coast-to-coast campaign promoting our national parks and scenic splendors. His slogan: "See America First!"

How did I become involved? The trail for this led back to the man who had sponsored my first trip to Alaska, George Hibbard of the Milwaukee & St. Paul. To kick off his campaign, Secretary Lane had called together a conference of western governors, congressmen, naturalists and national parks superintendents to meet at the Smithsonian Institution in Washington. Seeking somebody to represent Alaska, he turned for advice to his longtime friend, railroader Hibbard. Back came a wire: "Suggest you invite Professor Lowell Thomas from Princeton."

For so short a message there were several exaggerations: I was not a full professor; and though I could certainly speak about Alaska, there had to be others who knew it better. No matter—George Hibbard's crisp wire was the pivot on which my life next turned, and this time I was set on a course from which there was to be no turning back.

The first thing I did was to head for New York in search of a public-speaking coach, someone who might help me shorten my talk. My guess was that I might be introduced at the end of a long roster of speakers—each extolling the glories of his home region, and in such a situation brevity, wit and eloquence could be golden assets. The man I found had a studio in Carnegie Hall, which was appropriate, as his name was Dale Carnegey. In later years he would change it to conform to the better-known spelling of the concert hall and the Pittsburgh steel tycoon, and would go on to win fame and fortune with his book, *How to Win Friends and Influence People*. But first he did several stints working with me, starting on that January day in 1917 when his coaching helped me reshape my talk for Washington. Dale and I remained close friends until he died.

When I reached the hall at the Smithsonian, Secretary Lane was up front, presiding. During a lull, when I placed my card on his table, I could tell from his expression that he thought I was a page announcing the professor's arrival. My age then—twenty-four.

"Um—I'm Lowell Thomas," I said.

He looked again—hard. "I see," he finally acknowledged. "Well, as I understand it, you're to show some films, and as we don't want to darken the auditorium in midsession, we've scheduled you to speak last."

It was a long, all-day session. It wasn't that I was afraid to compete against the eminent gentlemen who preceded me; my big worry was that the soporific effect of all those accumulated superlatives they showered on us would put the audience to sleep.

Finally my moment came. "Mr. Secretary," I began, "distinguished guests: I think I can tell you something about Alaska, but I confess I feel a bit out of place in this illustrious company. You see, I grew up in a mining camp, where I got my start in an ore house."

There was a moment's lull before they got it, then came the laughter. Showing only my choice pictures, drawing on only the high spots from a talk I already had given more than a hundred times, I made my thirty minutes count. And when I was finished, I had them standing up to applaud. Instead of a dragged-out afterthought to the conference, my part had been a sort of climax, and, afterward, governors and senators came up to shake my hand.

It was a heady moment for a young fellow whose usual audiences were clubs and modest groups in Scranton, Altoona, Trenton and so on. There was Secretary Lane asking me if I would take over and run his See America First campaign.

"But I have classes until June."

"Starting in June, then."

I floated back to Princeton on an ecstatic cloud. Fran and I could be married; we would travel endlessly, promoting America! What could be better! What other prospect could be so full of shining excitement?

Then, on my twenty-fifth birthday, April 6, the United States declared war on Germany. No longer was there reason for Uncle Sam to encourage Americans to go anywhere except to work or war. Soon came another summons to Washington, again from Secretary Franklin K. Lane.

"Our See America First campaign is out for the duration," he said. "This is no time to tell about the quiet charms of Nature. How about going to Europe for us? Our people are not ready for this war." How right he was! For Wilson had been reelected with the promise that he would not take us into the war. "So," added Secretary Lane, "why not take your cameraman, quickly get what you can, and return to help with the war effort here at home."

This was how I became involved in World War I. This was what led to my experiences with all of the Allied armies from the North Sea to Arabia.

5.

With Allenby in Palestine

Today I entered Jerusalem.
—GENERAL SIR EDMUND H. H. ALLENBY

THERE was a complication. Secretary Lane pointed out
that while Congress was busily appropriating all sorts
of money to fight the war, they might be slow in allocating
funds to *tell* about it. Did I think I could raise enough
privately to finance such a mission?

I said I believed I could, for I was remembering Silas
Strawn and what the meat packers had said about our
Carlton Hudson exposé: "If there is ever any way in
which we can be helpful . . ."

So to Chicago I went. As I sat in the Strawn oak and
leather office, I couldn't help but wonder why anyone
should hand over to me a rather sizable sum of money.
Because, some nervy part of me replied, it isn't for me;
it's for our country; there's a war and we are in it. And
so I laid out Secretary Lane's proposal and my enthusiasm for it as forcefully as I could.

When Silas Strawn asked a question or two, I told him
I had come to him for advice because Secretary Lane
didn't think Congress would act quickly enough on such
a minor matter.

"How much will it cost?"

"Seventy-five thousand."

Although he didn't pull out his checkbook or reach for
the telephone, after a long moment's contemplation he

said, "I'll put myself down for three thousand and I'll give you a list of others to see. If you're still short, come back here."

I was a young man in a hurry then—Fran and I had hoped to be married in June, and here it was almost July and I was broke; and with every transport that sailed off to the war without us, I saw a dozen important stories slipping away forever. But, intentionally or otherwise, this eminent lawyer was doing me quite a favor. With his name as the passkey, I got into the executive offices and board-rooms of Chicago's most potent business firms, and the men I came to know there, as one of them noted when he saw my list, probably represented more wealth than all the directors of the House of Morgan.

Not one turned me down. Arthur Meeker, of Armour & Company, was being shaved in his private office when I was shown in. He listened a few minutes, then, through the lather said, "Would ten thousand be helpful? We owe you at least that, young man." E. P. Ripley, the patriarchal head of the Santa Fe Railroad, sat as expressionless as a monument while I made my pitch, and as soon as I'd finished he said, "I'll match the top amount on your list." And so it went with the heads of Swift, Wilson, International Harvester, Weyerhaeuser, Quaker Oats and so on. In two weeks I had a hundred thousand dollars contributed by eighteen different millionaires; I was amazed at how easy it had been.

The first thing I did was to go looking for the best cameraman around. I found him in soft-spoken veteran Harry Chase. Unhappily for me, he was already committed to the widow of travel-lecturer Frank Robison, and to get Chase I had to buy the entire Robison collection of stills and slides. There were thousands of them, and I never used one, but they would have been worth the price, no matter what it was. Inconspicuous Harry Chase turned out to be not only a crack cameraman but a mechanical marvel who could fix anything from a lady's watch to a half-ton movie projector, and he stayed with me for the next ten years.

While Harry was out rounding up equipment, I hurried back to Washington to get the credentials we would need. Secretary Lane cut through the inevitable red tape by taking the matter up with President Wilson. Within hours, while thousands scurried about the war-frenzied capital seeking this or that, I was on my way out, closely guarding my briefcase; inside were impressive letters from Secretary of War Newton D. Baker, Secretary of the Navy Josephus Daniels and George Creel, head of the newly formed Committee on Public Information. Addressed to all commanders and embassy personnel, they instructed the recipient in the name of the President, to "assist and expedite in every way possible the mission of Mr. Lowell Thomas." And that, I kept reminding myself, was me.

Fran and I were finally married in Denver on August 4. A few weeks before I had been broke. Now I had the hundred thousand and an important job to do. Instead of Alaska, I was offering Fran World War I for a honeymoon, and a few days later, along with Harry Chase for a chaperone and his padded trunks full of heavy camera gear and fragile glass negatives to worry about, we sailed for France.

More than a thousand others, troops and civilians, were crowded aboard the *Chicago*, an old war-horse of the French Line. All of us, in one way or another, were heading over "to make the world safe for democracy." Two we came to know were Mrs. Theodore Rossevelt, Jr., and Mrs. Kermit Roosevelt, Teddy's daughters-in-law, whose husbands were already "over there," as officers of our First Division. Both these attractive young women had joined the Red Cross and volunteered for overseas duty, and as I watched Fran studying their crispy gray uniforms, I could tell an idea was taking shape in her mind. Until then, neither of us had considered what she would do when I would go off to the battlefront.

If there were German submarines about, we didn't see them and landed at Bordeaux after an uneventful crossing. To celebrate, we went the first evening to dine in a fine Bordelais restaurant. Having heard there was some question about the purity of French water, and being inexperienced as well as a trifle gauche, I put it to a gentleman at the next table. Was the water fit to drink? I asked.

He was a white-bearded patriarch, surrounded by an array of wineglasses, and was somewhaat startled by my question. "I can't say," he replied. "I have nevaire tasted eet."

The following day we went on to Paris. There, I installed Fran at the Regina Hotel across from the charms of the Tuileries and the Louvre and off I went to the headquarters of General Pershing at Chaumont. Appointed commander in chief of a non-existent American Expeditionary Force in late May, Pershing had himself been in Europe a bare two months and obviously had other things on his mind. But my letters were persuasive and I was soon ushered into his austere presence. Here to my astonishment I found two old friends; one, Ed Bouton, a lawyer, had been a neighbor in Cripple Creek. He now was our A.E.F. Adjutant General. The other was a man I had known in Alaska when he was a major. Pershing had him as his Chief of Staff—Major General James MacAndrew.

I have met many professional soldiers in my time, of many armies, but never one who so completely looked the part as Black Jack Pershing, sitting stiffly behind his desk, his eyes cold and his olive-drab uniform immaculately pressed, planning strategy for an American army soon to number a million men. Even this interruption was accepted as a duty. What, he inquired crisply, were the specifics of my mission and how could he assist me?

I told him my assignment was to help bring the realities of the war home to the American people, first perhaps by focusing on the experiences of a single doughboy, with films and firsthand reporting. For the moment I required nothing beyond the courtesy he had already extended by consenting to this interview. Perhaps he would care to tell me something of his plans for the eventual deployment of the A.E.F.?

He had only one plan, he replied at once, and that was to use the American army as the spearhead of a coordinated drive that would sweep all of France clear of German troops. Nor did he intend, as some had already suggested, to dissipate this attack force by parceling it out, unit by unit, to every French or British sector commander who ran into trouble. The A.E.F. would stay together, he said brusquely, and fight together as a unified command under American officers.

This may have been the first public exposition of Pershing's soon to be hotly debated doctrine of holding the American forces intact and opposing either their amalgamation by small units into the Allied armies, or their diversion to secondary operations. And despite the most intense pressure, Pershing relented only once, at the height of the savage German attacks in the spring of 1918. He then released his forces to Marshal Foch, the Allied commander, but had them back in time for the final counter-offensive launched that summer.

I could have stayed at Pershing's headquarters with other American correspondents, waiting for the A.E.F. to be committed to battle. But it seemed to me that there had to be livelier things to do in the middle of a war than sitting around Chaumont swapping tall stories with my fellow reporters.

To begin with I took a trip to the village of Domrémy in eastern France. Here, almost exactly five hundred years before, Joan of Arc had been born, and from here she set forth to save France from the English invaders. Now the American First Division was encamped in Domrémy, preparing to go forth and save France from another invader. Then I went to Tours, about a hundred and twenty-five miles southwest of Paris, where a mammoth American supply center was being established. It was there that I interviewed Colonel Merritte W. Ireland, Surgeon General of the A.E.F., and afterward asked if it wouldn't now be a good idea to integrate those American doctors who had been serving with our Allies by giving them commissions in the U.S. Army. Yes, he replied, we are considering the idea.

"Well," I went on, pressing my luck, "may I suggest the name of an excellent surgeon, now with the British army in southern Italy, who is most anxious to join the A.E.F.?"

"Who?"

"Major Harry G. Thomas."

"Any relation?"

"My father."

He made no promise. But he smiled, and in a short time Dad was transferred to France, there to serve out the rest of the war as a colonel with the A.E.F.

A week or so later, I had my first experience under fire. After several requests, I had finally been granted permission to visit an active front and went with a staff officer into the trenches that crisscrossed that sliver of Belgium still held by the Allies. I barely had a chance to look around before the German artillery opened up.

"Your reception committee," the officer said sardonically as we crouched low in the mud and tried to disappear inside our helmets.

"If it weren't for the honor of the thing," I replied,

trying to match his wry humor in hopes it would keep my knees from shaking, "I'd just as soon they didn't make such a fuss."

Then talk of any kind became impossible. The barrage was a heavy one, the sky echoing with the whine of the shells closing in, and by thunderous explosions when they burst, showering us with rocks and dirt. Twenty yards to the left, the trench disappeared under a direct hit, and from the rubble came the anguished cry, "Aide man! Aide man!" And so I came to know something of this war I'd been sent to find out about. It left a man trembling in helplessness, naked to the shattering force spewed from the unseen guns on the far side of no-man's-land. For no matter how far down against the wet earth you pressed, there was really no place to hide. Those were some of the longer moments in my life, and when there came a lull in the barrage and my guide muttered, "Let's get out of here," I scrambled willingly to obey.

Back in Paris and still trying for some fresh and graphic approach to filming the war, I made up my mind to find an appealing young doughboy and follow him into action. When I heard that a classmate from Chicago-Kent law school, Ed Vesey, was already at the front with the British, I decided he would be my man. Ed was photogenic, easygoing and bound to be in the thick of things no matter where he was. So I located his outfit, made the necessary arrangements at headquarters and got permission for him to join Harry Chase and me for some preliminary shots. Alas, it was to become an old story: the day before my message reached him, a German shell came over with Ed Vesey's name on it.

Next I tried a young flyer named Tommy Ward. Harry shot a couple of thousand feet of film, but as there was no possibility of getting our heavy gear up into the air with him, we were restricted to his activities on the ground, and that certainly didn't convey the ferment or danger of the war. After more than two months in France, I had the feeling that we weren't getting anywhere.

Then a story that had been building in the military bulletins from Italy had come to a shattering climax in the disaster at Caporetto. There, in late October, the Austrian army, reinforced by seven German divisions, had launched an offensive meant to break a long and bitter stalemate north of the Venetian plain. It turned into one of the most devastating Allied defeats of the war. The powerful Austro-German force tore open the front and sent the Italian armies reeling back in disarray. Unable to stand and fight, they began a headlong stampede down the mountain roads under pounding artillery fire, not stopping until they got to the Piave River, just north of Venice, a retreat of more than seventy miles. Now, even as the French and British drained the hard-pressed Western Front to rush reinforcements to the crumbling Italian line, the urgent question was whether Venice could hold and, indeed, whether the gutted remnants of Italy's army could stave off complete collapse. Anyway, that was where the action was, and it sounded to me like the place for Fran, Harry and me to be.

We did not get off to an auspicious start. Our passports were picked up at the frontier and sent ahead to Rome where, we were told, we could collect them at police headquarters. But when we reached Modena we were arrested for traveling without papers. Given the nervous state of the Italian people following Caporetto, one could hardly blame the *carabinieri*, but that didn't make us feel any better as we sat three days under guard in a dingy hotel, worrying about our confiscated gear and whether anyone would respond to our call for help. Finally the word came to put us on a train to Rome.

To avoid such contretemps in the future, I asked Chaumont if they could assign to us an officer able to cut through our allies' bureaucratic vagaries. The man they sent was General Webb Hayes, whom I had known in Alaska and who was apparently not a vital cog in the war effort at Pershing's headquarters. The fact is that his high rank may have had less to do with his soldierly skills than with the fact that he was the son of our nineteenth President, Rutherford B. Hayes. But for our purposes he was perfect— distinguished-looking and skilled in the niceties. When necessary, I introduced him simply as the son of the President of the United States, provoking looks of utter awe and, invariably, an immediate solution to our thorniest problems. In fact, the Italian Under-Secretary for Foreign Affairs was so impressed that *he* assigned a permanent aide to our growing entourage, a charming Florentine artist named Pierro Tozzi. So knowledgeable and articulate was Major Tozzi that as we traveled through Italy and he entranced us with delightful commentaries on the local art and architecture, I felt guilty enjoying it so much. Tozzi was to become famous in art circles as the discoverer of a long-lost masterpiece by Michelangelo, a statue of the youthful St. John the Divine, which was exhibited at the most recent New York World's Fair.

But the pleasures of the country quickly took second place to the pressing realities of the war. The Austrians and Germans were then within fifteen miles of Venice, seemingly poised for the death blow. And that's where we made our base.

The city was being hastily evacuated, the glass workers to Florence, the lace workers to Genoa, and so on. The American Red Cross was at work trying to minimize the chaos of this transition and to assist the refugees in temporary shelters, sometimes badly crowded and often short of food. And one night, returning from a trip to the Italian Piave River front, I found Fran in a Red Cross uniform. She had signed up and was off to Genoa in the morning. I bid her good-bye with mixed feelings: our meetings would be few and far between now, but I had known for some time how she longed to make a personal commitment to the war, and especially to work among its bereft and uprooted victims.

As for me, I came to feel that I had to make myself an extension of Harry's cameras. An ordinary correspondent could sit on the terrace of the Gritti Palace overlooking the Grand Canal and write his dispatches from communiqués, headquarters' handouts and rumors. But to photograph the war you had to get where the fighting was, and you had to get close. And so we went scrambling through the trenches, recording the faces of men under fire and, with Tozzi's help, putting together a word picture of the precarious Italian front.

The only Americans in active combat in Italy were some scattered airmen under the command of a round little major from New York with a squeaky voice and a razor-sharp mind. He had left a seat in Congress to join the fighting. After talking to him for a little while, I made a note of his name, Fiorello La Guardia, because I had an idea I might be hearing it again. Years later, I was to feature "The Little Flower," the colorful mayor of New York, in my evening broadcasts.

The battlefronts weren't the only hazards Italy confronted us with in those bitter-cold winter days, when the rain turned to sleet in the mountains and the steep, endlessly winding roads grew slick with glare ice. Once we were riding just behind the limousine of a visiting congressman from Boston, George H. Tinkham; it suddenly skidded and spun out of control, plunging down an embankment, and rolled over and over. We went chasing down the mountainside after it, sure the V.I.P. and the British journalist, G. Ward Price, riding with him must have been killed. But the congressman got away with a broken arm, the chauffeur was unhurt and the Englishman came crawling through the shattered window with his monocle still firmly in his eye.

Another time, Chase, Tozzi and I hitched a ride to Verona in a camion loaded with artillery shells. We crawled up over them into the cramped space under the canvas roof and quickly dozed off. It almost turned out to be the Big Sleep. The deadly exhaust fumes, leaking up into the confined area where we huddled, had Chase and Tozzi sick and staggering by the time we got to Verona; I could not be roused at all. They dragged me into the cold air and slapped my face good and hard, and eventually I came around. But it would only have taken a few more whiffs of that carbon monoxide before nothing at all could have roused me.

That December we were taken to the Alpine lair of the *Arditi*, one of the first Alpine military ski outfits ever organized. That was quite an experience, especially for someone who'd grown up in the mountains, as I had. These crack troops had an elaborate *refugio* near the summit of Monte Rosa, a thirteen-thousand-foot massif at the Austrian frontier. To get there we had to cross a gaping chasm from another summit, hauled over one at a time in a hip-high basket suspended from a dancing cable. This they called a *teleferica*. Of course I had had an indoctrination into this sort of thing at the Grand Canyon, but Harry Chase arrived looking as though he had been pummeled by the hammers of hell.

The *Arditi* were nerveless young men who climbed cliffs with knives in their teeth and went silently down the powder-snow slopes on nine-foot skis, rifles slung and using a single pole for braking. Clad entirely in white, they simply vanished from sight in a scant two hundred yards. When would they finish their training? I asked. Arched eyebrows: their training *was* finished. Ah, well, when would they fight? An elaborate Italian shrug: fighting could be dangerous; across the valley was an equally well-trained Austrian ski troop.

The *Arditi* leader was the Marquis Degli d'Albizzi, a dashing young cavalry officer who was obviously chafing under these restrictions handed down by a higher headquarters. Of Russian, English and Italian descent—and uncertain citizenship—he had been trained in the Czar's army and gone to Italy in 1911 to volunteer his services for the war in Tripoli. His application would be considered, he was told. They would let him know. "Better let me know right now," said the irrepressible d'Albizzi. "If you don't want me, the other side does." From then on he was an Italian. Years later we were to be together—in another war.

During the several days we were with the *Arditi* the Marquis showed us their hidden quarters and artillery emplacements, impregnable galleries blasted out of the mountain wall. During the day, with a warning shot, the Austrian artillery across the valley would open up and we would all retire to the safety of our mountain shelter. Later the Italians would return the fire, but the enemy guns were equally secure. Sometimes one side or the other, in a tentative, gingerly way, would try a night raid; but few shots were exchanged and seldom anyone got hurt. Absolutely nothing happened on that mountaintop. It was as though each side had developed a new secret weapon and didn't care to risk losing it in combat. It was a static front, and finally Chase and I left.

By December, Venice was an all but deserted city. The streets had fallen silent and, except for a rare gondola carrying an Italian admiral and his staff, the canals were empty. One afternoon, in the vast expanse of the Piazza San Marco, I saw three British officers, one of whom seemed vaguely familiar. I walked over to say hello and realized he was the young Prince of Wales, sent to Italy after Caporetto to shore up the morale of an ally and of the British troops rushed in to plug the gap. When he heard I had just returned from the front, he questioned me, for though he had been on active duty since the outbreak of the war, he had not been allowed to visit any active front for fear he might be captured. Meanwhile Harry circled around, photographing us in earnest conversation against the background of the wintry and desolate piazza.

Several decades later I occasionally pulled the leg of

some Italian I met by telling him how I had "been with Garibaldi." Of course he knew I couldn't be that ancient. Then I explained how I had been with the Italian "liberator's" son, Pepino Garibaldi, at the Zenzon Bridgehead, at the Italian front on the Piave. A decade later General Garibaldi was our guest when, with Italian-born English novelist Rafael Sabatini, he came to spend a weekend with us on Quaker Hill.

Late one afternoon, just back from the Piave, we stopped at Saint Mark's church, where the latest military bulletins were posted on some sandbags. The thousand-year-old basilica, a triumph of Byzantine architecture, was now heavily banked with them. Amid the notices and dispatches was one with the word that General Sir Edmund H. H. Allenby had been named the new commander in chief of the stalled British army in the Middle East.

Even the little I knew about Allenby sent me back to my quarters in a thoughtful mood. A cavalryman with a dramatic Boer War record, he had fought brilliantly in the battles at Mons and Arras. But his persistent efforts to introduce elements of mobility and surprise on the static Western Front had not endeared him to the British general staff; there is a certain military thinking that shuns unorthodoxy even more heartily than defeat. That the generals were now willing to entrust the Egyptian command to him meant they were more concerned with the fumbling failures of General Sir Archibald Murray than with their private distaste for Allenby's heretical tactics. Now this seemed to herald imminent and dramatic new doings in the Holy Land. So I decided that was where I wanted to be and immediately sent off a long cable to the Foreign Office in London. In it I explained what Chase and I had been doing in France and Italy; I quoted in full my letters from the Secretaries of the Navy and War, and the head of our Department of Information. And finally I pointed out that while the war in Europe was being covered by an international corps of correspondents, the world knew far too little about the British campaign against the Turks. Crossing my fingers, I waited for a reply.

It was not long in coming. I was in Genoa, spending Christmas with Fran, when a message from the British ambassador, Sir James Rennell Rodd, caught up with me: would I come to see him in Rome at my earliest convenience? It had a certain ring to it. I sensed that the answer was yes, and kissing my bride good-bye, I took the next train south.

Later I learned how lucky I had been. The sheer length of my cable had caught the attention of John Buchan, Director of Information, a remarkable man as esteemed in the world of literature as he was in affairs of state. Author of *The Thirty-nine Steps* (one day to be an Alfred Hitchcock film), he later wrote one of the remarkable autobiographies of our time and, as Lord Tweedsmuir, ended a distinguished career as Governor-General of Canada. When I saw him in London after the war, he told me my cable had convinced him of what I proposed to do—throw a spotlight on the heretofore obscure struggle in the Middle East —something the British themselves ought to have been doing. And so his message to Sir Rennell Rodd, the British ambassador to Italy, had been terse and to the point: "Do everything possible to help this young man."

Nor had Sir Rennell dallied. By the time Chase and I arrived in Rome, he had arranged for a courier vessel, a converted destroyer, to speed us across the Mediterranean to Egypt. Even then it was standing by, waiting for us in the instep of the Italian boot formed by the Gulf of Taranto. Our conversation with the ambassador was brief. After a hurried handshake, Harry and I collected our equipment and continued south. I was off on what was, I suppose, the most profoundly affecting experience of my life.

We left Taranto in a storm, which gave us protection from German submarines but was otherwise unwelcome to Harry and me as well as to most of the crew. The Mediterranean is a shallow sea and can be one of the roughest when it kicks up. As luck would have it, the storm intensified to gale force and we were forced to detour into the harbor at Malta. There we sat for five days while the winds howled and wintry rain swept our island world. Finally the skies cleared and we dashed eastward, paralleling the North African coast to Alexandria at the mouth of the Nile, thence southward by train to Cairo, command post of the Near East campaign.

Cairo, exotic capital of Egypt and largest city in Africa, has historically been a focus of intrigue and political excitement. Now, as the nerve center of a vast theater of operations, with thousands of British, French and Colonial troops thronging the streets, it was a bedlam of activity. Allenby, we quickly learned, was "off in the blue," somewhere in the Sinai Desert with his army, but his whirlwind appearance had already sent morale soaring. Seeing numbers of British officers lounging in the lobbies of the great hotels—Shepheards, the Cecil, and Continental—he took to replying to their salutes with a crisp command: "Stand by for orders to leave for the front." And off they were sent.

In the early days of the fighting, Lord Kitchener, Secretary of State for War, had chided the first British commander in Egypt, whose army moved, when it moved at all, with rheumatic restraint: "Are you defending the Canal, or is the Canal defending you?" Now, at last, things were happening.

Allenby had been given the Near East command in the summer of 1917. By October his reinforced and thoroughly reinvigorated army—a polyglot array of Austrians, New Zealanders, Indians, Arabs, a Jewish unit, and Englishmen —was on the move. Profiting from the lesson of two stinging British defeats at Gaza, northern anchor of the Turkish defense line, Allenby struck at its southern end, Beersheba, with five full divisions. Stunned, the Turks reeled back, pressed so hard they hadn't time to destroy the town's wells, thus assuring Allenby a vital source of water for the desert campaign ahead.

Turning north, he rolled up the Turkish line toward Gaza, which fell on November 7; he then pushed on, sweeping along the coast to take Jaffa the following week. Now, at last, the great prizes of Palestine and Arabia— Jerusalem, Damascus, Aleppo—were within reach, and with them a chance to drive Turkey out of the war.

Two weeks passed, and still Harry and I were in Cairo waiting for permission to move up to the battlefront in Palestine. When we checked at headquarters each day the report was no word. They did not know—nor did I until after the war—that a minor battle royal, Allenby versus the Foreign Office, had resulted over our request to be allowed to cross the Sinai Desert so we could report on the operations of the British forces at firsthand.

Allenby, whose troops cheerfully—but privately—referred to him as The Bull, and of whom it was said that you could hear his roar all the way from Dan to Beersheba, had been incensed to learn that an American observer and his photographer had been sent out to Egypt. He promptly expressed this to London, his cable demanding to know who was running a war. Let it get out, he added, that he was letting members of the world press join his army, and the Foreign Office could confidently anticipate the claim of every sovereign state and religion in the Western world to be represented at the liberation of the Holy Land. As London had not even provided him with sufficient transport for his soldiers, he was certainly in no position to accommodate a small army of newsmen and religious zealots.

For his part, John Buchan switched from a head-on counteroffensive and took aim, instead, on Allenby's vulnerable flank. Civilization, he cabled back, deserved to have the details of the general's brilliant campaign, particularly as there was no comparably good news from France. Furthermore, the Foreign Office would hold off and not send any more "observers" without Allenby's specific approval.

Meanwhile, unaware of these cables speeding back and forth with our fate hanging in the balance, Chase and I tried to keep occupied. I followed the campaign from official dispatches; I sought out those who had been to the front and questioned them. For the moment, they agreed, all seemed quiet. But a few mentioned a mysterious young Englishman who had gone into the desert and was leading the Bedouin against the Turks. When I pressed for more information, that was all anyone in Cairo seemed to know.

Another thing I did to keep busy was to wangle my first airplane ride. It was a landmark moment in my life. Only fourteen years had passed since the Wright brothers had made history's first flight, yet here was I, soaring high above the desert. And on the airfield below, and on other airfields in France and Germany, pursuit, reconnaissance and bombing planes were changing the face of war. And with the coming of peace, their successors—the great transports and passenger jets—would inexorably change the life of every man and woman on earth.

Over the years I have often thought how my own life, which began in rural America during the agricultural age, has since spanned the entire industrial era, and that consequently I have probably lived through more great technical and scientific advances than had occurred in all the rest of recorded history: the automobile, the almost universal use of electric power and the telephone, motion pictures, radio and television, transcontinental highways, nuclear energy, startling discoveries in medicine, explorations of the ocean bottoms and man's first ventures into outer space. And yet none of these seem quite so remarkable to me as the first moment when a Breguet biplane lifted free of the earth and I realized that I was flying.

The headquarters of the Royal Flying Corps was at Heliopolis, a few miles from Cairo. An ancient seat of learning where Moses had been a student and Pythagoras a teacher, it now echoed to the impudent roar of those frail, fabric-covered, open-cockpit planes. My pilot was a South African, Major Edward Emmett, who put the Breguet through every acrobatic maneuver he knew. What he did was to make me a lifelong devotee of the airplane, for I loved every second of it—looking at the pyramids upside down as we looped over them again and again, seeing a whirling Sphinx rush up at my face as we spun down in a whirling tailspin.

"Are you all right?" Emmett asked after we'd bounced down on the landing field at Heliopolis.

"Yes," I replied at once. "When can I go up again?"

A few days later, I flew in one plane with Harry and his DeBrie motion picture camera in the cockpit of another, and we took the first pictures of the Suez Canal ever made from the air. I was already in a state of elation when we returned to Cairo, but my days of highest excitement were just beginning. For this time, when I checked at headquarters, the word was our clearance from Allenby had finally arrived; it had been arranged for Harry and our heavy equipment to travel to Jerusalem via the Sinai-Palestine railway—the "Milk and Honey Express," the Tommies called it—but I was to be *flown* there, from Egypt across the Sinai to the Holy Land!

My pilot was Major A. J. Evans, an engaging young man with a bent for adventure. England's top prewar cricket star, he was among the handful who had flown the first of those early box-kite planes across the Channel to France. Shot down behind the German lines and imprisoned, he promptly escaped. A few days after delivering me to the Holy Land, he would again be shot down behind enemy lines, again imprisoned—and again escape!

But military prisons, the war itself, were far from both

our minds as we flew over the Suez Canal and started across the Sinai Desert, the great triangular land bridge between Africa and Asia. I blessed Harry's foresight in pressing on me, at the last moment, a still camera, for as we went slanting beneath the clouds, there, stretched out below us, was a land where men had marched and fought and traded in the ages before there was a Western civilization. Here Moses received the Ten Commandments; here the children of Israel wandered forty years before they reached the Promised Land. Evans and I, covering the same distance in less than four hours, and with a swing out over the Dead Sea, circled over Jerusalem. We were among the first ever to gaze down from above on that hallowed ground and its holy places. Landing in a meadow near Ramleh, now the site of Israel's Ben-Gurion Airport, we taxied over the plain where Richard the Lion-Hearted had camped during the Third Crusade, longing for the Holy City he would never enter, and where Napoleon established his headquarters in a vain effort to sever the British route to India. What a revolution the airplane had wrought! Between morning and noon, three thousand years of human history had flashed beneath our wings.

I had been somewhat concerned lest they rush us off somewhere from Jerusalem, maybe to Jericho. Arriving, I learned that Allenby's striking force had been depleted by a crisis call for additional manpower from the beleaguered Western Front, his planned spring offensive called off. Instead, I was told, he was reorganizing, hoping for sufficient reinforcements to enable him to strike north toward Damascus by summer. He was rarely seen in Jerusalem, preferring his field headquarters.

For the time being I was satisfied with the chance to wander about experiencing at firsthand those long-imagined biblical settings. When Harry arrived, we traveled farther afield, photographing the bleak hill country and ancient towns of Judea, Samaria and Sinai, now swarming with Australian and British cavalry, Indian lancers and a camel corps from Rajputana. We took pictures of young Tommies in their khaki shorts wandering the streets of Gaza, where Delilah barbered poor Samson, and of Anzac Light Horse camped at the Vale of Ajalon, where Joshua ordered the sun and moon to stand still.

Jerusalem fell first. The City of God, the holiest city of Christians and Jews and one of the chief shrines of Islam,

Jerusalem had been in Moslem hands for a thousand years, and not nine holy crusades spanning the Middle Ages, nor Napoleon, nor Sir Archibald Murray's modern army, could wrest it free. But Allenby, having outflanked the Turkish position, surrounded the Holy City and marched in without firing a shot—which was precisely as he had planned it, for he had a horror of damaging any of the city's holy places. And so the age-old dream of Western civilization was realized.

Years later, on a worldwide tour, I told of my experiences during those epochal moments in history and disclosed some of the unreported episodes of the Palestinian campaign. General Liman von Sanders, the German who had been rushed in to command the Turkish force defending Jerusalem, was awakened to be informed that British cavalry had enveloped the city and that its capture was imminent. He fled in his pajamas.

Meanwhile, a cockney unit, the 50th London Division, had outpaced the line of advance and run short of supplies. At dawn, a mess sergeant and a company cook, scrounging through the hills for food, came upon a walled city. Nervous and about to turn back, they were hailed by a mounted cavalcade riding through the gate behind a white flag. At the head was the mayor of Jerusalem, eager to surrender. Of all the thousands of fighting men closing on the city, the two cockney kitchen NCOs had been first to reach it. Now dumbfounded, they listened while the mayor made an eloquent speech, at the conclusion of which, with a flourish, he presented the keys to "this holiest of cities" to the cook.

When the mess sergeant found his voice, he blurted: "Hi say, Guv'ner, we don't want any keys to this 'ere 'oly city. What we want are heggs for our hofficer."

Returning—without the eggs—they reported this remarkable encounter to their "hofficer," Major Vivian Gilbert, who rushed off to inform his brigade commander, General Watson, who promptly sent the two noncoms back to find the mayor and deliver the message that he would be in Jerusalem within the hour to accept the surrender! This time the mayor delivered a formal speech from the city's wall, flanked by most of the populace, who cheered and threw flowers. Of course General Watson had to report all this to his chief, General Sir John Shea, who was commanding the 50th Division. Naturally, he wanted the honor of accepting the surrender of the world's holiest city. So the next day the mayor went through all this for a third time. Again there were cheers and flowers, and again the mayor made his speech. But when Sir John made his report, Allenby told him the formal ceremony would take place two days later. When the modern Coeur de Lion came to the Jaffa gate, he dismounted from his charger and went in on foot as a simple pilgrim. Everyone in Jerusalem was there to greet him. The crowd sang and cheered and threw flowers in his path. For a fourth time the Moslem mayor made his speech, perhaps not so eloquently because he was hoarse by now. And so Jerusalem surrendered for the fourth time! A month later the mayor died of pneumonia, and the story was that he had died from exposure—from making his speech of surrender so many times.

The Western world thrilled to the news of the fall of Jerusalem. Men and women of all faiths imagined themselves amid its glories. But some of the footsore troops on the scene, having fought their way from Egypt through the forbidding desert, were more measured in their enthusiasm. Colonel Barney Todd's Tenth Light Horse, strung out in single file across half of Jerusalem, were taken on a tour of the fourteen Stations of the Cross along the narrow Via Dolorosa. Surely they could be forgiven a purely personal reaction to Christ's agony as He made his final journey toward Calvary. At the head of the column, the guide would point to a wooden cross and say, "This is where our Savior fell the first time," and this information would be passed back from man to man along the narrow, winding street: "This is where He fell the first time, this is where He fell the first time"—and so on. As the long line shuffled slowly forward—"This is where our Savior fell the second time," and so on and so on. After this had gone on for quite a while, at the fifth or sixth station, when the guide said Christ had fallen, the Aussie behind him sang out: "He's down again, boys,"—and so it was passed on down the street: "He's down again, He's down again, He's down again!"

And one homesick Tommy wrote to his mother in England, "I am in Bethlehem, where Christ was born. I wish to Christ I was in Wiggan, where I was born."

Again I heard the rumors of that shadowy Englishman among the desert tribes, a scholar, some said, without a day of military training. And yet the story was that his

Bedouin irregulars were harassing the enemy behind the lines and that the Turks had put a price of fifty thousand pounds on his head. But it was also said the Arabs had come to regard him as one of their own and that anyone who did harm to *El-Aurens,* as they called him, would face the united vengeance of disparate tribes who could agree on little else. How could I find out more about him? I asked nearly everyone I encountered, but learned little beyond what I had already heard.

Waiting for Allenby to reorganize and plan his final drive, Harry and I wandered where our fancy took us. One day, in a military flivver driven by the British lieutenant assigned to help us—and also no doubt to keep us out of trouble—we rattled down the road to Hebron and got into some serious trouble indeed. We wanted to photograph the mosque above the tombs of Abraham, Isaac, Jacob and their wives, Sarah, Leah and Rebecca. Slipping away from our young aide, we took our camera inside, which was a sacrilege, for even entering the consecrated shrine was strictly forbidden to nonbelievers. Blithely unaware that we had transgressed, we were busy photographing when a rising murmur of protest finally drew our attention to a crowd of Moslems, angry, swelling and moving toward us with clearly hostile intent.

"Let's get out of here," I whispered to Harry.

"One more shot," he replied.

"It'll be your last," I insisted, grabbing his arm and yanking.

We ran for the car, trying to skirt the edge of that out-reaching mob. When they failed to get their hands on us, they began pelting us with stones. Luckily, our lieutenant, watching grim and white-faced, had the motor running and went roaring off the instant we tumbled in.

There were repercussions, beginning with the lieutenant —"I say, sir, that was a bit unwise, you know"—and reaching all the way to Allenby's headquarters. The great man, we heard, fumed when he heard about our escapade, and for a time I wondered whether he would seize on it as a reason for shipping us back to Europe. Instead, incredibly, it led to a very cordial meeting. For the incident had apparently served to remind him that I was there at his headquarters, as an observer.

One day I walked alone down Christian Street in the Old City, fascinated by the swirl of faces and exotic dress, by the constant din. A group of Arabs approached, their faces, half hidden, swarthy and bearded. All but one. As they passed me in the narrow street, I could see that this one, though dressed like the rest, and even with his face beaten by the weather and burned by the sun, was different. He was smaller, clean-shaven, his features more finely wrought; his eyes were a startling blue. And he wore the short curved sword of a prince of Mecca. I watched them move away down the street and could see that the others deferred to him.

I thought it all strange. A blue-eyed Arab? Perhaps he was a Circassian, one of the storied people from the Caucasian Mountains who had abandoned Christianity for Islam in the seventeenth century, one of whom was Saladin who led the armies that threw back the Crusaders. A recollection of that elusive British desert warrior stirred in my mind. But such was the power of these surroundings to conjure up fantasy that in a little while I had forgotten my errand and turned back. I didn't know what I meant to do, but I felt sure there was a story in this mysterious figure, and I meant to track it down.

At the headquarters of the Military Governor, Sir Ronald Storrs, I went in. I wondered what he would have to say about my tale of a blue-eyed Arab on Christian Street. Shown into his office, I immediately began telling him of the encounter. Did he have any idea who the man could be? Was he, by chance, the desert fighter I'd been hearing about? And somehow I wasn't surprised when, without a word, Storrs walked over to another door, opened it, and there, sitting in the adjoining office and looking at us quizzically, my blue-eyed Arab, still dressed as a desert Bedouin.

Sir Ronald merely said: "I want you to meet the Uncrowned King of Arabia." I soon learned how Storrs and Lawrence had been old friends, from their Oxford days, and in introducing him in this way he was actually pulling his leg.

We spent only a short time together that first day—Lawrence was waiting to see Allenby—and I found him reluctant to talk about himself or the desert campaign. He seemed shy and kept looking over at Storrs, as though begging to be rescued from this American. Casting about for something—anything!—to say, I mumbled a few words about my enchantment with the antiquities of the Holy

113

Land and was instantly tuned in to an entirely different personality. For Lawrence, as I soon realized, was a scholar, an archaeologist, and had originally come to the Near East to study the architecture of the crusader castles. Now—as I silently blessed my father for awakening my interest in antiquity—he spoke eagerly and eloquently of his explorations into the ancient past, those blue eyes shining and the boyish, sensitive planes of his face reflecting his enthusiasm.

We arranged to meet again the next day. When he had gone, Sir Ronald told me something of the personal history of this remarkable young man, rejected for military service at the outbreak of the war and now, not quite thirty years old, legendary leader of the Bedouin revolt against the Turks. He had become, quite simply, Lawrence of Arabia.

Few knew him well. Sir Ronald was one who did, for not only had they been together at Oxford, but in 1916 they had been on the joint mission to the Hejaz that had bound Lawrence to the Arab cause and the Arabs to the support of the British in the Near East. Most important, the two were among a tiny minority of British officialdom —Lawrence called Storrs the most brilliant—who believed in an enlightened future for the Arabs.

Sir Ronald told me Emir Feisal, with Lawrence as his adviser, had been Allenby's right arm in the Palestine campaign—in a certain sense quite literally—for the Hejaz "regulars" and Bedouin irregulars had protected the British right flank in the advance on Jerusalem. Until now, the existence of a British officer as one of the leaders of an Arab force had been held secret; the Foreign Office wanted the world to believe the Arab uprising entirely spontaneous and only coincidentally helpful to British arms. Now it was seen that as this was essentially true and the effort so far successful, Lawrence's role could be revealed: England might well reap some credit abroad for championing a subjugated people. This of course did lead to confusion and bitterness when Arab claims were rejected during the peace negotiations at Versailles. But truth and honor are often among the casualties of a nation at war.

Meanwhile, said Sir Ronald, Lawrence had been called in from the desert by Allenby. Shortly before, he had been captured by the Turks in Deraa and before escaping had undergone a gruesome experience, about which Sir Ronald would say no more. Wounded in each of his last five battles, exhausted, convinced he had lost the confidence of the Arab leaders, he had returned to headquarters "to confess that I had made a mess of things, and had come to beg Allenby to find me some smaller part elsewhere."

"Will the C-in-C let him go?" I asked Storrs.

"It's not possible," he replied. "Just now he is worn out by a year and a half of guerrilla fighting, but the war is not over and there is only one Lawrence. He is an inspired tactician and the only man we have to whom the Arabs will listen. He must go back."

When he does, I decided, saying nothing at the time, Chase and I would join him.

Next day, knowing Lawrence had seen Allenby, I asked him what his plans were. He smiled ruefully. "I am ordered to return to the desert," he said.

When I told him I believed the Arab effort and his own contribution to be a dramatic new aspect of the war and I wanted to film and report it, he said he had no objection, but he had come and would return through the Turkish lines, and it was not feasible for us to attempt this. Although it looked hopeless, my every instinct told me I must not miss the chance to be first to tell the world his story.

For the moment I could only bide my time. After Lawrence left, Harry and I returned down the winding Jaffa-Jerusalem road, then on to the Plain of Esdraelon where the little band of British correspondents covering Allenby's campaign were encamped. They were four in all—two reporters, a photographer and an artist. The paucity of their number was astonishing enough—four men to cover a war involving hundreds of thousands of diverse troops and about to reach its climactic moments!—but it was their attitude toward their assignment that later made it clear I virtually had the field to myself. Fergus Ferguson, representing Reuters, had been born in Constantinople and spent all his life in the Middle East; he had long since ceased to be moved or even terribly interested in anything that happened there. The other journalist, William A. Massey of the *Daily Telegraph* and pool representative of the other London papers, seemed primarily concerned with dry facts and oblivious to the romance and color of a modern war in the ancient lands of the eastern Mediterranean. One of his dispatches, covering a cavalry charge by a regiment of Dorset yeoman over the very spot where the Bible tells us

David slew Goliath, made no mention of that intriguing sidelight, but remarked on the disposition of every unit involved, including a quartermaster company that never budged from its position seven miles behind the line, and noted the family background, school and previous station of each ranking officer.

Had they heard about Colonel Lawrence and his Arab irregulars? I asked Ferguson and Massey.

Yes, but it had all been a diversion. No one would ever hear of Lawrence again.

Had they tried to get his story?

What! Travel halfway across the Arabian desert to some godforsaken water hole? For what—to see a bunch of Bedouins on camelback? Wasn't Esdraelon bad enough?

As for the photographer, Harold Jeap, a gnome of a man straight from London's cockney East End, he found these new surroundings so alien and understood them so little that he didn't seem to know which way to point his camera. When Harry asked if he'd gotten any pictures of the pyramids, he said no, he could get all the mountain pictures he wanted crossing the Alps on the way home. Then Harold asked, "By the way, was it Mr. 'Spinx' who built the Pyramids?"

The exception in this fog of indifference was James McBey, Allenby's official artist. He was a Scot from dour, gray-granite Aberdeen, where he had been a bank clerk, and with his bulk and loping walk could have passed for a professional wrestler. In fact he was as gentle a man as I've ever met, soft-spoken, full of whimsy, and so sensitive to the drama of this war in the desert that the floor of our tent and the sand outside were forever strewn with his sketches. If I had only had the foresight to pick up a few! McBey, who was to turn up in my life later on, quickly gained a reputation as the greatest etcher of our time after Whistler. His work, some of it done while we were tentmates at Esdraelon, was to command record prices, and at least one sketch, a magnificent mood piece of Allenby's camel corps in Sinai entitled *The Dawn Patrol,* became a classic.

Not far from our camp was a pioneer Zionist settlement called Rehoboth. Today it is a city of forty thousand, center of a flourishing citrus-growing region and site of the Weizmann Institute of Science. But in 1918 it consisted of a handful of Jews from eastern Europe struggling against the arid earth and the hostility of the Palestinians, trying to forge a new life in the Hebrew homeland of the Bible. I went there several times, drank their rich, smooth wine and heard their stories. Most were from Russia, refugees from the anti-Semitic tyranny of the Czarist regime. There were several of these agricultural colonies, founded with the financial support of the wealthy Baron Edmond de Rothschild.

To them Palestine was a historic homeland, a last hope. They would cling to these scattered corners of Eretz Israel against all odds. Later they would be the forerunners of a flood of Jewish immigration, in the dark days of the Hitler holocaust, and their ranks would swell.

As for the Moslems, they had their claim on Palestine, too. Descendants of many earlier peoples, they had been there for many centuries and resisted bitterly first the trickle, then the tide, of Jewish immigration. There was to be sporadic but unremitting fighting over the next thirty years. Interested outside nations, locked to their own narrow self-interest, encouraged expectations on both sides that were incompatible. In 1948, with the creation of the state of Israel, the conflict flared into all-out war, armed truce, war again. The great powers took a hand; nuclear arms were rattled; oil, the lifeblood of our modern civilization, became a weapon. But Jew and Moslem in the Palestinian powder keg, there is right on both sides and justice for neither.

I might never have gotten acquainted with Allenby if it hadn't been for the Duke of Connaught. King George V had planned to fly out to Palestine and personally give out decorations after his army had taken the Holy City. But he fell ill and asked his uncle, the aged Duke of Connaught, to go in his place. The Duke arrived via Egypt over the same "Milk and Honey Express" on which Chase had made the journey across the Sinai. At Ramleh, the end of the line in the Plain of Esdraelon, when the Duke emerged he faced a sea of faces, thousands of Allenby's troops all wearing helmets.

Standing on the platform of his wagon-lit, he saw only one blot on the landscape. It was my American "campaign" hat. This was the same as was worn by the Royal Canadian Mounted Police. The Duke had served in Canada as Governor-General. He asked Allenby who was wearing the hat, and this reminded the C-in-C that I was with his army. A few days later he invited me to headquarters for luncheon.

When I arrived, I was much surprised to find I was to be alone with the modern Richard the Lion-Hearted and the uncle of the King. Why this good fortune I could only guess. Maybe the Duke had brought word of what Pershing's army was doing on the Western Front and how much now depended on America.

At any rate, here I was with a chance not likely to come again. At an appropriate moment, I mentioned Lawrence, told of my meetings with him and said I'd been disappointed not to be able to accompany him back to Arabia. Allenby then told how they had tried to keep the role Lawrence had been playing as much of a secret as possible. The idea was to have the revolt in the desert appear to be strictly an Arab affair. In this way they hoped many men of Arab blood would be influenced to desert from the Turkish army. He said they had succeeded in this, and he explained how it had been important to play down what the Arabs had been doing in the Hejaz and what Lawrence and his handful of associates had accomplished. He said it was no longer necessary to keep it a secret and if we wished we could join Lawrence and make the journey the long way around—back across the Sinai to Egypt, a few thousand miles up the Nile and then east across the Sudan and the Red Sea. He said he would give us permission to do this. Something about the way he said it, itemizing each turning point en route as though to emphasize the distance, suggested that he was wondering whether we would do it. But the fact is I could barely wait for him to finish so I could say yes.

Did I realize what this was to mean? I'm sure I did not. How could I know this was to be the big opportunity of my life, result in a speaking tour of the world, a book to remain a best seller for half a century, and affect almost everything I was to do for some six decades?

When I told Allenby we wanted pictures of him and his staff on the Mount of Olives, he told me to bring Chase the next day to the Augusta Victoria Stiftung, which with its high, square tower dominated the famous hill to the east of Jerusalem. A hospice and sanitorium built by the Germans and named for the *Kaiserin,* it reflected a sort of

Biedermeier gloom and belonged on the banks of the Rhine. Kaiser Wilhelm himself had come to dedicate it in 1910, entering the City of God in full, flamboyant military regalia, riding a white charger and wearing that menacing spiked helmet. He must have been especially pleased with the two mosaic ceiling panels in the Stiftung chapel; Harry and I were appalled. One panel depicted Christ and His disciples; the other, Kaiser Wilhelm and his entourage, also in biblical dress. They were still there when I visited the Holy Land in later years.

Allenby and some of his staff officers were waiting for us at the tower. We talked briefly about his campaign, but I could not keep him long on that subject. Like any other newcomer with a sense of history, he seemed totally taken with Jerusalem and its roster of conquerors and defenders. While Harry worked steadily around us, Allenby, the modern Coeur de Lion, now playing the combined roles of teacher and tour guide, noted the places in the golden hills and around us where the best and worst in humankind, through the ages, contended for dominion over the city and over the temporal and spiritual fate of its populace.

There, Allenby said, pointing, the Canaanites, seeing how the seemingly insignificant group of hills commanded the main route from the desert to the sea, had built a stronghold five thousand years before. The stronghold became a city and the city a coveted objective in the clash of armies at the crossroads of civilization. To this day the turmoil in the Holy Land is but ancient history in modern dress.

To the Jews, the Western Wall, all that remains of King Solomon's Temple, marks Jerusalem as the heart of their homeland. To Christians, it is the City of God, for here Christ was crucified, here buried, on the spot now sanctified by the Shrine of the Holy Sepulcher. And for Moslems, the Dome of the Rock, whence Mohammed is said to have ascended to heaven, makes Jerusalem almost equal to Mecca and Medina as the holiest of cities. Even with the city returned to the rule of the West, Allenby seemed to be prophesying the bitter clashes that would continue to our own day. Soon after he entered Jerusalem, he had received a delegation of quarreling Greek Orthodox monks, Catholics, Copts and Nestorians. Each was convinced it should have sole control over the Shrine of the Holy Sepulcher. Each beseeched Allenby's support. But he was a soldier, not a magistrate, and sent them away saying, "Who am I to set the world aright?"

Peace would come to the Holy Land, not by fiat, not even when men rose above their religious faith, but only when they truly began to live it. Such was Allenby's moral as we surveyed the panorama of Jerusalem.

Before heading back to Egypt on our way to Arabia, Harry and I had our first home-cooked meal of the war in the American Colony in Jerusalem. Bertha Vester, then in her thirties, was a striking blonde, regal and utterly lovely. That her face reflected an abiding composure—that she could even find time to feed and entertain two strangers—was something special for us. Her husband ran a unique mercantile establishment just inside the Jaffa Gate, conducted tours to all the far-flung biblical and historic sites of the Holy Land, and, most important, she directed the varied social services the American Colony traditionally provided to Jerusalem's sick and poor. Once we heard Bertha Vester's story, we understood the sources of her strength.

Her father, Horace Spafford, had been a prominent Chicago attorney. Then tragedy: his wife and four daughters aboard a steamer that went down in mid-Atlantic, the mother rescued, but all four children drowned; a year later, an infant son dead of scarlet fever. To the bereft parents, life turned suddenly meaningless and, worse, seemed to mock them for their concern with pleasure and the material things. They fell back on their religious faith and it sustained them. And finally, three years after Bertha was born, they gave up everything and moved to the Holy Land, to live close to the presence and spirit of the Savior.

The year was 1881. Soon a few friends followed, settling next to the Spaffords in northeast Jerusalem, in what came to be called the American Colony. Still others joined them, fundamentalist Protestants, some Swedes who believed in the imminence of the Second Coming, perhaps fifty in all, and all convinced that God's love was given most freely to those who served their fellow men.

Raised in such an environment, Bertha moved spontaneously into a long lifetime of benevolence. She was to live eighty-seven years in that intensely dramatic city, through two world wars and all the incessant upheavals that racked history's most tormented land. From the time of Abdul Hamid, the Ottoman sultan, until the Six Day

120

War of 1967, Bertha Vester was both spectator and partic- ipant in the Holy Land's turmoil and turning points. It was Bertha to whom the Arab mayor of Jerusalem turned when the Turks fled and the British stood at Jerusalem's gate. What should I do? he asked her. For answer, she tore a white hospital sheet in two and rode with him to sur- render, to Sir John Shea, to interpret for him. She came to know kings, presidents, princes and field marshals—and uncounted thousands of Moslems, Jews and Christians, who called her *"Ummuna,"* which in Arabic means "Mother of us all."

The enduring capstone of Bertha Vester's life is the clinic she established and ran through her American Colony Charities Association, which today is called Help for the Children of the Holy Land. Its real beginnings go back to Christmas Eve, 1925. On her way to lead the carol singing in a field outside Bethlehem, she had encountered a peasant whose sick wife had just been turned away from the Gen- eral Hospital. The reason? It was the Christians' holiday. The woman slumped weakly on the back of a donkey. The man, walking alongside and supporting her, carried an in- fant in a bundle of rags.

The irony, the mocking analogy to that time, this same holy night two thousand years before, when Mary and Joseph had also been turned away, struck Mrs. Vester like a blow to the heart. She immediately gave up her caroling plans and arranged to have the poor sick woman admitted to the hospital. But it was too late. On Christmas morning the man stood sadly at her gate; his wife had died. Now, he said, holding forth the ragged bundle, unless someone took his baby, it, too, would die, for he could not care for it in the cave that was his only home.

"I will take him," Bertha Vester said, and that moment began planning and working for what was to be a career unique in the annals of the decades to follow, caring for more than a million mothers and children.

For many years I was an inactive director of the Amer- ican Colony Charities Association which administered it, headed by Dr. John Finley, editor of *The New York Times,* later by the legendary Rev. Harry Emerson Fosdick and Dr. Edward Elson, Chaplain of the U.S. Senate. Eventually I succeeded Dr. and Mrs. Norman Vincent Peale as its president. As for Bertha Vester, having touched the troubled Holy Land with her healing hand for nearly a full century, she died in 1968 at the age of ninety. I was proud to have been her friend. It seemed to me she was the most impressive American woman of our time.

With Lawrence in Arabia

> I was sent to these Arabs as a stranger, unable
> to think their thoughts or suscribe to their beliefs,
> but charged by duty to lead them forward and
> to develop to the highest any movement of theirs
> profitable to England in her war.
> —T. E. LAWRENCE

THOMAS Edward Lawrence was born in Wales in August, 1888, and from the first appeared ordained for an
uncommon destiny. His parents were an Irish baronet, Sir
Thomas Robert Chapman, and a talented Scottish governess named Sara Maden. The only trouble was that they
were not married to each other. Sir Thomas had abandoned
his wife and children to run off with their governess, and
the two thereafter lived together as Mr. and Mrs. Lawrence.
They had five sons, of whom T. E. ("Ned") was the second.

The amateur analysts have made much of Lawrence's
illegitimacy, ascribing to it a warping of his psyche, an
unendurable sense of shame. Building on this frail foundation, they conjure up a character of dark introspection, of
confused sexual taste, a man whose feelings of inferiority
were masked by his plunging himself into the most dangerous situations and then, having won worldwide fame, by
renouncing the honors and the fortune in money offered
as reward. How else did it happen, these sages ask, that
he had no interest in women? Why, after the war, did he
twice try to bury himself by enlisting in the military ranks
under assumed names? Why did he appear to court death

so assiduously, finding it finally on that narrow roadway in the Dorset countryside?

Why, indeed? I don't know. I don't think anyone knows. And now that the Lawrence legend has become fair game we are apt never to find out, for considered speculation has given way to endless flights of fancy. There were many who insisted that I alone had launched the Lawrence legend with my Palestine-Arabia film production, which I presented in person for record runs in London, New York and on around the world. This was the first the public had ever heard of him, including his own countrymen. But the story I told of his desert exploits was based on what I myself saw and heard during the time I was with Lawrence in Arabia.

One of the most gifted and unusual men of our time, he was, above all, possessed of a clear and penetrating intellect. At Oxford, he took first-class history honors with a brilliant thesis, published as *Crusader Castles*. Fascinated with the Middle East, he was wandering through Palestine, Syria and Mesopotamia five years before the war, part of the time excavating the sites of ancient civilizations along the Tigris and Euphrates.

He was a natural for British intelligence and early in 1914, ostensibly exploring the Sinai, he was actually reporting to the War Office on Turkish troop dispositions along the Egyptian border. Once the fighting began, he was posted to Cairo. In November, 1916, a month after Hussein ibn Ali, Emir of Mecca, had proclaimed an Arab revolt against Turkey's rule, Lawrence set off on his singular desert mission; thereafter he dressed as an Arab, shared their food and their tents, and almost his sole contacts with British officialdom were in quest of money and ordnance for his Bedouin warriors.

Officially attached to the army of Feisal, ablest of Hussein's sons, as political and liaison officer, Lawrence was in fact the leader and inspiration. He injected vigorous new life into their rebellion, helping to unify the separate tribes, heartening both sheiks and nomads to believe they would prevail and, after four hundred years, throw off the Turkish yoke. He harried the enemy where they least expected him to appear, then vanished again into the desert. Having no military training, he fabricated a strategy that violated the textbook precepts—but happened to work perfectly for undisciplined irregulars operating in a vast and trackless expanse of desert. He cut railroad lines, blew up bridges and struck down strongholds the enemy considered impregnable. His raids diverted thirty thousand of Liman von Sanders's Turkish troops which could otherwise have been thrown into the fight against Allenby. And now, as Harry and I journeyed west, south, east and then north to join him, Lawrence was poised for the final blows.

Our ultimate destination, in a straight line, lay little more than a hundred and fifty miles south of our starting point in Jerusalem. We didn't know this, for the reason that we didn't know where we were going. To get around the Turkish line, as well as to preserve the secrecy of Lawrence's whereabouts—all Palestine swarmed with spies of both sides—we were obliged to travel a devious route of nearly three thousand miles by train, steamship and camelback. Not until we crossed the Red Sea were we told that we were bound for Aqaba.

It was an unforgettable trip. First we took the Milk and Honey Express back across the Sinai to Cairo. There we were put aboard a paddle-wheel steamer for the long journey up the Nile. When we reached Wadi Halfa some days later, we transferred to a train to continue our journey straight south to Khartoum, for at this point the Nile begins to meander all over the Sudan. That train belonged to a vanished era—three spacious, immaculately white compartments to a car, large fans stirring the heavy air, and smiling Sudanese to indulge us.

In Cairo, for travel reading, I had picked up a copy of Winston Churchill's account of the Anglo-Egyptian campaigns in the Sudan, *The River War*, with its tragic prelude, the story of Victorian England's odd man out, Charles George Gordon. Now, arriving in Khartoum, I found that beguiling city of white stone fraught with phantom images of "Chinese" Gordon, though it had been largely rebuilt since he was killed there more than thirty years before.

And it suddenly came to me that Gordon and Lawrence in some ways were two of a kind. Half a century before, someone had written, "If you wanted some out-of-the-way piece of work done in an unknown and barbarous country, Gordon would be your man." And so would T. E. Lawrence, as the War Office discovered in 1916.

Both were somewhat fanatic in the intensity with which

they pursued their assigned missions. Both were outsiders, bizarre in the eyes of their fellow officers, contemptuous of rigid army dogma, seemingly devoid of romantic interest in women, bored by London society—although there were patrician hostesses who would have built an entire social season around each—and prone to self-analysis and philosophical musings. Both did their best work with insurgent troops in alien lands, Westerners among Arab tribes, Christians among Mohammedans, and were more hindered than helped by the military establishment to which, officially, they belonged. And in the end, both having done the job they were sent to do, better, perhaps, than Whitehall ever intended, they were, in effect, renounced, pledges made by their government disclaimed, with the result that one lost his life, while some insist the other lost his honor.

Oh, yes, they also shared a postmortem misfortune. When Hollywood got around to doing their stories not so many years ago, they chose otherwise excellent actors—Charlton Heston for Gordon and Peter O'Toole for Lawrence—who no more represented the looks, character or personality of those titans than I do.

By the time he came to Khartoum in February, 1884, Major General Charles George Gordon had already done a fair share of "out-of-the-way" work for his country in China and Equatorial Africa. In putting down the Taiping Rebellion, he demonstrated a genius for commanding irregular troops and was ever after popularly known as Chinese Gordon. But in the Sudan, Gordon found himself pitted against an adversary fully as fanatical as he was, and perhaps a tragic outcome was inevitable.

An obscure fakir, a mystic named Mohammed Ahmed, had proclaimed himself the Mahdi, the messiah of Islam, and gathering together an inflamed army of zealots, the dervishes, he embarked on a holy war to drive nonbelievers from the Sudan. He had already destroyed one British-led army of Egyptians when Gordon was sent to Khartoum, his mission—whether simply to report on the situation, evacuate the remaining garrisons, or stay and fight—never made clear. In the circumstances, Chinese Gordon's reactions were hardly surprising: he evacuated two thousand women, children and wounded from the city, installed himself in the palace and declared that the Mahdi "must be smashed up." The problem was that Prime Minister

William Gladstone's cabinet was bitterly divided over what action to take, and though Gordon sat in Khartoum, convinced that his presence there would force the government to send a relief column, they took no action at all.

The Mahdi laid siege to Khartoum in mid-March. Over the long and harrowing months that followed, while British public opinion rallied behind Gordon and pressured the cabinet to rescue the beleaguered garrison, the ministers, in an agony of indecision, debated the matter endlessly, inconclusively. Meanwhile, night by night, Gordon sat alone in the palace, confiding his bitter disillusion to his journal: "If a boy at Eton or Harrow acted toward his fellow in a similar way, *I think* he would be kicked, and *I am sure* he would deserve it. I know of no parallel to all this in history." Each morning he would climb to the palace roof and train his telescope on the river, certain that *this* day he would see the smoke of a British flotilla steaming for Khartoum. But he saw nothing except the tightening army of dervishes.

Finally, in August, following the private intercession of the Queen—"Gordon must not be abandoned!" she told Gladstone—the government decided to move. But it was November before a relief force started south from Wadi Halfa, taking nearly three months to proceed up the Nile and arriving at Khartoum two days too late. On January 26, the Mahdist army had broken through the walls of the city, butchered the garrison of eleven thousand and hacked Chinese Gordon to pieces on the steps of the palace.

I could not get those two messianic figures, Gordon and the possessed Mahdi, out of my mind all the time we were in Khartoum. When I heard that the Mahdi's son still lived nearby, I sent a messenger to request an interview. Though his father had died only five months after the victory over Gordon, and though Kitchener in a famous battle at Omdurman, just across the river, had soundly defeated the Mahdists and reconquered the Sudan for England, the son of the Mahdi remained one of the most influential Arabs in the country.

He was an impressive, powerfully built man, who seemed entirely sustained by his sense of history. He outwardly bore no bitterness against the British masters of his land; at the end of the war he would offer his father's sword to King George V as a mark of his personal fealty. As John Buchan wrote, "The old unhappy things had become far

127

off and forgotten." But as we sat in the courtyard of his handsome villa some miles across the desert from Khartoum, this serene and perceptive man said he was absolutely certain the Sudan would eventually win its independence. He did not live to see it—more than forty years would pass before it happened—but in the end history bore him out.

A day or so later, Harry and I dined with the head of British intelligence for central Africa at his home, imaginatively called the House of the Hippopotamus Head. Suddenly his face tightened and he said, "I don't mean to rush you, but do you see what is coming in the distance?"

The air had grown ominously still. Overhead the sky remained cloudless and washed white by the afternoon sun. But as we followed his fixed stare to the east, we saw what appeared to be a mountain range moving toward us.

We were in for a haboob, our host hastily explained, a terrific sandstorm that periodically swept across this part of Africa, turning day into night and, with its whipping, lacerating sheets of sand, blinding and choking anyone unlucky enough to be caught abroad. He said we probably just had time to get back to our hotel.

Harry and I said a quick good-bye and ran for our donkeys, the Khartoum taxi of that time. Although the Charles Gordon Hotel was only half a mile away, the black wall was on us before we got there, the flying sand stinging our faces and hands so that they felt as though they were on fire. We bent low on the necks of our little mounts, hurrying them forward, but of course man rarely succeeds in urging a burro to do anything in a hurry. By the time we arrived I had a vivid idea of what it must be like to get caught in the desert by such a storm. Inside, with windows closed tight against the ferocity of the haboob, the heat was stifling. And still the sand sifted through every crack and crevice, coating the beds and floors, turning our eyes red and our mouths gritty. The storm lasted for hours and there was no sleeping until it ended. I have since lived through arctic blizzards, cloudbursts, cyclones and monsoons, but none as unforgettable as the Khartoum haboob.

From the Nile we crossed the Nubian Desert by train to Port Sudan on the Red Sea. Here the military commander, General Sir Reginald Wingate, put us aboard a much-torpedoed and barely navigable wreck of a steamer bound for the Arabian coast. Our shipmates included several hundred sheep, horses and mules, a platoon of Gordon Highlanders and a hundred or so Turkish deserters. The crew was equally eclectic—some Hindus, a few Javanese and Somalis and a whole band of fuzzy-wuzzies in native dress. As there were no passenger accommodations, we bunked on deck with the animals, and the animals, being somewhat testy in these odd surroundings, didn't sleep much. Consequently, neither did we.

In Cairo, we had stocked up on chocolate bars against the possibility that the farther east we journeyed the more likely we were to be confronted with a steady diet of delicacies like dried dates and fried locusts. And on the advice of a colonel who described the Bedouin craving for tobacco in most expressive terms—"If you offer them a 'gasper,' they'll love you; if you don't they might take it into their heads to go through your pockets while you're still wearing them"—we had also stuffed the odd corners of our bags with cigarettes. Unhappily, as we neared our destination, the temperature shot straight up. One hungry afternoon I opened my kit to find a fluid mass of chocolate, pencils, notebooks, bullets, matches, cigarette paper and tobacco.

We docked at Jidda, port of entry for Mecca, and as close to the Holy City as nonbelievers were permitted. Then we sailed north along the coast to the head of the Gulf of Aqaba. Here our ancient but honorable vessel anchored offshore and we transferred to a lighter, still in company with the livestock, for the trip to the beach. If we had any complaints about the crowded quarters, we kept them to ourselves after one of the mules fell overboard and within seconds was attacked by sharks and torn to pieces.

We had not absorbed this item of violence when, chugging toward shore, we heard the crackle of rifle fire and wondered if we were to land in the midst of a battle. But as we scraped ashore on a coral beach, we saw, to our considerable relief, that a thousand or more Bedouins were blazing away, not at the enemy, but at the blue sky in exuberance over our arrival. With their fierce beards, exotic headdress and gorgeously colored robes, shouting and firing as they wove toward us through palm trees and the great piles of supplies stacked on the sand, they seemed part of some fantastic Arabian pageant.

They were, in fact, part of what was called Lawrence's army. The first among them to reach us led the way to a nearby tent and gave us something to drink, and soon Lawrence himself, just back from one of his desert raids, appeared. Once again I was struck by the contrast between this blond, small-boned Englishman, his face benign, almost saintly, and the black-eyed Bedouin Arabs around him.

He seemed glad to see us. He introduced us to Emir Feisal, who had moved his base camp to Aqaba, and to the handful of British officers who were fighting the lonely desert war with him—Joyce, Marshall, Hornby, Buxton, Dawnay, Young. They were names, as yet unknown to the world, that would come to be remembered among the most gallant of England's soldiers. And before many days had passed, we were mounted on camels and off on a seventy-mile trip to the interior to see the action at firsthand. Standing on a mountaintop with Lawrence, Feisal, Nuri Sa'id and Auda abu Tayi, we watched the bombardment of Ma'an, a station on the Damascus-Hejaz railroad north of Medina.

In the weeks that followed, I slowly came to learn the story of Lawrence's astonishing desert campaign. Though we grew to be friends, I got little enough of it from him; he was always happy to talk about archaeology, poetry, literature or his companions, but remained difficult to draw out about himself. Luckily, his comrades-in-arms were not so reticent. From them, from what I saw for myself, I began to piece together an account of what proved to be one of the most unusual achievements of World War I.

In March, 1917, Lawrence had made a jolting six-day camel ride across the desert to the camp of Emir Abdullah, Feisal's older brother, carrying with him a plan of attack newly devised by General Sir Archibald Murray and his general staff in Cairo. He barely made it. Stricken with dysentery, burning with fever, he feared at every stop that he would fall into the hands of well-meaning tribesmen whose treatment of every ill was to burn holes in the patient's body at the sites where they believed the malady lurked.

As it turned out, however, his sickness changed the

course of the war in the Middle East. Until then, Lawrence had been too much caught up in the fighting to think beyond the objective directly in front of him. Now, reaching Abdullah's camp, he collapsed into a tent and for ten days lay sick and shivering, sometimes out of his head with delirium, but at moments able to see the whole complex nature of the Arab revolt with piercing clarity. Recovering, persistently thinking his way through those enforced hours of idleness, he came to understand the true strengths and weaknesses of both sides, how the vast desert was the Arab's ally, so far largely unused, and how the very massiveness of the Turkish army could be its own undoing.

Until that moment, the recapture of Medina had been an obsession with both the Arabs and the British military. It was the cornerstone of the plan Lawrence had brought from General Murray. To the Arabs, who had taken Mecca at the outbreak of their insurrection, Medina was an emotional issue, the second holiest city in Arabia. To Murray, who was in thrall to the Western Front orthodoxy of war—regiments, divisions, even whole armies thrown into big battles for big objectives—Medina seemed the biggest prize around.

"One afternoon," Lawrence wrote in his masterly account of the desert war, *Seven Pillars of Wisdom*, "I woke from a hot sleep, running with sweat and pricking with flies, and wondered what on earth was the good of Medina to us?"

It had no strategic value; it neither threatened the Arabs nor was it situated to serve as a base of operations. The fact was, Lawrence realized with the thrill of unexpected discovery, Medina was contributing most to the Arab-Allied cause just as it was—a remote enclave tying down a sizable Turkish garrison and consuming the huge quantities of supplies required to sustain it. And even if the Turks came to recognize it as a liability, swollen Ottoman pride would keep them from abandoning it. Why, then, should the Arabs do their work for them?

Now Lawrence's agile mind leaped ahead to further heretical questions and to answers fixed firmly in the realities of the situation. How could an undisciplined collection of desert tribes challenge a seasoned and numerically superior Turkish force led by war-wise German officers? Why should they try? In a jujitsu concept of war, the ponderous strength of the Turks could contribute to their defeat, for as long as their big bases remained intact, Constantinople would feel obliged to reinforce them, immobilizing substantial military power deep in the Arabian desert.

Battles in Arabia were a mistake, since we profited in them only by the ammunition the enemy fired off. Napoleon had said it was rare to find generals who would fight battles; but the curse of this war was that so few would do anything else . . . We had nothing material to lose, so our best line was to defend nothing and to shoot nothing. Our cards were speed and time, not hitting power.

And his trump card was the thousands of square miles of empty desert in which to operate, terrain the Arabs knew intimately, as the enemy did not. Instead of fighting pitched battles, he would lead a hit-and-run campaign, making the most of his mobility, striking quickly and, just as quickly, vanishing "into the blue." How could he thereby inflict serious casualties on the Turks? He could not, nor did he need to.

In Turkey, men [were] less esteemed than equipment. Our cue was to destroy, not the Turk's army, but his materials. The death of a Turkish bridge or rail, machine or gun or charge of high explosive, was more profitable to us than the death of a Turk . . . Ours should be a war of detachment. We were to contain the enemy by the silent threat of a vast unknown desert, not disclosing ourselves till we attacked. The attack might be nominal, directed not against him, but against his stuff; so it would not seek either his strength or his weakness, but his most accessible material. In railway-cutting it would be usually an empty stretch of rail; and the more empty, the greater the tactical success.

So was born Lawrence's desert strategy. It would rely heavily on "tulip-planting," a term he playfully invented as, in dead earnest, he invented the "tulip" itself—a thirty-ounce charge of guncotton that, emplaced under a railway crosstie, was powerful enough to rupture some thirty feet of track.

He had come to Abdullah's camp without any articulated opposition to the plan of his superiors in Cairo. By the time he left his sickbed, he was prepared to turn their doctrinaire rules of war upside down, having conceived a set of tactics entirely alien to the headquarters mentality—and these so carefully reasoned, down to the fine details, that they never had to be revised. And when the war ended, the defeated Turks were still in Medina, and Medina had remained a liability to them to the last.

The Hejaz railroad had been built by the Ottoman Sultan Abdul Hamid at the turn of the century as a monument to the Pan-Islamic ideal, the effort to revive Muslim power and unity under Turkey's domination. Until the war began, it was known as the Pilgrim Railway for the great number of the faithful it annually carried to Mecca and Medina. It also served, not coincidentally, to keep a tight rein on the Arabs by the swift transport of Turkish troops. Now it bore a steady stream of soldiers, supplies and military hardware south to the garrison of twenty thousand defending Medina.

Once he had devised his new strategy, Lawrence, at any time, could have put the Hejaz railroad permanently out of commission. But he did not want to dishearten the Turks; they might take a notion to quit Medina. He only wanted to keep them off balance. And of course it was a convenience to be able to replenish his Arabs' food, weapon and ammunition stores with the booty taken from derailed and blown-up Turkish trains.

He made his first raid only a week or so after those seminal days in Abdullah's camp. The target was the railway station at Aba el Naam, within a hundred miles of Medina. While his artillery opened fire from the hills, destroying the station and its water tower and thoroughly distracting the three-hundred-man Turkish garrison, Lawrence planted his tulips under the tracks, north and south. A sidetracked train, attempting to flee, touched off the charge and traffic was blocked for three days. Meanwhile the raiders had inflicted nearly a hundred casualties on the Turks and taken thirty prisoners, all at a cost to them of one man slightly wounded. "So," said Lawrence with his gift for economy of language, "we did not wholly fail."

133

In the months that followed, travel along the Hejaz rail line became a terror and an agony to the enemy. In Damascus, people scrambled for seats in the rearmost carriages, paying up to five times their normal value. Lawrence slipped into the city one night and posted a notice to the effect that henceforth good Arabs would use the railroad, in either direction, at their own peril, thereby extending his threat all the way to Aleppo. Civilian traffic all but stopped. Railroad engineers went on strike. Soon so much rolling stock had been destroyed that the Turks could not have evacuated Medina if they had wanted to. Supplies to their army at Jerusalem were also badly pinched—just as the British began their march on the Holy City.

Sir Archibald Murray, who had consistently viewed Lawrence as a noxious weed in his orderly garden of textbook tactics, was replaced by Allenby. The new commander in chief did not at first understand his desert warrior any better than had his predecessor, but one difference between the two men was that Allenby was willing to learn. He sent for Lawrence and asked him outright what, if anything, his tulip raids meant, beyond their obvious and melodramatic courtship of the Arab cause.

Lawrence explained his intention of harrying the rail line to Medina, in effect immobilizing it, for all but the purpose of feeding the Arab garrison and thereby keeping it there. This, he said, seemed to him a far less costly way of neutralizing an enemy than killing him or holding him prisoner in Cairo.

Allenby understood this at once. The two men would never be close friends—they were of two different worlds —but they now became each other's staunchest advocates. Allenby sent Lawrence back to the desert with a promise of as much assistance as he could manage, and henceforth the Arab insurrection was calculated into the overall concept of British strategy.

By the time Harry Chase and I came to Arabia, Lawrence knew as much about the handling of high explosives as he did about archaeology. He calculated and triggered his bursts with such devastating acuity that if a train were carrying foodstuffs and ammunition—which of course he spied out in advance—he could make the locomotive buckle so that the boxcars, charging on, tore themselves open and spilled their contents onto the right-of-way for his Arab cohorts to scoop up. If it carried troops, he would blow it sky-high. When the opportunity presented itself, he would mine a bridge, dumping the locomotive and lead cars into the watercourse below. For the Turks, these were aggravating and time-consuming repairs.

They intensified their patrols; they packed every train with heavily armed guards. It made little difference. So enormous was the territory over which the hard-riding marauders were free to rove that they could always find some unlikely spot to strike. And so meticulously did Lawrence plan the raids that even when the Turks came out fighting, they found themselves raked by strategically emplaced machine guns. From the beginning until they marched into Damascus alongside Allenby's troops six weeks before the war's end, Lawrence and his men, among other depredations on the enemy, destroyed fifty locomotives, twice as many boxcars and seventy-nine bridges.

Not that the enterprise was without risk, particularly to Lawrence, who usually set the explosive charges himself. It was characteristic of him to choose the most dangerous assignment; but he was also concerned that if his Arab friends became familiar with the use of high explosives, they would still be blowing up trains for fun and profit long after the war was over. And so he was always close by when the targeted train hove into view, sometimes hidden, sometimes sitting inoffensively on a hillside, staff in hand and looking for all the world like a Bedouin shepherd. But as the Turks' nervousness increased, they took to shooting at everything in sight, even innocent-looking shepherds, and Lawrence was hit several times. He carried a long-barreled Colt .45 in the folds of his aba and once used it to drive off a patrol of Turks that had surrounded him against a ruined locomotive.

Late in the campaign, near Deraa, Lawrence touched off his charge under the driving wheels of an unusually long train. As it careened and splayed off the tracks, more than a thousand soldiers poured out, firing wildly—the train was carrying Djemal Pasha, the Turkish commander in chief. Lawrence, who had only sixty men hidden in the hills behind him, ran for his life, bullets kicking up the sand at his heels. But as he ran—and this was typical of his self-possession—he counted his steps and, reaching his machine-gun positions, he could give the gunners the precise range. They poured a deadly fire into the Turkish ranks, killing a hundred twenty-five, enabling the little Arab band to get away safely.

Liddell Hart, among the foremost military theoreticians in the West between the two world wars, once undertook to write a book about the Arab rebellion, conceding that he began it with the conviction that Lawrence's role had been exaggerated and at least partly fabricated. But as he followed his research toward the essential truths, he was forced into a radical reappraisal. "I found him growing more distinct as the background faded, until the Arab revolt became an emanation of him. Thus I was compelled to recast the book and to make it primarily a study of him."

Hart was struck not only by the guerrilla operations that damaged and distracted the Turks, not only by the precision with which Lawrence dovetailed his means to the ends he sought, cannily choosing his targets for their vulnerability to the men and weapons he could bring to bear on them, but finally by the sheer tactical genius of this man who had had absolutely no formal military training. The capture of the Red Sea port of Aqaba was a graphic illustration.

Aqaba, unlike Medina, had real meaning for both sides. Held by the Turks, it commanded the Red Sea approach to both Palestine and northern Arabia. Taken by the Arabs, it could provide a splendid base to support a British drive east from Egypt. But the taking would not be easy. To the south and west, Turkish guns bristled along an impregnable shoreline. To the north and east, the rugged sweep of King Solomon's mountains provided a natural defense.

Lawrence and his handful of warriors set out on camelback from El Wejh, six hundred miles to the south, swung across the desert in a great counterclockwise arc, and two months later stood poised to strike from the heights behind the town. He had no orders to take Aqaba. His journey across the desert and through the mountains had itself been an incredible odyssey, during which his ragged band had been reduced to a choice between eating their camels and starving. But Lawrence had single-mindedly led them on, gathering new adherents as he went, retaking Arab villages long dominated by the Ottoman rule. And when at last they swept down into Aqaba—sheiks, tribesmen, nomads—the Turks and their German commanders were stupefied and, in a short, bloody battle, overwhelmed. The enemy's defense line was sundered, his defeat made inevitable.

If Aqaba was a military masterpiece of surprise, the battle at Tafileh shows Lawrence in the altogether astonishing role of the classicist in the art of war. Faced by a Turkish force in command of a fortified ridge—and, as usual, outnumbered—Lawrence opened up with his few pieces of antique artillery in a frontal bombardment. With the enemy thus occupied, he sent two flying columns to encircle both his flanks. Pinched off, caught in a vicious crossfire, the terrified Turks looked up to see Lawrence himself leading his remaining men in a headlong attack on their position. They fled, what had moments before been a well-organized and dominant body of troops suddenly transformed into a demoralized horde, running for their lives and leaving behind two hundred prisoners and twenty-seven machine guns. Lawrence, with his self-deprecating sense of humor, referred to Tafileh as a parody of the "old maxims and rules of the military text books." But Liddell Hart always considered it a paradigm of battlefield mastery—and took pains to point out that the master's proficiency at war was entirely self-taught.

Not that he enjoyed it. The killing of men, either in battle or by the remorseless desert, invariably left him shaken and torn. He never spoke of these feelings, as he avoided talk of all things that touched him most deeply. In fact, there were times when he seemed to mask his anguish with some outrageous observation on the travails of war. Once our camels rode side by side at the head of a thousand Bedouins. They were bound for a battle and were improvising war songs that lauded *El-Aurens,* the blond sherif who led them. Lawrence paid no attention. He and I were discussing the ancient Hittite civilization, and his discourse was so brilliantly lucid, and the fierce music behind so compelling, that I soon forgot the plodding, swaying beast under me and the bloody rendezvous toward which the column rode.

But Lawrence hadn't forgotten. Suddenly, almost in mid-sentence and apropos of nothing in our conversation, he said, "Do you know, one of the most glorious sights I have ever seen is a trainload of Turkish soldiers ascending skyward after the explosion of a tulip!"

I have always believed that he was consciously cleansing

137

his mind of a debilitating sense of sympathy at that moment. Anyone who saw him in the presence of death knew that it became a personal burden to him, even the death of an enemy, and that he bore it and inflicted it only at the cost of a constantly worsening wound of the spirit.

Sometimes one or more of his men wandered off and got lost in the desert, and then it was often Lawrence himself who went searching for them. For a death in the desert, as Lawrence himself has described it, is an appalling end:

> Not a long death—even for the very strongest a second day in summer was all—but very painful; for thirst was an active malady, a fear and panic which tore at the brain and reduced the bravest man to a stumbling, babbling maniac in an hour or two; and then the sun killed him.

Once he had to kill one of his own men. From the beginning, he had been called on by his followers to adjudicate their disputes, some of them not unexpected among antagonistic tribes suddenly thrown together with only an enemy in common—assaults, camel theft, arguments over loot from a Turkish train; some were more exotic—marriage settlements, cases of evil eye and one of bewitchment, which Lawrence satisfactorily resolved by counter-bewitching the accused. But this time murder had been done. A Moroccan, Hamed, had shot one of the Ageyl, and now the dead man's relatives and friends demanded "blood for blood."

> Then rose up the horror which would make civilized man shun justice like a plague if he had not the needy to serve him as hangmen for wages. There were other Moroccans in our army; and to let the Ageyl kill one in feud meant reprisals by which our unity would have been endangered. It must be a formal execution, and at last, desperately, I told Hamed that he must die for punishment, and laid the burden for his killing on myself. Perhaps they would count me not qualified for feud. At least no revenge could lie against my followers; for I was a stranger and kinless.

138

Lawrence made the condemned man enter a dank and narrow gully. At its end, where the vertical walls came darkly together, Hamed fell, sobbing, on the prickly weeds, and Lawrence gave him a moment's respite. Then he told him to rise and shot him through the chest. The bullet knocked him down, blood spurting from the wound, but it did not kill him. He cried out, rolling among the weeds, and Lawrence shot him again, but was by then so nearly undone that he only managed to hit the luckless man's wrist. Hamed kept calling out, trying to crawl toward Lawrence, who finally put his .45 under the Moroccan's jaw in the thick of his neck.

He called the Ageyl and they dug a hole in the gully where the body lay and buried it there. He did not sleep that night, and long before dawn, burning to be gone from that place, he woke the men and bade them load up. Sick with fever and an agony of the heart, he had to be lifted into the saddle.

Not long before I came out to the desert, Lawrence had undergone his most lacerating experience of the war. He had slipped into the town of Deraa as a spy, anxious to see for himself how best he could attack and destroy the junction from which three key rail lines spoked out across the desert. Almost at once he was seized by the Turks. They did not doubt his story that he was a Circassian—his Arab dress and speech bore him out; their mission was to provide a comely young man for the perverted pleasure of the Bey, governor of the province.

That night, soon after dark, the captive was taken to the Bey's quarters and, in a dimly lighted room, thrust toward a bed where a squat, sweating man in a nightgown sat trembling with passion. Dragged down to the bed, Lawrence endured the frantic pawing as long as he could, then thrust his knee hard into the Bey's groin.

From this moment, the sequence of events is made unclear, perhaps intentionally. In *Seven Pillars of Wisdom*, Lawrence tells us he was held fast by a corporal while the Bey spat at him, smashed at his face with a shoe, and finally twisted a bayonet through the flesh over his ribs. Later he was whipped bloody and left, passive and barely conscious, in a wooden shed from which he escaped that night. And fleeing, he found what he had come seeking in Deraa: a hidden valley road by which he would return

139

to raid the rail center. But there is little doubt that those hours left harrowing scars on his mind, as they did on his body. "In Deraa," he wrote, "the citadel of my integrity had been irrevocably lost."

"What was he *really* like?"

This, of course, is the question people began asking me from the time I came out of the desert and still ask me down to this day, well over half a century later. It is a mark of Lawrence's lasting appeal, the heroic legend standing intact despite the calculated, carping denigrations of the Aldingtons. He was the giant of a particular time and place, perhaps the last of his kind, and the world cannot get him out of its collective consciousness.

But the answer to the question—what was he really like?—is that I don't know. For the question implies that we can have some magical insight into the soul and spirit of another man, a key that will unlock the secret motivations for all his acts, and I don't think this is true. Certainly it is not true of someone as inherently private as was T. E. Lawrence. The question seems to beg me to tell why he turned his back on destiny, a brilliant career, why he spurned greatness. And I can't. Any more than I can tell why a man without military training became one of the great military leaders of World War I, and with a constantly improvised army of irregulars killed, wounded and assisted greatly in the capture of seventy thousand Turkish soldiers and, by war's end, controlled a hundred thousand miles of enemy territory. Nor can I say how this classical scholar, the same man who would translate Homer's *Odyssey* into English prose, also came to master the technical intricacies of aerodynamics and contributed importantly to the development of a seagoing motorboat.

I know *what* he did, said and some of what he thought—not why—during the period I was with him in Arabia. No other observer had this good fortune. And I have tried to tell about it in a way to help unravel some of the mystery with which Lawrence surrounded himself—I don't know why he did *that*, either. What I know about him I *do* know, for I have clung to the memory of our time together through all the long years, while those who claim some

140

special access to the innermost mainsprings of his psyche are working with fantasy.

He had a tremendous personal effect on me. Suddenly I could see what I felt was the reality of the desert. Before, if I had thought of it at all, it had been in terms of a forbidding obstacle, something to be avoided, endured or stoically crossed. And my first experiences in Arabia reinforced this. For there before me stretched an immense and arid land of rock and shifting sand. And when you reached the top of one ridge, there ahead was another, and then another, endless and barren all the way to some distant horizon.

And then, of course, one had to cope with the desert's ubiquitous and irrational beast of burden, the camel. A nineteenth-century chronicler, William Gifford Palgrave, called it "from first to last an undomesticated and savage animal, rendered serviceable by stupidity alone . . . never tame, though not wide awake enough to be exactly wild." My own comment would have been somewhat terser: the camel is an impossible creature that gives every sign, as has often been said, of having been created by a committee.

But the thing is that in the desert it works, as nothing else does. The same must be said for the kaffiyeh, the Arab headdress Lawrence wore, as did Chase and I, not as an affectation, but because nothing else was nearly so effective against the sun and the swirling sand. And as for the desert itself, it was Lawrence who finally enabled me to see it through Arab eyes, dangerous to any who challenged it in ignorance, but a refuge to those who learned to respect its awesome breadth, a source of nourishment to those who knew its oasis islands and the wadis that in season rushed with fresh water. Lawrence's friend, the noted Arabist Gertrude Bell, put it this way:

The Arabs do not speak of desert or wilderness as we do. Why should they? To them it is neither desert nor wilderness, but a land of which they know every feature, a mother country whose smallest product has a use sufficient for their needs. They know, or at least they knew in the days when their thoughts shaped themselves in deathless verse, how to rejoice in the great spaces and how to honour the rush of the storm.

141

The book I wrote about my experiences in the desert, *With Lawrence in Arabia,* eventually went into more than a hundred printings. The world tour during which I told Lawrence's story, until then undisclosed, brought me many other opportunities. But had I been compelled to keep it all to myself, pledged never to write or utter a single word about Lawrence in exchange for the opportunity to join him in Arabia, I still would have jumped at the chance, for it was an unforgettable time and it changed my life in ways that had nothing to do with fame or fortune. While with him I was in the presence of greatness, and I remain eternally grateful even though I may not have had the wisdom to know it at the time.

Lawrence turned aside a promotion to general's rank, had friends sidetrack a recommendation that he be awarded the Victoria Cross, and even declined knighthood. When I asked him why, he laughed and replied that if he were knighted his tailor would hear about it and double his bills. "I have trouble enough paying them as it is." Of course this was not the real reason, but it was as close as he was prepared to let anyone get, and he usually had an amusing comment to make about anything in which he was involved.

Another time I may perhaps have come a shade closer to the essence of the man. Aware of his disdain for money and nearly all the things money could buy, I was often fascinated toward the end of the desert campaign to see him casually stuffing thousand of pounds in gold sovereigns into a camelbag and riding off—for by this time the British government was gladly providing him with all the gold he needed to pay for men and material, with or without a receipt! So I asked him once to assume that the money was his: what would he spend it for? "Oh," he replied, "I'd like to have a Rolls with enough tires and petrol to last me all my life."

He could have had it, of course, and any of the daydream luxuries other men crave. But the real price—adopting the values of ambitious careerists, accepting their empty honors—was more than Lawrence ever seriously considered paying.

We had wonderful talks. During the long marches, or sitting by his tent as the day faded and slowly cooled, his conversation seemed to separate us from the world, his facility with the English language so exhilarating I found it hopeless straining to match him. Few men could: his command of English was burnished by his easy familiarity with six other languages—classical Latin and Greek, French, Italian, Spanish and German—as well as whatever Arabic dialects at his command. His extraordinary clear and versatile intelligence endowed what he said with solid substance, and that endlessly inventive wit phrased it for maximum impact.

There wasn't a question I could ask about this strange and exotic land we traveled that he did not effortlessly answer, from how to handle a recalcitrant camel to the future of the Arab people. He was gloomy about their chances of winning the nationhood and independence for which they had revolted. "When you can understand the point of view of another race," he once said to me, "you are a civilized being, but somehow this doesn't apply collectively."

For the governments of so-called civilized nations were often too much in thrall to narrow self-interest to honor the legitimate aspirations of a weaker people. Even as Lawrence encouraged the Arabs to believe their aims accorded with those of the Allies, even as he led them in the struggle to drive out the Turks, in his heart he knew the old bondage would only be replaced by a new one. The French were determined to have Syria; the British wanted Mesopotamia. Expediency had led to secret agreements and conflicting promises, and how were commitments of honor to be redeemed?

Surely not by any singleness of Arab purpose. Lawrence deeply admired the Arabs' courage and loyalty and inventiveness, but he knew that a gift for organization was not among their racial traits. Once he told me, "Everybody is a general in the Arab army. In British circles, a general is allowed to make a mess of things by himself, whereas here in Arabia every man wants a hand in making it complete."

In the end, when the promises had been broken, when he came face to face with his personal tragedy—that he had himself been used as the instrument of an Allied policy inimical to the best hopes of his friends and follow-

143

ers, he made a final effort to win public opinion back to the side of simple justice. In a profound and poignant letter to the *Times* of London he wrote:

> The Arabs rebelled against the Turks not because the Turk government was notably bad, but because they wanted independence. They did not risk their lives in battle to change masters, to become British subjects or French citizens, but to win a show of their own.
>
> Whether they are fit for independence or not remains to be tried. Merit is no qualification for freedom. Bulgars, Afghans and Tahitians have it. Freedom is enjoyed when you are so well armed, or so turbulent, or inhabit a country so thorny that the expense of your neighbor's occupying you is greater than the profit.

So he had foreseen the ultimate chaotic course of events in the Middle East. The inevitable and essential truth of his judgment would be confirmed by history, but not until long after he was dead.

The war in the desert now began moving swiftly toward its inexorable end. All during the spring and summer of 1918, Allenby had been training raw recruits, painstakingly rebuilding his depleted army until he had a striking force of nearly a hundred thousand. Meanwhile, with feints and several incursions across the Jordan, he persuaded his old foe, the German general Otto Liman von Sanders, that the main British thrust, when it came, would again be aimed at the Jordan valley. Lawrence's raids along the length of the Hejaz railway only strengthened this belief, and Liman von Sanders massed almost half his available Turkish troops on his inland flank. As he did, Allenby was secretly deploying the bulk of his infantry, with the cavalry just behind, north of Jaffa, preparing to strike at the Turkish right, along the Mediterranean coast.

This spectacular plan, calculated to knock Turkey out of the war and break the back of the Ottoman Empire, depended on the element of surprise and was known to only four people. Lawrence was one. His role was to cut the three rail lines radiating from Deraa, focal point of

144

the enemy's communications network, isolating his fighting force and depriving it of supplies and reinforcements.

Lawrence struck on September 17. Like maddening wraiths, his little band appeared and then vanished south, north and west of Deraa, and each time they left the railroad a shambles. Afterward, summing up the devastating effects of this final raid, Lawrence told me, "This, after all, was the main justification of our existence and of the money and time we had spent on the Arab revolt."

He had started out with a small, battle-hardened force of four hundred and ridden six hundred miles in just twenty-three days. Too weak in numbers to stand and fight, they led a precarious existence, shifting camp twice a night to avoid being ambushed. But again the vast and unmapped desert was their ally, and they came in out of the blue, miles behind the Turkish armies and with stunning unexpectedness. Two days before the British advance in Palestine began, they had cut the three rail lines and for five days permitted no trains to get through to the fighting fronts. The results were ruinous to the Turkish hopes of turning back Allenby's assault. Not only did they wait in vain for assistance, but when they began to retreat, they found all their advance food depots and ammunition dumps exhausted.

Allenby attacked early on September 19. His infantry punched a hole in the tautly stretched Turkish line and the cavalry poured through, sweeping behind the dazed defenders and closing their line of retreat to the north. Their position untenable, threatened front and rear with annihilation, the Turks fled eastward across the Jordan, then scrambled toward Damascus, harassed by British aircraft and Lawrence's Arabs, now swelled to a force of eleven thousand men.

For the first time, the British regulars had joined forces with their Bedouin allies, and together they marched into Damascus on October 2. On the thirtieth, the Turkish government requested an armistice. In one of the most dazzlingly executed battles in the annals of warfare, Allenby, with much help from Lawrence and Feisal and the Arabs, had destroyed the Turkish army, taking seventy-five thousand prisoners while themselves suffering little more than five thousand casualties, and finally won the war in the desert and hastened the end of World War I.

It all went very quickly then. Lawrence stayed in

Damascus only four days, its virtual ruler until Allenby's arrival. Then he begged the commander in chief to let him go.

> . . . I made to Allenby the last (and also I think the first) request I ever made of him for myself—leave to go away. For a while he would not have it; but I reasoned, reminding him of his year-old promise, and pointing out how much easier the New Law would be if my spur were absent from the people. In the end he agreed; and then at once I knew how much I was sorry.

By November 11, the day the armistice was signed, he was back in England. Knowing he would go, and that there was therefore no reason for me to stay, I too had returned to Europe.

Our paths were to cross again under far different circumstances.

7.

Inside Revolutionary Germany

If my government falls, Germany will turn to a dictator, and then you Americans will have to come back.

—Chancellor Friedrich Ebert

PARIS in November—the biting wind and the raw, rainy days and nights—was a contrast to the dry desert heat. Perhaps I caught a cold. Perhaps all the months of living out of a kit bag, of constant movement through chaotic events, and the intensity with which I felt it all, finally laid me low. I don't know and I never found out. But one evening, returning to my hotel room at the end of still another long day, I felt the stairway moving under my feet, like some surreal escalator, and I gave in to the gathering darkness and passed out. I probably would have fallen all the way back into the lobby of the St. James and Albany if a colleague, Webb Waldron, hadn't caught me by the lapels of my trench coat and gently lowered me to the steps.

When I came to some forty hours later, I was in the American Hospital in Neuilly, a Paris suburb, and at first no one seemed to know what was the matter with me. That was the winter the killer influenza epidemic of 1918 swept over Western Europe, taking some twenty million lives, and there was little doubt but what I had been one of its near victims. So I lay on my back in that hospital room, sicker than I had ever been in my life. Alone except when Waldron came to visit or when a nurse came along, I had plenty of time to think about the jumbled happenings of those last days and to ponder what to do now that the war was over.

Returning from Palestine on a Greek freighter, I had stopped in Genoa to collect my bride. But I learned that her Red Cross unit had completed its work and that Fran, having heard nothing from me during all those weeks when I'd been roving the desert, had returned to Denver, to her parents. I wrote her at length—it was only the first of many times in nearly sixty years of marriage that my unanticipated travels would separate us. Then I went on to London to express my gratitude personally to John Buchan at the British Ministry of Information, the man who had made it possible for me to cover the campaign in the Middle East, the journalistic coup of a lifetime. A few days later I was back in France, with the American First Army as it bulled its way toward the Meuse River in the final battle of the war.

The end was very near. Allenby's smashing assault in the desert had started a chain reaction that could have only one outcome. Within days of the Turkish army's flight, Bulgaria and the once mighty Hapsburg Empire, Austria-Hungary, fell, like dominoes in a line. For a little while the Germans stood alone, torn by internal strife, pressed relentlessly backward by the Western Allies. Then, at 5 A.M. on November 11, in a railroad car pulled into a woodland siding at Compiègne, their representatives signed the articles of surrender. The news came to us later in the day, less than a hundred miles to the east, in the Argonne Forest, and at 11 A.M. all firing ceased.

I sent Harry Chase back to the States to begin the monumental job of processing our film. But I was not yet ready to go back and returned instead to Paris: there was quiet at last on the Western Front, but peace was not yet assured. Allied ships continued to blockade the German coast. Nothing but wild rumors seeped out of Germany, its borders sealed by order of Marshal Foch. There had been a mutiny of sailors on the warships anchored at Kiel. It was said the revolt had spread to Berlin, with councils of workers and soldiers, in the manner of the Russian soviets, seizing power in dozens of other cities. The Kaiser had fled, and there was a crucial struggle going on inside the beaten land. The shape of the peace—if, indeed, peace there was to be—depended on its outcome. And *that* had to be a story!

One evening, when Webb Waldron came to the hospital to see me and I was reasonably sure I was going to survive after all, I put it to him: why didn't we go to Germany and get the inside story of what was happening there? Webb, a novelist and magazine writer who was then European editor of *Collier's Weekly*, had years of experience on me, and maybe I ought to have listened to him. He said every reporter in Paris had the same idea—the German upheaval was the hottest story in the world; editors were clamoring for on-the-scene reports—but getting them from so far away was impossible. No one was being granted authorization for German travel; the border was closed tight and headquarters was making no exceptions for anyone, particularly journalists. In fact, it appeared precisely the journalists that Foch meant to keep out. He wanted no softhearted stories out of Germany to rouse a gullible public in Britain and the United States to oppose the French intention to press for a rigorous and fully retributive peace treaty.

"What about going without authorization, then?" I asked naïvely.

Well, he replied, a group of correspondents had tried, had gotten beyond Koblenz, where the Germans provided them with a car and driver so they could head for Berlin. The correspondents were Fred E. "Doc" Smith of the *Chicago Tribune*, Herbert Corey of Associated Newspapers, Lincoln Eyre of the New York *World*, Cal Lyon of Newspaper Enterprise Association, and George Seldes of the Marshall Syndicate. After spending some days in Germany and getting a few interviews, including one with Field Marshal Von Hindenburg, they were picked up by our military people and hustled back to France. At first it looked as though they would be court-martialed for violating war regulations, but Colonel House got them out of that predicament. They could not release their stories while they were in trouble, so their material became dated. It must have been a frustrating experience for them.

In my ignorance, I persisted. Along the length of the Rhine River, I said, there had to be a place where two enterprising reporters could slip across into Germany without being noticed. And once we were there, beyond reach of the MPs, surely we'd find people to help us—surely the Germans would be glad to have someone tell the world their side of things for a change, wouldn't they?

Webb undoubtedly thought he was humoring a sick friend. "Listen, L.T.," he said, "let's see how long it takes you to get well. That's the important thing."

It was all the spur I needed. Two days later I was up and about. Once I was discharged from the hospital, Webb and I were on a train bound for Alsace, the Rhine province newly retaken from the Germans.

We arrived in Strasbourg, the provincial capital, with our hearts and hopes high. It was a busy, self-absorbed city and no one paid any attention to two Americans strolling along the river. But the Rhine bridge was heavily guarded and Germany, so close we could see children playing on the far bank, remained beyond our reach. We pondered the possibility of attempting a night swim. But it looked so ominously cold and swift-running we continued south, studying our map, wandering about in towns so recently reoccupied by the French that they hadn't even finished replacing the German traffic signs. In one, Mulhouse, capital of newly liberated Lorraine, we sat in a café bemoaning our luck—the frontier *was* sealed; we had not found a single unguarded crossing—and wondering what to try next. Confident that no one in this provincial border city could understand us, we made no effort to keep our voices down. Suddenly a French soldier, who heretofore had seemed to be devoting all his attention to a bottle of white wine, brought his bottle and chair over to our table and, in impeccable New Yorkese, said: "Sounds like you got a problem."

We parried. It was heartening to hear an American voice in the midst of this French-speaking wilderness, but how could we be sure he was as sympathetic as he sounded?

He was, he allowed after still another glass of white wine, an ambulance driver serving with a French infantry unit. His name was Tony, he came from Staten Island and at the moment he was on a dull, lonely assignment. His mission was to drive back and forth along the frontier and pick up Allied prisoners of war, now streaming out of German prison camps. In the post-Armistice chaos, they had simply been opened wide, and the POWs, turned loose, were straggling across the border in two's and three's from Switzerland to the North Sea. And what were we up to?

Webb and I took one look at each other and decided to tell him. If he turned out to be an MP, well, we hadn't done anything wrong *yet*. But if he really was an ambulance driver, maybe he could be our ticket into Germany. We were reporters, Webb said, trying to get the straight story of what was really happening inside Germany, but kept out by idiotic army rules and red tape. We needed help. Maybe it we hid in his ambulance. . . ?

He casually took another swallow and said, "Let's see that map you've got there."

Not only was our new friend more than willing to help, but his familiarity with the frontier provided us with a real plan in place of the fuzzy hopes we'd been going on. Our basic problem was getting across the Rhine—where it ran between France and Germany—and that seemed impossible. But only a few miles to the south, the fortuities of geography put both banks of the river well within Swiss territory; if we could get into Switzerland, all we'd have to do would be to cross one of the bridges in the city of Basel, then find a place to slip across the Swiss-German land border. Here was Tony telling us he would get us into Switzerland—maybe.

"Just don't mention my name in your dispatches or whatever you write," he said as we folded the map. "These French have no sense of humor."

We ate a hearty meal, drank some more wine and, around midnight, walked through the empty streets of Mulhouse to where his ambulance was parked. He had us stretch out in the back and buried us under a pile of blankets. Then we felt the creaky vehicle lurch forward. It was to be quite a night.

The ambulance was stopped twice by road patrols. We heard Tony's laborious French—*"C'est vide. Je retourne à l'hôpital"*—and they passed us through. Shortly before 2 A.M., he stopped again and let us out on a stretch he said was parallel to the frontier.

"The border's right there," he whispered, "about a hundred yards. Good luck."

We shook hands. The ambulance lights vanished around a curve and we were alone in the pitch dark of a moonless night. We picked our way through the brush in the general direction Tony had pointed until, one behind the other, we tripped over a low barbed-wire barrier and fell heavily into Switzerland. We picked ourselves up and stumbled on, coming on a road, then crouching in a ditch alongside as a pair of sentries went chattering by and we heard others whistling in the distance. Soon we could see a scattering of lights ahead—Basel—and just about dawn, after circling the city, we found an untended railroad bridge and crossed the Rhine where it was not an international boundary.

During the day, at the frontier, we watched as people were waved through the checkpoint without even slowing down, and I guess that went to our heads. Why should we go crawling around in the woods trying to sneak into Germany? We would march right up there and walk across like everyone else.

Well, we didn't. Everyone else—workers, mostly, who crossed every morning and night—was personally known to the guard. When he saw two strangers in American uniforms approach, he reacted by slamming the gate shut, and ten minutes later Webb and I were sitting in a Basel prison, under arrest.

Though it hardly seemed so at the time, this was one of the luckier things to happen to us on this expedition. The Swiss jailer gave us a decent breakfast and at our urgent request sent for an American consular official. He arrived as a second cup of coffee was restoring our confidence, an imposing-looking gentleman whose first question was: "What the hell do you two think you're up to?"

We told him. We said we were reporters trying hard to do our jobs but that wherever we turned officialdom blocked our way. All at once our fatigue and frustration gave us the effrontery to take the offensive. We bombarded him with questions, giving him no chance to answer.

Webb: "Wouldn't you like to know what's happening in Germany?"

Me: "Don't you think the men who fought this war and the people back home who paid for it have a right to know?"

Webb: "If the Germans are willing to let us in, why should Marshal Foch or the Swiss keep us out?"

Me: "What if they're plotting to start the fighting again? What if the Communists have taken over? Do we have to wait for the peace conference to find out?"

When we finally ran out of breath, he said he thought we were indeed on a worthwhile mission and wished he could join us. He would help us, he said, if only we'd, goddam it, shut up for a minute. We couldn't believe this rather crusty consular officer was going to stick out his neck for us.

152

But he did. He returned around noontime with the Swiss military commandant in Basel, a colonel, who asked us a few questions and then produced some papers. What had passed between those two Webb and I were never to know, except for a hint from the Swiss that he also would like to go along and see what was happening in Germany. A few hours later, having been given time to go on a bit of a shopping spree so we could stock up on coffee, chocolate and cigarettes, we were escorted to the railroad station and placed aboard a train. Once across the border, without anyone seeming to even notice our presence, we were deposited well inside Germany, in the city of Freiburg. Our elation was only tempered by the realization that we'd failed to get the names of our American consul and the Swiss colonel.

Little more than four years had passed since those exhilarating summer days of 1914 when Kaiser Wilhelm II, flaunting a pompous ferocity and concealing his withered left arm, whipped the Fatherland into a fever for war and sent German armies smashing into Russia and Belgium. Neither Germany nor the world would ever be the same. Eight and a half million soldiers died in those four years, nearly two million of them Germans—the greatest loss by any single nation in the history of warfare—and the toll among the civilian populations was even more harrowing.

Despite the awesome casualties, despite growing disillusionment inside the Reich—winters of near-starvation, protests and spreading strikes—the war ground on. Early in 1918, although a fresh American army was taking its place alongside the resurgent Allies, General Erich Ludendorff was telling the Kaiser that he would be in Paris by April 1. Not until the last days of September, when Ludendorff had no more troops to throw into still another sacrificial offensive, was the word *armistice* uttered aloud in the rarefied councils of the High Command. And even then Ludendorff, who had been virtual dictator of Germany for two years, was plotting only to withdraw to a shortened defense line on the frontier and rest his army before again taking up the struggle.

It was not to be. With the home front sliding toward chaos, threatened by utter breakdown on the right and bedlam on the left, the Kaiser appointed a new chancellor, Prince Max von Baden, and this humane and internationally esteemed statesman moved for peace. Ludendorff was dismissed and went to hide in a Berlin boardinghouse before escaping to Sweden, wearing a false beard. Against the Kaiser's will, his abdication was peremptorily announced and he went fleeing to Doorn in the Netherlands, the monarchy dissolved. But it was too late to turn back the gathering storm. Even as the articles of surrender were being signed—by a civilian cabinet minister, Matthias Erzberger; the generals, who had begun the war, refused to face up to their responsibility to end it—the despairing land burned with the fires of revolution.

No one can say how it began. In those fretful last days before the armistice was signed, as radicals and reactionaries wrangled over who was to blame for the downfall of the proud nation, rioting erupted across Germany—a seething protest, a cry of anger by defeated soldiers and civilians who were spent and broken by the intolerable demands of the war. Together they turned on those who had led them to disaster. In Kiel, when the Admiralty ordered the fleet to sea for one final, futile battle, the crews mutinied, turning hoses into their ships' boilers and hoisting the red flag of rebellion. Dock workers and garrison troops joined them. Within days the revolt had spread to Hamburg, Bremen, Cologne, Dusseldorf; and Berlin was locked in the grip of a general strike.

If this overthrow of the Hohenzollern Empire constituted a revolution, it was clearly not the revolution Karl Liebknecht had in mind. He was the most effective agitator in Germany. With Rosa Luxemburg, he had founded and now led the Spartacus League, the party of Germany's revolutionary Marxists. Even as a member of the *Reichstag* he was unremitting in his impassioned opposition to the war, and in 1916 he had been arrested and imprisoned. Then, in October, 1918, as the Empire crumbled and confusion degenerated into turmoil, he was released, returning to Berlin in triumph, the dissenter vindicated, blessed by Lenin and cheered by throngs as he paraded exultantly past the *Reichstag*.

Not for Liebknecht and his Spartacists the modest aspirations of Prince Max's government—peace, a true parliamentary system. Liebknecht called out for a government patterned on the newly triumphant soviets of Russia, "supreme authority to the Workers' and Soldiers' Councils." And as his strength swelled, as the more moderate Social

Democrats were confronted with a nightmare vision in which they traded a dictatorship of the right for one of the left, there seemed no way to forestall the Spartacists but to proclam a German republic. This they did, hastily, on November 9. And so Prince Max, the last Imperial Chancellor, turned his shaky control of the Fatherland over to the Socialist leader, Friedrich Ebert.

"Herr Ebert," Prince Max said, "I commit the German Empire to your keeping."

And Ebert, who had hoped to restore a benevolent monarchy to Germany, who had himself suffered cruelly from the war, replied, "I have lost two sons for this empire." And alone in the Chancellor's Wilhelmstrasse office, he began his monumental effort to save Germany from herself.

It was only a month or so after this pivotal day that Webb Waldron and I arrived in Germany. The world outside, indeed the German people, still had heard little of the background to these epochal events. As we wandered the streets of Freiburg, the thing we felt most acutely, more than the people's relief with the war over, more than their hunger for food and goods, was a sense of bewilderment. What was going to happen next?

A red flag flew over the *Rathaus,* the city hall. A revolutionary council headed by a butcher and a lawyer ruled the city but knew almost nothing of what might have happened outside Freiburg since the upheavals of early November. Still, they treated Webb and me cordially and told us what they could about the political ferment in southern Germany. As we were in uniform, perhaps they thought we were an advance element of an American occupation force. Nor did we have a language problem—it has always amazed me how so many Europeans speak excellent English while the average American has trouble getting by even in London.

When we persisted with our questions, someone suggested we visit Prince Max, who had returned to his Baden estate immediately after divesting himself of the chancellorship. It was easily arranged, the Prince graciously agreeing to see us the following day. Welcomed to his country home, sitting in his comfortable study and listening to him talk about those hectic last weeks, Webb and I could see how relieved he was to be free of the bitter conflicts of the chancellery, and how glad he was to get his version of events on the record.

A member of the royal family and a distinguished humanitarian, Prince Max had devoted himself exclusively to the Red Cross and the welfare of war prisoners—on both sides —during the four years of conflict, consistently refusing to accept a political role until the last month of the war. Then the Kaiser sent for him and told him he alone could save Germany from ruin: only his reputation for openmindedness and integrity could hold off the extremists; only his international stature gave Germany a chance to avoid a total and calamitous surrender.

He smiled ruefully and told us that he seemed to have succeeded at neither. "I believe the Allies want vengeance more than peace, and the harsh terms of the armistice have armed our fanatics, who always come to the fore in times of trouble."

He was also concerned about the High Command's pretense that the Fatherland had been betrayed on the home front while the army was still fighting strongly, the growing myth of the "stab in the back." It would torment the German people, he predicted, and some day be seized on to rehabilitate the military and start another war.

"We were beaten in the field," he said emphatically, and as his story unfolded, it was clear that few men knew the truth better. Unaware of the gravity of the situation on the battlefront, he himself had tried to hold out against the decision to seek immediate terms, fearing it would precipitate an internal convulsion. Summoned to headquarters to hear Ludendorff's demand that Germany accept an armistice, he had pleaded with the Kaiser for a week's delay so he could prepare the people and solidify his government. Wilhelm would not hear of it. "The Supreme Command requests it [the armistice]," he told the Chancellor, "and you have not been brought here to make difficulties for the Supreme Command."

We moved on to Stuttgart, then east to Munich, capital of Bavaria. At the Bayerischer Hof, one of Europe's great hotels, we seemed to be the only guests. Outside, the streets were eerily still, with only a rare automobile swooping by and the people, their faces pinched, silent and distracted as they hurried by the empty shops. Only ersatz, substitutes, appeared to be for sale in Munich—ersatz tobacco, ersatz coffee, even ersatz food. In one shop we saw clothing made of a paper product; it was wilting in the condensation of the display window, and I wondered how long it would stand up to a Bavarian snowstorm. I was glad to think about our bags stuffed with Swiss chocolate and cigarettes, but the fact is that our supply of riches didn't last long; we kept passing them out to hungry-looking people wherever we went.

Demobilized soldiers roamed the streets of Munich during those bleak days, uprooted, unemployed and unable to find themselves in the city from which they had jauntily marched off to war three or four years earlier. Goaded and used by the most reactionary elements in Bavaria, seeking scapegoats for their humiliation, they would soon turn to intimidation and violence in a scramble for political power. One of them, just returned to his adopted city at the end of November, was a thirty-year-old Austrian corporal without money or trade, seething with hatred for those, mainly Jews, whom he blamed for having brought the downfall of the Fatherland. He described himself as a revolutionary "who favored revolution for its own sake and desired to see revolution established as a permanent condition." His name was Adolf Hitler, and there, in Munich, he got his start.

For the moment, though, Bavaria was in the hands of the Social Democrats. Led by a Jewish writer, Kurt Eisner, they had forced the abdication of the Wittelsbach king and established the "People's State." Webb and I requested an interview with Eisner, and he saw us at once. He was a small man with red hair and an untidy beard, his pince-nez periodically popping off his nose as he relived for us the heady moments, only six weeks before, when he had walked through the streets with a few hundred men, occupied the Parliament and proclaimed a republic. It had been overwhelmingly confirmed in an election a few days later, and now Kurt Eisner, a Socialist Jew, ruled Catholic, conservative Bavaria. Suddenly he knifed forward in his chair and exclaimed, "And not a shot fired—no violence, none!"

It was only a few days before Christmas. As we were leaving, I told Herr Eisner how Webb and I had hoped to go to the Alpine village of Oberammergau, home of the world-renowned *Passion Play,* staged only once every ten years, but it seemed impossible because there was no transport. He at once said he would arrange it.

And he did. Though we had to scrounge for gasoline and tires, and though our car broke down in the mountain snows so we had to finish the journey in a farmer's horse-drawn sleigh, we got to Oberammergau on Christmas Eve—and brought first word to this mountain fastness of the war having ended.

The entire village looked more like the setting for a fairy tale than for the drama the outside world came to see—brightly colored houses poking bravely above the deep snow, gay Bavarian folk characters painted on every door. A bundled figure trudging forward to greet us turned out to be Anton Lang, whose portrayal of Christ was known all over Europe and America. Webb and I stayed the night with Herr Lang and his wife—and were visited by nearly everyone in the village—including Judas. How was it they hadn't heard of the armistice? Devout Christians, they had been exempted from military duty, and then forgotten during the snowy winter as the collapse of the mountain telephone line must have seemed the least of Imperial Germany's problems.

Webb and I returned to Munich and there expressed our thanks to Herr Eisner, the odd-looking little Jew who had made this very special Christmas possible for us. Two months later he was dead, shot down as he walked along the Promenadestrasse on his way to Parliament by a right-wing assassin, one of those heedless freebooters who, like Hitler, had long lived with violence and now believed loyalty to the Fatherland demanded murder and mayhem against the Republic.

Just before the new year, we came to Berlin, where a new war, for the possession of Germany, was moving toward a shattering climax. It was a curious and contradictory moment in history. Armed mobs defied the curfew; gunfire crackled from the rooftops. Yet the telephones worked and the streetcars were running and, as one Berliner put it, "If the streetcars are running, you know life is bearable." Though food supplies were short and people were reduced to making do with meals of boiled turnips, no one was starving. A new Ernst Lubitsch film, *Carmen*, starring Pola Negri, had recently opened and was playing to capacity crowds. Even the revolution followed a certain stoic and orderly pattern, entirely in keeping with that unquenchable

Germanic instinct to submit in the face of authority. According to a current joke, a planned assault on a government building went awry when the insurgents came upon the warning signs protecting the surrounding lawn—"Keep off the grass." Rules were rules: they turned back.

Still, the revolution went on and people were killed in the streets while Chancellor Ebert struggled desperately to restore order. A mob of three thousand rebellious sailors had seized the Royal Palace, then demanded two hundred thousand marks for "guarding" it. When Ebert called on loyal troops to drive them out, Liebknecht and the Spartacists responded by urging the citizenry to march on the palace and defend it against the "counterrevolutionaries." Thousands of shouting demonstrators—students, war veterans and angry women—heeded the call. And the soldiers, who had willingly bombarded the barricaded sailors, killing thirty, could not bring themselves to turn their guns on a crowd of unarmed civilians. Sullenly the troops withdrew; the milling horde in the palace square cheered exultantly and embraced the mutinous sailors.

Flushed with his victory, Liebknecht and his Spartacists, so named for the leader of a Roman slave revolt two thousand years before, united with other radical socialists to form the Communist Party of Germany. One of its leading theoreticians was an overweight lady of middle years who had been born in Poland and whose brilliance as a speaker and pamphleteer of the left rivaled Lenin's. Her name was Rosa Luxemburg and, unlike Lenin, she did not believe the German working class was yet sufficiently organized for revolution. But events were outpacing theory; Rosa Luxemburg and Karl Liebknecht, who sought to ride the tiger, would soon be devoured by it.

Extremists of the right were gathering strength, too, and their leitmotiv and driving force was hatred. At a meeting of army officers, when a government spokesman begged support for Chancellor Ebert's embattled Republic, a young air force captain in full uniform rose to make an embittered protest: "We officers did our duty for four long years; we offered our lives for the Fatherland. Now we come home and they spit on us. And so I implore you to cherish hatred, a profound, abiding hatred for those animals who have outraged the German people. . . . The day will come when we will drive them out of our Germany."

His name was Hermann Goering, and far to the south

the man with whom he would be linked in infamy, Adolf Hitler, burned with the same passion. "So it had all been in vain," he wrote in *Mein Kampf*, "in vain all the sacrifices, in vain the death of two million . . . There followed terrible days and even worse nights. In these nights hatred grew in me, hatred for those responsible for this deed. My fate became known to me. I decided to go into politics."

Webb Waldron and I certainly were getting our inside look at Germany in convulsion. We had checked into the Adlon Hotel on the Unter den Linden, not far from the Brandenburg Gate, which today divides East and West Berlin, and once again our American uniforms were the passkey to some exceptional experiences. Ignoring the curfew, we went walking and were stopped by a sailor carrying a rifle and wearing an ammunition belt festooned with potato-masher grenades. Who were we? he asked in English, and I had visions of a summary execution or, at the least, confinement in some dank dungeon, never to be heard from again. But as we haltingly told him that we were American journalists and went fishing for our papers, he laughed. He was from Hoboken, he said. He had been visiting relatives in Hamburg when the war broke out and the next thing he knew he had been drafted into the Imperial Navy and sent to sea on a U-boat.

And as we stood there grinning and shaking hands in the wonder of this small world, a machine gun opened up from a building across the street. It was apparently aimed at an approaching military patrol, but its wild torrent of fire sprayed a hundred-yard length of sidewalk and sent bullets ricocheting around our ears. We dived into the nearest doorway, tumbling over each other in the dark, huddling close as we tried to catch our breath. The shared danger solidified our friendship; when the machine gun quit rattling out there, we invited the sailor back to the Adlon for a drink.

We sat up most of the night, pressing cigarettes and brandy on our new friend and listening to a vivid account of his part in the revolution. He had been among those who mutinied at Kiel—"They wanted us to commit suicide for the Fatherland, and we said, 'That's not part of the bargain—go to hell!' "—and was now one of the sailors occupying the Imperial Palace. Most of them had no better place to go, he said. They were still hoping that somebody

L.T. and his parents.

Birthplace of L.T., Woodington, Ohio, a suburb of Greenville, the town where Annie Oakley was living when she died in 1926.

Facing page: Dr. Harry George Thomas, a man of many interests—1900, Victor, Colorado.

L.T. and his mother, Harriet Wagner Thomas. Picture taken in Greenville, Ohio, while awaiting word from Cripple Creek.

Dr. Thomas in his office at the gold mines.

The mass meeting of miners on June 6, 1904, that led to a riot in which sixteen people were killed. From the window of his father's office L.T. witnessed the shooting and the charge of the militia.

A moment of football practice in Victor. L.T. on right, with two shaft houses of the great Portland mine on the left and Stratton's Independence in background right.

Victor high school football team of 1908 with L.T., end and quarterback, second from right, second row, at the age of sixteen.

In 1907 L.T. rode nine hours a day for an assay office collecting ore samples from smaller mines.

At the University of Northern Indiana (Valparaiso) L.T. collected a B.S. and an M.S. in two years. In this photo he is with daughters of two professors.

After returning to Colorado, L.T. did what young scholars in mining camps have always done.

L.T. was offered a job at $95 a month as a reporter on the *Victor Daily Record*, of which he soon became editor. Here he is with his only sister, Pherbia.

In 1912, at age twenty, he went to Chicago to study law. This is the costume he wore into the office of the *Chicago Journal.*

Facing page: With the *Arditi* near the summit of Monte Rosa in December, 1917.

L.T. with General Pepino Garibaldi at the Italian front.

With Field Marshal Allenby after the fall of Jerusalem.

Lawrence of Arabia.

Heading down the old road to Jericho from Jerusalem to the Jordan in the turret of a World War I armored car.

L.T. mounted on an Arabian horse.

The armored cars of T. E. Lawrence could race across this desert floor at top speed from one mountain range to another. L.T. is in the group on the right.

T. E. Lawrence and L.T.

A foreign correspondent in the Holy Land needed quite a
bit of equipment to do his job properly.

L.T. and his wife, Fran, in
the Malay jungle.

Heading for the Malay forest on borrowed elephants.

L.T. on left and Fran, behind the three men seated on the ground, with a Malay pygmy tribe. Cameraman Harry A. Chase holding his hat in the foreground.

L.T. about to cross the frontier into Afghanistan, then a forbidden kingdom.

L.T. photographing the victims of a tragedy in the Khyber Pass, the occupants of an ambushed mail car.

Nearing the Afghan end of the Pass. The tents are those of British soldiers encamped at the Indo-Afghan frontier.

L.T. chatting with King Amanullah Khan (in black astrakhan) and his brothers in the grounds of the royal palace at Kabul.

L.T. with General "Hap" Arnold.

L.T. with the Army airmen who were first to fly around the world.

Facing page: Major Martin and Sergeant Harvey on arrival at Port Moller.

Mr. and Mrs. L.T. at Tempelhof in Berlin with Gustav Lindenthal, famous patriarch and builder of the Hellgate Bridge, and Otto Merkle, founder of Lufthansa.

L.T. at a gathering of some of the early Atlantic fliers.

Count Felix von Luckner, six feet three inches of supercharged energy and ebullient high spirits.

Floyd Gibbons and his replacement.

L.T. when he first said, "Good evening, everybody."

Amos 'n' Andy on the air.

Homer Croy, L.T., and Prosper Buranelli with the boxes containing the 265,654 telegrams that were received in response to a single radio program.

President Herbert Hoover and L.T. on the steps of Clover Brook Farm.

Lowell Thomas, Jr., timing a radio broadcast for his father.

Gene Tunney liked to pitch, and he had no intention of surrendering the baseball while the Nine Old Men were being photographed. Prosper, behind Gene Tunney, obviously wanted to get on with the game.

"Lowell, who's the chap playing first base for you?"

T.R., Jr., and Billy Van.

—Ebert or Liebknecht, it didn't really matter—would pay them to leave. Next day, as if to prove his companions were the most cordial of revolutionaries, he took us to the palace and conducted us on a tour of the pillaged former home of the Kaiser. We even had a glass of wine from the Emperor's swiftly dwindling private stock.

Next our uniforms attracted the notice of a young German, a reporter who had once worked for the Associated Press in Berlin. Eager to reestablish his journalistic credentials in America, he attached himself to Webb and me, willingly serving as interpreter and general functionary. It was to prove a mixed blessing. Without telling us, he took to sending dispatches back to the States via Copenhagen, not all of them famous for immaculate attention to facts. He used his own by-line, true, but as he frequently mentioned Webb and me by name and described our experiences with more zeal than accuracy, trouble was inevitable.

Webb and I were the first foreign correspondents to reach Germany and stay long enough to get shot at. This gave us a leg up. Like true veterans of street warfare, we learned to dive for cover only for a machine gun, and only when it opened up in our immediate vicinity; we soon came to recognize and discount automobile backfiring and to ignore isolated rifle shots, and mainly went routinely about our business of covering the revolution. Perhaps more to the point, we were around long enough to sort out the leading actors in the drama of Germany's power struggle and eventually to interview them all. For if, as has been said, luck is largely a matter of being in the right place at the right time, we were blessed to be on hand at precisely the moment in history when the contending factions were most anxious to get their version of events out to the world. Like Prince Max and Kurt Eisner in Bavaria, the political leaders in Berlin each had a story to tell, and they told it to Webb and me openly and at length.

One who seemed to know, even in the flux of the fighting, that his side had already lost was Count Johann-Heinrich von Bernstorff. He, too, was staying at the Adlon, and one day, as the three of us stood behind its massive iron gates watching a street battle, he patiently responded to our questions and reflected on his role in Germany's rise and fall.

It was a vivid moment of point and counterpoint. Beyond

those protective gates, a company of militia had just broken up a Spartacist rally to which Karl Liebknecht and Rosa Luxemburg had addressed impassioned revolutionary exhortations. Now the crowd was being driven down the Unter den Linden; we could hear scattered shooting in the Tiergarten just beyond the huge wooden statue of Von Hindenburg that for a year or more dominated the Unter den Linden and hadn't yet been toppled over. As Count von Bernstorff watched his world distintegrating before his eyes, he talked softly and calmly about a Germany he loved better and how it had come to this.

He was a gentleman of the old school, his aristocratic credentials impeccable, his forebears firmly established in the diplomatic service of Prussia and the Imperial German Empire. He had been born in London, where his father was ambassador to the Court of St. James. And Johann-Heinrich lived up to the reputation of the Bernstorffs; were it not for the autocratic vainglory of Kaiser Wilhelm II, he would have rendered the greatest service of all of them to Germany. For Count von Bernstorff became the German ambassador in Washington from 1908 to 1917, and had Wilhelm heeded his counsel, the United States would never have entered the war and Germany would not have lost it.

It was not the first time his advice had been spurned, to Germany's disadvantage. Convinced that an accommodation with France was not possible, he had urged close cooperation between Berlin and London and candidly supported the obvious corollary of no German challenge to British supremacy on the high seas. In the best Bismarckian tradition, he believed the elephant and the whale should avoid a confrontation; their vital interests differed and conflict between them was unnecessary. Unfortunately, the elephant decided to behave like a whale: the Kaiser ordered a German naval buildup, irritating Britain's most sensitive nerve ending and, inevitably, goading her into a protective alliance with France.

In prewar America, Bernstorff was one of the most popular figures of the diplomatic set, elegant, urbane and thoroughly charming. He was also chillingly effective at his job. After Germany invaded Belgium without provocation and precipitated war with England and France, he labored day and night to prevent a tide of pro-Allied emotion from sweeping the United States into the camp of the enemy. Germany must do nothing further, he cabled home insistently, to shock America out of her neutrality. Toward this end, he opposed the resumption of unrestricted submarine warfare and urged the Kaiser to accept President Wilson's offer to mediate a settlement of the conflict. But in Berlin, those who had the Kaiser's ear encouraged his fantasy of a Germanic Europe, and they prevailed. American merchantmen were wantonly sunk; the notorious Zimmerman note exposed a puerile Foreign Office plot to coax Mexico into war with the United States. When, in April, 1917, Congress finally voted to commit America's strength to the Allied cause, Bernstorff returned home in black depression, convinced that the German leaders had thrown away every chance to avert a catastrophic defeat.

He was sent to Turkey, an inferior post for a man of his experience, and a mark of the Kaiser's disdain. But he continued to serve loyally until Turkey's surrender, then came home again, this time to witness the final agony of his own beleaguered country. Now, as we stood behind the Adlon gates with gunfire punctuating his bleak soliloquy, Count von Bernstorff said, as had the Socialist Ebert, that the Kaiser had had to go, yes, but that the loss of the institution of the monarchy was a grave mistake. "It is the symbol of our nationhood. Without it, we Germans are like so many autumn leaves, blown back and forth by the winds of change."

In the years to come, he would serve the Weimar Republic, acting as chief delegate to the disarmament conference of 1926. But as democracy withered in Germany, as his dire prediction came true and the winds of change swept the German people toward the Nazi dictatorship, he gave up and chose exile in Switzerland. There he died in 1939, just in time to be spared the melancholy spectacle of Germany's second march to ruin.

No one in Berlin that gray and cheerless winter mourned the passing of the year 1918. On the other hand, there did not seem to be much promise for tranquillity in the first days of 1919. The city buzzed with nervous rumors that Liebknecht was about to stage a *putsch*. It was said that Ebert was giving serious consideration to abandoning the Chancellery and taking the government out of Berlin to some safe and distant place. "If the Liebknecht crowd takes this opportunity to seize power," he said, "they will find nobody here."

When Webb and I went to see him in those first days of the new year, he looked like a man on the ragged edge of breakdown. For two months it had been as though he were holding a sundered, struggling Germany together with his bare hands, and now the whole thing was getting away from him. Ebert was not quite fifty then, a plump man with haggard eyes whose slightly raffish gray goatee jarred an otherwise entirely bourgeois image.

Born into a poor Catholic family in Heidelberg, he had been apprenticed to a saddlemaker—"the saddler is in the saddle," the German people joked when Ebert became Chancellor—and worked as a bartender in his own tavern. He had been active in socialist circles before he was twenty. But Ebert's socialism owed less to Karl Marx than to his own personal convictions: he had little use for the fierce theorizing of the professional dissidents; not passion but common sense was his hallmark, and he devoted his best efforts to bringing order to the haphazard party organization and expanding its membership. As for political theory, he had a single simple belief: Germany and its working people would prosper under the Social Democrats and a constitutional monarch. Now here he was, thrust into the position once held by Bismarck, and struggling to avert a civil war.

Ebert's deputy, Philipp Scheidemann, was present at the interview in the Chancellery and told us how he had come to proclaim the Republic, almost by accident. He had been having a bowl of soup at the Reichstag the momentous November afternoon when a swarm of workers and soldiers came rushing in looking for him. Liebknecht, they said, was at the Royal Palace, about to declare the establishment of a Soviet republic. He must do something at once.

"I went upstairs to a window. There was a great crowd in the Koenigsplatz and I began addressing them. 'The war is over,' I said. 'The Kaiser has gone.' They cheered wildly, and before I quite realized what I was saying, I cried out, 'Long live the new Germany! Long live the Republic!' And so it was done."

Ebert had been furious; he still hoped for a restoration of the monarchy. But there was no turning back, and the two had since worked together tirelessly. Now both looked as though they hadn't had a decent night's sleep in a long time. And what of the future? Ebert shrugged. "I cannot even tell you what will happen tomorrow. There is only one

164

thing I know and it is this: if my government falls, Germany will turn to a dictator, and then you Americans will have to come back."

The next day, Webb and I went to see Karl Liebknecht and Rosa Luxemburg. For a time they had found a refuge with the rebellious sailors who held the Royal Palace, and night after night, within its ramble of lofty rooms and majestic corridors, they plotted the capture of the German government. Eventually, though, the sailors, in exchange for eighty thousand marks and a promise of amnesty, evacuated the building and Liebknecht and Luxemburg moved on, setting up new command posts wherever they happened to be. Nearly every day they marched out to another street demonstration where they whipped their followers into frenzies of enthusiasm. But for what? we asked them. What was their program? When would they strike?

Rosa Luxemburg spoke first. She made it clear that she opposed the use of force in pursuit of a political end. The people must bring down Ebert's government; then the Spartacists would take charge.

I reminded her that Lenin had not waited for the people. He had incited them to revolution and did not appear to mind the broken heads and worse that it took to achieve and maintain it.

Her look of scorn was eloquent. She was not an unattractive woman, despite her plumpness and a limp from an old hip injury, for the intensity of her feelings fired her eyes and her eyes illuminated her whole face. She disagreed with Lenin, she said, and had told him so. The Bolshevik regime had become a dictatorship of an elite. What was the use of overthrowing the existing power and replacing it with a couple of dozen new tyrants? If there was to be revolution in Germany, it must be democratic in methods as well as goals. Then, speaking clearly and looking straight at Liebknecht, she said, "The Spartacus League will never take power except in accordance with the clearly expressed will of the proletarian masses."

Unable to contain his agitation, Liebknecht jumped to his feet. "Yes, yes, the will of the people!" he exclaimed, pacing the small room in a sympathizer's house where we had gathered. "We will heed the will of the people later, when the militia is not on our necks. But democratic socialism doesn't grow on trees, available for just the plucking. We have to have power before we can offer it. We have to *lead!*"

It was almost as though Webb and I were no longer there; the two were clearly replaying an old argument for each other. Ignoring us, they wrangled on, Luxemburg cooly intelligent, but Liebknecht stronger, more caustic, wearing her down. He looked less like a revolutionary than a bank clerk—a slender little man with a clipped black moustache and a stiff white collar—but when he spoke he smoldered with passion.

I don't know about Webb, but at the time I was more interested in events than in polemics. What was going to happen? At the first break in their fiery dialogue, I interrupted to say that I had heard them both speak at street rallies and it did not seem there was any difference in their appeals. What did it mean when they called on the people to "arm for the final battle" and "destroy" the existing power structure?

"That is political rhetoric," Rosa Luxemburg replied.

"It is an incitement to revolution," Liebknecht replied.

As it turned out, he was right. Two days after our meeting with them, on the morning of Monday, January 6, the bloody rising known to history as Spartacist Week began with a general strike. It was called by Liebknecht and a "Revolutionary Council" hastily formed the night before. Its first act was a ringing statement in which the Ebert-Scheidemann government was "dismissed" and the Spartacists declared to have "provisionally taken over."

Rosa Luxemburg was not present. When she heard the news she was stunned. For Liebknecht to persist in precipitating the revolution despite her strong opposition was bad enough; that "he had seized power," as she derisively put it, "by means of a statement" was, to her, a public confession of his inability to hold it. Still, what was done was done. Perceptive enough to recognize her own responsibility for the disaster, utterly convinced of the rightness of their cause, she committed herself to the revolution. On January 7, writing in the Spartacist newspaper, *Die Rot Fahne* (The Red Banner), she again called the workers to the "final battle. . . . Disarm the counter-revolutionaries, arm the masses, occupy all important positions. Act quickly. The revolution demands it!"

But by then Chancellor Ebert was no longer the discouraged, demoralized leader Webb and I had seen only a few days before. He had taken a strong man into his government as Defense Minister, a master butcher named Gustav Noske, who had made himself the Social Democrats' expert on military affairs. To Ebert, Noske suddenly promised a last chance to stave off disaster. It was Noske, a no-nonsense nationalist to whom socialism and Kaiser Wilhelm were entirely compatible, who had put down the naval mutiny at Kiel. Now, with Ebert's nervous concurrence and the blessings of the High Command, he took over the Freikorps, an army of volunteers controlled by the Kaiser's most fanatic officers. "Someone must play the bloodhound," Noske said. "I am not afraid of the responsibility."

And so the lines of battle were drawn. Inside Berlin, electricity and public transport stopped, factories and stores closed down. Hundreds of thousands swarmed through the bloodily contested streets—demonstrators, soldiers and ordinary citizens so desperate for food or a chunk of coal to keep them warm that they dared the unending riots, the sniper fire and the retaliating machine guns to go out looking for them.

There was particularly bitter fighting at the Brandenburg Gate, for machine guns emplaced there could sweep the length of the Unter den Linden. Webb and I were shot at regularly, and once, scurrying back to the Adlon, a bullet whipped through my hat. This "news" was promptly sent out by our self-appointed A.P. interpreter and eventually reached the United States in slightly—but significantly—garbled form: "Lowell Thomas, the American journalist, was shot through the *heart* today during a street battle on the Unter den Linden." Whether it was an honest mistake —in German, hat is *Hut* and heart is *Herz*—or our man trying to embellish a story, the damage was done. A *Denver Post* reporter picked it up and telephoned poor Fran, who wept and, for the next two weeks, considered herself a widow.

Meanwhile, Noske, the bloodhound, was organizing his strike force in the suburb of Dahlen. On January 9, he sent the first Freikorps troops into Berlin, following two days later at the head of three thousand more. They began methodically to blast the Spartacists out of their strongholds with cannon and grenades, executing hundreds and imprisoning the rest. By the night of the fourteenth, the general strike was broken and more than a thousand on both sides were dead.

Liebknecht and Luxemburg, having fled the bloodhound's fury, were hiding in a working-class district west of the city. There they issued their last manifesto, and there a young Communist functionary named Wilhelm Pieck brought them false identity papers.

It was no use. They were ferreted out and arrested by Noske's Cavalry Guard on the night of the fifteenth and, along with Pieck, taken to a hotel near the Tiergarten for questioning. Later, a chambermaid told how the "questioning" had consisted mainly of "knocking the poor woman down and dragging her about." Liebknecht was badly beaten, too. Curiously, Pieck was not harmed at all and was, in fact, soon released. The reason was, as the evidence eventually made clear, because he had answered the Freikorps questions all too willingly, informing on other Spartacist leaders; it may even have been Pieck who betrayed Liebknecht and Luxemburg. These facts are never mentioned in the official biographies of the man who, in 1949, became the first president of Communist East Germany.

In the Adlon lobby late the same night, Webb and I heard how Liebknecht and Luxemburg had been arrested and brought to the Eden Hotel. We hurried over there and from a block away saw first one car, then a second, speed off from a side entrance. At the hotel no one seemed willing to answer our questions, so we started back. Walking along, we thought we heard some shots from inside the Tiergarten, but as there was still sporadic shooting going on all over Berlin, we gave it little thought. Those shots, as we later learned, ended Karl Liebknecht's life.

He had been driven into the Tiergarten by a group of officers, ostensibly en route to the Moabit jail. But once inside the deserted park, they dragged him from the car and shot him dead. Then they brought the body to a mortuary; they had found it, they said, in the street.

Rosa Luxemburg was in the second car. She was so badly beaten there was no need to take her from the car. One of the officers, a certain Lieutenant Kurt Vogel, just put his pistol to her head and pulled the trigger; when the car reached a bridge over the Landwehr Canal, they stopped and threw the body in. In their cover story they said they had surrendered her to an anti-Communist mob and didn't know what happened to her afterward. This led to tales of her escaping and hiding somewhere. But in May her battered body was washed up in one of the canal locks and no one, neither followers nor foes, could pretend any longer.

Ebert was appalled by the slayings and ordered a rigorous investigation. But things being what they were, only a single soldier, a private, accused of clubbing Liebknecht with his rifle, ever went to prison for complicity in the crime. He served four months. As for Noske, he told a cabinet meeting in March that he had been given a job to do and he had done it: he had broken the back of the revolution. Look at the excesses of the other side, he declared. If he had been forced to limit the zeal of the government troops, it would have sapped their willingness to risk their lives in the murderous street fighting. And I suppose there is a sort of grim logic to what he said—as long as human beings are willing to resort to force as a shortcut to reason in defense of what they believe, they have to anticipate animal behavior on the other side, too.

Certainly the elections called by Ebert less than a week after the abortive revolution justified the government's stand. The Social Democrats won a smashing victory. Ebert thereupon led a constituent assembly to the cultural center of Weimar to draft a new constitution—Berlin was still considered unsafe. He was chosen to be the Republic's first President and Scheidemann was named Chancellor. But the seeds had already been sown for a black harvest.

The document produced by the delegates after six months' hard work has been called by one historian a constitution in search of a people. It was humane, idealistic and thoroughly democratic—and pleased no one. The Weimar Republic, which it brought into being, infuriated the old imperialists and the new nationalists by "pandering to the rabble," and the feverish left was incensed because industry and the great landed estates had not been seized and turned over to the masses.

If there was one thing on which the German people did agree, even before their new republic came into being, it was that a massive and galling wrong had been inflicted on them at Versailles. There, in the resplendent Hall of Mirrors, where the German Empire was proclaimed in 1871, Ebert's plenipotentiaries were threatened with an Allied invasion of their country if they did not, within one week, sign a treaty heaping full blame for the war and all its

169

consequences on Germany. Having no other option, they signed—and thereby committed their struggling nation to the loss of twenty-seven thousand square miles of territory with a population of seven million, including Alsace-Lorraine and the rich Saar coal basin; military occupation of the Rhine's left bank; reduction of the army to a police force of no more than one hundred thousand volunteers; and reparations still to be determined, but to begin at once with a provisional payment of twenty billion marks in gold. The terms were staggering in their vindictiveness; but even worse, the economic and emotional burden they pressed down on the German people all but guaranteed the undoing of the peace the treaty was supposed to insure.

Ebert and his government had an additional burden: they were held to blame. The army, having left Germany defenseless, had deftly shoved the political power into the civilians' hands to avoid the responsibility. Now the Weimar Republic was inextricably linked with the shameful surrender. *They,* not the soldiers, had lost the war. They had brought this disgrace and suffering to the Fatherland. The myth of the stab in the back had come to full flower.

Scheidemann resigned. Overwhelmed by the strain of reparations, the German economy collapsed. By the end of 1923, it took four billion marks to buy one dollar—then it got worse. This was actually good news for some: certain industrialists paid off all their debts in worthless marks; the state cleared its war loans; and the army, stirring again, was financially unencumbered as it began planning the next war. But for the millions left bankrupt, their bank accounts wiped out and the buying power of their salaries shriveled, for those who pushed a wheelbarrow full of marks to the bakery to buy a loaf of bread, it was a time of the most profound misery.

It was a time, too, of violence from both the left and the right, with the threat of civil war hanging over the Weimar Republic like a cloud that wouldn't go away. Plundering Freikorps bands, wearing the swastika emblem on their helmets, terrorized the cities, beating those they considered enemies and innocent bystanders as well. From a dark underworld of conspiracy, there crept one political assassin after another to cut down some of Germany's most promising leaders. Eisner, Liebknecht and Luxemburg went first. Then Matthias Erzberger, who signed the armistice, was shot down in the Black Forest; Walther

Rathenau, Ebert's Foreign Minister, was murdered because he was a Jew; Hugo Haase, leader of the Independent Socialist Party, was killed on the Reichstag steps; Philipp Scheidemann was scarred by a thug who threw prussic acid at his eyes. And in almost every case, the assailant went unpunished.

As long as Ebert was alive, he managed, somehow, to keep the wallowing ship of state afloat. But when he died in 1925, to be replaced by the timeworn Field Marshal, von Hindenburg, not a whole parade of chancellors and cabinets could reinvigorate the besieged republic. Year by year, the extremist parties gained strength until, soon after the onset of the world depression, the Communists had the third greatest number of seats in the *Reichstag* and the National Socialist German Workers Party, called, derisively at first, the Nazis, had the most.

The rise of the Nazis was phenomenal. Starting as a joke—their 1923 attempt to take over the Bavarian government was called the "Beer Hall *Putsch*"—they clawed their way to notice by a calculated policy of obstruction in the *Reichstag* and brutality in the streets. In January, 1933, the weary old Field Marshal turned the Chancellery over to their leader, Adolf Hitler, and two months later an obedient *Reichstag* granted Hitler dictatorial powers. The Weimar Republic was dead.

Not many remember the city where it was so bravely born. But all men would have reason to recall another place, only a few miles to the northwest, for it was to become the symbol of the Germany that was born that winter of 1933. It is called Buchenwald.

In late January, Webb and I made our way to Hamburg, hoping to hitch a ride back to France on a merchant ship. We wound up, instead, on a sleek French cruiser bound for Le Havre. We had met the captain in a café, bought each other a few beers and then asked if we could tag a ride with him. *"Mais certainement, mes amis!"* he declared expansively, and for once I was grateful for the potency of German beer.

When we were well out to sea, we confessed that our papers weren't precisely in order, that we had never gotten clearance to leave France, hence had none to return. The captain was a good sport. He said we were allies and mustn't worry. He didn't worry either. Instead of docking at Le Havre, he anchored offshore in the dead of a winter night and put us over the side in a longboat. Whereupon we were landed on some deserted beach miles from the city and left there with nothing more than our luggage and a cheery *"Bonne chance!"*

It was the luggage that hurt, and it hurt me more than it did Webb. During those last frantic days in Berlin, I had finally found something I'd been hunting for from the time we arrived in Germany—good film footage of the street scenes, the rioting and rallies, during the revolution. At the UFA studio, where my American dollars must have seemed a fantastic treasure just then, I bought four reels of first-rate film.

It weighed at lot. So did the dress helmet I had gotten at the Reichschancellery and the Imperial Palace, and the ersatz suitcase full of ersatz goods I had found too fascinating to resist. All these things were to play an important role in my future, but as we set out toward the lights of Le Havre I seriously considered dumping the whole lot.

We pushed on at a slow pace and in a couple of hours came, finally, to a suburban railway station. There we simply plopped ourselves down and waited until a train traveling in the direction of Paris stopped. It was a local train, stopping at every crossroads village along the way, so what was normally a three-hour trip took six, and it was so packed with demobilized poilus that Webb and I were lucky to find places in the corridor to lie down. But at 7 A.M. it deposited us at the Gare St. Lazare, and even in the gray of a winter morning Paris was a welcome sight.

We had a problem. Here we were, sitting on a sensational story, a firsthand account of the German revolution, and Webb was anxious to start filing it at once. But how would the French and American military commands react to this blatant admission, the way we'd defied their orders against crossing the frontier? President Wilson and the American delegation to the peace conference had arrived in Paris and were staying at the Hotel Crillon, so we decided on a rather brazen strategy. We would report there and, like the patriotic Americans we were, bring to the President's attention all this information we had accumulated during our six weeks in Germany, information no one on this side of the border could possibly have. We might still be reprimanded—or worse—but at the moment it seemed our only chance to finesse the military authorities.

Once we'd made the decision, we didn't dally. We stuffed a briefcase with our notes and threaded our way through the traffic on the Place de la Concorde to the Crillon. There we asked to see Colonel Edward M. House, who had no official title but was known to be Wilson's most intimate adviser and chief deputy. Would he listen? Would he even see us?

The answer, to our immense relief, was yes. We started talking as soon as we were shown into his suite and didn't stop, except to give him time for a question, until an hour and a half had passed. Then he called in two other members of the American delegation, Herbert Hoover, United States Food Administrator, and General Tasker H. Bliss, wartime chief of staff, and gave them a twenty-minute briefing on what we had told him—the essence of the interviews we'd had with the top German leaders, the attitudes and living conditions of people in the major cities, and an up-to-the-minute account of what had really happened inside Germany since the armistice.

There were a few more questions, then Colonel House rose and expressed the delegation's gratitude for our report. "I will convey it to President Wilson this evening," he said. "It is going to be very valuable to all of us. Now, is there anything I can do for either of you?"

We said that we were both anxious to return home but knew shipping space was at a premium because the A.E.F., which had grown to nearly a million and a half men, was being sent back.

"Let me take care of it for you," he said. "You will hear from me."

I never learned just how important our information actually turned out to be at the peace conference, but Herbert Hoover later told me it was of significant help to him in the massive task of emergency relief to which he'd recently been assigned. In the first years of the war, Hoover had taken the lead in raising a billion dollars for food, clothing and medical supplies and had negotiated agreements to get them through the Allied blockade and past the German lines to the ten million people of Belgium and northern France caught in the invader's grip. Now he was charged with helping the starving and homeless millions throughout all Europe. Eventually he saw to the

173

distribution of eighteen and a half million tons of food in a dozen countries. In an article Webb wrote for an April, 1920, issue of *Collier's* he termed the Hoover achievement "more important than the work of any other man or group of men concerned with preparation for the war or its prosecution."

. . . Last year Hoover pulled central Europe through the worst crisis of her history. When you read [his] name you think less of a personality than of great storehouses of food, big American ships unloading needed provisions, and vast offices in which busy clerks keep track of American relief around the world. . . . In Paris I heard how Hoover, after sitting silent through hours of talk, talk, talk, endless talk all afternoon in the Supreme Economic Council, would finally write a few lines on a piece of paper and pass it on to Lord Robert Cecil, the chairman. Nine times out of ten, Hoover's was the plan adopted.

Yet this was only the beginning of Herbert Hoover's long service to America and the world. He was one of the most remarkable men I ever knew, perhaps the one I admired most, and that he became my warm friend in later years is an honor I will always cherish.

As we had anticipated, the imprimatur of Colonel House and the American delegation secured us from the danger of retribution by the military, and Webb got busy sending out his stories. I pondered my future. My original mission, to return to the United States and help stimulate the war effort with my films from the front, had been effectively canceled by the war's abrupt end. Could I still make any use of the thousands of feet of film Chase and I had shot in France, Italy and the Middle East, and the four reels I had picked up in Germany? Or would I simply have to content myself with having had an incredible experience and let it go at that? The answer would have to wait until I got home.

For a few days Webb and I seemed to be the most popular young men in Paris. Word of our German adventures had quickly gotten around, and everyone, particularly the other correspondents, still forbidden to cross the Rhine, was hungry for details of what was going on there. Then one evening we returned to our hotel to find a message from Colonel House: he had arranged passage home for us on the *Leviathan;* we were sailing in the morning.

I can unequivocally recommend allowing a presidential assistant to make your travel arrangements; thanks to Colonel House, the crossing was a voyage I will never forget.

Before it was taken over by the United States as a prize of war, the S.S. *Leviathan* had been the flagship of the Hamburg-American line, christened *der Vaterland,* the largest passenger liner afloat. Converted to a troop carrier, it could—and on this trip did—hold eighteen thousand doughboys, most of them forced to sleep in shifts.

But not Webb and I. Because of Colonel House's intercession on our behalf, we were assigned to the Kaiser's own Imperial Suite, a lavish top-deck lounge with two bedrooms and a private dining room. The other bedroom was occupied by a Chicago tycoon who had had some important logistical job in the war, but we only saw him when he came out to complain because we kept inviting some of the troops up to share our luxury—and he only did that twice. The second time, with doughboys sleeping all over the lushly carpeted lounge and those who were awake passing around a couple of bottles of my cognac, he said he didn't know why he had to be inconvenienced by having all those chaps cluttering up his quarters. It was then I really knew travel was broadening. I silenced him—slightly inaccurately but apparently effectively—by saying, "Say, don't you know there's a war on?"

8.

Telling My Story

Even Royal Albert Hall, largest concert auditorium in the world, is proving hardly large enough for the people who want to hear him.
—*The Times*

I returned to an America I barely recognized. Apart from the physical changes—new buildings going up everywhere; automobiles honking horses and pedestrians over to the side of the road—the people, in that typically all-or-nothing American way, seemed totally disinterested in anything to do with the war. They had fought it; they had won it—now they wanted to forget all about it.

This didn't bode too well for my high hopes and the hundred thousand feet of war film on which I'd built them. But as I did not want to join the ranks of the unemployed, I proceeded exactly as though our film was going to make our fortune, and after some travails it did.

First I cabled Fran and asked her to meet me in Chicago; I felt obliged to report to Silas Strawn and the other generous men who had made it possible. Then I got in touch with Harry Chase and told him to keep working away on the film processing. When he asked me what we were going to do with it, I had to confess that I didn't yet know.

Neither did Strawn, or any of my old newspaper pals—all agreed that the United States was suddenly caught up in a wild postwar mood and seemed to want nothing so much as to be entertained. I tried to forget my problem while Fran and I enjoyed a brief second honeymoon in Chicago. But once we were back in New York, I could see what I was up against wherever I turned. The war had been relegated to the forgettable past and the country had taken off on a binge of merrymaking. Broadway was building to the record theatrical season of 1919. Prohibition was on the way, but while the whiskey flowed, nightclubs were packed with people hungry for amusement. It was as though all America was saying, "We did our bit; now make us laugh."

Well, why not? One day, I don't remember where or just when, I quit thinking of my film footage as a somber chronicle of the war in Europe and the Middle East and began to see it as possible entertainment—moving pictures and stills to transport audiences to places they'd only imagined. And as the pictures appeared on the screen, I would tell them the dramatic stories that could never be conveyed by headlines and news dispatches, with appropriate music synchronized into the background. The result could be a wholly new and spectacular form of entertainment such as no one had ever before attempted in an elaborate way.

Exhilarated with the idea, Harry, Fran and I went to work editing the film. It took us weeks, during which Chase's skill as a film cutter and his genius at keeping our complicated equipment functioning were about the only encouragement we had to go on. Theatrical producers, already playing to packed houses, weren't interested; studio executives, hearing that the film had been shot in the war zones, shook their heads. Only one, Manny Cohen, head of Pathé News, was intrigued; he offered to buy my German revolution reels, for they were still news—and, nearing the bottom of my bankroll, I agreed. Cohen paid me a modest price and promptly built a reputation by scooping every other newsreel company in the world. Meanwhile I continued pounding the pavements looking for somebody to help me get my show in front of an audience.

Then Harry Chase had an idea. Before the war, his boss, Frank Robison, had done his travelogues in New York under the sponsorship of a newspaper, the *Globe*. Maybe the *Globe* would be ready to take us on. Ready or not, over to the *Globe* I hurried, for I had run out of other possibilities. And Fred B. Taintor, the editor, was interested; he saw our show as a circulation builder. I saw him as a savior. The trouble was, in all Manhattan there was only one theater available, a huge new white elephant of a place called the Century. It was up on Central Park West, well out of the theater district, and in its short life not a single production had ever turned a profit there. Should we try the Century? At this point I was willing to try Hoboken, New Jersey, but I didn't say so. I said, "Yes, sir," and we shook hands on the deal.

We didn't go uptown unarmed. For one thing Taintor gave the show plenty of space in the *Globe*. And when I told him I thought the souvenirs I'd brought home from Germany and the Middle East might be useful for promotion, he contrived to have them installed in the Lord & Taylor display windows on Fifth Avenue, then the most conspicuous showcase in New York. Flanking a Century Theater broadside—"DIRECT FROM JERUSALEM, BERLIN AND PARIS! LOWELL THOMAS! THREE WEEKS ONLY!"— were the Hejaz flag of Emir Feisal and the German flag Kaiser Wilhelm had once placed on the tomb of Saladin, adversary of the Crusaders under Richard Coeur de Lion —remarking with deathless swagger, "From one great emperor to another." Elsewhere, in stark contrast, were the ornate spiked helmets worn by Wilhelm and his palace entourage, and the tawdry ersatz clothing and food the German people had had to make do with toward the end of the war. Nothing like it had been seen in New York before; it was a sensation, the windows drawing such crowds that Lord & Taylor had to keep someone outside to keep them moving.

The Century was nearly sold out for opening night. I was nervous—I always am. But an audience which comes hoping an entertainer will do well is always your ally. When the theater lights dimmed, a swell of exotic Levantine music, chosen by Fran, filled the darkness. Then I stepped into a spotlight and said: "Come with me to lands of history, mystery and romance. What you are about to see is an untold story, part of it as old as time, and part history in the making."

My show was on at last. With only another introductory sentence or two, I stepped back into the shadows and the screen was lit with a sweeping, panoramic picture from the air. I could hear gasps out front and knew I had not been mistaken about the entertainment potential of our film. It was, remember, well before the age of television; even the movies were new and still silent. Yet here were motion pictures of faraway places and gripping events, described by an invisible narrator even as they happened on the screen.

Dr. Frank Crane, one of the best-known clergymen and columnists of his day, was in the audience our first night, and two days later a hundred newspapers carried his reaction:

> I have just seen and heard Lowell Thomas at the Century Theater, New York. I have been told of a flight by airplane (and have seen shown on the screen the airship flying) over the road it took the Children of Israel forty years to travel. I have seen generals in high-powered automobiles scurrying along the road past antique camels, and machine guns on the Mount of Olives. . . . No more amazing military campaign was ever projected and carried to a dashing finish. My head is in a whirl. The past and present have got tangled up.
>
> This is the most smashing picture I ever saw.

Still, we had a few problems, foremost among them our location. It was as though the mile between Times Square and Columbus Circle were an obstacle course few theater-goers dared traverse. The *Globe,* not New York's most potent newspaper, failed to make any overwhelming impression on the ingrained habits of the rest.

And then there was Editor Taintor insisting I put on a different show every night of the week—the A.E.F. in France, the Italian front, the war in the Balkans, Allenby and the Palestine campaign, Lawrence and the Arabs, and the German revolution. The people wanted variety, he said; never mind that editing our material into six separate shows and providing music and narration for each one had taken twenty desperate eighteen-hour days. The outcome? The house was generously spread with empty seats when we did the war in Europe, and only filled up on the night when Jerusalem and Arabia were scheduled. Finally Taintor saw the light and we shelved everything but the Middle East and the German revolution.

One night near the end of our run, limited to three weeks because of another commitment to the Century, I had visitors backstage after the performance. They were Baron Edmond de Rothschild and the Messrs. Jacob Schiff,

Paul and Felix Warburg, and Otto Kahn, with their ladies. At the time, I had no idea who they were, just some distinguished-looking people in evening dress. Editor Taintor did tell me they were the partners of Kuhn, Loeb & Company and among the most influential members of the Jewish world community. But I had never even heard of Kuhn, Loeb!

After congratulating me, Mr. Schiff, the Wall Street patriarch, asked how much it would cost to buy out the entire theater for a performance. I didn't know, but Taintor did: $3,500. Schiff didn't flinch. He simply said we would have his check in the morning; what he wanted was for us to fill up the house. And he promised to send us the people. "Jerusalem is a holy place for Jews as well as Christians," he said quietly. "When General Allenby freed it from the Moslems, he made our dreams come true, too." This wealthy banker simply wanted as many as possible to see it happen.

The two Warburgs at once fell in with Jacob Schiff's idea and promised to send their checks, as well. Otto Kahn begged off, saying he was involved in supporting the Metropolitan Opera. As for me, I hope I had the grace to thank them.

Taintor was so fortified by this vote of confidence that he decided the show must somehow go on after the Century run and went looking for another theater. What he found seemed like another white elephant, Madison Square Garden, then at Madison Avenue and Twenty-sixth Street, even farther from the theater district than the Century. Everything I knew about it warned me away; it was the New York habitat of gaudy spectaculars like Barnum & Bailey and those other traditional American circuses, the Democratic and Republican national conventions. How was *I* going to fill it? And in case I were inclined to read omens, it was also the place where Harry Thaw shot and killed Stanford White, America's most famous architect, for fooling around with his wife, the glamorous Evelyn Nesbit.

But I suppose the reason we don't all live by omens is simply because they don't always come true. As Madison Square Garden was the only place available, we took it, and though the smell of Barnum & Bailey's big show lingered on, we played to capacity audiences for eight weeks. In fact, Taintor had me doing daily matinees.

It was at one of the afternoon shows when I first noticed a man with a fur-trimmed hat in a front-row seat and realized that he had been there for three performances running. Of course I didn't know who he was then, but he later asked to meet me. He was an intense-looking man who wore his hair in ringlets, and he turned out to be a noted philanthropist and the owner of R. H. Macy & Company, largest department store in the world. His name: Nathan Straus.

He had been much taken with our films and account of the liberation of the Holy Land. He thought it deserved the widest notice and proceeded to advertise it as "the most wonderful motion picture production I have ever seen." He did something I now know was incredible. He chartered a fleet of Fifth Avenue's double-decker buses, sent them into Brooklyn and the Bronx, and brought thousands to the Garden—entirely at his own expense!

It was all pretty heady stuff, encouraging me to believe that out there in the great American heartland countless millions, though they did not yet know it, were waiting to hear about Lawrence, Allenby and the fall of Jerusalem. So I began planning a coast-to-coast tour.

Taintor's interest in us stopped at the Hudson River, so I now had to serve as my own manager. And with the big boom in entertainment sweeping the country, I was turned down by every legitimate theater from Philadelphia to Los Angeles—they were booked solid. The only places with any open dates were cavernous opera houses and out-of-the-way auditoriums. I took them all, signing up for dates in Philadelphia, Washington, Chicago, Omaha, Denver and San Francisco, paying out some twenty thousand dollars in deposits. It was quite a gamble, but an American tour seemed my only prospect for keeping us going.

Our coast-to-coast tour was to start in the fall—after the hot weather when theaters reopened. Meanwhile Fran and I were looking forward to a vacation in the cool Colorado mountains. But as it happened, neither a vacation nor a tour was in our immediate future. On the last night of the Madison Square Garden engagement, a stranger came to the dressing room and turned our lives completely around—praise to Allah!

He was Percy Burton, a British impresario, manager of such luminaries as Sarah Bernhardt, Sir Henry Irving and Eleanora Duse. He was in New York scouting new talent and, having heard of something unusual "packing them in" at Madison Square Garden, came downtown to see what it was all about. He was, so he said, "thunderstruck." Here was I, an American, telling of a British hero—Lawrence—of whom he, a Briton, had never before heard. I must come to London, with both my Lawrence and Allenby productions. He would present me.

Although interested, of course, I told him I had already booked an American tour. However, he insisted I had to appear in London right away.

Actually I was as eager as he was, but not knowing how to get out of my commitments short of sacrificing twenty thousand dollars, I told him there would be several impossible conditions. I said I would come only during the summer months—the worst theatrical period of the year—and only if he could book me at one of England's great national institutions, Covent Garden Royal Opera House or the Theatre Royal in Drury Lane. When he didn't blanch, I threw in still another. "Considering the nature of my material, how about under the sponsorship of the King?"

"What do you mean?" he asked.

"I mean how about an invitation from the King?" In saying this I was merely pulling his leg. But he took it seriously, as I was soon to learn.

Then days later, I had a cable saying he had booked Covent Garden and it did include an invitation from King George.

Later, when what seemed a publicist's pipe dream had all miraculously come true, I learned that it had not been all that easy. While the Royal Opera House was indeed to be vacant for what the British call "the dog days of August," the managing director was loath to lease one of the world's most esteemed theaters to a Yankee with a story to tell. And when he finally yielded to Burton's tenacity, Sir Thomas Beecham, the top conductor of his day, who held the lease on Covent Garden, warned Burton, "I say you stand no more chance here than a snowball in the Jordan Valley." Sir Thomas was in attendance for my first appearance and had the good grace to recall his prophecy of doom and apologize for it.

We didn't have much time. A first week in August opening had been set by Burton. Actually I was quite relaxed about going to London, because I didn't see how a brief August engagement was going to profit either of us financially. I did look forward to the experience, and of course a season at London's famous Covent Garden surely would be of value as promotion for our American tour.

There were many things to be resolved at long range: how to advertise the show—never, I cabled Burton, as an "illustrated lecture." I suggested a live prologue, an Oriental dancer and an orchestra. Could Burton arrange this as well as some appropriate scenery? Done! he wired back.

Meanwhile, I was preparing to make a radical change in my presentation. I had always believed my two Allenby and Lawrence productions could be woven together, for both were part of the same story. With Burton's encouragement, I now decided to combine the two. This meant cutting each by about forty-five minutes, with a complete rewrite job to be done during the Atlantic crossing.

Once more I sought out Dale Carnegie. At the time he was launching public-speaking courses in YMCAs around town, still a backcountry young man with a streak of Missouri humor trying to make it in the big city. Dale quickly put aside his own plans and fell in with mine.

I saw little of the sea and not much of Fran during the trip. All day and far into the night, Dale, Chase and I were huddled over our projector and scripts, working under the pressure of an opening less than two weeks off. But by the time we docked in Southampton, we had put together the two parts of a tight, swiftly moving show: *The Last Crusade—With Allenby in Palestine and Lawrence in Arabia.*

Burton had been busy, too. When we got to Covent Garden, the scenery was already in place and it was perfect, the Moonlight on the Nile set from Hilding Rosenberg's opera-oratorio, *Joseph and His Brethren,* loaned to us by Beecham. As for the orchestra, Burton had gone all out, hiring the Royal Welsh Guards Band, at the time one of the best known in the British Empire. One look at those forty stalwarts in their scarlet uniforms and I decided to put them onstage to play for the early arrivals before retiring to the orchestra pit.

And so the night of the opening rushed in on us. Peeping out from the wings into the resplendent opera house, all red plush and glittering crystal, filling now with handsome men and women in formal dress, I was suddenly conscious of how recently I had come down from our Colorado mountains. Then the Welsh Guards moved into the pit and began the overture, and I was swept into the mood of the moment.

The curtain opened on the Nile set, the moon faintly illuminating distant pyramids. Our dancer glided onstage in a brief Oriental dance of the seven veils. Fran had set to music the Mohammedan call to prayer and, from the wings, a lyric tenor sent this haunting, high-pitched melody sailing away to the farthest reaches of the theater. Two minutes later, I stepped into the spotlight and began to speak:

"What you are about to see, the journey you are about to make—all this was intended solely for presentation in America. Until your impresario, Percy Burton, arrived in New York and insisted I come to London, I had never even dreamed you British might be interested in hearing the story of your own Near Eastern campaign and the story of your own heroes told through the nose of a Yankee.

"But here I am, and now come with me to lands of mystery, history and romance."

My Yankee-nose remark, which I had thrown in on the spur of the moment, drew a burst of laughter, and I made a mental note to retain it. Then I stepped away, and as the spotlight went out, the screen came alight and we were on our way, by sea and air, to the eastern Mediterranean.

But surely not any of us, not in our wildest fantasies, have ever conjured up the reaction that came. Afterward, the audience stood and applauded for ten minutes. Next morning, Burton, who had arranged for every notable from the British newspaper world to be invited, came rushing to our hotel with the early editions. And there, not in the theatrical columns, but on the front pages of the *Times,* the *Morning Post* and the *Daily Telegraph,* were reviews full of such ardent tribute as to require even a prudent man to be helped back down to earth. This is what Alder Anderson, the most widely read drama critic in London, wrote in the *Daily Telegraph:*

184

I can conceive of no more invigorating tonic than two hours spent in the company of Lowell Thomas. . . . This illustrated event is a triumphant vindication of the power of moving pictures, accompanied by a spoken story, to charm the eye, entertain the spirit, and move to its very depths the soul of the spectator. Indeed it seems almost a national misfortune that this series of wonderful speaking pictures should ever have to be withdrawn.

Within hours, alert London scalpers had bought up blocks of seats, and soon it was almost impossible to buy tickets at the box office for current performances. When I went down to Covent Garden to check the mail on those first days, I found lines waiting on all four sides of the building. Later, people brought campstools; and throughout the entire run there were queues outside the theater all day, every day, until the box office closed. "They waited," as one observer noted, "through fog and rain, and thousands had to be turned away!"

Burton, who had launched us with a flourish, now went to work capitalizing on the flood of publicity coming our way. He organized special trains to bring people to Covent Garden from the provinces. He plastered posters on the sides of London's big red double-decker buses and doubled our advertising in the evening papers. Alongside an ad for *The Wild Widow,* a highly successful comedy at the Lyric Theatre, he took one twice as big:

WHY IS THE WIDOW WILD?
BECAUSE SHE HASN'T MET LOWELL THOMAS
AND BEEN WITH ALLENBY IN PALESTINE
AND
LAWRENCE IN ARABIA

Well aware that I was an outlander telling a British story to British audiences, I was astonished by the warmth of the people who came to Covent Garden. I couldn't see any faces beyond the first row or two, of course, but any performer will tell you that an audience's reaction is a tangible thing, its appreciation or hostility silently conveyed through the darkened theater and clearly sensed onstage. And each time I appeared, without fail, I felt the flow of enthusiasm from out front.

Each night, too, Burton came to the wings soon after we were under way and at a pause in the narration, when the orchestra took over, he would tell me the names of famous personalities in the audience. Whether he did this to be certain I didn't let down or simply to hearten me, I don't know, but he achieved both ends. One night it was Rudyard Kipling, another George Bernard Shaw; Georges Clemenceau, premier of France, came, and my old friend Emir Feisal with his flowing-robed suite of Arab dignitaries; and then a party from the American embassy headed by Ambassador John W. Davis, the brilliant lawyer who ran for the presidency five years later. Members of the royal family and both houses of Parliament, generals who had fought in the Middle East, theatrical stars, industrial tycoons and the titled elite of Mayfair—they all came, and some asked Burton to escort them to my dressing room afterward. I hope they were not disappointed with the backstage Lowell Thomas. As for Fran and me, meeting this galaxy of the world's great and near-great was still another aspect of the fabulous adventure we were having.

It was all pretty hard to believe. Late one night, heading back to the apartment we'd rented in Albemarle Street, I said to Fran, "Is this really happening to us?"

"I suppose it is," she replied, "since I read about it all the time in the newspapers. But I can't believe it, either."

One evening the Prime Minister came to Covent Garden, he and his party quietly slipping into the royal box after the house lights dimmed. But as we had had advance notice, as soon as he was settled I said to the audience, "Tonight we are fortunate in that we are to make our journey to the Promised Land in the company of a man, who like Moses, never saw it, but was largely responsible for his people getting there. I refer to your great Prime Minister, Mr. David Lloyd George!"

At my signal, the spotlight was thrown on the royal box and the Prime Minister rose, smiling, to acknowledge a standing ovation. After the show, he invited me to his box for a chat. I was impressed by this magnetic statesman who had led the British nation to victory in what until then was the greatest of all wars. With him was a young cabinet minister—his name, Winston Churchill—who was among those within the government who understood the importance of Lawrence's contribution; and he congratulated me for making it known to the world.

In response to a newsman's question, Lloyd George made a very generous statement about the show: "Everything that Mr. Lowell Thomas tells us about Colonel Lawrence is true. In my opinion, Lawrence is one of the most remarkable and romantic figures of modern times."

The result was a flood of publicity and still more plaudits from the press. Wrote *Lloyd's Weekly News:* "Many things contrive to get themselves overpassed. For once let the praise ring true. For two hours great audiences sit never moving; such is the enthrallment of the pictures they see and the thrilling story they hear."

The *Strand* magazine called it "the greatest romance of real life ever told." *The Manchester Guardian:* "It is history without dogma, without dullness, and filled with adventure and beauty." *Punch:* "Those who have heard the young American are full of admiration of the manner in which he handles his subject. Certainly it is a most entrancing one, but in the hands of an indifferent speaker much of the charm would be missing."

When three or four weeks sped by with no letup in demand for tickets, Burton asked what my plans were. He said it must be clear to me that something extraordinary was happening, and I could probably continue the London run indefinitely. Did I, in the face of such a happy prospect, still intend to return to New York at the end of August for our American tour?

It was a question I had been pondering ever since I first realized what was happening to us. Obviously I wanted to stay. But it takes a special sort of effrontery to sit down and voluntarily divest yourself of a small fortune, and, until Burton put it directly to me, I wasn't sure I could do it. But I did. That same day, I sent cables to each of the dozen or so theaters I'd rented telling how I would be obliged to cancel our tour of the United States. With those words, I forfeited those twenty thousand in deposits.

Once it was done, I didn't give it a thought; I had every chance to make twenty times twenty thousand in England. But there were complications. The Shubert brothers, those irascible theater managers from whom I'd booked the Hammerstein Opera House in Philadelphia and the Shubert Theater in Washington, decided to play it rough. They insisted I reimburse them in full for the rentals, no doubt calculating I'd pay up rather than interrupt my London run. Not knowing what to do, I did nothing; I still had some time to worry that one around.

One morning there was a note from Lawrence in the mail:

Dear L.T.:
   I saw your show last night and thank God the lights were out!

                                                        T.E.L.

A day or so later he came around for tea. With a wry smile that may have been intended to deny his words, or to emphasize them, he begged me to call off the London run, to pack up and go home. He said I was making life impossible for him. Whenever he ventured out on the streets, he was stopped by strangers, then swiftly surrounded by a crowd. His mail had become a nightmare, as many as a hundred letters a day, many from women proposing marriage and other, less formal couplings. "And it's all your doing," he said, again hiding his true feelings behind his smile.

When I told him I had just canceled an American tour to sign a long-term contract with Burton, and how painful it would be if I had to break it, Lawrence shrugged and smiled. Neither Fran nor I could decide if he was serious. He said the only way out now was for him to leave London, but there is some reason to believe he had already made such arrangements. In any event, he soon went up to Oxford, where he accepted a fellowship at All Souls College. There, still plagued by idolators and the merely curious, he retreated behind a work schedule he would follow for much of the rest of his short life, sleeping by day, writing all night and going out only when it was absolutely necessary.

Two things finally convinced me he had forgiven me for the part I played in turning him into a celebrity: first, we continued to see each other from time to time, although I always had the feeling that each visit might be the last; and second, his mother telephoned during our last week at Covent Garden and said she would like to meet us.

We invited her to tea at Albemarle Street. She was an

attractive, gray-haired lady whose Scottish reserve made it hard to imagine the tempestuous love affair with Sir Thomas Chapman that produced five illegitimate children. She was obviously filled with maternal pride for her son, whom she called Ned, and thanked me for bringing the story of his achievements to the public notice. We chatted about his boyhood—her reminiscences were not unlike those of any doting mother—and later corresponded for some years.

The engagement at Covent Garden, originally scheduled for two weeks, ran through the summer and into the autumn. Sir Thomas Beecham, our landlord, was sharing in the proceeds and kept his opera company on tour longer than originally intended, as day after day the great opera house was sold out. I presume I knew eventually he would have to bring the opera back to London, but I let Burton do the worrying while I threw myself into each performance, six evenings and two matinees every week, as though it were my last. Any one of them might well have been.

People continued coming backstage every evening. Eventually I began to feel the strain. Once, Sir Johnston Forbes-Robertson, England's most renowned Shakespearean actor, told me the role of Hamlet, which he considered the most demanding, did not call forth such effort as I expended at each appearance, alone on stage for two hours.

And finally it laid me low. One evening, the bright beam of the projector seemed to dance crazily in my eyes and, as I sagged back toward the wings, it vanished in a frightening darkness. Luckily Burton was on hand. He produced a bit of brandy that brought me around with only a brief interruption of the show, and somehow I got through the rest of the performance. Meanwhile, Burton and Fran, thoroughly alarmed, had rounded up London's leading heart specialist, who examined me in the dressing room and again the next morning at his office.

"I find nothing physically wrong," he finally said, "but from what I've heard of the pace you've set for yourself, I must tell you that you may well be dead of exhaustion in a very short time."

I asked what he recommended.

"Take your wife on a three-month holiday, and start this afternoon."

"But, Doctor, I can't give this up—it's the opportunity of a lifetime."

In reply he said: "I was sure you'd say something like that. Very well, then, here's your alternative: do your shows, if you must, but remain in bed all the rest of the time."

"During the day?"

"Around the clock!"

He then prescribed a diet consisting largely of raw eggs and sent me off to try adjusting to a strange new life, half invalid, half theatrical athlete. To make it easier, Fran and I gave up our Albemarle Street flat next door to Rudyard Kipling and moved out of London to the edge of Wimbledon Common. A Daimler limousine, just like the royal family's, chauffeured us back and forth. It was a graphic reminder of the affluence within my reach and, as such, maybe a help in keeping me to my stiff regimen; I certainly did not want to die just then.

Early in October, Allenby, who stayed on in the Middle East as High Commissioner for Egypt, returned to England for the first time since the end of the war. A few days later, he and Lady Allenby sent word they would attend a matinee at Covent Garden. The result was pandemonium in the streets. Naturally, Burton had let the newspapers know about the popular Field Marshal's impending visit; it was to be one of his few appearances. The pent-up eagerness of Londoners to catch even a glimpse of the Great Crusader was so intense that hours before his arrival every approach to Covent Garden was jammed with thousands of people, thronging the streets and blocking traffic all the way to the Strand.

Inside the Royal Opera, Fran had banked two first-tier boxes with roses, and every head in the packed house was turned in their direction when Lord and Lady Allenby entered. As the audience gave them an ovation, the Welsh Guards played "Hail to the Conquering Hero," which I later heard had much displeased the general from "Megiddo and Armageddon." However, he didn't indicate this to Fran and me.

Again there was a burst of notices and feature articles in the press. Burton, who had managed the great stars of his time in a long theatrical career and was not easily impressed, said he believed we could play the Royal Opera House successfully for the next five years. But Beecham and his company were due at Covent Garden in another week, so where could we go?

Burton had not been idle. Though every legitimate theater in the West End was booked in those postwar days, he had come up with a bold idea. How about huge Royal Albert Hall in Kensington? At the time this was said to be the largest concert auditorium in the world, with a seating capacity of over six thousand; it was used for exhibitions, major sports events and the single performances of great orchestras and choral groups; no one had ever attempted an extended engagement there. Said Burton: "Let's give it a try."

We did, playing to as many as ten thousand people a day. But we did have problems for which there appeared to be neither preventions nor cures. London was then famous—if that is the word—for its midwinter fog, a fog so dense it could even creep right inside a building. And this is precisely what it did at the vast, domed Royal Albert Hall, sometimes filling it with a haze that made it seem as though Allenby and Lawrence had driven the Turks from the Holy Land through a dense smokescreen.

I had also been cautioned about certain acoustical problems and was advised always to address myself to the Prince of Wales's box. Nor did this entirely solve the problem. One night a major who had been sitting in the center of the main floor came around and insisted on shaking hands with me three times because, said he, "I heard every ruddy thing you said three times."

When Lawrence discovered we had moved to Wimbledon Common, he turned up late one Sunday morning, unannounced and unexpected. A friend had loaned him a small hideaway apartment in Westminster and he had walked all the way, some twelve miles. Fran and I were delighted to see him and engulfed him with questions. Patiently he sorted them out and brought us up to date on his life. He was writing an account of his wartime experiences, although he assured us his book would not be published in his lifetime. He continued to work at night and sleep during the day, interrupting this routine only for occasional trips back to Oxford for research.

Doctor's orders to the contrary notwithstanding, Fran did not begrudge me the long, late, fascinating talk that followed, and Lawrence came frequently after that. We would discuss the aftermath of the war in the Middle East and his obvious frustration. He had attended the Paris peace conference as a member of the British delegation, with Emir Feisal—usually in Arab garb. Perhaps he was a forerunner of the anti-hero widely celebrated in today's literature. "Glory is, or should be, out of date," he said, "and the only hero of action we can endure in this age is the one who will himself take responsibility for the meaning of what he does in the public domain."

But despite his efforts, he was unable to deflect the tortuous maneuverings that were to divide the nations of the Near and Middle East and relegate their separate parts to dependency on the great powers. Blaming himself for having made promises to be broken as soon as the shooting stopped, after returning to England, he said, he expected never to return to the East, not even as an archaeologist, where he was sure he would again be drawn into Near East politics. For this he felt he no longer had anything to contribute.

Only afterward did I wonder if I might have missed an opportunity to do something for him. Suppose I had offered to back him in an expedition to, say, Central or South America, to study the Mayan civilization, or the pre-Inca cities of the Andes? It didn't matter where, and at the time I had the money. Would he have accepted? Would it have changed the headlong course of his life downhill to disillusion and early death? Probably he would have refused, already irrevocably committed to his particular destiny. Even so, it is one of the moments of my life I wish I had back, to do differently.

It was on an early morning visit to Wimbledon Common when, quite casually, Lawrence told us how he had lost the completed manuscript of his book on the Arab revolt. He had been carrying it up to Oxford in a briefcase, which he put down on the station platform while he went for a newspaper. When he returned, the briefcase was gone.

"What will you do?" I asked, appalled. "Have you gone to the police?"

He shrugged. "There is nothing to do. Whoever took it will have been disappointed to find nothing more valuable inside than several hundred pages of my scrawlings, and I suspect the whole lot has long since been chucked into the Thames."

Would he start all over again, then?

He said he hadn't thought about it yet. "My instinctive reaction was one of relief—it was all a great burden, you know—and I'm still rather enjoying that."

To history's great gain, he eventually did rewrite it, not once, but twice, himself destroying the second effort because he was dissatisfied with it. *Seven Pillars of Wisdom,* a literary masterwork and classic account of war in the desert, was issued privately in 1926, then published in a general trade edition after Lawrence's death. It has never gone out of print since.

It is almost impossible to convey the curiosity of the British public with this newfound and still mysterious demigod during those postwar years. All through our London season, publishers kept after me to write something about him, a magazine article, a book, anything. Sometimes I told Lawrence of these offers and he assured me he had no objection. But at the time I had neither the time nor the energy for such an undertaking, nor had I yet properly sorted out my impressions. In some ways, I came to know Lawrence best during those Wimbledon visits, but the essential core of him, his innermost force, still remains an enigma to me.

And to all the world. This, I believe, is how he wanted it. In his lifetime, he was called tough, compassionate, solemn, impish, secretive, outgoing, pro-Arab, pro-Zionist, a patriot, a foe of the established order—and I had known him to be all these things. But he never tried to sort out the contradictions for anyone, never seemed to care what others said, never made even the slightest effort to clarify his nature. Once I asked him to verify an anecdote I'd heard from someone who had known him in Cairo. He laughed and said, "Use it if it suits your needs. What difference does it make if it's true—history is seldom true."

Knowing history would render its inevitable judgment of him, he steadfastly refused to make his own case. "When I am dead they will rattle my bones with their curiosity," he said, and as with so many of his prophecies, this one has been abundantly confirmed.

To this day, more than half a century later, scarcely a month passes when I do not have a letter from an editor asking me to do an article or another book on Lawrence, or from someone seeking information about him. Scholars still comb through obscure archives hoping to find new facts, a clue to his personality. Around the world, people still want to know, "What was he *really* like?"—and there has been no shortage of those willing to tell them, or attempt to do so.

Where does all this leave us today? Some new information has come to light since the publication of *With Lawrence in Arabia,* the first book written about him, and many interpretations have been offered, some of them belittling and even demeaning. But none of the later books, or the hundreds of treatises and popular articles—and certainly not the distorted motion picture about him—has given me any reason to revise my opinion. He was a wonder and a rarity, true to himself to the end, one of history's last romantic heroes. I stand with Churchill, Liddell Hart, Bernard Shaw, Toynbee, Robert Graves, Gertrude Bell, Allenby and Wavell—all of whom ranked Lawrence with the great men of the century. I stand with John Buchan, the reserved Victorian statesman-scholar who wrote in his autobiography, "I do not profess to have understood T. E. Lawrence, but I could have followed him over the edge of the world."

After I left London, we corresponded. He once told me how he tossed away most of his mail unopened, yet whenever I wrote to him he responded. And so I knew when— but not why—he enlisted in the Royal Air Force under the name of Ross, obtaining a discharge a few months later when a newspaper learned his secret and gave it out. Soon, though, he reenlisted, this time as T. E. Shaw, still trying to lose himself in the anonymity of the military, still despairing of ever being left alone.

From his cottage at Clouds Hill in Dorset he used to blast around the winding country roads on his powerful motorcycle, "The Blue Mist," named for the Rolls armored car he used in Arabia. And on a spring afternoon in 1935, overtaking some children on the road, he wrenched his wheel to one side to avoid hitting them and crashed. Six days later, he died of his injuries.

Scanning through my old radio scripts recently, I came across the broadcasts in which I broke the news in America.

May 14. A profoundly tragic story has to be told tonight. It's about the serious accident to Lawrence of

Arabia that happened late yesterday in England when he crashed his motorbike . . .

May 20. Colonel Lawrence, Lawrence of Arabia, is dead. He put in most of the last fifteen years of his life trying to avoid fame. And now England wants to bury him in Westminster Abbey, Britain's hall of fame.

Later, a Lawrence crypt was placed in St. Paul's Cathedral.

While we were still playing to full houses at Albert Hall, I ran afoul of a veteran Wardour Street movie tycoon, Sir William Jury, who had fought the war in the British Department of Information, and I wound up broke. Sir William—not the title I would have given him—discovered, as I had never realized, that I was using a few hundred feet of War Office film. As a result, Jury managed to extract from me most of my share of the box office receipts. Not wanting to become involved in a legal battle—I hadn't the time for it, nor did I want to appear the Ugly American and cast a pall over what was one of the most exhilarating experiences of my life—I paid, and never regretted the decision. Later, when I could look back on the episode from the perspective of the years between, I concluded that Sir William Jury had actually done me a good turn.

Life, after all, is a game of high stakes. Surviving, bouncing back, gambling again with what talents you have—isn't it what the game of life is about? The great danger is hitting the jackpot when you are young, as I did, and coming to believe this is all there is to it. You age complacently. You sit on your jackpot, living from it, living *for* it. Then when you lose—and we must all lose sometimes—the blow can be fatal; you haven't the strength or the will to bounce back. Sir William saved me from such a fate.

Early in the new year, 1920, having played the cavernous Albert Hall for more than two months, we found a more manageable theater, Queen's Hall, near the center of London, and moved again. While there, Burton, following an inscrutable calculation understood only by publicists, announced to the press that I was about to present *The*

195

Last Crusade to our one millionth patron. Naturally he had reporters and photographers on hand for the historic occasion, and by—ahem—great good luck, Number One Million turned out to be a highly photogenic Anglican prelate, the Bishop of Gloucester, complete with silk topper and a most benign smile. When I congratulated Burton on all the press coverage he'd contrived out of it, he replied, "We'd have done even better with a good-looking blonde, but His Lordship was the best I could manage."

Finally, the fabulous London run had to come to an end. For one thing, we had signed to tour Scotland, Wales and the rest of England; for another, the menace of the Shubert brothers hung like a cloud over my head. But we certainly went out in a blaze of glory. Earlier, I had had what the British consider the ultimate accolade, a command performance—I was invited to appear before King George and Queen Mary at Balmoral Castle. But a miserably timed railroad strike made this impossible, so now the King and Queen came to the theater and, following the show, invited Fran and me to the royal box. I am afraid I was somewhat intimidated by Queen Mary's celebrated hauteur; if I said anything beyond, "Good evening, Your Majesties," I have forgotten what it was.

And finally, Burton arranged a banquet in my honor to be given by the press barons of England—John Jacob Astor, owner of the *Times;* Lords Rothermere, Northcliffe and Beaverbrook; with Viscount Burnham of the *Daily Telegraph* in the role of toastmaster. It was an elegant occasion, a glittering company of hundreds in the prestigious Criterion Restaurant atop Piccadilly Circus, and for a young maverick from the gold camps, slightly head-turning. Immodestly, I made a few notes of Lord Burnham's talk. He said he believed I had seen more of the World War than any other single person. He said I was "a great artist, a ripe scholar, a brave man and a true friend," and that "Lowell Thomas has almost created a new art." In rising to express my appreciation, I no doubt failed to measure up to his eloquence.

Back in the real world, I came to a decision about the Shuberts, who remained unwilling to release me from the Washington and Philadelphia dates although I had given them eight months' notice. Rather than meekly pay up the full rental, which is what they were expecting me to do, I would make a quick trip back to the States, fill the two engagements and be back in time for the tour of Britain.

As soon as we docked in New York, I dispatched Fran to a hotel and went directly to the Shubert office. Presiding over it was Jules Murray, who looked somewhat like Dickens's Scrooge, and who greeted me with, "What is this 'Allenby-in-Palestine — Lawrence-in-Arabia' thing — some new version of the Passion Play?" When I told him, he harrumphed and said maybe we'd do a 25-percent business in Washington. In one of life's more bizarre coincidences, Murray later became a patient of my father, who found him a charming and most agreeable gentleman. To fall back on a battered but serviceable truism, there is no accounting for tastes.

Anyway, we not only played to capacity in Washington, but the fire authorities looked the other way so we could seat people in aisles. "Lowell Thomas has created a sensation in Washington," said the *Times*. "It is entrancing entertainment." Not since Drinkwater's *Abraham Lincoln*, reported the manager after our two-week run, had the old Shubert Theater done such business. In Philadelphia, playing the huge and badly located Hammerstein Opera House, we did almost as well. And by the first days of spring, Fran and I were happily bound back to England.

The tour was a succession of crises and disasters redeemed only by the fact that we played to sellout crowds. In Liverpool, the theater was dreary and the hotel next door worse. In Glasgow, the whole house was bought out one day by the men of the 52nd Scottish Lowland Division, all veterans of the Palestine campaign. And all apparently stopped en route to refresh themselves in the pubs along Sauchiehall Street, with the result that long before I had the Turks out of the Holy Land I had a free-for-all in the main aisle. And then, in Usher Hall, Edinburgh, I lost my voice.

After frantically consulting with the learned professors in that renowned center of the medical arts, I was prescribed a remedy called Friar's Balsam that dated back to the Middle Ages. For three days I sat immobile in a hotel room, a towel over my head, inhaling the fumes from a kettle of boiling water liberally laced with balsam gum. On the fourth day my voice came back.

When our peregrinations were almost over, a cable from

the Prime Minister of Australia caught up with us. We were invited to present our show there, and in New Zealand, as guests of the Commonwealth government.

I handed the cable over to Fran and sat staring at the ceiling for a long time. Our plan had been to return home and finally take up the long postponed American tour. Financially, it was far the more sensible thing to do—Australia and New Zealand hadn't a tenth the population of the United States.

"What do you think?" I asked Fran.

"Well, it's another corner of the world," she replied. "And it's been a long time since we had an invitation from a Prime Minister."

I smiled happily. "I like the way you think," I said.

And we went out to cable our acceptance.

9.

East of Suez

If you've 'eard the East a-callin',
you don't never 'eed naught else . . .
—RUDYARD KIPLING

EVEN before the great voyages of discovery, some European geographers theorized there must be a continent beneath the Tropic of Capricorn, their argument being that the earth would be "unbalanced" without a substantial land-mass in the Southern Hemisphere. They even put it on their maps: *Terra Australis Incognita*. Had they been wrong, their theory would be remembered, if at all, as another of history's old wives' tales. But they were right—Australia was there.

And this was still nearly everything most people knew about it when the twentieth century was young. I considered myself somewhat better prepared for our journey; not only was I aware Australia was a land of oddities—the kangaroo, the koala, the boomerang—but I had actually read about it. During my Cripple Creek days, someone, surely not my father, had given me a copy of *Robbery Under Arms: A Story of Life and Adventure in the Gold Fields of Australia*, a rousing tale of derring-do by a transplanted Englishman, T. A. Browne, who called himself Rolf Boldrewood; and surreptitiously I also had devoured a series of lurid thrillers about the bushmen, by Bracebridge Heming. So I knew about cobbers, bushrangers, sheep stations and billabongs in the Outback. It was only the rest of the three-million-square-mile *terra incognita*—its people, cities, cul-

199

ture, government, history and economy—that I needed to learn something about. I looked forward to it, and so did Fran.

In the rush of preparations before we set sail, I made some rather important decisions and could only hope they would turn out well. At Burton's suggestion, I had our film duplicated and cabled Dale Carnegie an offer to return to England and organize two road companies of the Allenby-Lawrence show, he to coach my substitutes and act as manager. He promptly joined us, and in those hectic last days we tried to pull all the pieces together. At the same time, I was mulling an invitation to tour Singapore, Malaya and India when our Australian visit was over; with no way of knowing what our physical or financial state might be then, I accepted.

Finally, on a rainy morning in April our cumbersome equipment stowed aboard a faithful old steamer of the legendary Pacific & Orient line, Fran, Harry and I stood at the rail—a secretary ashore still taking dictation from me—and waved good-bye to Dale as we slipped away from Tilbury Dock and started down the Thames. I remember thinking he looked a little overwhelmed by the rush of events.

I suppose I should have felt the same. We were in for a six weeks' sea voyage, bound for a strange land half a world away, without any graspable idea of where we were to play or under what circumstances, or when we might be back. But the fact is both Fran and I were entirely delighted with the prospect, Chase poker-faced and silent as usual. It was another adventure; we were young and unburdened by any of the conventional cares—and should we run into trouble, we carried a courtly and comforting letter, broadly addressed to the American diplomatic and consular corps:

Embassy of the United States
London, April 20, 1920

Gentlemen:

I beg to command to you, by this means, Mr. Lowell Thomas who has attained considerable distinction with his "With Allenby in Palestine and Lawrence in Arabia." He is now proceeding to Australia at the instance of the government of the Australian Commonwealth.

I bespeak for him all facilities and courtesies which you may render consistently with your official duties.

I am, gentlemen,

Your Obedient Servant,
John W. Davis
Ambassador

It was a memorable journey, marked by new sights and experiences, and punctuated by tragedy. Our route took us through the Suez Canal into the Red Sea, then out in the Indian Ocean. We were headed toward Cocos-Keeling, two curving coral atolls of lovely isles almost a thousand miles south of the equator. There we heaved a barrel of mail over the side for the bronzed stalwarts who had put out to meet us in their outriggers. They were among the descendants of a mixed bag of immigrants, a company who contributed as gaudy a page as you'll find in the tumultuous annals of the South Seas.

A Scottish seafarer named John Clunies Ross, having once gazed on this island paradise and longing for surcease from the pressures of the early nineteenth century, in 1827 sailed with his family and a few like-minded Scots to make a new life there. Alas, someone had beaten him to it, the someone being Alexander Hare, an untamed Englishman who had made a fortune in the spice trade and spent most of it acquiring a harem of lovelies in the East Indian slave markets. These he brought to Cocos-Keeling, prepared to live happily ever after while his forty collector's items shook down coconuts from the palms and otherwise saw to his needs and amusement.

Aggrieved but not discouraged, Ross ran the Union Jack up on an isle within wading distance of Hare's harem and waited for nature to take its course. He didn't have long to wait. The brawny Scots and sleek East Indian sailors proved to be irresistibly appealing to the beautiful young slave girls, who soon defected by two's and three's across the shallow lagoon. Poor old Hare, owning up to the inevitable, soon abandoned the unequal contest and returned to Borneo, perhaps to rebuild his collection. And the girls he left behind became the maternal forebears of the some seven hundred people who now happily inhabit Cocos-Keeling. As for Ross, he finally found the peace he sought; he also established a dynasty that through five generations and down to the present day continues to rule benignly

201

the islands under Australian administration, its tenure endorsed by Queen Victoria in 1886 with a grant in perpetuity.

As we turned south and resumed speed, we came in sight of the German cruiser *Emden,* chased up on a reef at the beginning of World War I and still moldering there. From the outbreak of hostilities until a fateful November day some three months later, she had been a phenomenally successful raider, wreaking havoc on Britain's Pacific trade; in one incredible four-day stretch, she captured six ships, sinking five and imprisoning all their crews on the sixth. Then the Australian cruiser *Sydney,* alerted by a radio message from Cocos-Keeling, caught the *Emden* at anchor. Ironically, her captain had just sent a party ashore to destroy the wireless relay station. In a running battle, broadside for broadside, the *Sydney* drove the German raider up on the reef in flames and captured the entire crew. It must certainly have been the most exciting thing to happen in these tranquil islands since Alexander Hare left.

The war and its cost would soon be borne in on us again. A few days out of Perth, our first stop in Australia, the captain staged a costume party. It was a gay affair, enhanced by a soft moonlit night that encouraged dancing on the decks. But suddenly a chill cry—"Man overboard!"—shattered the gaiety and make-believe. As the ship reverberated under the stress of reversed engines, then began circling, the sad tale circulated among the passengers. On board was a group of Anzac veterans, so badly wounded that only now were they able to return home. One, blinded and despondent, finally unable to face his family, had confided in a comrade and then, before he could be stopped, gone over the rail.

We circled for hours, in vain.

There was bad news waiting for us when we docked at Melbourne—a cable from London reporting that the Allenby-Lawrence road companies had folded; poor Dale Carnegie had suffered a nervous breakdown over it. The details were filled in later—how Dale had hired thoroughly able people to do the narration and had trained them well, but the show had been so personally identified with me in the British public mind as to defy substitution. In the meantime, we had lost a good deal of money and poor

202

Dale was sick, blaming himself. There wasn't a thing in the world I could do about it at a range of ten thousand miles except to cable him my absolute confidence that he had done all anyone could expect. Once I sent this off, I put the loss out of my mind and we prepared to enjoy Australia.

This was easily done. We were welcomed with a dinner at Government House given by Prime Minister Billy Hughes, to which he had invited his cabinet, and there I made my opening appearance in Australia before a special session of the Commonwealth Parliament. Wrote the Melbourne *Graphic:*

> The interest taken by the advent of Lowell Thomas to Melbourne is indicated by the fact that welcomes and receptions to the distinguished traveler, explorer, war correspondent and his wife are being arranged on every side. In official quarters, his visit is regarded with the highest significance.

With such sponsorship, I could hardly fail; we played to full houses in Melbourne and in the cavernous Sydney Town Hall, which in those days had hopeless acoustics. I found Australian audiences extremely cordial but somewhat more outspoken than their reserved English cousins. One night, having gone through my by now well-polished line about being surprised to find that Australians would want to hear the Near East war story "through the nose of a Yankee," a voice from the balcony boomed out. "That's quite all right, old boy; just don't try to sell us your Yankee Prohibition." It got the best laugh of the evening.

In September we sailed off for a two-month engagement in New Zealand, returning to conclude the Australian tour with a run in Adelaide and an encore in Melbourne. It was during this second time around that I was saluted for the first time with something less than a rave notice. It appeared in a Sydney magazine of comment and satire called *The Bulletin*, and some of the remarks were close enough to target to make me wince, a not unnatural reaction as I was perhaps beginning to take the paeans of praise a bit too seriously. Anyway—given the calming effect produced by the passage of half a century—it now ranks among my favorite reviews.

A tremendous house heard Lowell Thomas through his first "talk" at the Royal on Saturday. Braziers burning incense and a shadowy water-carrier passing to slow music before the opening vista of palms created a temporary Oriental atmosphere which was quickly dissipated by the blinding spotlight hunting for the figure of the leading man. However, he soon came forward in dapper waiter's garments that seemed a little shy of his boot-tops, and poured out his talk with an occasional well-groomed jest to prevent the populace brooding unduly on his nasal inflections. The Yank's sense of humor, however, is not very alarming, while his crisp and easy narrative is mixed up with topographical sundries, scriptural references and Cook's tourist matter. The lecture is illustrated with lantern slides and cinema films. The films are good.

There were other Australian notices lavish enough to soothe my ruffled ego, but the one I appreciated most was about Harry Chase. A journalist with the perception to inquire about the technical side of our operation came away with quite a story.

Mr. Lowell Thomas has a silent partner in his projection box who must be nothing less than a wizard. One has merely to be whisked off on a magic carpet of their perfectly synchronized pictures and spoken narrative to believe Mr. Thomas when he says that his operator, Mr. Harry A. Chase, is the world's foremost projection engineer.

Mr. Chase was the first man in America to operate a cinema machine. Those used at the Theatre Royal are largely his own invention. The dissolving effects are his exclusive idea. He operates three different machines simultaneously and makes some thirty different movements per minute in order to "strike" all three arcs and, at the same time, dissolve his scenes and adjust his three machines.

All of which wasn't the half of it. He was also a cameraman with the insights of an artist. Eventually Harry and I would travel a quarter of a million miles together, but he alone had to see to the disassembly, crating and transport of our half ton of equipment, collapsible booths of sheet

204

metal—also of his design—to hold the huge carbon arc projectors and highly flammable nitrate film stock.

He had begun in the days when film ran through the projector and collected in a basket on the floor, to be rewound by hand. He fixed that. Now, even in an armory, he could fill the largest screen with a brilliant picture, a not inconsiderable factor in our success. He could also grind his own lenses, take his cameras to pieces after a desert sandstorm and banish the last particle of dust before putting them back together. Then he would unscrew the back of your watch and do the same thing—never complaining, rarely speaking, but forever there when you needed him. He has been dead fifty years now and I still miss him.

Quite by chance, something happened to me in Australia that had nothing to do with the show but was to play a part in my life—sometimes, I think, to blight it—ever after. Sir John Monash, commander in chief of all Australian armed forces in World War I, gave a luncheon for us at Menzies. It seemed strange indeed that Australia's foremost military leader in combat with the Kaiser should be a German Jew. Across the table from me sat Ivo Whitten, a former amateur golf champion, who invited me to play a round. It was my first. In those early 1920s, golf was still an esoteric pastime, indulged in by gentlemen of means, and only its built-in aggravations have remained the same.

Aspects of it puzzled me—and still do. In the foursome ahead, I noticed a player who spent most of his time in the rough. Later, in the clubhouse, he told of losing a dozen golf balls. The unhappy duffer was Cyril Maude, one of the most famous actors of his time.

While we were down under, the world's imagination was caught by the excitement of the London-to-Melbourne air race. It was a time when daring aviation exploits were much in the news: Alcock and Brown had recently won the twenty thousand pounds offered by Lord Northcliffe for the first nonstop flight across the Atlantic; now the Commonwealth government put up a similar prize for the first airmen to fly from England to Australia and make it in under thirty days. There were many competitors—four of whom were killed "throwing dice with death," as *The New York Times* put it.

The prize was taken by a four-man crew headed by Captain Ross Smith, who had flown for Allenby in Palestine and whom I had known. Flying a Vickers Vimy—whose identification letters, G-EAOU, said Smith, stood for "God 'Elp All of Us"—the brave foursome spanned half the world in twenty-eight days, surviving wind, rain, sandstorms, and in Persia irate Moslems intent on destroying their plane because nowhere were such huge birds mentioned in the Koran.

Fran and I were on hand to greet them when they landed in Melbourne and when the pilot was told he was henceforth to be known as Sir Ross Smith. Already in the thrall of anything to do with airplanes, I persuaded Ross to return and tell his story to British audiences, as I had told mine; it couldn't miss! Some film had been shot on the flight, and it took only a cable to Dale Carnegie to arrange for the two to meet and prepare a script for an illustrated show, I to put up the money.

Alas, my crystal ball was clouded again, my gifts as an impresario definitely flawed. Though Sir Ross did run for some weeks at London's Philharmonic Hall, we lost quite a few quid, as the cockneys put it; Dale again returned home in a nervous state, and I resolved to temper my enthusiasms in the future. As for the Smith brothers, Ross and Keith, King George had knighted both, and soon they began preparing for a flight all the way around the world. One day, testing his new Vimy, Sir Ross went into a spin from which there was no pulling out; he was killed in the crash, at his brother's feet.

The *Times* of Melbourne in a farewell salute said: "Lowell Thomas has made a success not only as an entertainer but also as an ambassador. He has added considerably to the popularity of the Americans." We sailed away vowing to come back—which we were to do, many times. Now we were bound for Singapore, hustling, polyglot, international crossroads of the South China Sea, first stop on our tour of the Malay Peninsula and India.

It particularly fascinated me, mainly because Sir Thomas Stamford Raffles, the audacious Englishman who won Singapore for his King and the East India Company, has always ranked in my imagination with the likes of Marco Polo and Clive of India. Arriving in 1819, accurately noting the ancient and half-forgotten city was "of much higher value than whole continents of territory," he built a new metropolis on the ruins of the old and made it the flourishing commercial center of southern Asia.

Early in 1921, when we landed at the "Lion City," it was a bastion of the British Empire, the Gibraltar of the Pacific. And despite the whirlwinds of time, the memory of Raffles was everywhere—the Raffles Hotel, the Raffles Museum, Raffles Square with a statue of the legendary proconsul himself brooding down on the teeming populace. The waterfront was an ever-changing panorama of ocean liners, tramp steamers, Chinese junks and sampans by the thousands.

We were booked into the Victoria Theatre where, among the largely British audiences, we could always count on a generous sprinkling of wealthy Malays and Chinese, Europeans in transit, American representatives of Standard Oil, General Motors and the Guggenheims, and a broad spectrum of missionaries. Some of these—not the missionaries—we also ran into at the far-famed Raffles bar, seemingly a mandatory stop in Singapore, like Customs and Immigration. There one could find Frank Buck matching stingers with anyone who mounted the next barstool.

The Sultan of Jahore was usually with him. Frank Buck must have left the Raffles now and then, for he had built quite a reputation for providing any animal found in the Malay jungle to any zoo in the world. Later, of course, he wrote the immensely popular account of his adventures, *Bring 'Em Back Alive*.

One day Madame Ernestine Schumann-Heink, the celebrated opera contralto, came sweeping into the Raffles. She was a person of awesome proportions and august presence. I had interviewed her several times in Chicago, so I reintroduced myself. She probably didn't remember me, for she had been busy shedding her third husband at the time and the divorce, a stormy one, attracted many other reporters. But she insisted she did and clamped me to her voluminous bosom. Then, to establish that there was nothing personal about it, she did the same to Fran.

The great diva was also on tour, and we became friendly during her stay in Singapore. When Fran and I learned her sixtieth birthday was approaching, we arranged a luncheon for her. Afterward, in her rich German accent, she announced a birthday wish to see the Chinese quarter, opium dens and all, so off we all went.

It was quite a procession. Schumann-Heink was so amply

endowed that she filled a double rickshaw; behind came Fran and I, Fran clutching an American flag in which Madame had wrapped all her jewelry, entrusting it to our care while we toured Singapore's sin section. Five or six other rickshaws carrying the rest of the guests followed, but it was the altogether imposing figure of the renowned contralto that stopped traffic.

Burton Holmes, in the early decades of this century, was our most sophisticated and widely known globetrotter. One day in Paris, when we were having coffee together at the Café de la Paix, he told me how, if you sat there long enough at this favorite sidewalk table, you would see everyone in the world of any "importance." In his "travelogues" (he coined the word) "B.H." gave much publicity to the corner table at this Place de l'Opéra café. Eventually the owners shipped it to him, and years later there it was in his museum-like home atop one of the Hollywood hills.

The same was true of Singapore. Sooner or later all travelers visit the crossroads of Asia founded by Sir Stamford Raffles. When we were there one of the all-time great violin artists, Mischa Elman, was thrilling the island audiences; and he too helped us celebrate Madame Schumann-Heink's birthday.

We really got the flavor of the city's nether reaches. British sailors seeking escape, and Chinese merchants trying to sell it to them, crowded the narrow, noisy streets. Sidewalk peddlers hawked drugs, black-market money, gold and silk —and anything else that men come by in shadowy ways. In an opium den we watched skeleton-gaunt Chinese rolling their pills, lighting their pipes, inhaling deep, deep puffs and then slipping off into oblivion. Singapore, with its vivid human drama, was only the stepping-stone to the strange new region we were soon to enter, and for the first time I began to regret we would be passing through so hurriedly; what an illustrated show all this would make!

We had done our four weeks at the Victoria and were preparing to move on when Harry, a fanatical fisherman, hired a small boat and sailed out into the lagoon to try his luck. He didn't have any. Alas, poor Harry: in the bush, snakes made for his bedroll; in the desert, scorpions found his shoes; in London, he had had a perpetual cold. And contentedly fishing away on a sunny day off Singapore, he let himself in for the most devastating sunburn I had ever seen. His skin blistered, his legs swelled to twice their nor-

208

mal size, and when I took one look I knew we weren't going anywhere for a while.

An American couple offered us the use of their guesthouse while Harry recovered. It was a thatched-roof cottage on stilts with lush coconut palms swaying all around and the gentle waters of the South China Sea rolling up on the beach a few yards away. I'm afraid Fran and I rather enjoyed this hiatus in our frenetic schedule. We had, after all, been busy tearing across continents and oceans almost constantly since the August day in 1917 when we were married.

During this peaceful interlude I suddenly decided that I did not want merely to flit through Asia as a performer. Since we had all our camera equipment along, why not film the exotic sights and put together a new production? When I broached this idea to the officials in Singapore, they responded by offering me a special train to use as our base. It would carry us all the way up the Malay Peninsula in style—a private locomotive, lavish sleeping quarters and a diner with our own kitchen. The following morning Harry tottered out of bed for the first time in two weeks and pronounced himself ready to go.

Our first stop was the ancient Portuguese city of Malacca, across the strait from Sumatra, where we were booked into the town hall. It was a far cry from the Royal Opera House at Covent Garden. Along with a full house of rubber planters, traders and British colonial officers, a squadron of immense bats was attracted to the performance, zooming in through the unscreened windows and making straight for the brightly lit screen. Now and then one dive-bombed into a punkah, an electric fan the size of an airplane propeller suspended from the ceiling, and came crashing down into the audience, adding some sound effects to my account of the Palestine campaign.

Moving up-country in a series of short runs and one-night stands, we filmed a crocodile hunt—the bait, dead monkey—also life on a rubber plantation. Malaya then supplied most of the world's natural rubber, a thriving industry that began with a few trees smuggled in from the Amazon. We played Kuala Lumpur, the tropical city from which the British governed the loose federation of Malay states, and moved on again.

At Ipoh, the Sultan of Perak invited us to a festival,

thereby providing Fran with a tale she—both of us—would tell ever after. The setting was a jungle glade to which we rode out in a procession of elephants. There were no howdahs, just a pad secured by broad straps, to which Fran, Harry and I, riding together, clung as we swayed and jounced along a trail through the dripping dense growth.

It was a grand party. Its feature attraction was a hundred-foot waterfall which plunged over rocks worn smooth where the Malays, seated on huge leaves, came tobogganing down on the churning cushion of water, howling with glee and ending up with a great splash in a pool at the bottom. An Afghan with a trained Himalayan dancing bear entertained the nonswimmers. When, presumably for our special enjoyment, the Sultan commanded the Afghan to take his bear down the waterfall, both seemed terrified. But after one swoop on the foaming slide, even the bear wanted to do it again and again.

Harry and I slid off our elephant to film the spectacle. The bear was coaxed closer to our camera. And the elephant, either offended at our interest in another creature or just plain frightened, suddenly trumpeted its outrage to the world and went lurching off into the jungle. The last we saw of Fran, she had flattened herself on the pad to keep from being swept into oblivion and was hanging on for dear life.

What do you do when your wife is a passenger on a runaway pachyderm? "There goes my wife," I said to the Sultan. "What can we do?"

"Nothing," His Most Gracious Majesty replied.

We had gone only a hundred yards or so into the tunnel of torn underbrush when we came upon the elephant calmly feasting on young bamboo shoots. Fortunately Fran was none the worse for her adventure.

"Are you all right?" I asked.

"Yes," she said, "but if you have that bear with you, please leave."

She was a good sport always. Our next expedition, to visit a tribe of Sakai pygmies deep in the interior, also called for travel by elephant, and she turned down the opportunity to stay behind. We set out from Ipoh in a forty-foot houseboat propelled by native oarsmen and skippered by an opium addict. Every couple of hours he would order the crew into a cove, then roll a pill or two, and drop off into whatever dreams you dream when you smoke opium.

Eventually we went ashore at a landing where there was a sign reading "Downing Street." A short distance from the river, we came to a large house with a sign over the door: "Number Ten." We were greeted by one of the best-known British District Officers in Southeast Asia, Captain Hubert Berkeley, from whom we were to borrow a string of elephants.

His Downing Street signs were his lighthearted way of saying that he considered his domain the center of the British Empire. Each morning at sunrise he would fire off a cannon and run up two flags, the Union Jack and the flag of the Berkeley Arms. He turned out to be one of the most colorful of all the picturesque characters we were to encounter in southern Asia, where we so often met representatives of the King who were straight out of Kipling. From him we borrowed our elephants, and off we went into one of the world's great forests, in search of the little people, the Sakai and the Semangs.

The Malay interior would live up to anyone's most nightmarish vision of a jungle. In those days, thousands of square miles of it remained untouched by civilization; even the trail we followed seemed only a tentative passage, to be reclaimed by the dense vegetation as soon as we passed. Towering trees closed over our heads to shut out sky; underfoot and everywhere around a tangle of creepers and vines thick as a man's arm imprisoned you where you stood, and it took an advance guard of machete-swinging Malays to enable the elephants to go crashing through. At home in this dank, dense wilderness lives the king cobra, largest and one of the most deadly of the world's poisonous snakes; the python, at thirty feet the longest of the constrictors; the seladang or gaur, a fierce wild ox standing six feet at the shoulders; also the Malay tiger, which will attack anything and, in default of easier prey, even stalks human beings.

Suddenly we broke out of the jungle's green gloom into a clearing with a dozen or so palm-leaf huts: we had found a Sakai village.

The people seemed a lighthearted group, café au lait in color and quite friendly, which was reassuring since each of their men carried a long bamboo blowgun and a quiver of poison-tipped darts at his waist. No one has improved on Kipling's description of their clothing:

The uniform 'e wore,
Was nothin' much before,
An' rather less than 'arf o' that be'ind.

No one knows where they came from or why only the tallest among them reach five feet, but the existence of pygmy tribes all the way from Africa to New Guinea is evidence enough that they are not freaks. It's true the first sight of a whole tribe of undersized people is a bit unsettling, but as we filmed away and I became absorbed in them as individuals, I soon forgot about their stature. The transition was hurried along, I think, when I imagined a pygmy sage describing *us* to his people: "Too bad for them, but they must suffer from some glandular disorder that leads to gigantism."

From Malaya we went on north to Burma, where from Rangoon we proceeded up the Irrawaddy a thousand miles to the China frontier on a stern-wheeler the British used for policing the backcountry. For ten weeks we put on the Allenby-Lawrence show, and we also filmed this storied country with its thousands of graceful pagodas and their silent, saffron-robed monks.

We played Mandalay, the royal city of King Thibaw and Queen Supayalat who only forty years before had ruled Burma by mass murder. On we went to Burma, southern terminus of the long trail through the Himalayas followed by Chinese smugglers, and from whence an endless supply of opium was disseminated all over the world. Returning, we stopped at Yenangyaung, center of a rich oil field, and put on our show for a full house of Texas and Oklahoma drillers, some of whom, we were told, had left America just one jump ahead of the sheriff. A full house? Not quite. Across the courtyard we could hear the expletives and imprecations of a group of nonstop poker players who would not be lured away from the temptation of drawing to an inside straight by Allenby, Lawrence or even the Second Coming.

From Rangoon we crossed the Bay of Bengal to Colombo, capital of Ceylon. It is said that when the Lord banished Adam and Eve from the Garden of Eden, they found a new paradise in Ceylon, and to us jungle wanderers this seemed believable. Here were immaculately maintained coconut plantations and the terraces where much of the world's finest tea is grown, also the most mannerly of elephants, first-rate hotels and superb beaches—and all enlivened by the warmhearted native Singhalese in colorful costume and bejeweled headdress.

Bandman, our London impresario, had provided us with a most unusual advance man, Willy Freear, who had been born in Kilkenny Castle. In his own performing days, Willy had parlayed an enchanting mix of comic songs, juggling and one-man skits. With his road show he had toured southern Asia for years. Even then, at seventy-one, he was sometimes given more publicity than he could get for us. But though Willy added endless gaiety to our party, he could not stave off a few disasters for us in Colombo.

To begin with, in this most Oriental of cities, we could not find an Oriental dancer for the prologue. Hesitantly, Fran said. "I've watched the dance so often, maybe I—I mean, it is an emergency and . . ."

"Could you?" I whispered. "I mean, would you. . . ?"

And so, in addition to having taken on the chores of company manager, she did the dance, veiled, anonymous—and looking pretty good.

We appeared at the Public Hall, which was a short rickshaw ride away—a graceful white building surrounded by banyan trees and palms. During the performance a monkey would occasionally throw a coconut down onto the tin roof where it landed with an explosive clang. When the tropical rain thundered down, it sounded like the world was tearing apart. One night all the lights went out in the middle of the proceedings and I had to ad lib for half an hour while a distraught Harry Chase prowled overhead, searching for the trouble.

Inside it was like a Turkish bath. All the fans had to be turned off so the audience could hear, and the temperature in the hall, jammed from footlights to foyer, must have been a hundred and twenty. Fran, once her dance was finished, sat in the wings with a stack of handkerchiefs which she dealt off to me so I could mop my face.

From Colombo we sailed on a Danish cargo ship to Madras on the east coast of India to begin our tour of the teeming subcontinent. It was a study in the starkest contrasts. The British raj was at the height of its glory and its resplendent nineteenth-century tradition infused the white man's India.

At Bombay, a babu, a subeditor of the *Chronicle*, mistook my picture in Arab costume for a South Arabian Sultan who arrived the same day. When the potentate from Mukalla and Shier saw the paper he sent his Grand Vizier to demand an apology. When I heard about this I sent our Willie Freear on a similar mission. Out of this came an invitation from the Sultan for us to be his guests in Mukalla, Arabian Nights capital of the Hadramaut, a seldom visited part of the Arabian peninsula. When we finally did so more than thirty years later, the Sultan had departed for his Mohammedan paradise.

In Calcutta, the theater program was printed on white silk. And when we were invited to dine with the governor of Bengal, we were awed by the magnificence of the palace and the guests, the splendor and graciousness of their way of life—brilliantly uniformed military guards lining the approaches, the broad staircase with its brilliant red carpet, attendants all in gleaming white and red, marble terraces, glittering chandeliers and the ladies in regal gowns.

Then the next day, in the heat and dust of Calcutta, in the streets where sacred cows were blocking traffic, we were stepping over naked Bengalis asleep on the sidewalks. Everywhere there were beggars, lepers and impoverished holy men, and we were glad to leave.

In Lucknow, our standing-room-only audience at the Mohamed Bagh Club was in full formal finery, the civil and military officers in dress uniforms complete with white tie and decorations, and the 16th Lancers band supplied our music.

Harry's wife joined us in India. Except for a few brief intervals, they had been apart ever since Harry and I teamed up in 1917, and I thought it would be in order for Fran and me to invite Emma to share our Indian adventure. She was most helpful at looking after the box office, but she was not what you would call a born traveler. In fact, almost from the day of her arrival, she was pining for her own particular Garden of Eden, East Orange, New Jersey.

Strolling in a park in Lucknow, Fran tried to pick up a baby monkey, and we were instantly surrounded by a simian militia. But for the intervention of some sympathetic locals, they might have carried us all off into captivity. In Delhi, attempting to photograph the thousands of followers of the Prophet as they worshipped at the Jama Masjid, largest mosque in the Moslem world, we were somewhat disconcerted, to put the best face on it, when all those prayerful thousands suddenly turned on us with what may have been mayhem in their eyes. Once again we had defiled a holy place with our presence, and once again we may have been fortunate to escape with our lives.

At least our audiences continued to receive us kindly, as did the critics. I was especially pleased with a review written in what was called Babu English, in the *Eastern Mail:*

> . . . His recitative skill, apparent from a voice that quickly went from humour to pathos, swayed his audience from laughter to sadness. It is difficult in this appreciation to single out for administration the several con-comitants of the exposition last night. The prevailing feeling on its closure was that no gap was left for the imagination to supply.

In the Punjab, the governor invited us to tour the Lahore bazaar by elephant, and so we came to know and love Primrose. One morning she was waiting outside our hotel, a tall elephant all painted and gaily caparisoned, with a howdah on her back impressive enough for the lordliest of maharajas. We climbed aboard and went lurching and swaying down the narrow streets.

Primrose had toured the bazaar before. While Fran, Harry and I enjoyed the spectacle—indoors as well as out, for we had a clear view into Lahore's second-story windows—and Emma Chase's stiff upper lip turned rigid, Primrose swept her great trunk left and right and wrought havoc on the sidewalk stalls we passed. Nuts and fruits, baubles and beads, all went flying through the air and came cascading to the ground, to be eagerly snatched up by the trail of youngsters who followed in our wake, while one of the governor's retainers ran behind to hand out copper and silver largesse to the stoic shopkeepers on our route. Everyone, apparently, was familiar with Primrose's capricious ways.

It was all quite gay and we were having a fine time until we noticed poor Emma, sitting up there in the Punjab governor's plush howdah, crying bitter tears. It was awful, she sobbed. She was frightened and hated it and wanted to go home.

Stricken, Harry flung out his arm as if to undrape all the enticing pageant for her and cried out, "But, honey, what

215

could be more fun than riding your own elephant through a bazaar in India?"

"Riding the East Orange streetcar to my mother's house!" the good woman wailed.

And that was it. A week or so later we put the unrelenting Emma on a train for the coast and, alone, she began the long voyage across the Arabian Sea, the Mediterranean and the Atlantic, back to her earthly paradise, East Orange, New Jersey.

In Calcutta, we visited the site of the infamous Black Hole, where one day in 1756 a hundred and forty-six Europeans were imprisoned in a single cell by the Nabob of Bengal; by morning a hundred and twenty-three were dead of suffocation. Calcutta, then, became the key and the Black Hole the spark to touch off the British conquest of India. Given his head, the young and moody military genius, Robert Clive, drove out the French, subdued the nabobs and established the supremacy of the East India Company. Rebellions were put down and India eventually came under the direct administration of the Crown; in time, some responsibility was even given to native officials, and seemingly the brightest jewel in the British Empire was secure. But of course it wasn't. A people craving to choose their own destiny, to walk their land as the equal of any foreigner, was not to be appeased by minor civil-service appointments.

An incident at a railroad station when we were on our way to Karachi seemed to epitomize the approaching clash of mutually exclusive ambitions. Our train was crowded; a pair of British noncoms, looking for seats, simply commandeered a compartment. It had been occupied by a distinguished-looking Hindu—a judge, it turned out—but they just tossed his baggage onto the platform and shoved him out after it. In the last seconds before the train pulled out, we made room for him with us. Later I heard that precisely the same thing had happened, in East Africa, to a young Indian lawyer named Mohandas K. Gandhi.

At the time of our tour, Gandhi's name was already on everyone's lips, revered by his own people, half scorned, half feared by the British. His religiously inspired passive-resistance movement had given a unique cutting edge to the nationalist unrest; he became the leading spirit of the All-India Congress Party. Gandhi, under arrest, was held at the Connaught Hotel at Poona, a hill station near Bombay. But this didn't matter; the Indian people had a leader and, for the first time, a real weapon against the British raj.

In the Punjab we felt the reverberations, both of a turmoil centuries old and the trouble to come. Along the wild and mountainous Northwest Frontier, now part of Pakistan, raiding was a way of life and seemed to have been given fresh license by the unsettled politics of the day. In Peshawar, the city at the eastern end of the Khyber Pass, fabled gateway to central Asia, our hotel was surrounded by a wide swath of barbed wire. At every performance there was the threat of violence.

All the rugged country west to Afghanistan was inhabited by fierce fighting tribes—Afridis, Wazirs, Mahsuds and Momands, all well armed and as dangerous to outsiders as they were to each other. No matter how many troops the British posted in the Khyber and along the frontier, they couldn't keep the tribesmen from blazing away from the overhanging cliffs and mountaintops. No wonder the Tommies called the Khyber the Valley of Sudden Death.

Still, we intended to have a look at this historic route, the pathway for invading legions of Persians, Greeks, Tatars, Moguls and Afghans. No other pass in the world has had such strategic importance. Even then, the Khyber was the key to such control as the British could maintain over the warlike tribes ranging the wild country east of the forbidden Afghan border.

They were understandably not entranced with the prospect of three Americans moving down into the vulnerable chasm. After persuading the governor, Sir John Maffey, that it was an essential for our film, we borrowed a Model T Ford. A British captain went along with us, and a Tommy to drive. The captain, uneasy about the whole idea, said Fran would have to stay at Peshawar. I could have predicted how this would turn out, but the captain, dubious to the last, finally won a minor point: Fran agreed to disguise her sex in a soldier's uniform. And off we rolled, just a contingent of British going about their official business.

In those days, long camel caravans wound along the floor of the gorge from Afghanistan bearing the silks and rugs of Bokhara and Samarkand to India. They still do. British motorized traffic traveled a higher road cut into the cliffs, its hairpin turns precarious enough but high enough to be safe from flash floods. It was a spectacular trip, the jagged peaks of the Safed Koh towering above us, and the snow-covered peaks rising from a solid wall of granite into the cloudless sky.

We sped through a narrow gorge to the walled fort at Landi Kotal, where a British brigade, the Khyber Rifles, was stationed. From there we dropped down to the desert floor and soon reached the Afghan frontier, at which point we faced an emphatic sign reading:

IT IS ABSOLUTELY FORBIDDEN TO CROSS
THIS BORDER INTO AFGHAN TERRITORY.

Here the Amir's poker-faced soldiers made it clear that no *feringhi* was to go farther.

We had now covered little more than twenty-five miles from Peshawar and had come to the end of the world as we knew or could imagine it. Beyond was a strange proscribed land where in our time—except for a British military invasion—only a bare handful of Westerners had ever set foot. And as we turned to start the journey back, I wondered if I would ever have a chance to cross this forbidden boundary.

From Peshawar we saw much of what is present-day Pakistan. We played Quetta where, a few years later, a devastating earthquake killed fifty thousand in one of history's worst natural disasters. At Karachi, where, in the same newspaper, I was hailed as a throwback to an ancient past and a herald of the future, one writer said:

Mr. Lowell Thomas is indeed the lineal descendant of the minstrels who, in castle halls, sang the sagas of great warriors to the accompaniment of their own harps.

A few columns over, a second critic, sounding like a man who had had a secret preview of television, still a quarter century away, wrote:

His production is sheer futurist journalism, an earnest of the time when newspapers, no longer smug black and white, will be pictured vocal and vibrant.

Our final stop in India was a revisit to Bombay, where the irrepressible Willy Freear once again had outdone himself. As he drove us through the city, we came upon an impressive palace to whose tall iron fence he had affixed what surely must have been history's most conspicuous advertisement. For the length of a city block, in letters four feet high, ran the inescapable legend:

SEE AND HEAR LOWELL THOMAS—
WITH ALLENBY IN PALESTINE AND
LAWRENCE OF ARABIA
AT THE ROYAL OPERA HOUSE.

Two weeks later, after nearly a full year in southern Asia, our tour was over—and I didn't want to leave. India, with its vastness and infinite variety, India in those crucial days when the long and glittering rule of the British and the maharajas was beginning to be tested by a gathering swell of popular resistance—India seemed to me the number one human adventure and the most exciting place in the world. It was as though all the months we had spent there were a mere introduction, the film we had shot a bare start. I wanted to step ashore at the far southern tip of the Hindustan peninsula and see it all, from the equator to the glaciers of the Himalayas.

And this is just what we did. First we returned to England to make some necessary financial arrangements and restock our film supply, and there Fran joined her mother for a leisurely European tour, while Harry and I went back to New Delhi, hoping to enlist the support of the British raj.

10.

Crossing the Forbidden Border

> Some men are at ease in a London club. To me
> such places are torture: I see dim acquaintances,
> talk clumsily, run away. But I am at home
> amongst horsemen, airmen and Hindu ascetics.
> —FRANCIS YEATS-BROWN, *Bengal Lancer*

THE newly appointed Viceroy of India had begun life as
Rufus Isaacs, son of a London merchant. A singular
man, he was the first Jew to become Attorney General,
Lord Chief Justice or Ambassador to the United States.
Now he was the Earl of Reading, the King-Emperor's own
deputy in India, ruler of the second most populous country
on earth.

He was understandably preoccupied. Nearly four hundred
people had recently been killed by troops during an insurrection in the Punjab; and the Sikhs were rioting over access to their holy place. Mahatma Gandhi, the apostle of
nonviolence, safely incarcerated at Poona, posed the most
dangerous threat of all, one that a face-to-face conference
with the Viceroy had failed to defuse, for the simple reason
that there were only two solutions to their conflict—for the
British to leave, or for the Indians to give up their aspirations to independence—and neither was acceptable to both.
Across India, the tinder waited for the spark.

I would not have troubled Lord Reading except that his
aides, as sometimes happens with those in lesser positions
of authority, gave in to self-doubt, caution and even resent-
ment. Instead of assisting me, they blocked me at every
turn. When I asked for an appointment with the Viceroy

himself, he promptly invited me to luncheon, and afterward, in his study, I put my case before him. I wanted to film India in all its diversity and contrasts, I said, but as the land was so enormous and its transportation network so uncertain, I needed help with special trains and a steamer or two to take us along the great rivers. I even wanted the cooperation of the Indian army on the Northwest Frontier. And most of all I wanted to borrow the services of an officer I had known in England, a remarkable young man who spoke a number of Indian languages and knew more about the people and history of the country than anyone I had ever met.

"Who is this paragon?" Lord Reading asked with a smile.

"Major Francis Yeats-Brown of the Seventeenth Bengal Lancers."

"Well, you shall have him, and everything else you've asked. I heard you at Covent Garden in London and went back a second time. If you can do for India what you've done for Palestine, possibly I can justify my appointment just by helping you."

He of course was pulling my leg a bit. At any rate, Harry and I were on our way. Our first stop was Cawnpore on the Ganges where Yeats-Brown was posted with his cavalry. He was delighted with the prospect and full of ideas. I had not been mistaken about Y.B., as everyone called him. In the months that followed he played a major role in our filming expedition, his gift of tongues and a special knack for winning the cooperation of all manner of people proving invaluable. He was our guide, our guru.

As with many men of both soaring intellect and considerable physical prowess, he was not prepossessing. Of average height but with a stoop that seemed to shrink him, he had a hawk nose that was at odds with a somewhat remote, even ascetic expression, and he spoke with a slight stammer. This last may well have been the result of his having early been bound over to a career in the army despite his obvious feelings toward literature and the arts. But that's how it was done in those days; the four Yeats-Brown brothers adhered to what was then hallowed English tradition—the eldest followed the father, a distinguished diplomat, into the Foreign Office; the second was committed to the navy, the third to the church, and Francis, the youngest, to the military academy at Sandhurst.

Y.B. may have downed his share of whiskey and sodas

in secret disappointment—or because, like most Englishmen posted too long in India, he found it the handiest way to stave off the heat and boredom—but he was a rare individual, a man of parts. He became a crack officer, a member of the all-India polo team and, as a wartime RAF pilot, a first-rate fighting man. Sent behind the Turkish front in Mesopotamia to bomb telegraph lines, he had crashed in the desert, been captured and escaped to fight again.

It is true that his fellow officers of the Bengal Lancers considered him an oddball, slightly mad. He had the distinctly un-British habit of periodically donning native garb and disappearing among the people. He had a flair for getting along with them; he recognized the folly of the patronizing British attitude toward India, and particularly toward Indian philosophy and religion. Ordinary common sense, he would say, ought to indicate the basic worth of the people and their beliefs, for both had proven their durability over the ages of adversity. And so, while his comrades were off pig-sticking, the traditional diversion of the military in the time of the raj, Y.B. was somewhere conversing with the holy men, poring over classical texts, pulling together primitive strands of Indian thought.

He was, finally, a gifted writer. He had already written a couple of books when I met him, and later, when our travels together were over, I had a part in encouraging him to resign from the Indian army to do the book closest to his heart, *Lives of a Bengal Lancer,* from which a spectacular movie was produced, and both made Y.B. famous.

All in all, he was quite a man to have along on an odyssey such as I planned, although he put his role modestly enough in an article he once wrote about me:

I was attached to L.T.'s party as interpreter and liaison officer. My desire was to see that he met the right people and took the right pictures from the point of view of the Indian government. However, he generally did what he wanted and saw whom he pleased. His energy was immense, and he spared no money or trouble to obtain the best pictures and information.

But of course a good deal of the credit for our achievement in India goes to him. And in addition to his own talents, he brought along an Afridi noncom named Naim Shah who stood six-foot-four and wore a peaked native hat that made him seem as gigantic as Aladdin's genie. Wherever we went, Naim Shah, in full regimental regalia, walked in front of us clearing the way; at night he carried a lantern and a heavy stick, peering sharply ahead, and if ever a cobra crossed our path, I didn't know about it.

We went first to Cape Comorin, southernmost tip of the Hindustan peninsula, so I could fulfill my dream of traversing the entire length of the great subcontinent. I stood alone on a massive rock at the water's edge looking off into the empty distance, knowing there was nothing between us and the far Antarctic but the Indian Ocean and its few remote islands. Then I faced about and tried, in a single flash of expanded comprehension, to catch the immensity, the abounding farrago of humanity and hope that stretched away to the north. I could not.

How could anyone grasp the limitless panorama of India? How could a writer capture the centuries, the cults and customs of the magnificent and squalid people who lived here? How could I hope to do justice to the astonishing contradictions—the Taj Mahal and the Black Pagoda, Vedanta philosophy and serpent worship, the jungles of Bengal and the gleaming Himalayas?

"Mother of history, grandmother of legend and great-grandmother of tradition," was how Mark Twain described India. Intimidated, feeling dwarfed and dazzled, I climbed into a bullock cart with my companions, the driver cracked his whip and we went plodding up the trail leading who knew where.

Toward evening, we passed through a dark forest, twisting branches overhead cutting the red sky into weirdly contorted patterns. Oil lamps flickered in the huts we passed; I sensed dark eyes surveying us from the shadows. In a little while we stopped to let the bullocks drink from a roadside pond. Nearby there was a shrine to Kali, Goddess of Death, portrayed as a four-armed demon dancing on the dead body of her husband, a knife in one hand and a human head in the other. Why, I asked Y.B., did this female monster number her Indian worshipers by the millions?

"Answer that and you may have a clue to the Hindu mind," he replied.

We were not the only Westerners drawn east by India's mystic appeal. Near Madras, we stayed a few days in

223

Adyar, a community of Theosophists guided by a colorful Irish crusader, Annie Besant. The transcendant enthusiasm at Adyar was reincarnation, each person who lived there believing himself to be the modern materialization of someone, usually of conspicuous celebrity, who had lived in an earlier age. This gave us an opportunity to shake hands with such historical sages as Euclid, Aristophanes, Ptolemy and Aristotle. "Have you noticed," Y.B. remarked to me *sotto voce* over a Scotch and soda one evening, "that the place is full of high priests and heroes? How is it no one ever turns up as the reincarnation of the temple bottle-washer or the harem housemaid?"

Many of Mrs. Besant's votaries were European Theosophists, but her particular protégé was a handsome young Indian named Jiddu Krishnamurti who was in training to become her successor to Jesus Christ. The one problem, as she sadly confided to us, was that the boy's main interest seemed to be tennis. Apparently it was a valid problem, for after she had taken Krishnamurti to England a few years later and introduced him as the new Messiah, he declined the honor. But her faith in him was not entirely misplaced, for later he became one of India's leading philosophers.

Wise men and saints, fakirs and fakers, hereditary thieves and religiously inspired murderers—all had their place in the Indian mosaic. Within the memory of living men, a sect of stranglers, practicing thuggee, the art of ritual murder, had roamed the length of the land. Worshipers of the deadly divinity, Kali, they paid her obeisance by snapping a ceremonial scarf over a victim's head from behind, twisting a supple wrist—and a vigorous man was dead before he even realized he was in trouble.

The British finally suppressed this demoniac practice by executing hundreds of Thugs, but they never made much headway against the criminal tribes. Estimated to be ten million strong, these devout souls were born into a caste which believed the soul's needs are satisfied by strong-arm burglary and confidence games of the most perplexing intricacy. Mind you, they had no stuffy prejudices against murder if the occasion seemed to warrant it, but for the most part they were more partial to stealing than killing. At Bapatla, on the Bay of Bengal, we met a celebrated member of this enterprising caste, a man now old and emaciated but still revered for a famous exploit. It appears that he and his men had once kidnapped six policemen sent to arrest them, donned their uniforms and, thus disguised, proceeded off on a crime spree of epic magnitude. Now he was respected everywhere as The Man Who Stole Six Policemen.

As every traveler should and does, we journeyed to Agra, city of the Taj Mahal. The Taj is, quite simply, a masterpiece of white marble and minarets reflected in an oblong pool. It has been said it is within more measurable distance of perfection than any other work of man. Certainly not in the more than three hundred years since it was built by the Mogul emperor Shah Jehan as a tomb for his beloved wife, Mumtaz Mahal, has anyone conceived a structure so sublime.

I was captivated on my first visit and glad to return again and again so Harry could film it by day and by night, under a sparkling clear sky and with those swelling monsoon clouds for a background. I returned some thirty times, and of course pilgrims from around the world travel great distances to stand in the shadow of its magnificence. But one man's wine is another man's vinegar. During World War II, I knew a colonel at the nearby American air base whose duty it was to escort visiting dignitaries to the Taj. After doing this many times, he would take them to the vicinity of the Taj and, from where he couldn't even catch a glimpse of it, he would sit reading a newspaper until his VIPs returned.

Little more than a hundred miles to the northwest, alongside the red sandstone splendors erected by the Moguls at Delhi, the British were building a regal new capital to reflect their imperial rule. *New* Delhi, already ten years under construction then, was to be a city of broad avenues and stately public buildings. Obviously the architects were men of discernment and vision, but as Yeats-Brown wryly remarked, the British might have done better to consult a soothsayer, for an ancient Indian proverb had it that whoever built a new city at Delhi would perish in its ruins. History had validated the unequivocal prophecy five times; a sixth upheaval was already blowing in the wind.

The sahibs from Britain, secure and comfortable in their exclusive clubs and compounds, seemingly oblivious to the sea of swarthy faces through which they moved as they passed between restricted white enclaves, fell victim to the illusion of permanence. They seemed to think the raj would be there for centuries to come. They knew all about the frail dark man in the loincloth; they discussed him of course, but always as a passing disturbance in the calm waters of British rule. Mahatma Gandhi indeed!

Y.B. knew better. Nothing was permanent in India except the people and the land. He saw the British raj as only a moment in the long view of Indian history, a phase even then coming to an end. And of course he was right. The magnificent new capital at New Delhi was completed in 1931; seventeen years later six hundred million Indians clapped their hands and the British raj vanished.

In Delhi, as in every other city we visited, I sought the help of British officials and American envoys in gaining permission to cross the forbidden border into Afghanistan. Nowhere were the answers encouraging. I wrote to Secretary of State Charles Evans Hughes in Washington; I even sent messages to the Afghan ruler, Amir Amanullah, in his capital at Kabul. No answer. We moved on.

At Benares, we saw thousands of Hindu pilgrims, weary but exalted, washing away their sins in the sacred waters of the Ganges. We spent weeks at Darjeeling, the most favored hill station in Bengal, filming, writing, unable to tear ourselves away. Here maharajas and British merchant princes came to escape the heat of the plains, and here, nine thousand feet up into the Himalayas, we gazed out on the splendors and spectacles of the world's mightiest mountain range—the Arabian Nights land of Sikkim below, dazzling Kanchenjunga and unconquered Everest aglow in the sunset, and beyond, Tibet, remote, mysterious, another forbidden realm I was assured could not be entered.

Less interested in British India than in Indian India, Yeats-Brown rejoiced when our tour took us to Puri on the Bay of Bengal. Puri has given us a word meaning an irresistible object that crushes everything in its path—the word *juggernaut*. The original juggernaut was the car of Jagannath, a temple on gigantic wooden wheels in which the idol of this Hindu divinity, one manifestation of Vishnu, rolled through the streets once every year, and still does. Worshipers used to seek Nirvana by throwing themselves under the wheels. The tiresome British called a halt to this particular manner of showing one's religious devotion.

The car is actually a temple some twenty feet high, on

sixteen wheels eight feet in diameter. In former times the streets of Puri were littered with the bodies of men, women and children who deliberately threw themselves in its path. A police inspector led us to a housetop from which we could film the ceremony. In the distance stood the temple of the deity, an architectural phallic symbol. Before the temple three gigantic carts were ready to move, the car of Jagannath gleaming in red and yellow.

Suddenly a chant went up from hundreds of thousands of throats: "O Jagannath, Lord of the World, have pity on us, release us from our woes!" Then the juggernaut of Jagannath was on its way! The god's sister's car came first, then the brother's and then his own. People in the vicinity surged forward to get their hands on the heavy ropes. Guiding the first car was a European, Captain H. R. C. Guise, the Puri Superintendent of Police. We saw him signal at one point for the emergency brake when devotees threw themselves in front of the huge wheels. A log dropped and brought it to a stop just in time.

From Puri we went to nearby Karnak, an overnight journey in a palanquin, where we hesitated to film the Black Pagoda at close range. All around the outside of the temple ran a continuing series of tableaux representing men and women indulging in sexual pleasures in every conceivable mode and manner, explicit eroticism executed with meticulous concern for detail. It was impressive, but not a single segment of the wall could then have been reproduced in the West without bringing the cameraman or publisher to the prompt attention of the police. How different today!

Inside, the artistic motif changed from hectic pornography to serenely philosophic contemplation, the statues and bas-reliefs expressing the soaring metaphysical and moral precepts of Hindustan. In answer to my unspoken question, Y.B. explained how Hindu thinkers, having divined the essentials of psychoanalysis centuries before Freud, believed man must frankly face the crudest material level of experience before taking off into the loftier reaches of reflective thought. Such was the moral of the Black Pagoda.

As we were about to end our visit, out from behind a sensual group slithered a Russell's viper. Was this poisonous snake warning us that we shouldn't have been there in the first place?

227

I had a good deal to mull over as we started back, each of us in a palanquin carried by four bearers, an overnight trip over a jungle trail, in those days the only access to the Black Pagoda.

By this time, nearly a full year had sped by since the dusky evening when we started north from Cape Comorin; we had covered more than sixty thousand miles exploring India's farthest reaches and were fast running out of money. I told myself it was a good thing we were entering the last phase of our journey—another visit to the Northwest Frontier—but I didn't mean it. Nor was I oblivious to the fact that our presence within striking distance of the Khyber Pass would put us in position for a trip to the Afghan border, should the elusive permission finally come through.

Those rugged, untamed badlands especially intrigued me because, except for the advent of the rifle, life there had changed little since the dawn of history. The fiercely independent, barely civilized tribesmen gave the British fully as much grief as they had given the Moguls over four hundred years before, and the Tatars and Persians in the dim past. Although the Indian army had thirty thousand men in the region, the fighting went on and raiding remained the way of life. Native towns, like the medieval strongholds of Europe, were surrounded by walls twenty feet high; inside, each family had its own walled enclosure, for when the people were not battling the infidels they were engaged in blood feuds with each other. It was not uncommon for a man to sit perched in a tower atop his mud wall for weeks, even months, taking his meals and sleeping there, peering through a slit, rifle always ready, just waiting for a shot at his particular foe—who lived nearby.

We stopped first at Tank in Waziri country, the bare brown land of the Mahsuds. One day the raiders struck, creeping stealthily along the wall until they reached the courtyard of a Hindu merchant. A scrawny pariah dog slept fitfully. Behind bolts of cloth, bags of dried peas and skeins of yarn, the unsuspecting merchant and his wife and daughters were stretched out on their string beds, asleep.

Down dropped the shrouded Mahsuds, noiselessly, knives unsheathed. In a moment two were on the sleeping merchant, the others storming through courtyard and shop to seize the cashbox, grain bags, account book, camel, wife, daughters—everything. Then came the hue and cry, policemen and townspeople swarming through the bazaar, rifles crackling, all just as it had happened countless times before.

But this time there was a difference; this time the raid had been carefully staged for our benefit. With the help of Captain T. K. Wodehouse of the Frontier Police and a puzzled populace, the terror was simulated so Harry, from a nearby rooftop, could get it all on film for the later edification of audiences in London, Paris, New York and Chicago. There were no casualties, except for a veiled lady who fainted, no doubt because the re-creation was all too vivid, and had to be revived by her husband with several severe pinches.

Afterward, Wodehouse collected his Mahsud ruffians, distributed our cash payments and dispersed the crowd. But that same evening, after we had left for Bannu, he was sent out to seek a band of Mahsuds who had "gone ghazi," the frontier expression for those who take up arms against non-Muslims. Then, in a gorge only a few miles away, he was ambushed and killed.

Northeast of Bannu, we were in the domain of the Afridis. They are tall, fair-skinned, shaven-pated people, blessed by Allah with a glorious climate, fertile valleys, herds of cattle and many camels. But the blood of fighting men runs in their veins, and as thieves they are in a class by themselves. More than once, while we slept in a tent in the midst of a detachment of troops, the stealthy Afridis visited us, making off with anything they could carry in two hands. British soldiers in Afridi country had learned to sleep with their rifles chained to their wrists, but many a man awoke to find the bedclothes stolen out from under him in the night. Even when the intruders were detected by sentries, even when hands were actually laid on them, they usually got away, having had the foresight to grease their nearly naked bodies from head to foot.

We heard a good deal about Multan, a legendary figure in those parts, an Afridi Robin Hood who robbed rich Hindus and dispensed handsome benefactions among the Moslem poor. Always carefully watched by the Frontier Police, he appeared one evening at a caravan court near the banking bazaar in Peshawar. But all was well; he was unarmed and had apparently come only to watch the dancing boys. A troop of musicians strolled by and joined the crowd around the fire; four Afridi litter bearers carrying a sick man to the hospital beyond the bazaar put down their burden to watch the frankly lascivious dance—nothing that would excite special notice in sin-saturated Peshawar.

But suddenly Multan stepped forward into the firelight. Forty men, including the musicians and the dancing boys, converged on the sick man, who threw back his blankets, leaped to his feet and began handing out the forty rifles concealed in the litter. Half the force made straight for the bazaar, overpowering the police guard there without a shot; the others secured a line of retreat. In less than an hour, Multan and his brigands had looted the banks—and the silversmiths and moneylenders, quartered in the same district—of four hundred thousand rupees, more than a hundred twenty-five thousand dollars, and were on their way back to the hills. Pursued, they fought a brilliant rearguard action and made a clean getaway. Many years were to pass before Multan was finally gunned down —in a personal quarrel during which he first killed four men and wounded two others.

Yeats-Brown, who had soldiered with Afridi troops, told us the story of young Yakub Khan and the sniper. Constantly at work on the roads through the Khyber, the British offered handsome wages to any tribesman willing to lay aside his rifle for a pick or shovel. But money wasn't everything: hidden somewhere in the crags above Ali Masjid, a lone sniper had been picking off two or three soldiers a week and nobody knew how many road workers. When this had gone on for three months, or to the point of official embarrassment, the British offered a reward of a thousand rupees to anyone who brought the sharpshooter in, dead or alive.

Yakub Khan volunteered. Of course everyone laughed, for he was barely old enough to qualify for the Khyber militia, a guileless-looking lad, milk-faced, as the Afridis say, with down on his cheeks. But as all he asked was leave for the day it was granted, and in the early morning he climbed up into the heights. And before the sun had fairly cleared the Safed Koh, the echo of a rifle, just one shot, reached down to the British encampment. Soon enough a sentry reported by field telephone that he had found the outlaw's body; it had come pitching down from the escarpment high above. Yakub Khan returned to fervent congratulations, new respect—and a thousand rupees.

How had he found the sniper? an officer asked. How had he managed to waylay him when the best British soldiers could not?

"It was no trouble," replied the boy, counting his reward. "I knew all his little tricks and hiding places. He was my father."

Finally our time ran out. With my cash supply near zero and still no word from Afghanistan, we had to pack our gear and return to Bombay before we were stranded. There Harry and I booked passage on a P & O steamer for England; it had been a rich and unforgettable experience, but now I had to face some hard realities. As Yeats-Brown later put it:

> We had gone everywhere. We interviewed agitators and saints—were blessed by the Three-Breasted Goddess at Madura and drank tea with Afridi free-booters at Kus; it was a marvelous trip from my point of view, and I think from L.T.'s, although I wondered whether the large sum of money [was it a quarter of a million dollars?] which he spent making "Through Romantic India" could ever yield him an adequate return.

I don't recall how much money I had spent—a failing that was to afflict me until years later when I finally put my financial affairs in more competent hands—and at the time I wasn't thinking about any recompense; I just hated leaving with my hopes for getting to Afghanistan unfulfilled. Then, a few hours before we were to sail—we had already said good-bye to Y.B. and Naim Shah, who were to return to their regiment in the morning—there was a message from the American chargé d'affaires, Cornelius Van H. Engert, in Persia: he had just been informed that Amanullah, Amir of Afghanistan, would welcome a visit from Mr. Lowell Thomas and his party.

I caught up with Y.B. before he got away, and maybe we did exchange a discreet cheer, but we quickly got down to our logistical problem.

Y.B. thought it might be possible to drive an automobile across the Afghan desert. The distance from Peshawar to

231

Kabul was less than two hundred miles, so a few extra cans of petrol strapped to the outside should see us through. There had been keen competition for the Indian market between Ford and General Motors, and an American I had met in Calcutta, a jute broker named David King, might be able to help us. Furthermore, King, one of only sixteen survivors of the original French Foreign Legion in World War I, surely would be an ideal companion on such a journey.

King was intrigued by the chance to visit Afghanistan, and a friend of his at General Motors agreed to furnish us with a new Buick, which we shipped by rail to Lahore. There the five of us—Harry, Yeats-Brown, Naim Shah, King and I—climbed aboard and again headed for the Northwest Frontier and Peshawar.

Soon, if Allah willed it, and if Amir Amanullah Khan, Light of the World, did not change his mind, and if his zesty subjects did not shoot holes in our car, and if none of the disasters that usually overtake travelers east of Suez befell us—why, then we would pass out of the old Bajauri Gate at Peshawar and journey to mysterious Afghanistan, where so few Westerners had preceded us. But tomorrow might never come. "Life is but an hour," said Akbar, the Mogul emperor who once traveled this golden road. And what better way could we devise for spending our hour of life than to see as much of this world as possible before passing on to the next? And so, like the countless millions who have recovered their strength in this fabled caravan stop during the past five thousand years, or lost it altogether, in Peshawar we tasted the dubious delights of charas from a water pipe, visited the *serai* of the dancing boys and the streets of the daughters of Jezebel. We had not come to sit in judgment on the mecca of the hedonistic tribesmen; we were merely curious onlookers, pausing, bound on for the remote land beyond the Khyber.

Standards of morality differ. What happens in Poughkeepsie or Paducah would perhaps startle the burgers of Peshawar. But let us be frank and say that of the thousand and one sins of Peshawar, most are unmentionable and some are unbelievable. They are those that will not bear transcription to the printed page, and the sins of opium and hemp and dancing boys and acquiescent girls of every libidinous persuasion, of jealousy and intrigue and the deviltry which gets into men's blood in certain latitudes; they also are the sins of gluttony and gambling and strange intoxications, the passion of blood feuds and the lust for revenge, of endless battle and sudden, satanic death. And they are all on public display.

We sit on a balcony with Y.B.'s friend Abdul Ghani above the Street of the Storytellers. He puffs dreamily on his water pipe, and an incredible stream of humanity swirls below. Between puffs Abdul Ghani points out three ruffians whom he identifies as escaped criminals; on their heads is a substantial reward. Will he turn them in and claim it? Abdul smiles. He is not interested in the reward, nor are any others in the crowd who recognize the trio. Everyone in Peshawar knows that even with the best protection of the British raj, such a failure to mind one's own business is an assurance of waking up some morning beside the fountains of paradise. And Abdul thinks *this* world not a bad sort of place. Unlike those wandering Hindu saints, naked as rats, over there begging rice, he does not believe in torturing his body to save his soul. Abdul prefers one Kashmiri handmaiden in this world to a dozen virgins in the next.

The crowd parades beneath us. Here comes a group of gay lads from Tirah, bent on charas and the other delights of Peshawar. In front of them saunter the more sophisticated youths of the plains, hand in hand, with roses behind their ears and their collyrium-painted eyes coquettishly glancing about, returning stare for stare. Beggars, thieves, dwarfs, clowns, fakirs and purveyors of charas move elbow to elbow with Roman-nosed Afridis, bob-haired bandits from Black Mountain, shaggy men from Yarkand and Rajput sepoys in scarlet turbans.

On the adjoining balcony, a group of men cough in endless chorus. They are smoking charas, the mordant resin made from the crushed flower heads of the hemp plant. They will have only a short life, and it will be given over to coughing. Under the clamor of the bazaar, the labored hacking of the charasi beats a steady, insistent rhythm.

Abdul sends a servant for some charas. Taking a lump about the size of a dime, he mixes it with his tobacco and a red-hot piece of camel dung. To show us how it is done, he takes the first pull on the long, flexible tube of the narghile. Slowly, he inhales rapturously, the essence of camel, nicotine and hemp, hubble-bubbling through the water of the pipe. Then, as he coughs up the smoke, he passes the tube to me. One puff is quite enough to satisfy my Western curiosity. A certain giddiness comes over me; I feel as though I am riding through bumpy air on a magic carpet.

Many fantastic tales are related in Eastern bazaars of the strange effects and mental aberrations that come from smoking charas. Abdul tells of three travelers from Afghanistan, anxious to reach Peshawar before dark. But night comes on them before their arrival at the Bajauri Gate; they find it closed and locked. One of the three is a whiskey tippler, the second an opium smoker and the third a charist. Yearning for the comforts of the city, they sit down outside the wall to drink and smoke and talk the matter over. Soon the whiskey drinker says, "Let's break down the gate."

The opium addict toasts his pill, yawns and says, "No, let's go to sleep; let's wait till morning."

Then the charas smoker, inspired by a few drafts from his narghile, speaks: "I have it! Let's crawl through the keyhole!"

I understand it; one puff has made me a believer. I breathe deeply and try to remember that at dawn tomorrow our caravan leaves on the golden road to Samarkand.

At the very last we had bad news. Yeats-Brown was denied permission to enter Afghanistan, no doubt because as an officer of the Bengal Lancers he roused the suspicion of the Amir. Fortunately for us, he was able to send Naim Shah. We bid Y.B. a sad farewell; he would be returning to his regiment, having seen more of India during our journey together, he said, than in all his previous eighteen years in the East. And in the cool of early morning we set out for the Khyber Pass.

By 9 A.M. the sun beat down on us with a ferocity to fully justify Fort Jamrud's reputation as the heatstroke capital of the world. Every few miles across the sunbaked plain the British had erected stone shelters, but as many as a hundred travelers a year perished before reaching one of those oases of shade. At each of the British forts along the route, we were obliged to seek water for our boiling radiator, and two-thirds of the way through the Khyber, an officer shook his head with astonishment when he learned our destination and suggested it was not too late to switch to a string of camels.

We saw camels aplenty, for it was Tuesday, one of the two days the British provided military escorts to protect caravans from the local brigands. They wound back and forth on the serpentine parallel road below, with asses, bullocks and shaggy ponies among them, all carrying the riches of Bokhara, Samarkand and Afghanistan.

It took us until midafternoon to pierce the mountain barrier and cross the desert. Miles of the road had been washed away by summer floods, and sometimes we had to push through drifts and sand. Tacks from the heavy looped shoes of countless generations of Central Asian caravaners punctured our tires at the average rate of one an hour, so we spent considerable time patching inner tubes. But at last we were there, Landi Khana, a cluster of tents and stone huts at the bottom of the valley, the barbed wire and the sign at the frontier:

IT IS ABSOLUTELY FORBIDDEN TO CROSS
THIS BORDER INTO AFGHAN TERRITORY.

The Amir's soldiers let us through. Ahead, shimmering in the relentless afternoon sun, the scorched, stony terrain looked no different than the wasteland we had just crossed. But, we were in Afghanistan, the forbidden kingdom! Now not even the long arm of the British raj could protect us. Dave King took the opportunity to remark that it must have been about this point that a German engineer, returning from Kabul after completing work on a special project for the Amir, had recently been murdered by his Afghan escort.

Soon we came upon a soldier, crisscrossed with bandoliers of cartridges and obviously waiting for us. He climbed up on the running board and, gesturing, directed us to a nearby fort. There an officer told Naim Shah we were to spend the night at the Amir's winter palace in Jalalabad; he would accompany us. On we rolled, the landscape softening only imperceptibly from the harsh glare of the desert until, all at once, we found ourselves bowling along a tree-shaded avenue. It was as though we had been shot up from the fires of hell into a suburb of paradise—Jalalabad.

Half a mile above sea level, luxuriating in a subtropical climate in which date palms, orange groves and pomegranate orchards flourished, Jalalabad had long been the resi-

235

dence of the Amirs of Afghanistan during the months when mountain-locked Kabul was buried under snow. Arriving at the palace, we felt like modern Sinbads for whom this Arabian Nights splendor had been expressly conjured up. We bathed and were handsomely fed; we went to bed on cool silken sheets feeling voluptuously content—all of us pointedly not thinking about Amanullah's father, the late Amir Habibullah, who had been assassinated in this same palace three years before.

In the morning we drove the last hundred and ten miles to Kabul, via the Gate of the Trumpet and Drums. Here we were quartered in a stately but strange octagonal palace built by Amanullah's uncle, Nasrullah Khan. He had no present need for it; having made an unsuccessful attempt to seize the throne after Habibullah's murder in 1919, he was now in prison. A court chamberlain, assigned to our company, immediately began keeping a record of every move we made, every person we spoke with and everything we photographed. He spoke no English—or so he claimed—and though Persian was the language of the Afghan court, in the Kabul bazaar he kept our path clear by assaulting pedestrians with a stream of Pushtu, the amalgam of Central Asian tongues most of the people spoke.

We had just sat down to dinner on our first evening in Kabul. Under a huge candelabra with hundreds of glittering glass pendants the table was laden with highly spiced saffron pilaf, sour milk and cheese, mysterious sweet concoctions, unleavened bread baked in the ashes of the fire and mountains of delicious fruit—all brought from the Amir's own kitchens. Then there was a rumble as of heavy artillery nearby. The building rocked. The massive candelabra swayed and the dishes slid across the table and crashed to the floor. The servants, faces blanched, wheeled and fled through the door; thinking they must know something, we were hot on their heels.

The awesome rolling rumble lasted more than a minute, then all was silent; the earthquake was over. There would be others during our stay in Afghanistan, at least some quaking every evening, but nothing like the blockbuster that welcomed us to Kabul.

After some days of filming in and around the capital, we were driven to Paghman, twenty-seven miles north in the Hindu Kush mountains, where we would finally meet

236

the Amir himself. There we saw, kneeling in front of a gathering of robed Afghans at prayer, a heavyset young man wearing a black tunic, light twill riding breeches and black boots. We had come upon the royal court at Friday devotions; leading the service was none other than His Majesty, Amir Amanullah.

Afterward we were ushered into his private park. He came forward to greet us, followed by his brother and a group of cabinet ministers, all of whom he introduced to us. He seemed a jovial man, though long accustomed to having his way. Dark, questioning, protuberant eyes suggested a penchant for the good things of life.

"I am very glad you have come to Afghanistan," he said through the interpreter, "and I desire you to have every facility to see and photograph our country. Tell me if there is anything you want."

"I want to go to the headwaters of all the rivers of Afghanistan," I replied.

He laughed. "It is better that you do not. Are you married? Then it is also better for your family. I could not guarantee your return, for we are still in a disturbed state here."

Amanullah had not overstated the case. Afghanistan, a land the size of Texas, locked between more powerful nations, split east to west by the massive Hindu Kush range, had been conquered by Genghis Khan and Tamerlane and fought over for the past hundred years by Great Britain and Czarist Russia; only the year before had the British finally recognized its independence. In between, Afghan tribesmen regularly swarmed into India (now Pakistan) to pillage and plunder. And all through the ages, violence within maintained a bloody pace with foreign invasions. As an object lesson to other warring tribes, Abdur-Rahman Khan, Amanullah's grandfather, once built a tower of Shinwari skulls at Kabul.

After the assassination of his father, Amanullah had ascended a precarious throne, treason and conspiracy forever at his elbow. Among his numerous relatives, all of whom lusted for power, half were kept busy on the Amir's payroll and half were in prison. An Amir dared not leave the country, even for a short holiday, lest his enemies stage a coup in his absence. Amanullah was so closely guarded, night and day, that once, during some filming, when I took his arm to shift his position, rifles snapped up and were trained on me. "It is better if you *say* where you want me to stand," said the Amir gently.

Still, he seemed to be taking forceful steps toward the modernization of his remote and backward land. He was building schools and seeking trade links with the West. He was a fanatical believer in home industries and insisted his people wear clothing made in Afghanistan. Part enlightened leader, part Oriental despot, he had his own ideas about how to enforce this policy. He carried a razor-sharp knife, and whenever he spotted someone wearing clothes of foreign fabric or design, he would slip up behind and cut out a piece.

"This country is rich in men and material resources, both as yet undeveloped," he said to me. "It is my hope to invite experts from all over the world, including America, to help us. Frankly, that is why I am glad you have come and will tell the Western people something about us. But tell them, too, that Afghanistan is for the Afghans; I intend for my people, not foreign capitalists, to enjoy the fruits of their labor."

We filmed the Amir in Paghman and Kabul, alone and with his family, in the garden, on horseback, among his friends and especially at the wheel of one or another of his automobiles. He had quite a fleet of them to drive over the fifty miles of road in the vicinity of his capital. Once, waylaid by assassins while in his Rolls-Royce on the Kabul-Paghman road, his driving skill saved his life; swerving back and forth across the highway and accelerating to seventy miles an hour, he lost his assailants in a storm of dust. He was, incidentally, also an aviation enthusiast and had recently bought some airplanes in Italy; they arrived about the same time we did, by camel caravan.

We photographed the military procession to the Great Mosque, where prayers were to be said in the presence of the Amir. Turkoman cavalry, handsome youths on prancing, long-maned Mongolian mustangs, led the way. Next in the spectacular parade came Tajiks, Uzbegs, Kafirs—all the races of the kingdom, men whose warlike ancestors had periodically made a shambles of Hindustan—all in blue or scarlet full dress, maintaining ranks that would have done credit to the Coldstream Guards. Behind them were regiments of infantry, mountain guns, files of royal elephants—twenty thousand men in all, and only a fifth of the force kept permanently under arms.

Afterward we filmed an exhibition of tent-pegging. Galloping ten abreast down the tracks, the Afghan cavalrymen came on like rolling thunder, calling on the name of Allah. "Ye de!" they cried when their hands struck true, turning in their saddles and looking up to the pegs impaled on their lance tips, and "Wa! Wa!" when they went wide. A sham cavalry battled followed in the terrific midday heat. The Foreign Minister, Feizi Khan, who had called out the mounted squadrons for our cameras, began to wilt in his tight-fitting court dress. When he perceived that even this was not the end and that we were now to witness a display of horseback wrestling, he took off his fez and quietly collapsed into the arms of an attendant. A stretcher carried him away, and when we left Kabul the poor man had not yet recovered.

In the afternoon there came a royal command for our attendance at the palace; Chase was to photograph the Amir in formal dress. Having shed the cares of state for the moment, His Majesty was in a playful mood and posed any way either of us suggested. But once when my back was turned, out of the corner of my eye I saw him crouching behind me with his tongue stuck out.

When we were finally finished, Amanullah said to me, "You have ordered me about more than any other living man. I hope you are satisfied and have everything you want."

I assured him we had, and so we took our leave of the high-mettled young monarch who sat on the throne of what was then the most turbulent country on earth. He was to hold it only a few more years. His efforts at modernization stirred up violent opposition, and early in 1929, after bandits had seized Kabul, he abdicated and went into exile in Italy, where he died in 1960.

Our visit to Afghanistan had exceeded my farthest-fetched notions. Now I wanted to leave, and quickly, before Harry's film melted away, and we did, too; before the Amir should decide to invite us to stay a few more moons, as is the Central Asian custom with favored guests; and before we were completely destitute. So at daybreak one morning, without formality, we loaded the Buick and headed for the Khyber Pass and the plains of Hindustan.

Leaving the Kabul plateau and dipping down into the valleys leading to India, we had the usual punctures and mended them in the usual hundred-and-twenty-degree heat.

239

We drove on through the twilight and again slept in Amanullah's winter palace. Next morning we passed the frontier post of Landi Khana and continued on through the Khyber.

The gardens of Peshawar looked calm and English. We passed some subalterns riding back from polo, moustachioed majors in mufti driving pink and white girls to tennis. A church bell pealed. In the garden of the governor's compound, a terrier romped with a well-washed goat. Over them all the Union Jack flapped confidently. Suddenly the distance from Kabul to the Khyber seemed a good deal farther than from Peshawar to London.

11.

London to Leningrad—by Air

Garde à vous, monsieur! We are going to—how
you say it?—crash!

—French pilot over Andalusia

THE winter of 1922 had already established itself in London by the time Henry and I returned. Fran was waiting patiently, and we had a gala reunion. But I had barely begun to tell her about our Afghan adventures and to answer all her questions before I had to rush off to an important session—with a banker. We were broke—almost. And I had a new responsibility: just before leaving India I had casually asked Naim Shah, our loyal Afridi companion, how he would like to go to England with us, and just as casually he'd said he would like it very much. So now we were four.

The banker was sympathetic. Well aware of the record season we'd already had in London, he agreed to advance me the cash to put together a new show and enough to carry us until it began producing a return. However, he ahemmed, there was the matter of collateral.

I went back to the hotel to think it over. But thinking didn't produce the collateral; Fran did. Just like the valiant heroine in the fiction of every nation, she brought out her few jewels and said, "Go get the money." In this case, the jewels consisted mainly of the pearls I had bought her at Australia's famous oyster beds off Thursday Island, and I was never at ease over all those next months until I got them out of hock.

But we were in business again. With the speed born of

necessity, we edited our India-Afghanistan film and were ready to go in a matter of weeks. Once again Percy Burton booked us into the Royal Opera House at Covent Garden, and once again people came by the hundreds of thousands to see our show—despite its interminable title: *Through Romantic India and into Forbidden Afghanistan.*

One day the flights of fancy at Covent Garden were enlivened by an irate woman who came to discuss a wide range of iniquities. When I was somewhere between Peshawar and the Khyber Pass in my narration, she suddenly stood up in the main aisle and began shouting, "Down with the salt tax! Down with Lord Reading! Down with Lowell Thomas!"

I was not entirely in disagreement with one of her grievances, but after she had shouted them two or three times, attendants, in the gentlemanly British manner, led her outside into Bow Street. Next day she was back, and the day after that. For my part I enjoyed her immensely—she spiced the proceedings with the drama of the unexpected—and by the fourth day she was even getting a scattered bit of applause. I began to think about hiring her on a weekly basis. But then our Scottish assistant manager returned from booking us in the Provinces. He didn't realize I didn't object. He called the police and they took our gray-haired rebel away to the Marlborough police station and locked her up. But I promptly bailed her out.

Next day I went to court to testify in her behalf. I said that she had really disturbed nobody, least of all me, and had, in fact, rather brightened the show. And so she was released without even a fine. But apparently we had offended her; alas, she never came back.

Meanwhile, poor Naim Shah was finding life in London a puzzle. The long journey from India had been a trial, until I persuaded the P & O officers to let him cook his own food on deck, and then he weathered it in good style. In London he started out well enough, finding himself modest lodgings in the Chinese quarter of Limehouse and taking readily to the employment we devised for him: he stood in the lobby of the Royal Opera House in his native costume and, seven feet tall from the ground to the top of his striking Afridi headdress, was surely the most dazzling theater attendant in all London.

It was the English women who did him in. Since none of them were veiled, he made the natural assumption of a Central Asian; surely they were available. When waitresses or shopgirls smiled at him, he took it to mean they were offering themselves as concubines. And as Naim Shah was often willing, Fran or I were often in court apologizing for his transgressions and trying to explain their innocent origins.

Naim Shah could not grasp the subtleties of Western culture. Where he came from on the Afghan frontier, no man spoke to a woman outside his harem unless he wanted to add her to it. Here men spoke to women, the women replied—even smiled—and nothing happened. He would stand in Piccadilly Circus for hours watching this phenomenon, and every now and then he would try again. And Fran or I would have to go back to court.

To distract him, Fran sometimes took him to see the tigers in the London Zoo. They seemed to sense that here was someone from their own land and they would sniff and roar and follow wherever he moved along the bars of their cage. But this only made our Afridi more homesick than ever. After little more than a month, he told me he wanted to return to India, and I provided the passage.

Following the London season, we took the show to Manchester, Birmingham, Glasgow and Edinburgh. Then we went over to Paris, to do a version in French at what was then a famous theater, the Alhambra. My part in this Gallic enterprise lasted only one week, despite the efforts of a Berlitz professor. At the first Saturday matinee, I noticed a bearded gentleman in the second row cupping his ear as though he were having difficulty hearing. When I raised my voice it didn't seem to help. He turned to his companion, and in one of those whispers you can hear yards away, he asked, *"En quelle langue parle-t-il?"* I finished the performance and then and there turned the narration over to our Parisian producer, Victor Marcel.

It was just as well; Fran was going to have a baby within a few months and we wanted to get away from the hectic temptations of Paris. We moved out to Versailles and checked into a hotel within strolling distance of Louis XIV's fabulous palace and matchless gardens, and in this ineffably romantic setting we whiled away the summer and early fall.

When Fran's time drew near, we returned to London. I was signed to open with the Allenby-Lawrence show at the Theatre Royal in Dublin on October 7, and for a nervous time it looked as though there might be a crucial conflict in the scheduling. But Lowell, Jr., didn't let us down; the morning before I was to leave for Ireland, he made his own debut at a central London nursing home in Wigmore Street, just off Portland Place.

Obviously October 6, 1923, was a momentous day in our lives. But it was made even more memorable by something that seemed of only peripheral interest at the time. In the afternoon Harry came to see Fran and the baby. He had rigged up a contrivance of earphones, wires and whatnot. He called it a "crystal set" and said it might amuse Fran and help pass the time.

She put the earphones on; I remember the look of astonishment that crossed her face. Then, not speaking, as though under some spell, she passed them over to me. Whereupon I heard Lord Curzon, the former Viceroy of India, addressing the House of Lords. All this was taking place miles from where I stood, you understand, yet I heard every word as though I were at Westminster in the gallery of the Mother of Parliaments. It was a strange, portentous sensation, listening to my first radio broadcast. I think I sensed something of the potency of this instrument, almost as new as my son, some glimmer of its possibilities for the future. But of course it had nothing to do with me personally; I had no idea of the extent to which it was to move into my own life.

As soon as I arrived in Dublin I was advised to take the next boat back to Liverpool: the newspapers had been attacking me as a British propagandist, and my appearance on an Irish stage might well precipitate a riot. Instead, I went straight to my hotel and began preparing for the opening performance.

However, I was not discounting the danger. The failed Easter Rebellion was then only seven years old; the fires of Ireland's passion to be free burned hotly, fanned by wholesale executions and the terror spread by the British Auxiliaries ominously known as the Black and Tans. Though the Irish Free State had been created in 1921, the British presence remained gallingly felt; and of course there was the matter of the six counties of Ulster, still tied to the Crown. And so a murderous civil war raged on. History has few sadder examples of fanatics on every side drowning out the voices of reason, and the world is haunted to this day, in Northern Ireland as elsewhere, because the moment of reconciliation passed unheeded.

But I did not want to run; I had come to Dublin, not to be a combatant or an issue, but simply to do my show. Yet I confess I was not entirely at ease when I stepped to the edge of the footlights. The Theatre Royal was packed, every seat taken, even the standing room sold out, and no one could be sure whether the Irish were in particular need of entertainment or had come to see violence done. In self-defense I made two departures from my usual address. I said, first, that although the story I had come to tell was about the valor of British arms, I was an American who believed in Woodrow Wilson's principle of self-determination for all people, including the Irish.

Stony silence.

I took a deep breath and plunged on. "I also wanted to let you know I am married to a wonderful girl whose family name is Ryan, and who yesterday presented me with a fine baby boy, so now the Lowell Thomases have their own little Irishman." That one brought the house down. I of course also told how T. E. Lawrence's family had come from Ireland.

Thereafter the audience was as friendly and responsive as any I've ever had, and the twelve weeks I spent in Ireland turned out to be a welcome success.

Just after Christmas, Fran, Harry, young Lowell and I boarded the venerable White Star liner *Adriatic* and set sail for home, at long last. For a while it looked as though we wouldn't make it. In mid-Atlantic we ran into the record winter storm of 1924, and for two days we lay hove-to, the ship rolling up on her beams and the decks awash. I quit counting my sea voyages after a hundred, but this one was easily the wildest. Blinding sheets of rain whipped by seventy-five-mile-an-hour winds turned the world into a gray maelstrom. Dishes, chairs, passengers—whatever wasn't tied down—went crashing into the nearest bulkhead; no one slept—except Lowell, Jr., twelve weeks old, happy as a clam in his laundry basket, securely wedged into a corner—and at mealtime Fran and I had the dining salon almost to ourselves. Finally the winds subsided and we came limping into New York harbor. The lady with the torch was a welcome sight.

At first we moved in with my parents in New Jersey, where Dad had established a new medical practice down the coast at Asbury Park. We were short of funds again and this time I turned my hand to writing. I had finally decided the time had come to put the Lawrence story on paper; there was enough distance between us then, enough perspective. Working at full speed, I finished in time to meet a magazine serial deadline, and my first book, *With Lawrence in Arabia*, was published to heartening reviews and to a future of some one hundred editions and in many languages.

By this time we had moved out to Forest Hills on Long Island, but this, too, was a temporary arrangement. In those days Fran and I talked constantly about establishing ourselves permanently, somewhere; we had never had a home, having traveled continually since our marriage. But now there were three of us, and a real home, after all, is little enough to provide for a baby. Though we could easily name plenty of places where we *didn't* want to live, we hadn't come to a conclusion about the one place where we'd be happy to spend the rest of our lives.

One evening, having been to a play, we were walking past the jauntily lit marquees of the theater district when I noticed a familiar name heading the cast of *Saturday's Children*, the hit of the day. I stopped to stare at it, and when Fran inquired what the matter was, I said, "Beulah Bondy."

"Beulah Bondy what?" she asked.

"I knew a girl at college in Indiana named Beulah Bondy. I wonder if she's this one—Beulah Bondi with an *i.*"

"It certainly isn't an everyday name."

Beulah Bondy was certainly not an everyday girl. In addition to being a student of the drama she had been something of a mystic in those days, like her mother, who believed that numbers ruled our lives. It was always a little weird to hear those earnest divinations from someone who looked more attuned to a prom than a crystal ball. But remembering how the Beulah I had known had been an ardent student of dramatics, I took Fran's elbow and steered her toward the stage door.

And sure enough, my Indiana Beulah it was—and the one who was to become one of the best character actresses of her time, first on the stage and later in motion pictures. It had been nearly fifteen years since our Valpo days, and though she was glad to see me, she didn't seem in the least surprised. I introduced her to Fran and we chatted a moment, then she looked into a corner of her dressing room and said, "I knew you'd be coming to see me soon, Tommy."

I didn't know what to say. The first thing I'd told her was how I'd just chanced to recognize her name on the marquee. "Well," I finally managed, "it was a pleasant accident."

"That was no accident." She sat us down and with all her marvelous sense of the dramatic began to tell us how she had been spending some time in Dutchess County, New York, on Quaker Hill, near the village of Pawling, and how she had noticed a particular white house there, a lovely house with a wide porch.

"So?"

"So I've seen you and your wife living there."

"But . . ."

"I know—we haven't been in touch for years and I hadn't even heard that you were married. But, Tommy, there are some things we just *know*. Will you go and see the house?"

"Sure, Beulah." I laughed, much relieved that it wasn't anything more ominous. "I'm taking off on a tour in a couple of days, but when I get back we'll all go up to— where? Quaker Hill?—and look at 'our' house together."

Same old Beulah. Before we left I'd even forgotten the name of the place. At the last I asked her why she had changed Bondy to Bondi. She said something about the numerological advantages of *i* over *y* that I didn't grasp, and Fran and I walked up Broadway chuckling about love-ly, talented Beulah Bondi—the mystic!

Anyway, house-hunting had to take second place for the time being; I'd signed to do a coast-to-coast tour with the Allenby-Lawrence show, starting in Boston. We opened at the Tremont Temple, then the largest auditorium in the city, and with the help of enthusiastic reviews and plenty of advertising, ran six weeks and again broke attendance records. When one day His Eminence, Richard Cardinal O'Connell asked me to tea, I assumed he, too, would have something kind to say about the show. In fact he did, but he had invited me to his home for another reason.

You didn't have to be an unusually astute observer to know that Cardinal O'Connell was a force to be reckoned with in Boston. In a city where Lowells, Cabots and the other Brahmins had long ruled as by divine right, the

Catholic Church was now representing and defending the aspirations of growing numbers of first- and second-generation Irish. And in effect, the Church in Boston was His Eminence, Cardinal O'Connell.

He looked the part. He was built like a Notre Dame fullback and robed in the red and black of a prince of the Church; extending the great ring of his office, he was a formidable figure indeed. He poured the tea—I suspect both of us would have preferred a good jolt of Jamison's—and abruptly came to the point. He wanted me to delete a small segment of film and commentary from my show.

What segment? Had I somehow blasphemed against the Lord, profaned a sacred belief?

No, it was the part showing the mosaic ceiling panels in the chapel of the hospice built by the Germans on the Mount of Olives in Jerusalem. Of the two panels, one represented Christ and the twelve apostles, and the other Kaiser Wilhelm II and twelve of his advisers, also in biblical garb. The implication was heavy-handedly obvious, sacrilegious, I thought, and when the Kaiser's picture appeared on the screen the audience always hooted scornfully. I would then say something about the Savior looking a bit uncomfortable in such close proximity to the apostle of militarism.

Was the Cardinal troubled by this sacrilege? Oh, no—the *British* troubled him, and as any enemy of the British was a friend of the Irish, he resented the derisive laughter I was directing at good old Kaiser Bill.

I suppose I would have been even more shocked if, in Ireland, I had not seen for myself the depths of the anti-British feelings. Now here in Boston, headquarters of Irish sentiment in the United States, I found the passion running equally deep. I told His Eminence I would have to consider his request, but in truth I never really considered it at all. In the first place, I had a built-in resistance to any suggestion of censorship, no matter how politely put; and in the second place, I had no intention of giving up a sure-fire laugh. So the segment stayed, and maybe in Boston I had fewer Catholics in my audiences than I might have had. Over the years I have been on friendly terms with three American cardinals, and even with one Pope, but Cardinal O'Connell I never saw again.

When our Boston engagement ended we headed west and played just about every American city and town with more than five thousand people. Then we went north to Halifax in easternmost Canada and did the same thing all the way across the Dominion. By the time those trips were over I was so tired of the sound of my own voice and the swimming seas of anonymous faces that I vowed never to face an audience again with my Allenby-Lawrence production.

Mostly my North American tours are a scramble of disconnected memories—one-night stands, being shaken out of my Pullman berth to change trains in the middle of the night, and unending plates of chicken. The date in Denver stands out in my mind, not only because it was Fran's hometown and practically mine, but because *The Denver Post*, my sponsor, staged a parade for us!

It was quite an affair. Up Sixteenth Street from the railroad station we rode, Fran and I perched up on the back of a big open touring car, while confetti flew, people cheered, and bombs were fired off from the *Post* building. Looking for familiar faces, I spotted Bill Post, a Victor schoolmate, and waved. I hadn't seen Bill in twenty years, and as his special interest was Kelly pool he probably had no notion of the reason for the festivities. Finally I caught his eye and his jaw dropped in astonishment. He didn't even wave. Instead, he turned to the man standing next to him and, although I couldn't hear the words, I'd bet anything he said: "What the hell is *he* doing up there?" Come to think about it, I wondered the same thing.

The Denver Post, one of the West's great newspapers, had been founded by a couple of buccaneers, Harry Tammen, a saloonkeeper, and Fred Bonfils, who failed to complete his career at West Point and who found his real vocation running a lottery in Kansas City. Now Tammen was dead and Bonfils, almost respectable, ran the sensation-mongering *Post* like a dictator. A day or so after our arrival, he called me into his office and closed the door.

"Lowell," he asked, "how old are you?"

"Thirty-two."

"Well, you're a little young. But if you come back to Colorado and settle down here, I promise to send you to the U.S. Senate within five years."

I was nonplussed. It was a king-size compliment, but before I could even thank him for it, he was launched into painting a rosy picture of what such an opportunity could mean to me. He didn't say anything about what it would mean to him, but I wasn't gullible enough to believe he was proposing me for this great honor because he liked the wave in my hair.

True, I had once been taken with the idea of politics as a career; there were some things I felt strongly about and wanted to help legislate—a comprehensive system of interstate highways (now we have too many), also the elimination of all outdoor billboard advertising, still a monstrous blight on our land. But my idea of politics did not include returning to Colorado to become Fred Bonfils's man in Washington, D.C. So I told him I wasn't sure I was ready to settle down, but if I changed my mind I would be in touch.

Soon after, when we were playing Chicago, I went to see Silas H. Strawn, the great attorney who had really started me off by backing my World War I filming expedition to Europe. I told him about Bonfils's offer but not my decision; I wanted to hear the reaction of someone whose judgment I valued. It was emphatic.

"Lowell," he said, "if you really want to get involved in politics, wait until you are financially independent. The truth is that for twenty-five thousand dollars I can buy almost any member of either house of Congress. And I don't mean by bribery."

What he meant was that with the enormous power exerted by his law firm and its prestigious clients, by the business they could channel this way or that, it would take a strong—or rich—legislator to resist their influence. I wonder how much this has changed in the intervening half century. Maybe the price has gone up—inflation!

For much of the year 1924, Americans were most interested in the preparations and adventures of eight army airmen who set out to become the Magellans of the sky, first to fly all the way around the world. Their four DH-4 biplanes had been built by a young aeronautical engineer named Donald Douglas who, only a few years before, had taken all his assets, six hundred dollars, and gone into the arcane business of building airplanes. Due in no small part to the luster of the first world flight, for years Douglas aircraft dominated the skies—especially the DC-3.

One of the Douglas amphibians, lost in fog, crashed on an Alaskan mountaintop early on, and it took the pilots ten days to hike through the snow to a Bering Sea cannery.

But the others flew on, island-hopping across the Pacific, scraping over the Asian highlands and jungles at treetop level while vicious air currents threatened, as one of them put it, "to impale us on the horn of a rhino." Every leg of their incredible journey had its palpitations and mishaps, which is hardly surprising when you undertake to fly around the globe only twenty years after man first took to the air and the best equipment available is a single-engine plane with a speed of seventy miles an hour. But the fliers' blithe high spirits remained unruffled; they even picked up Linton Wells, a journalist-hitchhiker in Calcutta, and would have flown him all the way back to the States if a stern message from Washington awaiting them in Karachi had not forbidden it.

At every stop they were feted and wined; later the airmen said their "ordeal by banquet" wore them down more than did the twenty-six thousand miles they flew or their three hundred sixty-three hours in the air. Eventually exhaustion took its toll. In Paris, at the sexy *Folies-Bergère,* they fell sound asleep. In London, they had to turn down an invitation from King George to visit him at Buckingham Palace. Then they were off on the most dangerous leg, history's first east-to-west flight across the Atlantic. Leaving the Faeroe Islands for Iceland, one of the planes went down in the Atlantic after an oil pump failure. The pilots were picked up by an American cruiser, but their World Cruiser was lost. The remaining two planes, with a third replacement, flew on to Labrador and then Boston. Now they had only to cross the United States to complete the epic trip. At this point I joined them for the final four thousand miles of one of man's greatest adventures.

Many publishers and writers were eager to do the story of the first world flight and, with my enthusiasm for anything to do with aviation, I was one of them. The competition was keen, but I had a commitment from Houghton Mifflin for the book and from the McClure Syndicate to do the newspaper serialization—provided I could get the appointment as the flight's official historian. Thanks to the help of General Billy Mitchell of the infant Air Service, then an arm of the Signal Corps, who had been impressed with the success of my recently published book on T. E. Lawrence, this was arranged. I was assigned an army plane and a veteran pilot to fly me the rest of the way with the round-the-world airmen.

As there was a spirited dispute about the historic flight's point of origin between Santa Monica, where Douglas had built the World Cruisers, and Seattle, from which point they had lifted off into the unknown, climactic ceremonies were to be held in both places. Today it is hard to grasp the tremendous excitement that gripped the world at those pioneering feats of airmanship. The sky was then as much of a mystery and challenge as outer space is today; in addition, a dozen nations, not just two, were striving to fly farthest and fastest, to be first to send their brave young aviators through the frontiers of the air. Britain, France, Italy, Portugal and Argentina all had had planes and crews in the race to be first to circle the globe, and some of the fliers perished in the effort.

Now, messages of congratulations poured in on the Americans who succeeded; everyone wanted to see them and hear every detail of their fantastic achievement. As one admiral who rose to toast them said, "Other men will fly around the earth, but never again will anybody fly around it for the first time."

Meanwhile, I was having a fair round of adventures myself. Major Corliss C. Moseley, who was winging me cross-country to the receptions for the round-the-world team, was as good a flier as the army had, but the planes were still a long way from measuring up to their pilots. Taking off from New Orleans, the engine on our DH-4, known among airmen as the Flying Coffin, cut out at a hundred feet and we almost went right back into the barn that had served as our hangar—the hard way. At the last second Mose coaxed it back to life and we sputtered up into the air.

A couple of hours later, the engine again gasped for life and we had to make a forced landing in a cotton field near Natchez. Some field hands who had never seen an airplane were working nearby. One approached, looked us over, and with a certain wisdom said, "Mister, before I ever got into one of those things, I'd write a letter to the Lord. And I still wouldn't go until he wrote back!"

We had another forced landing at Allentown, Pennsylvania, a close call landing in the dark at San Francisco and a thrill a minute in between. But we finally made it all the way to Seattle. Afterward, I put together a film and narrative of the world flight and, sharing the platform with one of the world fliers, "Smiling" Jack Harding, we did a coast-to-coast tour.

There was a pioneer radio station in Pittsburgh then. KDKA invited me to do a one-hour impromptu talk on the flight. Of course there were no tape recording devices in those days, and I don't even have any notes on what I said. But I remember the date, March 21, 1925. It was the first time I ever stepped up to a radio microphone and began talking.

By the spring of 1926 I had finished writing *The First World Flight* and a book about my Afghanistan adventure, *Beyond Khyber Pass*. Having been deskbound for a year, I felt an urgent need to pack a bag and get going. Flying was still on my mind and, as I had been reading about the development of some embryo European airlines, I suggested to Fran a journey such as no one had ever made before: to crisscross Europe by air, flying via every available plane, going wherever they would take us. She wasn't long thinking it over, and soon we were looking for a suitable place to leave young Lowell.

The place we found was Locust Farm, a country home and school run by three sisters with experience looking after children whose parents needed to be away; it was in Dutchess County, about seventy miles north of New York City. And so Fran and I had our first glimpse of the lovely low hills of the Taconics. As our train passed through the village of Pawling, I suddenly remembered Beulah Bondi's strange vision of the Thomases living in a certain white house—hadn't it been somewhere near Pawling? But I was too preoccupied with my guilt at leaving Lowell, Jr., behind to think about it much. I would have given anything to take him with us, but two and a half is a little young for barnstorming across Europe in the war-surplus, single-engine planes used by those early commercial airlines. I still remember the sad look in his eyes when we left him, and we sailed for England with heavy hearts. Today, in light of his own fabulous adventures, I take comfort in the hope that eventually he came to understand why we did.

The Americans had won the greatest air race of all time, a major milestone in man's conquest of the air, but it was the Europeans who had gotten the jump in commercial aviation. The reason was basic: although we had our share of war-trained pilots, nearly all the planes they had

253

flown were built in Europe. Now those planes and the aces of World War I were pioneering air routes between London and Amsterdam, Paris and Berlin, Bucharest and Moscow and dozens of other cities. Otto Merkle, who had spent two years studying auto assembly-line techniques in Detroit and returned to Germany to found the airline called Lufthansa, told me the Americans would get going in commercial aviation within a year or so and then would soon outfly the rest of the world. But for the moment, the Europeans had a monopoly on air travel.

As for me, I figured if small planes could circle the planet without loss of life, an aerial tour of Europe must be safe enough for your grandmother. Having no available grandmother, I took my wife—and we both would have reason to question my sanity. Before it was over, we covered twenty-six thousand miles by air, breaking the record for passenger miles flown, often traveling in open-cockpit planes held together with baling wire and devout thoughts, and more than once it seemed likely we would never see our son again. But it was an adventure such as was given to few, and neither of us would have missed it for anything.

When we arrived in London I went to see G. E. Woods-Humphery, General Manager of the newly organized British Imperial Airways, and explained our purpose. He said he envied us such a journey and would gladly start us off with places on the next day's flight to Amsterdam. But by the next day, in the perverse manner of an English spring, the weather had turned foul and blustery and the flight was canceled. Nor did it improve the day after, or the next day. Each morning Fran and I would wait, packed and ready, until a polite call from Woods-Humphery regretfully announced another cancellation. We began to think we would never get off the ground. But on the fourth day, though the weather had not noticeably improved, the managing director sent his Rolls to take us to Croydon Airfield for a takeoff at 11 A.M.

And we did, in a Handley-Page, a wartime bomber now fitted with a cabin to accommodate six passengers, with the pilot and copilot up front. We roared up into a driving rain, the visibility so bad and the ceiling so low we had to fly right down on the deck all the way across the English Channel and along the coast of Belgium. We came in over Holland at minimal altitude, and as one of the unhappy passengers said, "We were looking up at the windmills."

It was a rough ride, and only Fran and I among the six souls bunched into the improvised cabin were spared the tortures of airsickness. At one point the copilot summoned me forward to take his seat while he went back to comfort the sufferers. But not until we landed and were all given a much needed shot of schnapps were any of them comforted. Three years later, when I chanced to run into the copilot in Bermuda, I finally learned the true depths of their misery—they were British Imperial employees, had no business in Amsterdam and would have to turn right around and go home. In a way it was all my fault. After our three-day delay in London, Woods-Humphery, sure we would get a bad impression of Imperial Airways service if we were held up any longer, ordered the pilot to fly us to Amsterdam, no matter what the weather. There were no other passengers booked, and to make a showing he sent the first four office employees who fell under his gaze to fill up the seats, and so they became our unwilling fellow travelers on the harrowing first leg of our trans-European air trip. I can only hope they forgave us.

The strength-giving schnapps we gulped at the Amsterdam airfield had been dealt out by Albert Plesman himself. Plesman, a bluff and hearty giant of a man, was already on his way toward becoming a Dutch legend. He was a founding father of commercial aviation with his airline, *Koninkyke Luchvaart Maatschappy*—today, happily, known simply as KLM—and remained an innovator and persistent champion of new and better aircraft and even farther-flung air routes.

It was Plesman who launched Fran and me on the red-carpet treatment we were to receive wherever we went in Europe. Air travel was still so new, almost invariably we were the only passengers on our flights, and the enthusiastic people who operated the fledgling airlines were as glad to see us as if we had been royalty; they entertained us accordingly. And those interludes of wining and dining and theater and concerts turned out to be a striking counterpoint to some of the white-knuckle hours we spent in the air.

From Amsterdam we flew to Paris, and from there to Bucharest in a French Spad, the pilot's face swathed in bandages and only his eyes peering darkly through the white mass. I made a point of not asking him what had happened. Landing, the Spad bounced hard, spun and went over on its nose. "Are you well?" asked the bandages.

"Oui," said Fran, looking straight down at the back of his neck.

Next day, another Spad, another French pilot. Preparing to take off across the Black Sea for Istanbul, I asked him in what I hoped was a casual way what would happen if our single engine conked out over the water. I don't know what sort of reply I expected, but frankness, not reassurance, was this pilot's strongpoint. "Oh, *on tombera quelque part dans la Mer Noire."* And no matter how I twisted the translation around in my head, it still came out as a flat assertion that we were bound to come down somewhere in the Black Sea.

Well, the engine didn't conk out. We made it to Istanbul and moved on from there, rarely in any one place more than a few days. It was still spring when we became among the first to land at Tempelhof, the new airfield in the heart of Berlin. I had plenty of opportunity to show Fran around the city, for we were waiting for the ponderous Russian bureaucracy to give us permission to fly into the USSR. As soon as it came, we took off for Leningrad, flying via Latvia, Lithuania and Estonia.

Our plane this time was a Fokker, a small cabin slung under its single wing. There we were kept company by the flight engineer, who could open a forward port and get directly at his engine for checking and lubrication. Ah, but the engine was lubricated with castor oil and the fumes inundated the cabin, and for the first and last time in several millions of miles of air travel I was good and ill. Nor could I try to forget my malaise by looking out at the scenery; the suspicious Russians had all the cabin window curtains drawn, as if the endless miles of forest below might reveal dark secrets of their latest five-year plan. All in all, I had good reason to remember our castor oil trip to the Soviet Union.

On our return flight the delicately lubricated Fokker engine began to splutter and fume over Poland, and we went spinning toward violent contact with the city of Krakow. Luckily the pilot managed to pull out and we landed wheels down. Soon after, en route from Nuremberg to Berlin in a Dornier Wall flying boat, we came within a whisker of hitting a mountain in the Thuringian Forest. Two weeks later the same plane, carrying the German ambassador to

America, hit the same mountain. All on board were killed. Was fate closing in on us? Indeed it was.

Thus far, each city we visited boasted an opera company and we had gone to the opera everywhere, for Fran always had an insatiable enthusiasm for music. I enjoyed it somewhat less, and all our flying, much of it in open cockpit planes, made it hard for me to stay awake indoors after dark. Not Fran. She watched bright-eyed and absorbed while I slept through great arias and cadenzas in London, Paris, Berlin, Dresden, Budapest, Milan, Rome, Warsaw, Leningrad and Moscow. So when we returned to Paris with Fran ready for still more opera—as well as some serious shopping along the rue Faubourg St. Honoré—I flew off to Morocco on my own. And it was on this jaunt, as the fliers in Alaska put it, "I almost bought the farm."

I was to fly with Latécoère, a small airline pioneering the routes across the Mediterranean from France to her colonies in North Africa. A few years later Latécoère was absorbed by Air France and forgotten, but one of its pilots, Antoine de Saint-Exupéry, will be remembered as long as man remains fascinated by the challenge of the skies. He was the poet laureate of aviation, capturing in words the danger, exhilaration and mystery of flight. In his masterpiece, *Wind, Sand and Stars,* he described the essential oneness of a pilot and his aircraft better than anyone ever has:

> The motors fill the lighted chamber with a quiver that changes its substance. The clock ticks on. The dials, the radio lamps, the various hands and needles go through their invisible alchemy. From second to second these mysterious stirrings, a few muffled words, a concentrated tenseness, contribute to the end result. And when the hour is at hand, the pilot may glue his forehead to the window with perfect assurance. Out of oblivion the gold has been smelted: there it gleams in the lights of the airport.

Soon after the start of World War II, Saint-Exupéry wrote, saying, "War is not an adventure. It is a disease." Infected with the disease, volunteering for active duty though well past military age, he disappeared on a reconnaissance flight over the Mediterranean, vanishing forever into the wind and the stars.

Unfortunately, it was not Saint-Exupéry but another

257

Latécoère pilot who was flying the mails to Morocco that summer day in 1926. Our plane was an open cockpit Breguet, a two-seat observation plane left over from the war. Crammed into the rear cockpit between my knees was a Latécoère mechanic, bound for a new assignment in Fez. We took off in the early morning, landing at Lyons and Marseilles, and followed the Spanish coast to Barcelona and Alicante. Then we set course for Málaga, cutting southeast over the Andalusian desert.

Somewhere east of the Sierra Nevada Mountains the engine suddenly quit. Overtaken by a frightening silence, gliding irrevocably to earth, we came down in a rattling, hard, deadstick landing on the red sand. After we had exchanged a few nervous jokes to dispel the tension, after the mechanic tried to coax the defiant engine back to life but could not, the pilot said he would go for help. Although it appeared to be an utterly desolate region, he said he believed he knew of a mine a few miles away where he would telephone the *pilote en chef* in Alicante.

The mechanic and I crawled under a wing to take shelter from the blistering heat of the Spanish desert in summer. Soon the pilot returned with good news: he had found the mine and gotten through to Alicante; the *pilote en chef* himself was already on his way with another plane. And little more than an hour later, there he was in the sky above us. We lighted a small fire to indicate the wind direction, and soon he dropped down and rolled to a stop beside the crippled Breguet.

The mail was transferred and the three of us prepared to take off; the *pilote en chef* would wait for the arrival of a new engine. But we couldn't take off. Our plane was overloaded and the air was at its thinnest in the midafternoon heat. After racing five hundred yards toward a menacing mass of boulders without lifting the wheels from the bumpy desert floor, the pilot taxied back to our first Breguet.

There followed a good deal of gesticulating and spirited French, which indicated that our pilot wanted the mechanic to remain behind, and the mechanic was wailing his resistance. The *pilote en chef* seemed to favor whichever currently had his attention. Still overloaded and with the mechanic on board, we tried again, but only succeeded in coming even closer to a violent end among those boulders. This time we dropped some mail sacks, and the *pilote en chef* encouraged us by shouting, *"Allez-y, décollez!"* And, on the third attempt we staggered up into the air.

But we were never out of trouble. Only a few hundred feet off the ground, the pilot went into a flat turn and the plane bucked and began falling. He had the presence to cut the switch, then twisted in his seat and shouted, *"Garde à vous, monsieur!* We are going to—how you say it?—crash!"* I remember thinking this hardly qualified as a hot news flash, and an instant later we hit like a bursting shell, and sand exploded all around us.

Somehow we all scrambled up out of the cockpit and tumbled to the ground. I was the only one to get up. Frantically I dragged the other two away, certain the plane would burst into flame at any second. But it did not, and when we had all recovered our senses and made sure we had no mortal injuries, we sat in the sand and surveyed the spectacle.

The plane was a wreck, with the Moroccan mails strewn over the desert for fifty yards or more. And as there seemed nothing else to do—we were too badly hurt to move—we just sat where we were and waited for someone to come to our aid.

The *pilote en chef* and some peasants who had seen the plane falling arrived about the same time; the peasants put us in a springless cart and took us to a hospital in Murcia, some miles away. Days later another plane came for the pilot and the mechanic and flew them on to Morocco.

But I had had enough. All those months of flying in every conceivable kind of aircraft, all the twenty-six thousand miles and all twenty-one countries, had finally caught up with me. I was bruised and cut from the accident, also exhausted. Now I was in the land of Valencia oranges and good red wine, and I intended to stay there and let my battered bones heal.

A few days later, bent over to favor my sore ribs but able to walk with the aid of a cane, I went up into the mountains to Granada, a city woven into history and spun with sheer magic. And there, beside the lovely fountains of the Alhambra, the glory of the Moors and their last citadel in Spain, my strength and spirit returned. By the time I got back to Fran in Paris I could make the crash sound like a joke. But I was glad transatlantic air service was still in the future. Sailing home on the leisurely old *Rot-*

terdam, I didn't do much more than eat, sleep and watch the flying fish from a deck chair.

In the early fall of 1926, Fran and I again took up our hunt for a permanent home. The look we'd had at Dutchess County when we took young Lowell to Locust Farm drew us back there, and one day we found ourselves driving along a dirt road leading to a place called Quaker Hill, a few miles east of Pawling. When we came to a handsome white New England house in a peaceful setting of fields and fine old trees, we were both immediately struck by the same thought—*this could be it!*

There was nothing to indicate the house might be for sale. But I jumped a fence and knocked at the door. A butler answered, and when I asked for the owner of the house, he showed us into a charming sitting room of chintz and solid country furniture. There I was joined by a handsome Virginia grande dame named Wise, a woman past middle age who looked as serene as her house. I introduced myself and said, "My wife and I have been traveling around the world for many years. Now we have a little boy and we would like to settle down in a home of our own. We wondered if by chance this place could be for sale?"

Her eyes had widened as I spoke. "This is the strangest thing," she said. "My husband and I lived in this house almost thirty years. Our three children were born here. And now you come along and . . ."

"I'm sorry," I said, my heart sinking. "I didn't mean to offend you."

I started to get up, but she motioned me to stay where I was, seemingly unable to speak for the moment. Then she said, "My husband passed away several years ago. Now the children are grown and gone and I am mostly alone here. Just this morning—I still have not mentioned it to a soul—I made up my mind to sell the house and take an apartment in New York City. And then suddenly you knock at my door and—well, it's as though you were fated to be the new owners of Clover Brook Farm."

I brought Fran in, and Mrs. Wise then showed us around and invited us to stay with her for a while so we could be absolutely sure Clover Brook Farm was where we wanted to live.

We were sure. Soon I was making the trip out to Garden City, Long Island, to promote an advance from Doubleday

260

on some books I hadn't written so I could meet the closing date. On the way back, Fran and I picked up Beulah Bondi and, without saying any more, told her to direct us to the house where she'd envisioned us living. She went straight as an arrow to Clover Brook Farm, as we'd known she would.

12

The Clover Brook Crowd:
a Prince, a President, a Pirate

> Mr. Thomas, would you be interested in writing
> my story? I am one of fourteen survivors of a
> shipwreck; we drifted thirteen hundred miles
> across the South Seas in an open boat; when we
> ran out of food, we ate the chief engineer.
> —FIRST ASSISTANT ENGINEER FRED HARMON

CLOVER Brook Farm consisted of a thirty-two-room
house, a home for the superintendent, two barns, and
eighty acres of fields, to which we soon added another three
hundred fifty of woodland. Clover Brook ran through the
property on its way to the Croton River. The house had been
built in Colonial days, and in all the years since then we
were only the fifth family to own it. One of our predecessors
was an innovative, aggressive magazine publisher,
Ben Hampton, who when he went broke in the 1890s sold
it to a Virginia family. Then he had made a second fortune,
in tobacco, and lost it. Subsequently he made a third producing
the Zane Grey films in Hollywood, and soon after
we moved in, Hampton tried to buy the house back. Failing,
he settled for the farm next door, later to be the home of
the Hogates of the *Wall Street Journal*, then of the Edward
R. Murrows, and now the Orin Lehmans.

Although we were almost broke at the time, I made a
thousand-dollar down payment on Clover Brook. Then a
Doubleday book advance enabled us to meet the December

30 deadline for the balance. So Fran, Lowell, Jr., and I had a home at last. I also had a commitment to write six books, none of which had been researched or even outlined, and not until after I finished at least one of them could I look forward to any sizable fresh flow of cash. I figured I needed help.

It came in the person of a round little man with the unlikely name of Prosper Buranelli. He looked like a screen director's version of Friar Tuck, measuring about five feet two in any direction, or perhaps like a not quite debauched Falstaff. But behind the endlessly engaging wit was a computer brain that seemed to me to have absorbed the total sum of human knowledge and stood ready to call forth even the most obscure bits on demand. Prosper was an authentic genius with a most unusual and attractive personality, a marvelous companion, altogether one of the most remarkable men I have ever known. Our meeting was one of the luckiest things ever to happen to me.

Not long after I had signed the Doubleday contract, I had run into a friend from London, Captain John B. L. Noel, a mountaineer-photographer, who had been a member of the first Mount Everest expedition in 1922 and the ill-fated 1924 attempt when Mallory and Irvine vanished forever near the summit of the world's highest peak. When I told Noel I'd undertaken to write six books and was so far floundering in the attempt to get started, he said he recently had solved a lesser, similar problem. John O'Hara Cosgrave, one of the editors of the New York *World,* had asked him to write a series of articles on Mount Everest. When Noel told him he hadn't the time, Cosgrave countered with an offer to send him someone who would relieve him of most of the work. Enter Prosper Buranelli.

"We spent a few hours together," Noel told me, "then he went off and wrote the articles, and when I read them I thought I had written them."

Within the hour I had Prosper on the telephone. That weekend he came up to Quaker Hill where I explained my problem and invited him to join me. "Well," he said, "let's give it a try." And so Prosper was with us for the next thirty-four years, until the night of June 19, 1960, when he died in our house.

He came from Temple, Texas, one of seven children born to an Italian immigrant from the Levant and a Wisconsin girl of German and Scottish parentage. Obviously they were not an ordinary couple. Another son, Vincent, became one of the world's foremost aeronautical engineers and invented the all-wing airplane. And their choice of a name for Prosper was as prophetic as it was surprising. They named him for Prospero, the incredibly wise Duke of Milan in Shakespeare's *The Tempest*—Prospero, who embodied Shakespeare's philosophy toward the end of his life; Prospero, who is given one of the immortal bard's most famous and illuminating speeches:

> Our revels now are ended. These our actors
> As I foretold you, were all spirits and
> Are melted into air, into thin air . . .
>   We are such stuff
> As dreams are made on; and our little life
> Is rounded with a sleep.

Prosper's schooling was interrupted in the sixth grade. Having borne as much as he could of the rote and endless repetition of things he already knew, he stood up in his classroom one day, broke a ruler over his knee for emphasis and walked out, never to return. When he was still only in his teens, in New York he spent three years experimenting with musical composition. With his sprightly intellect and bonhomie, Pros became a favorite in the Greenwich Village studios where the writers and artists of the day congregated, and soon a wealthy friend, awed by the seemingly limitless capacity of his mind, offered to sponsor him at Yale. So Prosper went off to New Haven. He lasted one semester, then returned to New York. He had enjoyed being at Yale, he reported, but there was little they could teach him that he couldn't learn more easily by himself. The rich friend persisted. What about Cornell then? Surely Cornell would stimulate him. So again Prosper boarded a train, this time bound for Ithaca. Same result. He didn't even make it through the first marking period, though there may have been distractions—this time he came back with a wife. In any case, that brief experiment was the end of Prosper's formal education and he decided he'd better go to work.

Cosgrave hired him as a specialty writer for the *World,* his specialty to do those cerebral pieces too taxing for other reporters. In 1919, Editor Cosgrave gave him an additional assignment: He was to introduce *World* readers to something called the crossword puzzle, a word game then enjoying a limited vogue in England. Pros was not too happy about this, he later said, because "the crossword puzzle was regarded in the office as beneath a sensible man's consideration." This he changed, developing a new numbering system and elevating the level of challenge so the crossword began intriguing even unabashed intellectuals. In the process, he became the father of the crossword-puzzle craze in America, taking on two assistants and turning out new and better ones for the next ten years. In 1924, when two enterprising young men, Dick Simon and Max Schuster, started a shaky publishing venture, their first offering was *The Crossword Puzzle Book*, edited by Prosper Buranelli. It established their firm by becoming a runaway best seller; so Prosper also can be considered at least the godfather of Simon & Schuster. More than a hundred million copies were sold of the crossword puzzle book, and Pros should have become a modern Croesus. However, money meant nothing to him.

He was also a chess master who could take on five men at the same time while discussing archaeology with a sixth. He haunted the Metropolitan Opera, knew most of the singers and musicians and, apparently, almost every line of music ever written. If you hummed a few bars for him, he would identify the composition, then proceed with a brief account of the composer's life. He was a brilliant conversationalist, always able to pluck a gem of relevant information from his incredible memory, no matter what the subject, and offer it with style and wit. In later years President Herbert Hoover called Pros his favorite fishing companion, and I suspect F.D.R. tried at least once to lure him to Washington.

Prosper had some shortcomings to go with his great gifts, most of them to do with the practical aspects of life. Our relationship may have flourished partly because he no longer had to concern himself with finance, which bored him. A main task of Mary Davis, who ran my New York office, was to retrieve the bills Pros threw into the wastebasket and pay them. She also periodically assembled and sent to the laundry the socks and shirts he stuffed into our filing cabinets.

He had an ideal if unusual marital relationship. Although he and his Mina loved each other dearly, although Pros took an inordinate pride in his growing family and a close interest in his children's education, he was rarely home. When we were at work on a book, he stayed at Quaker Hill; later, during the radio and Fox-Movietone years, he spent most nights in a small hotel across from the office.

Meanwhile, Mina was at their suburban house in Ridgefield Park, New Jersey, where she was somewhat disconsolate because the house seemed to shrink as the nine Buranelli children grew. Finally, in the 1940s, I scouted a larger place in nearby Tenafly and bought it for them. Weeks later, Prosper told Mary he was going home and asked her to write his new address on a piece of paper. This he gave to a taxi driver, who drove him all the way out to Tenafly. But when Pros saw the expansive grounds and the big, brightly lit house, he said to the driver, "Somebody's made a mistake. This must be where the mayor lives." And he went back to New York.

Over the years we had quite an array of guests at Quaker Hill—three presidents, a justice of the United States Supreme Court, several governors, actors, airmen, admirals, generals, artists, authors, explorers and opera stars. The first, arriving only a few weeks after Fran and I moved in, was Prince William, second son of the aging King of Sweden, Gustavus V. My booking agency, the Alber-Wickes Bureau, had scheduled the Prince for a series of talks on his African travels. At nearly the last moment, His Royal Highness, Prince William, admitted he had never spoken in public. Would I take him on for a couple of weeks, the Alber-Wickes people asked, and get him ready for the American tour, or at least let them know if he threatened to be a disaster on the platform so they could cut their losses?

At this point, I suppose any sensible man would have said he had his own work to do, having just moved into a new home, still sparsely furnished and lit by kerosene lamps against the day when electric power lines were brought close enough to be utilized. In our then rather remote area the roads were still unpaved and even a moderate snowfall reduced the meager population to dependency on horse and sleigh. However, I blithely checked with Fran—whose contribution was a gay "Why not?"—and soon a Prince of the royal House of Bernadotte, along with his aide-de-camp, was standing at our doorstep.

He was six feet eight inches tall, a telephone pole of a

man. Looking down on the world from such an Olympian height, he scarcely seemed in contact with it. In anticipation of his visit, while filling a speaking date at Montreal, I had invested in skis, poles, waxes and the other gear required for such Scandinavian enthusiasms as jumping and cross-country skiing. But in all the time Prince William was with us, he left the house only once, and then not to ski. He had enjoyed winter sports in his youth, he told us loftily, but he was now in his forties and it had been ten years since he'd skied or skated. I wonder what he might have said if, later, I had told him that in my mid-eighties, from November to May, I ski every chance I get. Luckily his aide, an army captain, was more than willing to join me on skis, and with him as a companion I was soon bitten by what was to become my number one sports addiction.

Prince William's current interests were literature and travel—and nervously preparing for his American speaking tour on a recent expedition to Africa. Prosper and I worked with him every day, shaping his manuscript into easy, idiomatic English and helping him to feel comfortable with it. When I suggested he try it out on a live audience—explaining how even a Broadway show went to New Haven or Philadelphia for a final tune-up—he agreed, provided he could read from the manuscript. This was bad news—there is no surer way to put an audience to sleep—but I said nothing.

The preview was easily arranged. Dr. Frederick Gamage, headmaster of the Pawling Boys School, was delighted with the prospect of having an explorer-prince address his students and invited us all to dine at his home on the appointed evening. This was the day William unbent and came down from Mount Olympus to join the brotherhood of man. He told amusing stories at dinner and charmed us all with his old-world urbanity.

I suspected one reason for the transformation: the Prince was finally relaxed about his lecture; the typed manuscript he'd carefully slipped into his inside coat pocket was to his liking and gave him confidence. I also knew, as he did not, that the manuscript was lying on the hall table back at Clover Brook. I had removed it from his pocket as I helped him on with his coat. I did this on the theory that the sooner he took the plunge the sooner we'd all know whether he was going on a speaking tour or sailing back to Sweden, so I had purposely left it behind.

After an enjoyable dinner he walked lightheartedly through the snow to the auditorium. There Prince William removed his coat and, about to step onstage, reached for his manuscript. He seemed to rise away from us again, his face growing remoter than ever. We could hear Dr. Gamage beginning his introductory remarks to the boys. As Prince William turned toward me for a lifeline, I discovered something important to say to Prosper and walked off to the side.

The Prince was not sailing back to Sweden. He was, after all, a Bernadotte, the son of a king. Squaring those royal shoulders, he strode out in front of his audience and began to talk, from the script when he remembered it, and improvising with style and humor and sheer elegance when he did not. The students were spellbound as he described his adventures and applauded long and hard when the talk was over.

On the way home the Prince was plainly exhilarated. His first platform venture in America had been a rousing success—as all the others would be—and he had done it without the use of a manuscript or even any notes. When he wondered aloud what had become of his script, I confessed my misdeed. Laughing, I added, "Since it all turned out so well, I hope Your Highness will find it in his heart to forgive me."

"Mmm," he replied from his great height, as though thinking it over, and finally uttered a grudging, "Yes."

I don't think he really did, though. Which may explain why, in thanks for the hospitality of my home and two weeks of our time, not to mention the services of Fran and a secretary, I received in the mail, some weeks after Prince William's departure, his autographed photo. However, the chances are he thought his bureau, the Alber-Wickes people, had engaged me to help him. Our only reward was the photo! And the honor of having a real prince as our first houseguest.

The legendary Arctic explorer Vilhjalmur Stefansson sometimes came to Clover Brook, after first exacting a promise from us for Fran never to have more than eight for dinner when he was there: Stef wanted to be in every conversation. And how right he was!

Soon after surrendering the White House to Franklin D. Roosevelt in March, 1933, Herbert Hoover, then at the nadir of his popularity, forsaken, even reviled, came to

Clover Brook for some days of quiet and contemplation, also some fishing. Thereafter for many years he was a regular visitor. We had met first during, and again just after, the war, when I reported to the American delegation in Paris on the situation inside revolutionary Germany. In 1928, in the one and only political speech of my life, I had spoken in his favor at a meeting of the Dutchess County League of Women Voters. But of course that wasn't why the Chief, as he was known to his friends, took to visiting us. He came because he knew no one on the Hill wanted anything from him but the pleasure of his company. The warmth he could never convey while in public office defined his personality when he was among friends; he was a gifted storyteller, and his vast experience in the affairs of nations, his personal involvement in the history of our times, made each of his visits a high-water mark for all of us.

Time heals all wounds. Eventually Herbert Hoover was rehabilitated and he came to be loved once more by the American people he served so valiantly. He was an all-out football fan and there was one memorable Saturday. We took him to West Point to the Army-Cornell game, and a few minutes before it ended, we left so President Hoover would not be held up in the usual pandemonium and traffic jam at Michie Stadium. We had been sitting on the visitors' side and were in full view of the crowd when we started to leave. All forty thousand who were there stood and applauded. It was a thrilling moment, for it was the first time he had been given such an ovation in the years since he had left the White House. Long after this he died full of years and high honor. And among things of which I am proud is that I could be his friend through the difficult time when he had been prematurely consigned to the dustbin of history.

Some of the guests who stayed the longest in those early years were the subjects of my books. My method of research was simple and direct: I invited them to Clover Brook and started them talking, and months passed before Prosper and I felt that our notes were full enough to start writing. One of the first was an army regular named Sam Woodfill, whom General Pershing had called the outstanding soldier of the war.

During the last great American offensive at the Meuse-Argonne, Woodfill, leading an advance patrol, found himself pinned in an open field by encircling machine-gun fire. Certain he would be killed, he scrawled a last message asking that his "darling wife Blossom" be notified that he had "fallen on the Field of Honor!" Then he got up and wiped out five machine-guns nests, picking off the five-man crews with murderously accurate rifle fire, killing four Germans who came at him with bayonets and pistols, capturing three more and returning unhurt to the American lines. For this Woodfill won the Congressional Medal of Honor, but ten years after the Armistice his identity was as unfamiliar to Americans as that of the Unknown Soldier. Everyone knew Eddie Rickenbacker and Sergeant Alvin York, but Sam Woodfill, a taciturn professional soldier who had quietly served his country from the Philippines to Alaska, consistently shrank away from the public eye.

At first I had no better luck than earlier would-be chroniclers of the Woodfill story. Then I put the problem in the hands of his "darling Blossom"—didn't she agree that her husband deserved the notice of his countrymen?—and soon the Woodfills appeared at Clover Brook, to stay until I had all the material I needed for *Woodfill of the Regulars*.

Not long after I finished the book, I was filling a speaking engagement in Cleveland and, as was the practice with visiting authors then, I was invited to Halle's book department for an autographing session. It was only a few days before Christmas and the store was crowded with holiday shoppers. Sitting at a table behind tall stacks of *With Lawrence in Arabia* and *Beyond Khyber Pass* and signing away, I didn't see the hulking, heavily perspiring man until he thrust his scarred face between the stacks and, rushing through the words as though afraid someone would drag him away, muttered, "Mr. Thomas, would you be interested in writing my story? I am one of fourteen survivors of a shipwreck; we drifted thirteen hundred miles across the South Seas in an open boat; when we ran out of food, we ate the chief engineer."

As opening gambits go, it was a blockbuster. I assured him I was certainly interested in hearing the rest of his story, and we arranged to meet later in the day. When he came to my hotel he was still sweating, and the scar, the effect of a burn, made the left side of his face look more livid and menacing than before. But Fred Harmon, lately the first assistant engineer of the wartime merchantman *Dumaru*, was not a menace. He was a tormented soul, unable to exorcise the demons of his own memory. He had survived a horrible tragedy at sea, lived through an ordeal that claimed a score of weaker men, but was not yet finished paying the price.

He showed me the journal he had written in an effort to lay the ghost of the *Dumaru* to rest. It was an extraordinary document, the story simply told but with compelling intensity, with the brutal candor an unschooled man can achieve when he conveys the impressions engraved on his heart and mind by some shattering experience. Yes, I wanted to do a book about the wreck of the *Dumaru*, and I invited Fred Harmon to Clover Brook.

He arrived early in January, still sweating, the scar pinching his face into an unsettling leer. Fran didn't even make it through lunch the first day. She paled as Harmon began telling Prosper and me about the cannibalism practiced by the *Dumaru*'s survivors, as did Helen Hamlin, my fragile-looking secretary. But when Harmon went on to describe how some men had drunk the blood of a corpse, Fran took a last look at the leg of lamb the cook had just put on the table, rose, put young Lowell in the car and drove off to New Jersey to spend the week with my parents. Poor Helen had to stay and make notes.

The *Dumaru* had been a war baby, one of hundreds of ships built in haste, often badly, to replace those sent to the bottom by German U-boats. In the summer of 1918, she was christened by Mrs. Woodrow Wilson and launched on the Willamette River at Portland, Oregon. Her name was a Multnomah Indian word meaning Bright Morning Star.

It was a misnomer; the *Dumaru* was cursed from the start. Sliding down the ways, she hit the water too fast and shot clear across the river to smash a number of houseboats tied near the far shore. Made of green Oregon fir straight from the forest, she soon split her seams and it took constant pumping just to keep her limping along. When she was assigned a cargo of gasoline and high explosives for Honolulu, Guam and Manila, the crew raised a hue and cry. They were a bizarre collection of castoffs and misfits—experienced seamen preferred the smart-looking iron ships coming out of San Francisco and Seattle—and most had signed on only to escape the draft. A few capable hands, like Engineer Harmon, were supposed to whip them into shape. When told it was either the *Dumaru* or the trenches, the crew sullenly went back to their posts, and on September 12 the *Dumaru* sailed off on her first and last voyage.

Halfway to Hawaii, in moderate seas, she nearly capsized when a heavy deckload of coal began shifting. A few days later, her steel rudder supports cracked. In Honolulu, a dozen crewmen decided they'd rather take their chances in France. They were replaced by Hawaiians and Filipinos, and the specter of racial animosity was added to the *Dumaru*'s troubles. In Guam, all hands were confined to the ship because of a flu epidemic ashore. By the time they hove anchor on the evening of October 16, officers and men openly feuding, the *Dumaru* was a tragedy just looking for a place to happen.

Two hours out of port the fates obliged. The ship was enveloped in a sudden thunderstorm, bolts of lightning dimming the lights and the roiled sea pitching the wooden ship up at the bow and smashing her down into the troughs with beam-cracking force. Then a bolt made a direct hit on the number one hold, filled with gasoline drums. There was a tremendous explosion, and flames quickly engulfed the forward section.

From the tangle of rope and tackle on the boat deck, two lifeboats and a raft were launched. Almost immediately they lost each other in the raging dark. Harmon, his face badly burned when he went over the side, found himself one of thirty-two men crowded into a boat built to hold twenty.

They rowed for their lives, straining to clear the *Dumaru* before its cargo of munitions went off. They had put about a mile between themselves and the doomed ship when a giant fan of flame lunged out at the sky. The men ducked their heads against the thunder of the following shock wave and the shower of burning debris. When they looked up again, the *Dumaru* was gone and the sounds of the storm seemed tame compared to the violence of the explosion.

Now they began rowing toward Guam, hopeful of making land before daybreak. But when morning bleakly dawned and the worst of the storm had blown itself out, the wind shifted and began blowing off the island with gale force. Pull as they would, taunted by the sight of land and a safe harbor only a few miles off, the tattered survivors were pushed inexorably out to sea. The dark line of land vanished. They were at the mercy of the northeast trade winds, and every hour carried them farther from safety.

For six days and six nights the men of the *Dumaru* struggled against the inevitable, pulling vainly toward land, subsisting on some sea biscuits and a meager ration of water from two emergency casks, one of which had sprung a leak and was practically empty. Cold rain gave way to blazing tropical heat, and the men suffered painful blisters and sea boils, and those who had been burned escaping the ship developed ulcerous running sores. They wrangled endlessly over who should sit where in the jammed life-boat, who should row and for how long, and whether the pathetic store of rations was being fairly shared. Fistfights threatened to swamp the boat, and "Graveyard" Shaw, the black cook, raged, shouting he would not, by God, be any white man's slave.

On the seventh day, First Mate Waywood, in nominal command, told his shipmates they had to come to terms with reality: they could continue the all but hopeless strug-gle to reach Guam, there being an outside chance they would be seen by a passing ship; or they could turn around and, taking advantage of the trade winds, set a southwest course for the Philippines, thirteen hundred miles away. There was another argument, but eventually the men, weary of laboring at the oars, voted to let the wind take them where it would. They hoisted a makeshift sail and were soon riding briskly before the trades.

The days passed without change—the eternal, endless sea, the hot blue sky—but the biscuits and water were now gone. Secretly, Graveyard Shaw had begun sipping sea water, and the more he drank the thirstier he became, the more he craved. By nightfall of the eleventh day, he had gone out of his head; by the twelfth day, his agonized rav-ings held all the others in fearfull thrall. Mercifully, he died the following afternoon, his swollen tongue thrust through lips split to the gums, the skin of his face drawn tight as a mummy's. When the body was slipped overboard, the sharks were on it like a flash. Said Harmon: "Thereafter the sharks followed us constantly, and we supplied them well. The nightmare days really began."

Despite Shaw's horrible example, two more men were driven to drinking sea water—it looked so cool, so tempt-ing. Within two days they, too, died in torment and fol-

273

lowed Shaw over the side. The following night, a young seaman died of exposure. Half a dozen more were critically ill. Worst off was Howell, the chief engineer, who had lapsed into a delirious coma.

On the seventeenth day, George-the-Greek, the hulking tyrant of the engine-room black gang, suddenly seized the boat's only weapons, two hatchets and some knives, and, backed by the Filipinos, proclaimed himself in command. Standing in the bow, he told how when Howell died he was going to boil his flesh to make a broth. "Them's as want to live can have some, and them's as is against it can say so now!" He hefted a hatchet in each hand.

But he didn't need to threaten anybody. Every man grasped at the grisly plan as a last chance for survival and was glad George was willing to wait until Howell was dead before proceeding.

It didn't take long. Howell gasped out his life the next morning and, while the body was stripped of its flesh, a fire was started under the biscuit drum, which had been filled with sea water. All hands waited wolfishly for the contents to come to a boil. Then it was passed around, each man allowed a few sips and a strip of flesh. "It was not repulsive," said Harmon. "The salt in the sea water had been absorbed by the flesh, leaving a decent broth, and the meat tasted like tough veal. It put some strength back in our bodies."

Carefully rationed, the life-giving concoction might have lasted several days. But George-the-Greek, already half demented, his huge body ravaged, waited until the others slept, then fell on the biscuit pot and drained it in gulping, gorging, mouthfuls. Almost at once he vomited it all back up. Then, screaming insanely and waving a knife, he began slashing at anyone in reach. It took four men to hold him and two more to tie him to the mast where, on the twentieth day, kneeling with his hands trussed before him as in prayer, he died.

Now the others began to go quickly—the veteran seaman Jennings, followed within hours by his son, the boy making his first voyage; a youngster named Weiland whose entire back was an open sore; and then Christensen, the steward, who decided to choose his own fate and slipped quietly over the side. From then on Harmon lost track. By the twenty-third day, only seventeen miserable creatures remained alive, and one of these, a Hawaiian known as Honolulu Pete, was out of his mind. When he died during the night, five of the men cut off his head and drank the blood welling up from the severed arteries. The others could not bring themselves to follow this; Harmon turned away until it was over.

At dawn of the twenty-fourth day, they saw a cloud on the horizon. "We prayed and God must have pitied us," Harmon recalled. "In a little while it began to rain. It poured down on us and we scrambled about the boat, spreading the sail and shaping it to funnel the water into a cask. We drank and drank and poured water into the mouths of those too weak to swallow."

A few hours later they sighted land. No one spoke. One or another of them had seen mirages before on this nightmare voyage, and all were afraid this might be another. It was easier to believe all the world was drowned under the malevolent sea, that they were doomed to sail on until, one by one, they all died. But after thirty minutes of stifled, silent hysteria, First Mate Waywood gave their hope life. "Yes," he said, "there's land ahead. I see a palm tree on a hill."

It was the island of Samar in the Philippines. The men of the *Dumaru,* those who still lived, had completed an incredible open-boat voyage of thirteen hundred miles across the Pacific. But their saga was not yet over. Even as their hearts leapt with joy at being saved, two more were lost, drowned in the surf when the boat was swamped crossing a coral reef. In the end, just fourteen men, salt encrusted, half naked, only half alive, staggered ashore.

The story has a final irony. The second lifeboat also made it to the Philippines. It was the one stocked with ample provisions—and carried only nine men. As for the four men on the life raft, they remained in the vicinity of the *Dumaru*'s wreckage and were rescued within a few days.

When Prosper and I had enough material for the book, Fred Harmon went back to his ship on the Great Lakes. I heard from him from time to time. Poor Helen Hamlin took off on a well-earned vacation, Prosper went to see his wife and children, and Fran and young Lowell came home from New Jersey. And *The Wreck of the Dumaru* became the third of the six books I had promised Doubleday. Since then, half a century has gone by and I still get letters from people telling me the story of the *Dumaru* is a classic.

Clover Brook, decreed Fran, was not going to become a museum. So all the curios and mementos we brought back from our travels, the wood carvings, gongs, drums, spears and boomerangs, went up to my fourth-floor study, a room sixty feet long and twenty-five feet wide. But I never had time to admire my collection, for the room also contained four desks, each one lodging a book in progress. Well organized and with Prosper's help, I was turning out the material at a steady pace. Doubleday was pleased. My first book for them, *Count Luckner, the Sea Devil,* had been the hit of their 1927 publishing season, a best seller translated into many languages.

Then, not long after I'd finished the *Dumaru,* an old Chicago friend, Burt Massee, who had made millions as one of the organizers of the Palmolive Company, told us he was getting married and invited Fran and me to go along on a honeymoon cruise. Indeed, he wanted me to arrange it. Burt Massee wanted nothing less than to charter Count Felix von Luckner's big four-masted sailing ship, the *Vaterland,* for a leisurely cruise of the Caribbean.

Thought of work fled. To see von Luckner again, and his lovely Swedish Countess, to sail the Spanish Main with the man who had taken a sailing ship through the Allied blockade and terrorized their wartime shipping, was too good an opportunity to pass up. I promptly cabled Massee's slightly wild idea to Hamburg, and a day later received a typically Lucknerian reply:

BY JOE! CAPITAL IDEA! SEND DETAILS!

And so we were set for a fantastic voyage.

Everything about Luckner was fantastic, larger than life, like the man himself—six feet three inches of supercharged energy and ebullient high spirits. The first time I ever saw him, a total stranger at a faraway airfield, he made so striking an impression on me that I decided on the spot I'd like to do a book about him.

The year was 1926 and Fran and I were making our survey of the budding European airlines. One day, delayed at Leipzig by a cranky Dornier Wall engine, we watched a silver plane circle the field, bank and loop and finally glide to a gentle landing. By the time its propeller quit turning, it was the focus of every eye. Then a strapping, big man opened the cabin door and a scattering of applause swept the field. He wore a chinchilla coat and a rakish naval cap, and when he bounded down a ladder to the ground, an equally improbable figure appeared behind him, a graceful blond lovely who looked like a fairy princess brought to earth on a sunbeam. To round out the illusion, she leaped daintily out of the plane into the man's arms, whereupon he set her down and they started off on a triumphal procession across the field, his voice booming out greetings to mechanics, attendants and travelers, including, when our eyes met, Fran and me. Even as they slipped into a waiting limousine, he was still calling *"Wiedersehen! Wiedersehen!"* in every direction.

"Who was he?" I asked the field commandant, standing nearby.

He looked at me as though I had just arrived from outer space. "Why, der *Seeteufel.*"

"Who?"

"The Sea Devil—Count Felix von Luckner. He commanded the *Seeadler* during the war."

"And the woman?"

"The Countess, of course."

If I'd known little about the Sea Devil before, I was to hear little else during the next several weeks. He was making a tour of Germany, seeking to reinvigorate his downcast and defeated countrymen, and wherever he went, half-holidays were declared in his honor. Great crowds turned out to hear him, especially the young people, for he was a legend in his homeland, this amiable buccaneer who had sunk twenty-five million dollars' worth of Allied shipping in two oceans without taking a single life or harming even a ship's cat. And everywhere, in his resounding voice, he kept telling his people to "Stay with the pumps—do not abandon the ship!"

Once Fran and I were established at Clover Brook, we invited von Luckner and his Countess to visit us. Just above our entrance hallway there was a bathroom. When the Count refreshed himself from the train journey, he left the water running in the washbasin. A half hour later the plaster in our hall ceiling crashed down. The place was flooded. They stayed two months, as lively a time as the old homestead was ever to know, for the irrepressible von

277

Luckner, now playing the clown, now the philosopher, regaled us with salty tales in which he acted out every role, his dialogue studded with vigorous exclamations of "By Joe!" the Count's self-imposed substitute for the sulfurous profanity of his youthful days at sea. In between, Prosper and I drew from him the story of his remarkable life.

He was the scion of an old and honored military family but yearned for a life at sea. At thirteen he ran away from home to become a cabin boy on a Russian schooner, roaming the world under an assumed name, surviving shipwrecks and suffering the beatings and deprivations that the merchant marine visited upon its children in those days. He took a few turns ashore, too, trying his hand as an assistant to an Indian fakir, as a kangaroo hunter, a prizefighter, magician and beachcomber; he also served with the Salvation Army in Australia and soldiered with the Mexicans under Diaz. He "walked the ties" across much of our country and made his way to Wyoming, hoping to meet his boyhood hero, Buffalo Bill Cody.

But there was salt water in his veins. Inevitably he went back to sea and rose in rank to command a series of rustbuckets under sail. As a result of saving several lives he eventually came to the attention of the Kaiser himself, who thereupon enrolled him for training in the Imperial German Navy and paid the costs out of the palace purse. The Emperor, fascinated with his gifts for comedy and legerdemain, made him his Falstaff for a time. He even plucked eggs out of the Czar's beard.

In the third year of the war, as one of the few officers in the navy with long experience under sail, after the Battle of Jutland, von Luckner was taken from a ship of the line and given the desperate mission of running a windjammer through the blockade to prey on enemy shipping. The vessel was a captured American three-master, but by the time the German shipwrights finished with her she had been transformed into a fighting ship, secretly armed and ready for plunder. At twenty yards she looked for all the world like an innocent sailing vessel of Norwegian registry, her deckload of lumber, according to her papers, bound for Australia. But in fact she bristled with hidden cannon and machine guns and had been fitted with two powerful Diesel engines, provisions to last out a two-year cruise and quarters for a large number of prisoners.

Two days before Christmas, 1916, the newly named

Seeadler—Sea Eagle—slipped out of Hamburg harbor and sailed straight into the teeth of a North Sea hurricane. While Allied patrol vessels ran for cover, the German raider, unmolested, bucked her way through the storm and out into the open sea. When she was hailed by a lone British auxiliary cruiser, von Luckner's false papers and a contingent of specially picked Norwegian-speaking sailors won the day. "Carry on," signaled the British after the boarding party reported back, and the *Seeadler* turned south for the Azores. One of the most flamboyant episodes in naval history was under way.

Nine days into the new year, the Sea Devil struck for the first time. Intercepting the British steamer *Gladys Royal* west of Gibraltar, von Luckner ordered the German colors raised and a false rail dropped, revealing a heavy gun. One shot across the steamer's bow and the battle was over. The stunned crew of the *Gladys Royal* was transferred to the raider, along with the best of its cargo. Then the captive vessel was sunk by gunfire and the *Seeadler* sailed on.

In quick succession, she captured and sank three more enemy ships, taking each of their crews aboard and providing every man with a good berth and three solid meals a day. The captains were shown to a special "Captains' Club" and treated as deferentially as they had been on their own ships.

The master of a Nova Scotia schooner presented von Luckner with a special problem: his supercargo included his bride of two weeks, sailing with him on a sort of honeymoon cruise. It was one she would never forget. Von Luckner, who first feared that the lissome Canadian might have an unsettling effect on his "passengers," later said, "She turned out to be the best fellow you could want for a shipmate. She had one of those temperaments that spread good cheer wherever she went. She had a smile for everyone and everyone treated her like a sister—which, on a ship crowded with men who hadn't touched port in months, was certainly a good thing."

Meanwhile, the *Seeadler* continued marauding the waters of the South Atlantic, racking up a mounting toll of Allied ships, evacuating each one and then sending it to the bottom with a well-placed shot or two. But only those brief moments of gunfire betrayed the fact that there was a war on. Aboard the corsair, prisoners had the run of the ship, and as each of their vessels contributed its stores to the

Seeadler, food and drink remained plentiful and varied. When a second woman was taken aboard from still another captured ship, von Luckner introduced her to the Canadian bride with elaborate gallantry, as though he had arranged the whole thing to provide companionship for both, then presented them with flowers from the diminutive greenhouse on his bridge. In the evenings, he had his musicians play "Tipperary" and "There's a Long, Long Trail," bringing tears of nostalgia to the eyes of his largely British "guests." In all, the voyage of the *Seeadler* was more like a holiday cruise than a war patrol.

But all good things must end. By late March, 1917, with the raider deep in the Southern Hemisphere where winter was fast coming on, von Luckner had two hundred sixty crew members and passengers from eleven sunken enemy ships aboard, rubbing elbows at increasingly close quarters. An earlier pirate skipper might have cleared the decks with a plank-walking ceremony, but the Sea Devil hit on a happier solution. Up over the horizon came a French bark, the *Cambronne,* to become his twelfth trophy. But this one was not sunk. Instead, von Luckner assembled all his prisoners and told them he was going to transfer them to the *Cambronne,* which would take them to Rio de Janeiro, the nearest port. He asked for the captain's promise not to communicate with another ship or reveal the *Seeadler*'s existence until they reached Rio. In light of von Luckner's astonishing chivalry, the promise was gladly given and kept.

That night there was a gala farewell party aboard the pirate ship, and no one went thirsty for champagne. In strict accord with international convention, von Luckner paid the prisoners for the time they had spent aboard the *Seeadler,* and they gave him three heartfelt cheers from the deck of the *Cambronne.* Then the bark set sail for Rio while the *Seeadler,* with the South Atlantic soon to be churning with speedy destroyers seeking her ruin, made for Cape Horn and the broad Pacific under every stitch of canvas she had.

By the time the Sea Devil reached his new hunting grounds, the United States had declared war on Germany, and in short order he captured and sank three American merchantmen, including one owned by Mayor Rolf of San Francisco, who years later became his warm friend and made him an honorary citizen of the Golden Gate city. Once more the *Seeadler* took on the bustle and exhilaration that came when she had a complement of prisoners aboard, this time forty-five men, one woman and somebody's pet opossum. As it happens, the woman was not married to the skipper she was traveling with, and one evening he came to the bridge and confessed as much to von Luckner. "My real wife is in San Francisco," he said despondently, "and she'd be awfully unhappy if she found out about this. Could you leave my—uh—lady friend out of your official report?"

"By Joe," replied von Luckner with a sly wink, "my superiors would not be too pleased either to know I had taken a woman aboard—after all, this is a ship of the Imperial Navy. So if you will keep your mouth shut, I'll certainly do the same."

And so the *Seeadler* remained a happy ship for a while longer. Then the fates turned against her. For weeks she roved the empty Pacific without even sighting another vessel. The men grew weary and discouraged. As stores of fresh food vanished, some of them came down with scurvy, the sailing man's disease. The eight-month cruise began to tell on the ship, too, its sails rotting and jury-rigged repairs a poor substitute for a shipyard refit. Finally, late in summer, when they made a landfall at Mopelia, an uninhabited atoll in the Cook Islands, von Luckner ordered the anchor dropped. Eagerly prisoners and crew scrambled ashore and found a palm-shaded paradise, abounding with wild fruit and, in the lagoon, an abundance of excellent fish. Quickly all hands regained their strength and will.

Then, disaster. One morning the eastern horizon seemed to swell, and moments later a forty-foot tidal wave had driven the *Seeadler* high up on the coral reef. The raiders were marooned. Stoically they set about building huts with the *Seeadler*'s shattered timbers, consoling themselves that at least their creature comforts were well provided.

Von Luckner would not be consoled. After two weeks of this languid Garden of Eden existence, the Sea Devil declared that he was a naval officer, not a beachcomber, by Joe. He had had all he could take of pineapples and swaying palms. With five volunteers he set sail in one of the lifeboats, his destination the Fiji Islands, his goal, to capture a sailing ship, come back for the others and continue raiding.

It was one of those incredible epics of the sea, six men naked to the weather in a cockleshell of a boat, fighting wind and hunger and the ravening thirst that overtakes castaways in the infinite world of salt water. And all in vain. After covering a thousand miles to the outer Fijis, after stumbling ashore half dead, they roused the suspicions of the authorities and, rather than risk capture, clambered back into their little boat and put to sea again. Landing finally at Wakaya weeks later and thirteen hundred miles farther on, they were arrested by a patrol and taken to a prisoner-of-war camp in New Zealand. Twice they escaped, only to be recaptured. "If the war had lasted another week," said von Luckner, "there would have been another escape."

Ending his account of his astonishing year, musing, the Sea Devil told me: "In the greater scheme of things, I suppose we inflicted only small injuries on our foe. But we had done what we had been sent to do; we had done everything you could expect of a lone windjammer. And there is this"—he leaned forward—"no one, no mother, wife, child or father ever had to shed a single tear because of any harm we brought to a loved one."

The years passed. Von Luckner, idolized in Germany and decorated by Allied governments for his unfaltering humanity during the war, married the beautiful Swedish heiress Ingeborg von Engstroem and became a citizen of the world. When my book about him, *Count Luckner, the Sea Devil*, appeared in 1927, he made a triumphant tour of the United States. My friend Burt Massee heard him speak in Chicago and never forgot it. As a result, two years later there was a hurried exchange of cables, and in midsummer, 1929, von Luckner and his Countess set sail for Bermuda aboard their four-masted schooner, *Vaterland*, there to pick up Massee's honeymoon party for what was to be an unforgettable cruise of the Caribbean, one of the zaniest episodes of the zany 1920s.

The original plan had been for von Luckner to sail directly to New York. But Massee, a onetime Milwaukee newsboy turned overnight millionaire, ordered the *Vaterland* stocked with enormous quantities of luxurious food and drink—two hundred Westphalian hams, three thousand bottles of Moselle and Rhine wines, three thousand more of French champagne and ten thousand bottles of Munich beer. The tax levied at the port of New York on all this would have been more than steamship fare to Bermuda for the entire honeymoon party.

By the time we finally set off, the honeymoon party numbered a something less than intimate twenty-six. For the beaming groom, who brought his Katie east to spend a weekend with us before sailing, insisted on inviting everyone in sight. I was working on a book then with Dan Edwards, the swashbuckling A.E.F. sergeant who had gone into a World War I court-martial for insubordination and come out with a Congressional Medal of Honor, the man who deserted from a military hospital to get back to the trenches, who, by war's end, had lost an arm and wore a gruesome scar from a gunshot wound in the face—none of which dimmed his zest for life nor diminished his ability to enjoy it to the brim.

Burt Massee had never met anyone like Dan—how many of us have?—and promptly invited him to join the honeymoon cruise. He also invited Prosper and three more of my staff; the British explorer Carveth Wells; McClelland Barclay, the artist whose portraits of stunning women were then in such vogue; and a clutch of his own friends from Chicago.

We arrived in Bermuda late in July. The *Vaterland* stood offshore in a flaming red sunset, towering masts reaching toward the gods of wind, gleaming white hull resting lightly on the water, like a giant seabird about to take flight. It was easy to imagine her as some sleek pirate ship of an earlier day just waiting for us, a doughty band of adventurers, before sailing off to pillage and plunder.

Once aboard, such an illusion was hard to sustain. Von Luckner greeted us—by Joe!—with a champagne supper and showed us to lavish staterooms. The *Vaterland*, a full three hundred feet from stem to stern and fitted for fun, carried a crew of thirty and a full-time captain so the Sea Devil himself need never be distracted from his social obligations. In fact, it was the Bermudians themselves who came closest to perpetrating an act of piracy. As part of their summer carnival, they dressed in appropriate regalia, swarmed out to the *Vaterland* in small boats and carried "the notorious buccaneer, Felix von Luckner," ashore in chains—for a mock trial presided over by His Majesty's Governor, General Sir Louis Bols, whom I had known when he was a junior officer on Field Marshal Allenby's staff. So heartily did the Sea Devil play his role that they made him an honorary citizen of Bermuda.

Such were the enchantments of the lovely British crown colony that no one was anxious to hoist anchor. By day we swam and sunned, Dan Edwards amusing himself and terrifying the rest of us by climbing up to the crow's nest with his one arm and diving fifty feet into the sea; by night we sought the pleasures of Hamilton, the capital city. It was, after all, the era of wonderful nonsense, a time when the dizzying spiral of prosperity was supposed to last forever. After dinner at the rooftop restaurant of the Hamilton Hotel, bridegroom Massee and his Chicago friends sat around matching hundred-dollar bills. One night, when we'd all danced until the small hours, Massee suddenly turned to von Luckner and said, "Felix, you don't have a piano aboard! How can we sail without a piano?" Whereupon he marched up to the orchestra and bought theirs. By the first light of a shiny new day, the entire string section, having been handsomely paid, carried it out to the *Vaterland*.

Von Luckner, of course, loved every minute of this phenomenal foolishness. He had lived a hard and dangerous life and meant now to enjoy all the rest of it. On the night we finally set sail for Santo Domingo, we stood together at the windward rail and he said to me, "You know, Tommy, we all came into this world crying while everyone else was laughing. By Joe, I mean to go out laughing—let the others do the crying!"

Santo Domingo, the oldest city in the Americas, is the capital of the Dominican Republic, which shares the island of Hispaniola with French-speaking Haiti. In many ways it still looks like the Spanish colonial town founded by Columbus's brother Bartolomé in 1496, narrow streets lined with low houses all pressed together, and a white fortress on a bluff overlooking the city, said to have been built by Diego Columbus, the discoverer's son.

Neither the look nor the lore of Santo Domingo particularly intrigued Dan Edwards. He wanted to go hunting. Somewhere he had heard there were wild pigs in the hills behind the town, and one day he set off wearing shorts and a teetering red fez, a rifle slung over his shoulder. No one was surprised when word came back to the ship that he had been arrested.

But Dan needed no one to intercede for him. Charged with carrying a loaded firearm in violation of the civil code, he demanded to be taken to the Commandant. Dan never said what passed between the two—perhaps he didn't really know, as the Commandant spoke only broken English—but when he came out of the conference the charge had been dropped and the Commandant had been invited to have dinner with us aboard the *Vaterland*.

This was only the beginning of their friendship. Before we sailed on, Dan was made a colonel in the Dominican army, which was then called out to pass in review for his left-handed salute. Further, the Commandant presented him with a thousand acres of land on a mountaintop which, though inaccessible, was said to be beautiful. These were lavish gifts for a young officer to be passing out, and we all wondered about the source of his power. Then Dan, only half joking, invited him to sail away with us, and only half joking he replied, "Very sorry. If I leave island only for a day or two, the President, he dies of fright."

In this land where revolution was practically a semi-annual occurrence, the Commandant and his troops were the main prop upholding the current regime. But only for the moment. Before another year passed, our new friend—whose name, incidentally, was Rafael Trujillo—had seized the presidency for himself, establishing a corrupt and ruthless dictatorship that dealt with political opponents by murdering them, and lasting until he himself was assassinated more than thirty years later.

Who could have foreseen it? To the honeymooners of the summer of 1929, Trujillo was the soul of kindness and consideration. He arranged for the President to receive us in his palace. He came each night to dine and dance with us. He solved all our little problems. When the local orchestra Massee had hired to play for us all bought themselves formal evening wear and tucked the cost in with their bill, Massee had only to mention it to Trujillo. The bill disappeared, the orchestra was arrested and, in final retribution, there they all stood on the wall of the prison fortress overlooking the harbor as we sailed off to Jamaica, still wearing their new tuxedos, with picks and shovels on their shoulders, to give us a salute. Later, as we neared Jamaica, the radio clattered out a slightly frenzied final salute from Trujillo:

WAS VERY PLEASING TO ATTEND. GENERAL EDWARDS IS WORTHY GREATEST ESTEEM. ADMIRE MR. BARCLAY EASY

We sailed on and on. In one port or another, the name
Vaterland had incited some narrow, nasty remarks, and
even intentional obstruction, by-products of a still smolder-
ing anti-German feeling, though the war had ended more
than ten years before. At my suggestion, von Luckner had
decided to change the ship's name to *Mopelia,* for the
South Pacific island where the *Seeadler* had been wrecked,
and somewhere between Jamaica and the Bahamas Charlie-
the-Bosun clambered out on the bowsprit and broke a bottle of champagne across the bow. That wasn't a trickle to
what was consumed on the foredeck during the rechristen-
ing ceremony.

At the island of San Salvador, we chanced on a Dominican monk who, because we were American, burdened us
with responsibility for correcting a grave historical error.
As we sat on the beach sharing a bottle of rum with him,
on the very spot, he assured us, where Columbus had made
his epochal landing on October 5, 1492, he told us the
schoolchildren of Chicago way back in 1892 had contributed their dimes and quarters for construction of a
heroic statue of the Admiral of the Ocean Sea—a Chicago
Tribune project. But alas, when the noble monument was
finished it was emplaced, not here, where Columbus actually landed, but all the way around on the wrong side of the
island. He sipped sadly and asked if we could do something.

Someone produced another bottle of rum and suddenly
there seemed only one thing to do. *We* would rescue Columbus. Loading chains, crowbars, the rest of the rum and
our holy friend into the longboat, we rounded the island
and, around midnight, full of fervor and spirits, we beached
near the misplaced statue, which looked massive and
spectral in the moonlight. It was at least fifteen feet high
and must have weighed tons, and though we pried and
tugged we failed to budge it. As long as the rum lasted we
kept trying, but finally even the unhappy Dominican had
to concede the inevitable. As we rowed back, we consoled
him by pointing out how when Columbus left Spain he

didn't know where he was going and when he landed he didn't know where he was, and when he got back to report to Queen Isabella, he didn't even know where he had been. So perhaps it was only fitting that he should still be in the wrong place.

No one ever suggested our enchanted voyage should end; I wonder how long it might have lasted if fate hadn't taken a hand. Summer had already passed, but in the Caribbean every day remained a golden replica of the one before. One morning when we were sitting around after a late breakfast, someone brought Massee a wireless message. He read it quickly, took his Katie's hand and, with a rueful smile, said, "I guess the party's over."

It was, and not only for Burt Massee. Wall Street had been hit by the greatest stock market crash in history, and as the dreams of millionaires and thousands of small investors went up in smoke, an era ended and another, far grimmer one began. Massee, said his broker's message, had lost sixteen million dollars in the market. He was wiped out.

In time he would go into the insurance business and make a partial recovery. But no man ever had a finer moment than did Burt Massee when the news of the crushing financial blow reached him. "Cheer up," he said to us, "we've had a good time, haven't we? I don't have a regret or a thing in the world to worry about—all the bills for this trip are paid."

One of the most impressive of the Massee honeymoon group was our host's doctor. Bill Jack, head of the medical department of the Burlington Railroad, stood six one, weighed 280 pounds and was a most genial companion. The President of the Dominican Republic at the time was Horacio Vásquez, who, no doubt at Trujillo's suggestion, gave a luncheon for us at his palace. When he told Dr. Jack of a chronic ailment he had been troubled with, Bill told him about a former colleague on the faculty at Johns Hopkins who probably could solve his problem.

A month after our return, President Vásquez flew to Baltimore, where Dr. Jack met him and helped with the operation. It proved a complete success. Not long after Vásquez returned to Santo Domingo, Burt Massee and "Doc" Jack received a joint telegram from the President and the dictator. Wanting to express their gratitude, they said they had done so by giving the orchestra another month in prison!

One day in August, 1930, my telephone rang and a highly overwrought voice at the other end said, "Mr. Thomas, you don't know me, but I figure you're the only man in the world who can save my job."

"Who is this?"

"My name wouldn't mean a thing to you, but I'm the head of sales for the Columbia Broadcasting Company. I heard you speak at Covent Garden in London and—well, if you can come to New York for just a few minutes tomorrow I'll explain everything. Maybe you'll be doing both of us a tremendous favor."

A little mystery, the promise of something new and exciting—there probably isn't any better way to get me moving. "Where?" I asked.

"The Columbia Broadcasting Building, Madison and Fifty-second Street. Can you be here at two?"

"Yes, all right."

And so began my more than forty-five years in radio.

13.

Good Evening, Everybody

When you hear the buzzer, start talking.
Talk fifteen minutes—I don't care
about what. Then stop.
— WILLIAM S. PALEY, President, CBS

ON Tuesday evening, November 2, 1920, station KDKA, Pittsburgh, the nation's first commercial radio station, went on the air with up-to-the-minute returns from the presidential election between Warren G. Harding and James M. Cox. It was clear before midnight that Harding was the overwhelming winner; it took somewhat longer for Americans to realize why the broadcast was more important than the election: the introduction of a revolutionary new medium of communication, a way of conveying information instantly, and entertainment so far-reaching that it would profoundly change the way of the world. First there had been the printing press; now there was radio.

Within two years, more than five hundred commercial stations across the country had been licensed to operate, with hundreds more scrambling for a wavelength on the suddenly precious broadcast bands. For, as in most of the great innovations of human history, the profit motive came into play. Not only was there money to be made in the manufacture of radio receivers, but it was soon seen that the makers of coffee, automobiles, cigarettes, soap and shoe polish—anything!—would pay handsomely to reach the swelling radio audience with their advertising messages.

In 1928, with the National Broadcasting Company operating three stations in New York, a wealthy young Philadelphian bought the fourth, then known as the Columbia Broadcasting Company. Young William S. Paley was determined to give General Electric, Westinghouse and Radio Corporation of America, joint owners of NBC, a run for their money. Soon he set out to capture their prize program, the only daily news broadcast on the air. It was sponsored by the staid *Literary Digest,* and its radio newsman was the freewheeling, hard-drinking, colorful war correspondent, Floyd Gibbons. This had been an unlikely marriage from the start; Bill Paley saw his chance in its imminent breakup.

Floyd Gibbons was one of the best-known reporters of the time. He had survived the torpedoing of the *Laconia* and lost an eye at Belleau Wood, and now, wearing a trademark eye patch, he was fast becoming an American institution with his evening news broadcasts. His instant radio success was due, at least in part, to the happy scheduling of his program in the fifteen-minute time period immediately preceding "Amos 'n' Andy," one of the longest-running and by far the best-loved radio show of all time. Still, the fact remained that Gibbons, rattling off the news with machine-gun rapidity and a certain racy irreverence, had a wide and growing audience.

For six months the *Literary Digest* and its dictionary-publishing parent company, Funk and Wagnalls, put up happily with Gibbons's flamboyant ways because he produced results: sagging magazine circulation had begun to climb. But the company president, a fervent teetotaler named R. J. Cuddihy, found it increasingly difficult to smile when the irrepressible Gibbons would march into the firm's board room for a daily news briefing, open his shirt, head for the water cooler and expansively announce, "Well, boss, your big boy broadcaster was out on one hell of a toot last night."

In the Great Beyond reserved for demon reporters where Floyd went on permanent assignment in 1939, I'm sure he is still chuckling about it all. Nor will he mind if I tell the story of how he finally got the ax. It seems that one 2 A.M., Floyd, a pal and a pair of lady friends found themselves in the vicinity of the Cuddihy Locust Valley, Long Island, home and in need of liquid refreshment. Pounding on the door until R. J. appeared, appropriately attired in nightgown and cap, Floyd said: "How's about a li'l old drink for my friends?" Surprisingly, publisher Cuddihy asked them in—probably out of fear they'd be arrested otherwise —although I never heard what drinks he served them. But Gibbons's radio days were inevitably numbered.

He was not an easy man to replace. As the final weeks of his contract sped by, R. J. Cuddihy auditioned dozens of platform people, authors, and journalists, and, dissatisfied with all of them, was about to cancel his program altogether.

I knew none of this when I went to the Madison Avenue and Fifty-second Street building one August afternoon in 1930. I knew someone had intrigued me with a mysterious telephone call and nothing more. Ironically, I never did make a note of his name or what ultimately happened to him. Our total contact was brief. He introduced me to William Paley, disappeared and, long after the excitement of my first months on the air had subsided, when I tried to find him no one remembered who he was.

Bill Paley whisked us up to a twentieth-floor studio, put me in front of a microphone and said, "When you hear the buzzer, start talking. Talk fifteen minutes—I don't care about what. Then stop." Then *he* disappeared.

I looked around. Three musicians, obviously standing by in case of a programming emergency, watched me from the corner of the room. "Did you hear what the man said?" I asked them. They nodded. "Well, I don't know what this is all about, but if you would play something, something Oriental, when I start talking, it could help."

The buzzer sounded. The musicians began to play "In a Persian Garden" and I started talking. I talked about T. E. Lawrence, India, some experiences in the Khyber Pass and in Afghanistan—whatever came into my head. Fifteen minutes later I stopped. Paley reappeared and said, "Come along. I want you to meet some people."

And so I finally found out how the *Literary Digest* had been looking for a replacement for Floyd Gibbons on their nightly news show; how on another floor R. J. Cuddihy and some eighteen of his editors and executives had been listening as my voice was piped down from the studio.

I didn't have the job locked up. Cuddihy, a rather stern-faced man, told me how they had soured on the whole project because neither of the two networks had been able to bring him anyone who came close to Gibbons's distinctive style. Obviously America had taken a fancy to Floyd, and it seemed he couldn't easily be replaced.

"Well, why bother replacing him at all?" I asked. R. J. Cuddihy was nobody as far as I was concerned, and I was feeling somewhat indifferent about the role into which I'd been cast—a piece of property dangling before these people, none of whom I knew. At the time radio meant little to me. I seldom listened. I was busy on several books and enjoying Dutchess County rural life.

Paley may have been trying to smile through it all, but the publisher pretended I hadn't even spoken and went on with his colloquy. He said I had made no attempt to imitate Gibbons, had spoken in my own, more casual style, and—would I come back on Thursday and do a summary of the day's news? "We'll listen to you at six P.M., then we'll listen to Gibbons, who is still on the air, and give you our decision right afterward."

I presume it was Bill Paley who answered and the answer was "Yes, of course!" Then he hustled me off. "We mustn't fail! We'll get you the best brains in the business to prepare this broadcast. It has to be a masterpiece!"

For him, luring the *Literary Digest* program away from NBC would be a million-dollar triumph and he was prepared to go all out to do it. But for me, having been involved in journalism and public speaking all my working life, it was a little confusing. How many brains did it take to prepare a fifteen-minute news broadcast? Thinking to protect myself, I said, "Okay, Mr. Paley, you round up all the best brains you can find and I'll round up some of the best brains I can find and we'll make an event of this audition."

Later in the day I called Russell Doubleday in Garden City and asked if he had any brains to spare. He asked if I was sober. Backtracking, I explained as much of the story as I understood. Mr. Doubleday, who also wondered aloud how big a brain pool it took to tell the day's news in fifteen minutes, promised to send me some people nonetheless.

Thursday at 9 A.M. we assembled in strength at the penthouse of the old Princeton Club on East Thirty-ninth Street, which I had taken over for the day. From Columbia came a trio: troubleshooter Nick Dawson, who had started out with the circus, as salutary a training ground for radio as any; Jesse Butcher, a *New York Times* man turned CBS chief of public relations; and Paul Kesten, who eventually became the first network chairman of the board. My own contingent consisted of Prosper, also called-to-the-colors-again Dale Carnegie and, from Doubleday, editor George Elliman and a young manuscript reader named Ogden Nash. I also brought along a stenographer, but hours passed and no one seemed to come up with anything worth writing down.

Perhaps the fault was mine. Knowing something about the partialities of writers of all kinds and the great thirst begat by Prohibition, I had brought from our Dutchess County farm a couple of jugs of applejack. Everyone had a sample sip, approved and dove in for more. Soon inhibitions were being shed all over the place and the geniuses paired off for a hot and lengthy debate on the best way to begin a news broadcast. And there we stayed, hung up in the starting gate.

Only poker-faced Ogden Nash, who sat quietly in a corner scribbling away, eventually produced a couple of lively paragraphs. He was still an unknown then, but his work was already characterized by the qualities that would make him one of America's best-read humorists, his marvelously controlled madness transforming all our provincial concerns into haughty, perfectly poised comic verse. Of his attitude toward flying, he once pronounced that "Two Wrights made a wrong." And when thieves broke into his car in Boston, he wrote the inimitable quatrain:

> I'd expect to be robbed in Chicago,
> But not in the home of the cod.
> So I hope that the Cabots and Lowells
> Will mention the matter to God.

But Nash's witticisms did not prevail against the heat and acrimony generated on our memorable audition day. When it got to be 4 P.M. and we still had lots of noise, mounting fury but no script, I got up and quietly walked out. I don't think anyone even missed me. I headed uptown, picking up a couple of evening newspapers on the way, trying not to think about anything but what a relief it was to be out in the fresh air again. When I got to Madison and Fifty-second Street, I went up to the twentieth-floor studio, made a few notes and at 6 P.M. I walked up to the microphone and said, "Good evening, everybody." Then I told the news. At the end of fifteen minutes I said, "Good night," and sat down.

Paley came in beaming. He could barely contain himself

until Gibbons's broadcast was over. Then he rushed me down to where R. J. Cuddihy and his aides had been listening to us both.

And Cuddihy was beaming at me, too.

Friday, September 26, 1930, was when my predecessor did his radio news broadcast for the last time. He had lost out on what had been the most impressive and by far the highest paid of all his spectacular experiences as a newspaperman. He had built up a huge coast-to-coast audience —which I now inherited. I don't blame him, and never did, for what he did to me just before he signed off. By then he realized what a disaster had befallen him. He was an unhappy fellow. And he made this obvious as he passed the "mike" over to me.

He said he was to be succeeded by a professor. He listed the four colleges I had attended, the four degrees I had, told how I had been on the faculty of two of them, and bore down heavily on the five or six social and honorary Greek-letter fraternities to which I belonged. Not a word did he say about my many years as a news reporter and newspaper editor in Cripple Creek, Denver and Chicago. No mention of my having been a war correspondent in World War I. No reference to my having had the exclusive story of the fall of Jerusalem or how I had scooped every journalist in the world with my account of the Arabian campaign and my exclusive story of Lawrence of Arabia, and also of the German revolution. He was telling his millions of listeners how he, a newspaperman, was now turning over the number one news program to a *professor!*

Although we both had been reporters on Chicago papers at the same time—he on a morning paper, the *Tribune,* and I on an evening one, the *Journal*—and although during the war we had often crossed each other's trails, we had never met. When he signed off for the *Literary Digest* I at once went to the phone, thanked him and wished him the best of luck. I was unhappy but not sore. I knew it was a tragic moment for him, although I hadn't even a faint idea of how fabulous an opportunity had been passed on to me—the only network daily news program! For the time being at any rate, for news I had all the air of the whole wide world to myself alone and was to continue on and on until all of my early contemporaries had gone to their Valhallas. And of course I didn't realize what endless opportunities this radio program would bring to me.

Some time was to pass before Floyd and I did meet. It was after I became president of the Advertising Club of New York. He came to one of our special luncheons. He was most genial and gracious, and from then until his untimely demise we remained the best of friends.

Floyd Gibbons was a giant of his era. And having been a cub when he was a star reporter for the prestigious Chicago *Tribune,* I stood in awe of him and still can hardly believe I had the good luck to be his successor.

At 6:45 P.M. on September 29, 1930, NBC *and* CBS announcers, Ed Thorgersen and Frank Knight, introduced me on the air as "the *Literary Digest's* new radio voice, informing and entertaining you with the latest news of the day." Then each spent several minutes saying some highflown things about my background and I in turn spent a few minutes thanking Gibbons for the handsome send-off he had given me on his final broadcast. As for the news that long-ago day, it dealt with a fire-snorting Fascist leader in Germany named Adolf Hitler.

There are now two Mussolinis in the world [I reported], which seems to promise a rousing time. Adolf has written a book *(Mein Kampf)* in which this belligerent gentleman states that a cardinal policy of his now powerful German party is the conquest of Russia. That's a tall assignment, Adolf. You just ask Napoleon.

Nearly half a century later, it is still hard to believe there was ever a time when one broadcaster had the world's airwaves all to himself. I also had both networks, for Cuddihy chose to keep NBC for the eastern half of the United States, with CBS taking the west. So far as I know, this was the only time in radio history that a single program was shared by rival networks.

But remember, this was radio's dinosaur era when all sorts of strange things went on, including the dogged insistence of otherwise sensible businessmen that the whole thing was a fad, like flagpole sitting, and similarly would soon pass on. Another way of appreciating how long ago all this was is to consider what today's sages of broadcasting were doing in the year 1930. Eric Sevareid had not yet entered college; Walter Cronkite had not yet entered high school; John Chancellor and David Brinkley had not yet entered long pants, and Tom Brokaw, Dan Rather and others later to become well known hadn't entered the world.

Actually there *was* one news analyst broadcasting when I took over from Floyd Gibbons, a man who was outstanding in his day, Hans von Kaltenborn. But "H.V." was on only twice a week, and his was a program of commentary. Nor—to my great good fortune—was there any real comparison between the numbers of our listeners. Not only was I the lucky heir to the audience of the immensely popular Gibbons, but, as I have said, it was the time slot immediately preceding "Amos 'n' Andy."

For all Paley's efforts, so powerful was the lure of Freeman Gosden and Charlie Correll with history's first situation comedy that six months after I went on the air, R. J. Cuddihy decided to move the program back to NBC altogether. Soon along came competition. The impressive likes of Edwin C. Hill, John B. Kennedy, Gabriel Heatter and Boake Carter joined me on the air, and within ten years more than a thousand other broadcasters from coast to coast were giving highlights of the day's news. And of course CBS presented a fair share of them. Now they number more than ten thousand!

Few later programs had the same tremendous impact on the public as those trailblazing broadcasts of the early 1930s. There was a visit I had from the old Marine hero General Smedley D. Butler, not long after I had gone on the air. "Old Gimlet Eye," as he was universally known, was then the Philadelphia Commissioner of Police and had made a special trip to New York to caution me to handle my awesome responsibility with wisdom and care. "My boy," he rumbled, "you have the ear of America as no one has had it before. Why, with a few words, or even an inflection of your voice, you might start a revolution."

Well, I have never started a revolution of the sort he had in mind, although over the next forty-five years, I have been told, my voice has been heard by more people than any other in the history of mankind, around a hundred and twenty-five billion, say those who calculate such irrelevancies. After a year and a half, the *Literary Digest* ran into financial trouble and dropped out of radio for some months, whereupon I was taken over by the Sun Oil Company. In 1946 I switched over to CBS and have been there ever since, by far the longest-running daily program in the annals of broadcasting. And I initiated some strange doings, which was inevitable if you start at the beginning and hang around as long as I have. So it was that I was first to broadcast from a mountaintop, a coal mine, an airplane, a helicopter, a ship and a submarine. Once, in Quebec, on a ski trip to the Laurentians, the only place available as a temporary studio near a telegraph key was the ladies' room at the St. Jovite Canadian Pacific Railroad depot.

In the beginning, we didn't buy the news but, as Floyd Gibbons had done, we swiped it. That is, we bought the afternoon papers, took the stories we wanted and rewrote them for the broadcast, always giving full credit to newspapers and wire services for the material we used. At first they were all enthusiastic about the arrangement and even assigned someone to listen each evening and count the number of credits, each one vying to be mentioned most often.

Then one day Frank Mason, head of Hearst's International News Service, called me and said I was no longer to use any INS material on the air. William Randolph Hearst had decided to build his own chain of radio stations and saw no reason to help the competition. Soon after, both the Associated Press and United Press also decided I was a threat to the existence of all newspapers and they, too, cut me off. In an eloquent speech to an AP convention, Roy Howard, president of the Scripps-Howard chain and head of UP, said the rival news services now had to "march shoulder-to-shoulder to destroy this radio monster before it destroys us!" So the decision was made: Lowell Thomas was to be denied use of wire service material, and since L.T. was not a newspaper, he was not to be allowed to subscribe for it. And this, of course, would drive him off the air.

Yours truly, who naively believed his daily deference to the press on a nationwide broadcast was helping to sell newspapers, could have been in trouble. But the rumblings reached us in time for countermeasures. For starters, we subscribed to Reuters and several other foreign press agencies. Then, casting about for some way to cover the national news, we came up with Abe Schechter, recently a reporter with the *Daily News*. He joined us at NBC, and our hope was to give broadcast journalism its own unique image and direction, maybe even boost our show to a new height of popularity. And so it actually worked, for we now personalized the news and gave it a stamp of timeliness and exclusivity.

Every day we would still comb the newspapers and decide which stories to feature. Then Abe and Prosper would sit at the telephone and become a two-man news center, our link with whoever was making headlines that day. Was the bonus bill coming to a vote in Congress? Al Capone arrested in Chicago? Jimmy Doolittle flying from Canada to Mexico City? Abe would put in long-distance calls to a key congressman, to the Cook County sheriff, to the Ottawa airport manager—and these worthies, flattered to have attracted the notice of a New York radio station, would provide us with fresh and exclusive material right up to air time.

To be sure, our telephone bill was sizable, but the system gave us a coast-to-coast reach and the kind of last-minute deadline no paper or wire service could hope to match, and one by one the press associations came around to make peace. The United Press was first, and when they set up an office to sell news to radio, they gratefully supplied it to me free of charge, even providing me with a teleprinter which remains to this day in my Quaker Hill studio. They said I had opened up a lucrative new field for them! So, without ever intending it, we did each other a good turn: the press agencies had forced me to find new ways to cover the news for the broadcast medium; when I did, they finally realized radio wasn't going to go away like a bad dream and they began organizing to provide news services specifically for broadcasting, which soon became a tremendous new business for them. The networks learned a lesson, too. Determined never again to be totally dependent on outside sources, they built up their own news departments, and today these are at least coequals with the graphic press in gathering the news and preeminent in beaming it across the world, not to mention the way they now earn a substantial portion of radio and television income. Incidentally, our Abe Schechter became head of the news department of NBC, the first ever established, and during World War II, as a major, he handled press relations for MacArthur.

For some reason, the people who have worked most closely with me during the radio years delight in telling tales about how I would come dashing to the microphone at air time with hardly a split second to spare. The tales are true, but the circumstances were sometimes extenuating. For example, our location was a problem. For a time our office was high up in the RCA Building in Rockefeller Center, which on its lower floors also housed NBC, and still does. There was no way to get to NBC except down forty-one floors in the elevator, across the lobby and up eight floors to Studio 8F. Several times I arrived to hear the announcer already intoning my name in introduction. And one day during the Christmas season I snatched some packages from my desk, made the headlong dash for the studio, reached the microphone in time to take a deep breath and say "Good evening, everybody"—only to realize I had picked up the packages but had forgotten my script. You can be sure there was some wild ad-libbing re the joys of the holiday season until breathless Mary Davis arrived with the sheets of news.

In winter, I had the additional difficulty of getting to the Pawling railroad station when heavy snows buried our country roads. Usually I could manage it with a horse-drawn milk wagon on runners, but once, when a record blizzard confined even the horses to the stable, I had to resort to skis. Cutting overland, following the slope of the land, I finally reached the New York Central tracks well south of Pawling. When the train hove into sight, there I stood, flagging it down with my ski poles. My fellow passengers cheered, and one of them called out, "The triumph of Lowell Thomas over the Vanderbilts!"

Not long after I took over from Floyd, I persuaded NBC to let me do my broadcasts from a rural studio at Clover Brook. This was not because I wanted to lessen the wear and tear on my producers' nerves; it was merely a desire to work in the country—and because of skiing. There were comparatively few amateur skiers in North America in those days, and of these Lowell, Jr., and I were two of the most ardent. As soon as winter came, we were off to one mountain area or another, bringing personal encouragement and sometimes even a cash investment to those game enough to back the new sport. Neither NBC nor, later, CBS objected—I always provided some local color which I presumed boosted the audience—but since my contract called for me to broadcast from New York City, I was obliged to pay the network and AT&T for line charges, plus travel expenses for a secretary, radio engineer and telegraph operator. Usually a few friends rounded out the party. I once calculated how over the years this cost me a round million and a half dollars. But when I remember the thrills I've had skiing from the Laurentians to the Rockies, and from Alaska to the Atlas and the Andes, I don't begrudge a penny of it.

Between longer trips I haunted the Berkshires, the Green and White mountains, and the Adirondacks, and the studio at Clover Brook made this easier. On a routine day I'd check the day's news by telephone with Prosper, rough out a broadcast outline and head for the slopes. By late afternoon I was back in our Quaker Hill fourth-floor study going over news dispatches sent up by teleprinter, redoing them to suit my style. At six forty-four I would hurry out to a studio a hundred yards out beyond the barn, where I would climb up a ladder to the mike, usually getting there just about when the engineer, who was in a room below me, yanked on a cord to signal my "Good evening, everybody."

Of course, if you play on the same fiddle for forty-five years, you're bound to hit a sour note now and then. Once, during my first year, I dropped the script and recovered it with the pages completely out of order. This meant for a while I had the abdicating King Edward VIII involved in the Miss America Pageant at Atlantic City— as if the poor guy hadn't enough trouble. It was quite a scrambled broadcast. Another time I inadvertently transposed the two vowels in the first and last names of the eminent British statesman Sir Stafford Cripps, tried again, did it again—and burst into such a paroxysm of laughter I knocked the microphone over. When I finally recovered, I moved directly on to the next item and didn't mention Sir Stafford again for months.

Then there was the fluff that broke me up when I happened to be broadcasting from the New York studio and I took the announcer, the engineer and all the production assistants into convulsions with me. The story was about a woman in Flint, Michigan, who had just given birth to her twenty-second child. At a certain point in the story my subconscious took over and out came a tribute "to

300

this Blue Star mother made of Flint," who I said had been a circus bareback rider.

Though every listener heard laughter, few actually caught the boner which was even bluer than indicated above. Within a week we had a flood of letters, all asking, in effect, what was so funny? So I had to devote part of a subsequent program to confessing my sin.

Over the years, I have had only two absolute rules on the air. The first is not to confuse opinions with hard news or be drawn into taking sides, not even when my friend and Quaker Hill neighbor, Thomas E. Dewey, was running for president. I have aways left the sermonizing to those among my colleagues who are divinely guided, or think so. Perhaps I don't deserve praise for playing it so. The *Literary Digest* always followed this policy and asked me to do likewise, and so I have done all these years. My second rule has been to remember always that the disembodied voice behind the dial comes from a human being. And so once, when President Roosevelt chose my time spot to make one of his fireside chats on every other station and, accidentally I suspect, allowed me to be his only competition, I opened as follows:

Good evening, everybody—or maybe *nobody*. I make this dubious reservation because right now President Roosevelt is on the air . . . so maybe at this moment I'm talking to *nobody*. However, a schedule is a schedule, so here goes . . .

And I closed with:

. . . maybe *nobody* is listening to me. Maybe everybody is listening to President Roosevelt. Maybe I'm just saying to myself, "So long until tomorrow."

As it happened, an avalanche of mail proved otherwise. It must have been at one of those rare moments when even F.D.R.'s rating had fallen off. One listener told how he listened to me, then went to a Masonic meeting where he asked his lodge brothers whether they had heard the President's speech; most of them said no! they had me tuned in. It was a Michigan crowd, so maybe most of them were Republicans who just disliked "that man."

Fluffs, scoops, a broadcast from some mountain aerie—

any of these could bring ten thousand letters in a given week. But never before had anyone generated such a massive response—nor has any broadcast since—as the time my announcer, Jimmy Wallington, casually said that Western Union had offered to transmit to us without cost any telegram sent by a listener.

It all began with a phone call from Newcomb Carlton, Western Union's chairman. As one of our regulars, Newcomb Carlton questioned my occasional references to Mackay Radio, the overseas arm of Postal Telegraph, his arch rival. I of course told him I was simply crediting Postal for relaying some short-wave messages to me from Admiral Byrd in Antarctica, with no favoritism intended.

Mr. Carlton then adroitly turned the conversation around to the virtues of Western Union. One word led to another, and within a week our NBC crew was down at his Hudson Street headquarters in lower Manhattan. While scores of telegraph keys tapped out marvelous sound effects for my show, and wire baskets bearing urgent messages went spinning overhead, and girls with rubber roller skates zoomed by, I did my broadcast. Newcomb Carlton, assuming I'd hear from some relatives and a few long-lost school friends, told Wallington to invite anyone in the audience to send me a free wire.

Before the night was over we were buried under an avalanche of telegrams, 265,567 of them, more than ever summoned up by any event in history, before or since. The messages ranged from thrifty expressions like "Keep up the good work" to a whole chapter from the Book of Job, sent by a pious skeptic who doubted it would go through. It did, as did several thousand sent in ironic error via Postal Telegraph, for which Western Union had to pay in hard cash. Had the whole lot been charged at the regular rate, the bill could have come to around five hundred thousand dollars.

I was going to answer those telegrams, every one of them. I had them bundled up and carted away to a frame building I owned at Quaker Hill. The building where they were stored was one I had loaned to Dr. Norman Vincent Peale and my brother-in-law, Raymond Thornburg, when they launched a new magazine, *Guideposts*. One day the building caught fire and the telegrams all went up in flames. So if you were one of the 265,567, belated thanks, and now you know why you never got an answer. It was a four-story frame building, rather ancient, and there may have been a defective flue. When I told about this on the air, how my telegrams had been burned as well as all the *Guidepost* files, names of subscribers and so on, many people wrote in, and overnight the list of subscribers doubled. *Guideposts* today has some two million on its list.

Radio cast me in a new role, which sometimes left me ill at ease. When strangers took to rushing toward me with slightly glazed eyes to say, "What a *thrill* it is to meet you!" I tended to look over my shoulder to see whom they meant. Press agents, who seemed to be lurking behind every closed door, suddenly closed in on me, offering endless possible news items which always included a plug for their clients. Their persuasiveness and imagination impressed me; they outdid each other inventing ways to promote their wares. Invited to address a charity banquet, I would find the advertised cause worthy enough, but the whole affair was the brainchild of a press agent trying to bring some cash into the coffers of the Depression-hit hotel he represented.

One wizard of this sort of legerdemain was Frederick Darius Benham, also known as Freddie "Delirious" Benham in salute to both his middle name and his frenetic air. Freddie even organized a sorority of executive secretaries in New York and Washington, and not altruistically because he thought the girls needed a social outlet. As the Seraphic Club's godfather, he gained ready access to many of America's most influential bosses. It still flourishes. It was Freddie, too, who dreamed up a luncheon club called the Circus Saints and Sinners. The first year we met at the Gotham Hotel to help the handsome old Fifth Avenue hospice survive the Depression. He even talked me into becoming the first president. But what started as a gimmick outlived Benham and became a long-lasting American institution: his Circus Saints and Sinners grew and grew until eventually it took over the Main Ballroom of the Waldorf-Astoria and for forty years was one of the best-known luncheon clubs in the country.

America's most eminent entrepreneur of the day offered me office space in the brand-new Empire State Building, rent free, and for a while we were both pleased with the outcome—I know I was. It was the glamour building of the 1930s, the tallest man-made structure in the world and still the most impressive. But it had been begun in the heyday of the boom and completed just in time to be

303

caught in the economic debacle of the bust. So there it stood on the corner of Fifth Avenue and Thirty-fourth Street, shiny new, soaring up to the sky—90 percent vacant. Former New York Governor Alfred E. Smith, who had been defeated by Herbert Hoover in a run for the White House, became president of the Empire State Corporation. Al Smith asked me to drop over to his office.

For a while we just chatted about mice and men. Governor Smith had by no means ruled out a try for the 1932 Democratic nomination, if for no other reason than to stop his onetime ally, Franklin D. Roosevelt. He remained an enormously popular national figure and was well worth the fifty-thousand-dollar annual salary paid him by John J. Rascob and the other owners of the Empire State to stave off its insolvency. Al Smith waved a cigar around his elegant office and said, "Lowell, this is the only occupied space for three floors up and seven down!"

In response I said I'd heard commercial space was going begging all over the city.

"Ah, but this is the *Empire State Building!* How would you like to move in here, take any space you want, any floor? Be our guest—no charge."

It was quite an offer, but not entirely rooted in altruism. Governor Smith didn't need to explain. Once I moved in, my radio program would, they hoped, bring a kind of reflected glory to this magnificent white elephant—maybe even lure some tenants. The idea of being in the world's tallest building was appealing. The price was right. Also I was eager to escape from the *Literary Digest* building, where I was more or less under the thumb of R. J. Cuddihy. So we shook hands, and a week later I moved in.

I had chosen the eighty-seventh floor—only the observatory was above us—and as there were no partitions, we seemed to be afloat in the sky over Manhattan Island. We used the corner on the south side, where we were in plain view of anyone who stepped off the elevator. And as the Empire State Building was one of New York's prime attractions, we had plenty of visitors. Still, the excitement of working a fifth of a mile above the city—the skyscrapers of Wall Street, the sunsets, the harbor and the Statue of Liberty far below for our contemplation—made it all worthwhile.

During our two-year stay at the Empire State, we staged one broadcasting extravaganza. Bertram Thomas, British explorer and Orientalist, who had recently made the first crossing of the unknown South Arabian desert, the Rub al Khali, was visiting the United States, and I gave a dinner in his honor. The place: my eighty-seventh-floor office in the clouds. Among the guests, some of the top explorers of the day—all representatives of other deserts—Roy Chapman Andrews, Martin Johnson, Dr. Isaiah Bowman, Sir Hubert Wilkins, Kermit Roosevelt, Vilhjalmur Stefansson. My idea had been to seat these modern trailblazers at a round table and, at broadcast time, spin the table and microphone and have each recount something of his own adventures. It went off smoothly—except when two of the guests missed their cues, these intrepid explorers who had penetrated the world's farthest, most exotic reaches, because they were held spellbound by the lights of the city below.

During our second year Al Smith said, "Lowell, in order to heat your office we have to heat eighteen vacant floors. Much as we want you here"—there was a long pause—"we can't afford this."

So we moved on again.

The mail was fascinating in those years when radio was new. It was an intimate medium then; all around the world people tuned in as though opening the door to an old friend. And like old friends they felt free to scold, for radio also made it possible for a broadcaster to step on millions of toes at the same instant. Early on, Funk and Wagnalls published a book of the letters I had received with the rather vapid title *Fan Mail*. I wanted to call it *Making Millions Mad*, but publishers, like parents, always know best.

But of course not everyone wrote to complain. Some, like Gladys Sniggs, a lady in Broome, Australia, and the sea captain off the Madagascar coast, only wanted to tell me I was coming in loud and clear. A Canadian Mountie on Ellesmere Island told of the broadcast being heard by the farthest-north man on earth—him. An American geologist came in person to thank me for making him rich. Deep in the Canadian bush, he'd picked up my broadcast by short wave. Hearing me report a gold strike in northern Ontario, he had immediately chartered a plane and staked a claim right next to "Discovery," before anyone else could get there.

One day a former United States naval attaché named

Harold Grow gave us an account of how he had been imprisoned in Peru, during the Leguía revolution, and how for weeks my broadcast had helped him hang on to his sanity. When I had begun reporting the excesses of the Peruvian revolution, he persuaded his jailers to listen in; they had been so concerned by their unfavorable image in the outside world that they released him. Now, in thanks, he pressed an Inca amulet on me, his good luck charm.

I don't recall it doing anything special for me, but not having it certainly brought a series of misfortunes down on Harold Grow's head. His glamorous blonde, Betty, left him; and he lost his money trying to break into the automobile business. When I next ran into him in Detroit, he was really down on his luck, and I insisted on returning the Inca amulet. I don't think he ever let go of it again. The next thing I heard, he had pulled himself together and was back in the Navy, promoted to the rank of captain. During World War II he made a brilliant record and wound up in command of the Japanese island stronghold at Truk.

As the years passed, other observers, expert and amateur, have submitted their analyses of why, of all the thousands of programs on the air since 1930, mine alone is still heard. Magazine writer Al Hirshberg said it was because I had a voice like an organ. Damon Runyon in his famous column said it was because I gave the impression of saying, "Now here is the news with some human slants on it and you can interpret it to suit yourself." Playwright Russel Crouse said it was because radio and I were invented for each other, and since I was invented first, I was able to make the new medium do my bidding. I wonder. . . .

Let me also offer for consideration the estimate of one-time columnist Cy Caldwell. Cy was a caustically comic sort who was irreverent about everything except "Amos 'n' Andy." Once, when we invited him to The Hill for a weekend, he stood on the far side of the threshold and asked me if we tuned in at 7:00 P.M. I told him we seldom listened to radio and would rather talk to each other or to our guests. He had already climbed back into his car when Fran came out to promise him we would listen to "Amos 'n' Andy"!

In any case, Cy once weighed the theories advanced to explain my longevity in radio and dismissed them all. Instead, he came up with a piece of doggerel which he said explained everything and was also suitable as an epitaph:

> Here lies the bird
> Who was heard
> By millions of people—
> Who were waiting to hear
> "Amos 'n' Andy."

14

End of a Golden Age

> Dear Lowell, I am afraid Hitler has ended our
> ball games for the duration. . . . As ever yours,
> —F.D.R.

A pun making the rounds in the early 1930s had an
aristocratic young potato seeking her parents' permission to marry Lowell Thomas. "But that's impossible, dear,"
they replied, aghast. "He's just a commen-tater." Forty
years ago "Bud" (H.C.) Fisher of Mutt and Jeff fame used
me in one of his cartoons with the above, and it still turns
up occasionally in my mail.

I cite this now, not necessarily as a paradigm of humor,
but in illustration of the fact that when I began broadcasting and had all the world's air to myself, my name
seemed to pass into the public domain. I was swamped
with invitations to speak at banquets and commencements,
to endorse commercial products and candidates for public
office, to join cabalistic societies, invest in esoteric inventions and both edit and narrate commercial films—one
faintly pornographic.

I had been on the radio only a few months when someone from the oddly named Jam Handy company got in
touch with me. Jam Handy, to my considerable surprise,
was not in the business of preserving strawberries; it was
one of the largest filmmakers in our little-known, number
two American film center, Detroit, Michigan. Its clients
were the major automobile companies and other business
concerns, and its products were sales and promotional
movies shot on an elaborate scale. Could the Jam Handy

people interest me, asked their man, in appearing in a film they were about to make for Frigidaire, a division of General Motors?

Sure! That was, after all, a whole new arena for me. But I told him I had always prepared my own scripts and had reservations about speaking someone else's words sight unseen. He assured me Jam Handy would be open to any suggestions for change, and he would send the script off to me at once.

I had never seen anything quite like it before. It was full of the verbal twists we came to associate with Madison Avenue—verbs wrenched into the form of nouns, like "freezability," euphemisms in place of plain old reliable words, like "home food center" for "kitchen," and convoluted sentences endowing inanimate objects with human characteristics and making sense only if you didn't think about them. Still, I was sufficiently intrigued by this exotic medium to take a train to Detroit—where I promptly antagonized everyone in sight. Introduced to the dozen or so gentlemen in the Jam Handy board room and asked my opinion of the script, I said, "Well, first of all I'd like to know if there is any reason why it shouldn't be in English?"

This produced some weak smiles. Then someone—to my chagrin, I later learned he was the script writer—asked what I found so obscure about it. I told him. There followed a babble of sound out of which I comprehended a unanimous conviction that, as a neophyte, I couldn't be expected to understand the need for the specialized language of commercial movies on which I subsequently worked. In reply I said English was English and was almost always best understood when used according to the tried and true rules of orthography and grammar. There was some desultory argument, but eventually changes were made and we got down to work.

The most pleasant aspect of my first venture into the world of commercial film was the girl cast as my secretary. She was charming, cheerful, and unusually efficient around our stage-set office. So when the shooting ended I tried to hire her as my real secretary. Smiling, she assured me her office skills were make-believe, like the prop office itself; all she really knew was acting, which she certainly did know. Her name was Martha Scott, and the next time I saw her she had become one of Broadway's and Hollywood's brightest stars.

Enter the Cohn brothers. They, too, were on the verge of bigger and better things, movie moguls in the making, Harry on the West Coast where he became known, not always lovingly, as King Cohn, and Jack holding down the New York end. But in those early days they were still seeking a foothold for their fledgling company, Columbia Pictures, and sometimes grinding out obscure features and documentaries, sometimes skillfully combining the two and leaving it to the audience to figure what was fact and what fiction. I knew nothing of this when Jack Cohn telephoned me. He said Columbia had a picture they were convinced needed my touch. It was about the aborigines of northern Australia, he exuded, shot by a University of Hawaii professor of anthropology, authentic but exciting, a revelation. Anyway, it would only take me a few weeks.

In my innocence, I agreed to do it. Then I compounded my mistake by accepting an unrealistic contract. Many in the film world regarded Harry Cohn as a brigand and Jack a buccaneer. The deal they came up with required me to edit their uncut film, write the narration and record it, all for a sum I'm now embarrassed to set down. But as I did not have an agent or a lawyer to protect me from the consequences of my own ineptitude, I signed; years still had to pass before an accumulation of experiences convinced me that, as the aphorism goes, a man who acts as his own lawyer has a fool for a client.

Nor was this the end of the lurid episode. When months, not weeks, had gone by and Prosper and I were working on the last of the ten reels they had given me, and when I was already deep in the red on the whole project, they presented me with two more reels. And whereas the originals at least had the virtue of having been shot in Australia, the last two were as phony as a Cecil B. DeMille sunset. Suddenly deciding to juice up the story line, the Cohns sent up to Harlem for a busload of black extras—who looked about as much like the Down Under aborigines as I did— and shipped them out to Montauk Point at the tip of Long Island for the shooting of a "breathtaking and sensational climax." Are you ready to hear it?

It seems this pearling vessel is wrecked off the Australian coast. The captain's beautiful blond wife, cast adrift and separated from the others, is captured by the aborigines. Naturally she is wearing very little, what there is kept good and wet. Meanwhile, the frantic captain scours the north coast searching for his beloved wife. Does he ever find her? At the risk of spoiling the picture for you should it ever come to your neighborhood theater, I will tell you he does. I will even tell you how, although you may not believe it. One day he spots an aborigine chieftain wearing a pair of familiar silk step-ins. Aha! He follows the step-ins home, and of course they lead him straight to the demeaning hovel where his blond darling is held prisoner. Swelling music! Rescue! Clinch! The end!

Apart from my contractual commitment to finish the foolish thing, I suppose I did it because I never believed anyone would actually pay money to see it. But in so doing I had still failed to gauge the ingenuity of the brothers Cohn. They entitled their epic *The Blonde Captive;* they plastered the country with twenty-four-sheet billboards showing me watching benignly as the lady, flimsily clad as always, is dragged off in chains by elephants—elephants! And in kangaroo land! The Cohns proceeded to clean up. They netted half a million right off the bat, big money then, and eventually a lot more. Every five years or so they would send it around again and it would always make money, none of it for me, thanks to my ingenuousness at the trading table. It may still be coming around for all I know. I don't pay attention anymore; I finally decided there was no point in going into hiding every time it turned up in Times Square.

One day during those halcyon years before World War I, a parachutist named Rodeman Law took a swan dive off the Statue of Liberty. The jump was an artistic failure; Law's chute opened late and he barely escaped with his life. But four cameramen were on hand to film the event, whose significance lies in the fact that it launched the newsreel industry in the United States.

Filmed news was already going strong in Europe. As early as 1889 William Friese-Greene was aiming his primitive camera at strollers in Hyde Park and making "actualities." In Paris, Charles Pathé had the inspired idea to cover the events of the day with a camera, just as journalists covered it with words, and he went around filming elections, strikes, disasters, sports events and glamorous personalities. Soon all France could go to *le cinéma* and see the headlines come to life.

Then Pathé sent the newsreel across the Atlantic. When

311

it caught on, American filmmakers, some with more enthusiasm than talent, rushed to cut themselves a piece of this new pie. Many quickly disappeared, taking fortunes down the drain with them—filmmaking has never been an inexpensive venture—but Pathé's crowing rooster, Paramount's steadily cranking cameraman and Fox-Movietone's montage of athletes, airplanes and ships at sea would continue heralding the news in theaters all over the world for the next fifty years.

Today it is hard to believe there are millions of young Americans who have never seen history's great events flashing larger than life across the big movie screen of their local movie palace. Before the age of television, the newsreel, more than any other medium of communication, enabled people to *see* and hence understand the twists and turnings of our times. During the half-century heyday of the newsreel, five hundred staff cameramen and thousands of stringers regularly turned in miles of raw film from which the big companies culled the thousand feet, maybe ten minutes' worth, to provide sixteen thousand theaters from coast to coast, twice a week, with the biggest news stories of the day.

A Fox-Movietone cameraman was at Roosevelt Field in the early morning hours of May 20, 1927, when Charles Lindbergh's Ryan monoplane lifted off a muddy runway and turned east to fly the Atlantic. Others filmed his triumphant return; eighty million Americans thrilled to hear the Lone Eagle speak when he was greeted by President Coolidge, who also spoke, a noteworthy event in itself. And ten years later the devastation of modern war was first brought graphically home by the poignant footage of a Chinese child, sitting alone and weeping amid the ruins of the Shanghai railroad station after a Japanese air raid.

Fox, the giant of the newsreel field, was launched in 1919. When sound was introduced, it became Fox-Movietone, and I was its "voice." Thus began seventeen years of new and special excitement for me.

The year was 1932, and within a short time Fox-Movietone had put together a crew whose faces became as familiar as Gable's, Garbo's and Mickey Mouse's. Ed Thorgersen did sports—sometimes also Paul Douglas and Mel Allen—Lew Lehr comedy pieces and Louise Vance fashion. As chief commentator, I brought Prosper in with me to write our scripts: a made-for-each-other arrangement. With his encyclopedic mind and flair for pungent expression, Pros enlivened our commentary with humor and high style, and as he was a born night owl, the long hours of waiting for film to arrive gave him many a legitimate opportunity to play poker half the night, check in at the local tavern or just sit around swapping stories with the newspapermen who invariably sought him out.

Twice each week, around 10 or 11 P.M., we repaired to the Movietone studios on Tenth Avenue and Fifty-fourth Street. There we would screen the film that had already come in, cut it, and begin preparing the script. As the night wore on, the pressure intensified, especially if there was a late-breaking story due. We cut and spliced, wrote and rewrote, recorded and rerecorded. Toward dawn, when everyone was ready for a hot bath and a warm bed, we had to pull it all together and do the final version. I think only the fear that we would sound the way we felt perked us up.

Our third-floor screening room was often crowded with journalists, politicians and celebrities, come to have first look at film just in from a war front, the World Series or an ocean liner on fire. We had other visitors as well. Not infrequently Twentieth Century-Fox would borrow our studio for a test or a screening, but mostly we were too busy to notice. Once, though, Gypsy Rose Lee came to do a late night test, and as she seemed to require a live audience for her striptease act and I was free for the moment, she asked me to do the honors. It was beguiling.

But such diversions were rare. It was a pressure-cooker business, continuously charged with the high drama of human events. Periodically, a bannerline story or a scoop would blow the lid off altogether. One of the earliest of these produced some of the most spectacular footage ever set down on film. It was October, 1934. In Marseilles, King Alexander of Yugoslavia had just arrived to begin a state visit, the French premier, scholarly Jean Louis Barthou, on hand to greet him. Two Fox cameramen, the brothers Mejat, assigned to record the official welcome, were shooting away as the motorcade moved down a broad avenue.

Suddenly, pandemonium. A blurred figure brandishing a pistol breaks through the police line and leaps up on the running board of the royal car. At point-blank range he begins firing at the King and at Barthou, sitting alongside. The camera trembles as the crowd surges toward the assassin, but the cameramen, who have the story of a lifetime locked in their lenses, keep grinding away. We see the stunned expressions of Alexander and Barthou; we see them slump down on the seat, bleeding and mortally wounded. Next day, black headlines, the newspapers full of stories about the assassinations—a plot by Croatian terrorists. In only a few days the film arrives at Tenth Avenue and Fifty-fourth Street, and a few hours later all America actually sees it happen.

Less than three years later, even those sensational pictures were topped—twice in the span of a few months. Early in May, cameraman Al Gold was grousing because he had drawn the assignment to cover the arrival of the German zeppelin *Hindenburg* at the Lakehurst, New Jersey, naval station. It was an out-of-the-way location and, besides, it was hard to generate any excitement over still another transatlantic crossing by a dirigible; the Germans had done it many times before. A few hours later—and for the rest of his life—Al Gold had a new standard for measuring excitement.

The *Hindenburg*, pride of Nazi Germany's commercial air fleet, had left Frankfurt three days before, carrying thirty-six passengers and a crew of sixty-one. Strong headwinds had slowed her crossing, but by seven twenty on the evening of May 5 she was hovering two hundred feet over the ground in light rain, dropping her nylon landing ropes to the ground crew. Routinely, Gold turned the handle of his camera.

Then it happened. In an incredible instant, there was a muffled detonation near the stern and the graceful airship, filled with flammable hydrogen, turned into a crumpling mass of bright, heaving flame. Some passengers and crew jumped before the ruined craft settled to earth; others somehow crawled to safety through the fire. But in little more than half a minute, thirty-six were dead in the inferno that marked the end of lighter-than-air travel, and our reluctant cameraman, Al Gold, got it all.

Then, in December, we had the stunning film of the Japanese air attack on the *Panay*. Busily devastating China without a declaration of war, Japan, in the sway of militarist extremists, had bombed the American gunboat in the Yangtze River, killing two and sinking the vessel, then claimed it was all an accident. But Eric Mayell, our cameraman in the Far East, and Norman Alley of Universal

314

were both aboard and shooting away. Their film was delivered directly to President Roosevelt and clearly showed the American flag flying in plain view as the Japanese airmen swept low over the *Panay* to drop their bombs. As a result, Japan paid an indemnity of $2,214,007.36, the precise amount of the American claim for the loss of life and property. And the American people had striking notice that they faced a ruthless foe in the Pacific. Though a showdown had been avoided for the moment, it was obvious dark times lay ahead.

There was a golden age on Quaker Hill in the years before the war. It was no longer the sleepy, shut-away little community of Colonial days, nor was it the summer resort that boomed just before the coming of the automobile. Instead, for a favored handful, a few old-timers and those, like us, who came to blend our lives with its orderly rhythms, the high ridge above the Harlem Valley became a haven of unblemished tranquillity. It cast a particular spell. True, we newcomers sometimes jarred the tranquillity—I'm sure I did—but even our transgressions were perpetrated with the idea of making a real Shangri-La.

By this time I had built a special broadcasting studio, the first such out-of-town facility in the history of radio. This helped make it easier to go skiing, for Fran and me to cut horseback trails and to try our hand at running a dairy farm, all in descending order of proficiency. We built new sheds, remodeled barns, moved stone walls, put up miles of additional fencing, planted tens of thousands of trees and dug a battlefield of trenches for two new water supplies. In addition to the gymnasium, a tennis court and two swimming pools, we completely remodeled our thirty-four-room house and endlessly landscaped the grounds and gardens. I was in the money now, and with every passing day I became more expert at getting rid of it.

One local venture began when I was doing a second speaking tour of Canada—which as usual included submitting to the warm and inevitable hospitality of local committees. Nearly always I would be invited to dine before my talk. This meant being plied with questions, the answers to which were the substance of what I would have to say later on the platform. In self-defense, I adopted the practice of asking someone in whose company I was left to tell me about his own work, and life, in Halifax, Medicine Hat,

Calgary, or wherever. In this way I learned a good deal about Canada.

In New Brunswick I was briefed about fur farming by a genial newspaper publisher. C. C. Avard had been a pioneer in what was then proving to be a new Eldorado, supplying the London market with silver fox furs. By the time we had finished our coffee, I was in business with him. The arrangement we made was for Avard to provide the animals and an experienced fur rancher. I was to furnish space and pens at Quaker Hill, also do what I could to establish a New York market for our pelts without—so we hoped—going through profit-draining middlemen. We shook hands on the deal and before long I had several thousand mink and foxes—plus one black bear about which more later.

To shorten the story, the venture in some ways was a success. Raising animals is absorbingly interesting. It isn't always the financial return that thrills me. I like trying new things. Everything about this was foreign to anything we'd ever done. As for the family Avard sent to us, the Fred Wards, they fitted perfectly into our Quaker Hill-Pawling scene. To the community's gain, many of them are still here, including their unusually capable eldest daughter.

When Electra graduated from high school, I asked if she'd like to do secretarial work for Prosper and me. Soon she had taken over the office altogether. After some years she married Gene Nicks, my radio engineer, raised two stalwart sons and today, forty-two years later, she is still with me—secretary, social director, tour guide, travel agent and a wonderfully good friend to all of us. Because of the endless procession of celebrities who have trooped across the Hill, from presidents to punchinellos, some say Electra may be the best-known secretary in America. I only know for sure that she's the best.

There had long been touchy feelings between the country "squires" on the Hill and the merchants and tradespeople below in the Valley, at Pawling. Then several of us organized a softball team called the "Debtors." Our number one opponents were the "Creditors," from Pawling, of course. For a while all went well enough, normal Hill versus Valley rivalry expressed only in the swings of our bats. Then came a day when one of ours, the acknowledged Squire of the Hill, with too many under his belt, started making needling remarks—caustic and loud. This had the

316

Pawlingites seething, reinforced by their traditional belief that the Hill folk were basically snobs anyway. Following a close play at home plate, suddenly fists were flying and, but for a few cool heads, what had started as a friendly neighborhood game came near ending in a non-Quaker Donnybrook.

I proposed a merger of our two teams—use the name Debtors *and* Creditors, and henceforth play only in competition with teams from nearby Millbrook, New Milford, Brewster and Poughkeepsie.

Among those now regularly in the lineup were Ken Utter, a hefty farmer; Bob Petrie, a young athlete and banker; Munn Slocum, a garageman who could have played third base in the major leagues; Em Addis, editor of a weekly paper; Eddie McGrath, genial owner and chef of the Pawling Railway Restaurant; Casey Hogate, the three-hundred-pound publisher of the *Wall Street Journal;* Carl Ray, a former Dartmouth All-American; and round, waddling Prosper, of whom it was said, though he couldn't hit at all, his fielding was worse. But he loved to play, so we often let him pitch, which certainly kept the outfielders busy—if batters could solve his style. My secretary Electra managed the team and handled details of scheduling and equipment. Right through the thirties we had a lot of fun, some fair baseball and plenty of excitement.

Then came the summer of 1933. President Roosevelt, in office six months, had already declared a bank holiday, taken the country off the gold standard and orchestrated a pyrotechnic display of legislation and executive acts aimed at stemming the worst economic depression in American history. By August it was still with us, but as the dog days began smothering Washington, F.D.R. decided to escape for a few days to the family estate at Hyde Park on a bluff overlooking the Hudson. After him trailed a hundred and thirty reporters, for this was one President who rarely let a day go by without making news.

Washington was bad, but Poughkeepsie, where the unhappy press corps was jammed into the ancient Nelson House, was worse, languishing in the grip of a typical Hudson Valley heat wave. Meanwhile, twenty miles across Dutchess County, in the upper Berkshire foothills, a refreshing breeze usually blew, and I got to feeling sorry for my sweltering colleagues. So I picked up the telephone and called one of the President's secretaries, Marvin McIntyre.

"Mac," I said, "if some of your flock want to beat the heat for a couple of hours, come on over to Quaker Hill." I expected Charlie Hurd of *The New York Times* and maybe six or eight of my other old friends to accept the invitation. Instead, all hundred and thirty showed up—plus F.D.R.'s four sons and his daughter, Anna.

How do you entertain a hundred and thirty-five unexpected guests? Applejack and other spirits was the obvious answer, but by midday we had run out. Then an uninhibited young lady in the group managed to find the key to our wine cellar, and at the first gurgle a stampede of thirsty humanity went thundering down the stairs. In this critical moment I had the flash inspiration that cast such a long shadow. "Everybody outside!" I said. "We're going to have a ball game." Then I phoned my Debtors and Creditors teammates, whereupon our local history took a dramatic turning.

It was a hilarious game. The correspondents, many of whom hadn't done anything more athletic than climb up a barstool in years, floundered to a 10-0 deficit. When we loaned them some of our men to even things up, ineptitude overtook *them*, too, and we soon quit keeping score so players and spectators alike could concentrate on having the time of their lives watching two grown men sliding into the same base, several brilliant national affairs pundits wandering together under a fly ball until it hit one of them on the head, and an overstuffed columnist swinging so vehemently at a third strike that he popped his belt and went down in a heap, entangled in his own trousers.

I would like to believe our laughter was heard clear across the valley at the summer White House. At any rate, the Roosevelt boys carried the tale of our merrymaking and mayhem back to the President. The one-of-a-kind voice boomed in my ear when the phone rang early the next morning: "Lowell, how come I wasn't invited to your ball game?"

"My apologies, Mr. President. Your team could have used some extra encouragement."

"Well, how about doing it all over again? I need a good laugh. So round up your team and come over to Hyde Park next Sunday."

As it turned out, the game was not played on the Roosevelt acres. Someone asked the President how it would go over in the Bible Belt if they heard the President not only condoned Sunday baseball, but even staged a game on his own place? F.D.R., who had a mind of his own, responded with a story about Andrew Jackson. "Will he go to heaven?" a contemporary asked a man who had done political battle with that earlier President. "He will if he wants to," was the reply.

F.D.R. wanted to, so although the game wasn't played at Hyde Park, it was played. He also took an extra measure of perverse delight in sending Major Jarvis and his Secret Service men over to a vacationing neighbor's place to lay out the diamond. The neighbor: Ogden Mills, Secretary of the Treasury under President Hoover, an implacable political foe.

The President's big open touring car was parked alongside first base, and from this vantage point he ran his team as though it were a Federal agency, boasting of its virtues while constantly changing the lineup. In and out of the game went a bewildering array of White House correspondents, Brain Trusters, Secret Service men and Roosevelt sons, F.D.R. exhorting them all and Mrs. Roosevelt, like some Madame Defarge of the diamond, sitting on the running board, stoically knitting.

Naturally, everything in the roistering revelry of a game was endowed with sham political overtones, and particularly by the Brain Trust, those university professors and reformers whose social and economic advice shaped the New Deal. Harry Hopkins, chasing a home run into the next field and finding himself confronted by a nettled bull, came tumbling back over the center-field fence—to be greeted with the cry, "The capitalists' revenge!"

Then F.D.R.'s starting pitcher, Professor Rexford Tugwell, ran into hot water. Flashiest and farthest left of the Brain Trusters, Tugwell had become an instant celebrity, and now extra base hits were whistling past his ears. Finally, Roosevelt, laughing so hard he could barely get the words out, yelled, "Tugwell, you're through!" and sent him to the showers—a Secret Service man taking his place on the mound.

Next day, in an editorial written by Frank Knox, publisher of the Chicago *Daily News,* the President was congratulated for his good judgment in sending Tugwell to the showers. "Now," urged Knox, "finish the job and get him out of the administration altogether."

Virtually every newspaper in the country ran a front-

319

page story about the game. Since there was no other news at the time, with the President as a participant and a hundred and thirty reporters present, I suppose it could hardly have been otherwise. *The New York Times* headline was typical:

ROOSEVELT'S TEAM LOSES DESPITE AID
White House Team Bows to Lowell Thomas Debtors and Creditors—President Coaches Hard

So what had begun as a Sunday afternoon pastime became something of an event—indeed for a decade it was almost a national institution. Thereafter, every summer when President Roosevelt came to Hyde Park seeking diversion from the burdens of office, he sent ahead to challenge the Debtors and Creditors to another game. After the first one they were all played at Quaker Hill to minimize the political repercussions, and each one attracted more spectators than the one before, nearly a thousand people eventually, as well as newsreel cameras and radio coverage.

In 1937 we changed the name of our team. It was the year Roosevelt came up with his court-packing scheme, shedding crocodile tears for the nine elderly justices of the Supreme Court and their heavy burden of work. What he really wanted, as everyone knew, was to pack the high court with enough new members who shared his political philosophy so even his most controversial New Deal measures would be ruled constitutional. With the idea of giving the President a ribbing, we renamed our team the Nine Old Men. But someone leaked this to F.D.R., who could always be counted on for a trick of his own. When next his team trotted out on the field at Quaker Hill, emblazoned across their sweatshirts was *their* new name: The Roosevelt Packers.

Celebrities drifted in and out of both our lineups. One was Jack Dempsey, who looked fearsome at the plate, then popped up or fanned out, but brought enthusiasm to the game. Jack couldn't hit or field, as you would have expected of a world-famous athlete. Later, he confessed how when most kids had been playing baseball he had been working, living as a hobo or fighting.

Gene Tunney liked to pitch, and that settled that. If the former heavyweight champion of the world wants to pitch, who's going to argue with him? Gene really took the game seriously. He even bought his chauffeur a catcher's mitt, and whenever they were driving from their home in Maine he would have the car stopped and for fifteen minutes or so he'd warm up with his driver.

Then there was Branch Rickey, who spelled me behind the plate. There are those who say Rickey had the most brilliant baseball mind in the history of the game. He won innumerable championships as general manager of the St. Louis Cardinals and the Brooklyn Dodgers; he broke baseball's color line by signing Jackie Robinson to a contract. But Rickey was a devout man, and in a baseball career lasting half a century, even as an executive he never appeared at the ball park on the Sabbath, no matter how crucial the game. However, occasionally he did come to the Hill and played with us.

Our umpires now and then added color to the games, especially when we had some well-known lovely take on the role for an inning—some, like Geraldine Farrar, Gloria Swanson, or even Sally Rand, who was required to officiate sans fan or bubble—and they loved it. That is, all but one, glamorous Anna May Wong. A line drive off the bat of Homer Croy sailed right through the pitcher's box, and *gong!* Down went Miss Wong, out cold.

Not surprisingly, our games against the Roosevelt Packers provoked a lot of political repartee. Just before one game, F.D.R. called the amply padded Casey Hogate over to his car and said, "Mr. Hogate, they tell me you have to hit a home run to make it to first base."

Replied Casey to F.D.R. with a GOP gleam in his eye, "Yes, sir, Mr. President, that's what any American businessman has to do under the New Deal."

Then he proposed to the President, "Let's play for a bit of a stake: if your Packers win, you double the income tax; if we win, you abolish it." Said F.D.R.: "I have no more confidence in my team than in the Supreme Court."

Another time, when Congressman Hamilton Fish, a conservative and a bitter Roosevelt opponent, was at first base for us, the President called me to his side, and in a voice you could hear at home plate, he asked, "Lowell, who's the chap playing first base for you?"

Of course he knew who it was, and in reply I merely remarked, "I guess you know him!" To which he replied: "I want to buy him from you. I'll give you thirty cents for him!"

321

Ham laughed, too. But he wasn't laughing when in a subsequent election F.D.R. managed to have him defeated by gerrymandering his district.

We played one memorable game in Griffith Stadium, then the home of the Washington Senators, against a team of congressmen who chose Vice-President Henry A. Wallace to be their pitcher. When they fell behind, they replaced him with a ringer, onetime famous major-league fast-ball artist Walter Johnson. Mrs. Wallace had thrown out the first ball, and later between innings she said to Fran: "I wish Henry had stayed in Iowa, on the farm. That's where he belongs."

In the evenings F.D.R. invited all of us to a dinner at the Carlton Hotel. At the time, my sponsor was the Sun Oil Company, owned by the Pews of Philadelphia, politically, a powerful Republican family. F.D.R., sitting just across the table from me, suddenly stopped, wagged a finger at me and exclaimed, "Ah ha! The enemy! Before midnight, Lowell, I'll bet you will have given Joe Pew an account of everything said here."

During the summer of 1940, an election year, when we assembled at the Hill for the annual game between the Packers and the Nine Old Men, the campaign was already heating up. Wendell Willkie had just been nominated by the Republicans, it was an open secret that Roosevelt would run for a third term and politics was on everyone's mind. No doubt there were people on the Hill who felt Roosevelt's presence had more to do with the election than with baseball.

After the game, his car was driven to our barbecue area, and as we were chatting he said, "Lowell, I hope you don't have any false notion about why I'm here. I know I can't get ten votes on Quaker Hill."

Then he told me how, years before, when he had first gone into state politics, he had driven over every one of the Hill's hundred miles of road trying to drum up support for his candidacy. But it was a traditional Republican stronghold then and remained so, as did the entire area. Not once in his long and spectacular political career had he ever carried Quaker Hill or Dutchess County, or even his own Hyde Park township. "You know," he said wistfully, "I'd give Willkie almost any three western states if I could carry Dutchess County."

Of course he defeated Willkie soundly in 1940, and our

Quaker Hill neighbor Tom Dewey much more narrowly four years later—the only time in American history that both candidates came from the same county. But he never did carry Dutchess County.

I wonder if any team as haphazardly put together as the Nine Old Men ever received such publicity. As a result we were bombarded with challenges, many of them from similarly impulsive softball practitioners, hoping to have some fun or maybe raise a little money for charity. These we often accepted, and for many years we were at it almost every Sunday afternoon from spring through early autumn, often playing a double-header. Among our opponents were Robert L. Ripley's Believe-It-or-Nuts, the Connecticut Nutmegs, the New York Artists and Models Guild, the Circus Saints and Sinners, the Explorers and a team of Republican Roosevelts from Oyster Bay, Long Island, led by T.R.'s son Ted and called the Oystervelts.

It was the Nutmegs or, more specifically, columnist Heywood Broun who introduced the appealing innovation of allowing some lissome lass to run for the batter. Broun, who weighed around three hundred pounds and saw nothing heroic about lumbering around the bases, proposed that his wife do it for him. As he took his stance at the plate, Connie Broun, who had a pair of smashing legs, strolled onto the field wearing shorts—during the pre-shorts era. "Attention, please," intoned the announcer without bothering to check with either captain. "Mrs. Heywood Broun now pinch-running for batter 'Babe' Broun."

This sensible emendation of the rules was carried to its logical conclusion when we played the Artists and Models. In this game, the masters of putting pulchritude to paper, like Russell Patterson and James Montgomery Flagg, not only brought their inspiration along, but had the girls run for them, the better to bedazzle the Nine Old Men. It was all too much for Fox-Movietone comic Lew Lehr, playing first base for us. When one batter hit a ground ball to shortstop and his runner, musical-comedy star Fifi d'Orsay, began undulating up the first-base line toward him, Lew was undone. Paying no attention to the shortstop's throw, which flew right by him, he grabbed the delectable Fifi instead, tucked her under one arm and made for the deep brush.

This may also have been the game in which Tom Dewey,

recently moved to Quaker Hill and a softball devotee, tore his pants. There was nothing memorable about it except that he was on his way to a Providence, R.I., speaking engagement and was dressed in his Sunday best; he had only stopped by to watch the game for a few minutes. Soon, though, he had shed his jacket and I put him in as a pinch hitter. Whereupon he lashed one into left field and stretched it into a double with a slide that tore his pants and left him otherwise covered with grime and glory. Of course he had to dash back to his farm and change clothes, but I have always believed that Tom Dewey—who was the warmest guy in the world but, some said, projected the public image of a suspicious department-store floorwalker—would have beaten F.D.R. in '44 if only someone had taken a picture of him barreling into second base and put it on all his campaign posters.

Once we played before fourteen thousand exuberant fans at Madison Square Garden, until then the largest indoor baseball crowd ever assembled. Our opponents were Bob Ripley's Believe-It-or-Nuts, and the beneficiaries of the copious box-office receipts were the Boys Club and the sandlot teams of New York City. Both lineups were studded with celebrities—Babe Ruth, Walter Johnson, Ted Roosevelt, Grantland Rice, Jack Dempsey, Father Flanagan of Boys Town; the umpire was Mayor Fiorello La Guardia. I had issued new uniforms to our team for the game—Sweet Orr farmer overalls, floppy straw hats and white goatees. The last, besides drawing laughs, served to camouflage a ringer we had in the lineup, "Cannonball" Baker, then the fastest pitcher in the country.

When the immortal Babe Ruth stepped to the plate, the crowd cheered expectantly. But softball is not hardball; the mound is closer to the plate and there are some speedball pitchers who can throw the ball right by the best batter. Well, the Babe had himself three Herculean cuts and didn't come close to connecting. Later, he confessed he didn't even see the ball.

It was not hard to sense the crowd's disappointment; they had come to see the Sultan of Swat, the mighty Ruth, blast one. So the next time the Babe came to bat, with two men on base, I took "Cannonball" out and sent Gene Tunney in to pitch. The eager Babe swung at the first pitch and poled it so hard and so far that if there hadn't been a roof on Madison Square Garden it might have landed in the

Hudson. The fans roared with glee, and not even Tunney begrudged the three runs.

We played a whole series against the Oystervelts, both at Sagamore Hill, the wonderful old home of President Theodore Roosevelt, and at Quaker Hill. Of course F.D.R. was never present for those games. Though the two families were closely related, there was a longtime antagonism between them, both personal and political. T.R.'s sons referred to themselves as the Oyster Bay "out-of-season" Roosevelts, and their references to their cousin Franklin are best left unrecorded. The Nine Old Men-Oystervelt encounter I remember best is the one in which, taking this family feud into account, I perpetrated some mischief.

There was a vaudevillian in those days named Billy B. Van who bore an eerie resemblance to President Roosevelt. Cleverly made up to enhance the illusion, wearing a felt hat and waving a long cigarette holder, he had made a night-club success imitating F.D.R. With only my secretary privy to the secret, I arranged for Billy Van to come to Quaker Hill.

The occasion was another game with the Oystervelts. The grandstand was packed that day, and hundreds of additional people lined the foul lines. Suddenly, with Ted Roosevelt at the bat, into the outfield rolled a black open touring car flanked by state troopers; inside, beaming at the crowd and waving the ever-present cigarette holder was—was it? Yes, of course!—President Roosevelt!

Ted's jaw dropped. Obviously he didn't know whether to laugh or cry. He certainly couldn't leave—not even a Roosevelt can turn his back on the President. For a moment I thought he would solve his dilemma by crowning me with his bat. Then, as the car was driven across the infield, the players and the crowd were completely taken in, bowing to the "President." I went up to the plate and whispered in Ted's ear.

With a broad grin and still carrying his bat, he ran out to the car, hopped up on the running board and shook the "President's" hand. While the crowd, still not too sure what was happening, cheered and applauded, the newsreel cameras filmed the scene. I have always wondered whether F.D.R. ever saw this Quaker Hill "reconciliation" between the estranged branches of the Roosevelt family.

These days, a slightly more jaded interval in the human

parade, I marvel at the fun and enthusiasm those games generated, the crowds that turned out to see us play, the teams thrown together at the drop of a challenge, the luminaries, many of them highly unlikely ball players, who came to enliven the games—Sir Hubert Wilkins, Harold Ross, Grantland Rice, Eddie Rickenbacker, Vilhjalmur Stefansson, Roy Chapman Andrews, Rube Goldberg, Henry Morgenthau, Jimmy Doolittle, Deems Taylor, Bernard Gimbel, Westbrook Pegler, Lawrence Tibbett, Lanny Ross, Jimmy Walker, and I could go on and on.

Of all the good men who ever pulled on a glove for the Nine Old Men, the best player—and one of the most thoroughly decent human beings I have ever known—was the air ace, Captain Frank Hawks. Always good natured and unaffected, he was a joy to be around, and many of us were in his debt without even knowing it. Although he was our most expert pitcher, I remember one game in which he let a rather inept opponent get four straight hits off him because the man's wife was watching. And one day, when Winthrop Rockefeller was looking the other way, Frank Hawks sent him spinning, fully clothed, into the pool. Whereupon tall and husky Winthrop returned the compliment. He had climbed out, dripping and spluttering, to administer the same dose to Hawks, the famous speed flyer who a few years before had been a carnival high-dive artist.

On another occasion Frank had flown to our game in an experimental plane. Afterward, en route to Buffalo, he stopped somewhere to refuel and, taking off, flew into some high-tension wires he hadn't seen. I wept at the funeral service, and those who didn't wanted to. Though none of us could realize it, an era was ending.

Those glorious days at Quaker Hill are much on my mind now, though forty years and more have rushed by since the heyday of the Nine Old Men. Long past are the evenings of stimulating talk with the likes of Tom Dewey, Ed Murrow, Norman Vincent Peale, Casey Hogate, Ralph Carson, Charlie Murphy, Ralph Lankler. Most of them are gone.

As for the Hill itself, it hasn't changed too much. Of course most of my special friends, and my bride of fifty-eight years, are no longer there. But I can drive past the empty ball field and hear again the crowd laughing and cheering. Or if I look across at Strawberry Hill on a winter's day, I can just about see Tom Dewey stepping onto skis for the first time. For years I had pleaded with him to give it a try. Alas, he finally chose a cold day after a January thaw, when the Hill was a sheet of ice. I should have told him to stay in bed. The moment he was released from friendly supporting arms, down went the Governor of the Sovereign State of New York and, despite my best efforts and those of ski pro Jim Parker, there he was, flat on the ice. Although he did persist, he spent most of the next hour on his derriere. In time, shaken, cold and thoroughly disillusioned, supported only by his sense of humor, Tom Dewey said, "Tommy, I thought you were my friend." Whereupon he shed his gear and so far as I know never went near a ski slope again.

Time and again I am asked, of all the unusual events in which you have been involved, which one stands out most vividly in your memory? To this there is no easy answer. The Palestine campaign, when Allenby took Jerusalem from the Turks, could head the list, or going to Arabia and bringing back the story of T. E. Lawrence might be number one. Then there was the German revolution, one of the major events of the same era. As for the speaking tour of the world we did following the great war, what an incredible experience it was! Our long and unusual journeys in Malaya, Burma, India and little-known Afghanistan were high adventure to the nth degree. The list is long and would include the first flight around the world and the Caribbean cruise aboard Count von Luckner's sailing ship. Earlier adventures as a gold miner, as a newspaperman in Colorado and Chicago, and early travels in Alaska would have to be considered. Then in later years there were more wars, a dozen or so expeditions to the Arctic, the Antarctic, to the tropics of Africa, South America, New Guinea, Australia, Siberia, Central Asia, and across the Himalayas to Tibet. I also would have to include the launching of Cinerama which resulted in a worldwide screen revolution.

But one event that still stands out vividly was the abdication of the young King who sat on the throne of the far-flung British Empire and the coronation of his brother George VI. Since I had known him as a young prince in World War I, and years later had been with him for a short time in India, for drama and pageantry this has to approach the ultimate.

Through the crackle of static, the voice reached us from across the sea, thin but unwavering, strengthened by conviction. The date was December 11, 1936, and the radio broadcast climaxed what many called the news story of the decade—not knowing what the decade still had in store for us—Edward VIII abdicating the throne of the British Empire for an American divorcée, Wallis Warfield Simpson. He was saying to his people, and to the listening world:

> You must believe me when I tell you that I have found it impossible to carry the heavy burden of responsibility and to discharge my duties as King as I should wish to do without the help and support of the woman I love.

Perhaps we should have seen beyond the titillation of an international romance between king and commoner. In truth, it was a portent of things to come, a beginning of the demise of the order the victors had so painfully built on the ruins of the First World War. This same year, the Spanish Civil War erupted with bombs falling on innocent cities; Mussolini completed his conquest of Ethiopia, and Hitler remilitarized Germany in defiance of the Versailles Treaty and was soon to send his troops marching into the Rhineland.

In May of 1937, when there was an eleventh-hour decision to outdo our competition by going to London to cover the coronation of King George VI for Movietone, I arranged to spend the preceding ten days with a firsthand look at Europe's descent toward the abyss, a grim counterpoint to the pomp and panoply we were to film at Westminster Abbey.

Upon arrival, my first move was to arrange interviews with several of Europe's leaders. Even to the casual observer they offered a dispiriting contrast. While the dictators solidified their standings with bluster and iron fists, the governments of England and France wavered uncertainly. Stanley Baldwin, who had been in the eye of the storm surrounding Edward's abdication, was to resign as Prime Minister a week after the coronation, and the name he was to present to the new King as his preferred successor was Neville Chamberlain. Léon Blum had become the French

328

premier only days before, and he would be out in little more than a year.

I was surprised and much pleased when Premier Blum agreed to go on the air with me, for this was an unheard-of departure from protocol for national leaders. It seemed to me there were serious matters to discuss, but Monsieur Blum had other ideas and turned the program into a promotion for French travel and tourism.

A few days later I was in Rome for an interview with Mussolini. He received me in the Palazzo Venezia, in one of those vast, magnificent Renaissance rooms. At the far end, across an acre of marble floor, Il Duce sat glowering behind a desk. There was not another stick of furniture in the entire room.

I wondered if Benito was disappointed when I negotiated the vast distance from door to desk without slipping on the glossy floor. Although he did rise to greet me, he provided no chair and I simply stood there as he responded to my questions with the fiery phrases the world was growing accustomed to hearing from the dictators: "The masses must obey; they cannot afford to waste time searching for the truth." If Italy was to have a Fascist empire, the people would have to be worthy of it; they must be proud to live in Mussolini's time. "If I advance," he had told them, "follow me. If I retreat, kill me. If I die, avenge me."

We walked through the fifteenth-century door out onto the famous balcony overlooking the historic piazza. Almost at once there was a crowd, chanting, *"Duce! Duce! Duce!"*

The day before I flew to London for the big event, I sat at a window in the Paris Ritz with two famous men. One was Michael Arlen, who had made a fortune from his novel *The Green Hat*. The other was one of Britain's press lords, an ex-Canadian, Lord Beaverbrook. When I asked the publisher of the *Daily Express* whether all British nobility would be on hand for the coronation at Westminster, he said they all would be there—but one. He also had no intention of attending, so fed up was he over the way his countrymen had treated their young King.

Prior to leaving New York I had written to several of my friends in London, men I had known in World War I days when they were young and who now were occupying government posts of importance. I told them I knew all seats in the Abbey had been assigned, and I didn't want them to do anything for me as a friend. But I said my coronation broadcasts would be heard throughout America, so—if they had any suggestions as to what I might do— and so on and so on. Little did I dream how lucky I was going to be.

The American to whom the British felt most indebted in those days was J. P. Morgan, who had raised the vast loans so vital to their war effort. He had fallen ill in Scotland, and at the last minute I was given his seat. When I got to Westminster Abbey I found I was almost directly above the throne. Directly across was the box occupied by the royal family. Below on one side were all the lords in their robes and ermine, and on the opposite side of the throne were their ladies in similar array, waiting to put on their glittering coronets the moment the Archbishop of Canterbury placed the Imperial crown on the head of his King-Emperor.

King Edward's equerry sat directly behind me. Others nearby included the Aga Khan, a number of potentates from distant lands, and behind a nearby pillar sat the tall, irascible and autocratic founder and head of the BBC, Lord Reith (then Sir John Reith), who would have looked even more glum had he known I had a far better seat.

To accommodate as many thousands as possible, the temporary tiers of seats were built so you were tightly wedged between your neighbors. Since you were there for hours, you soon became acquainted with those near you. On my right I was rubbing elbows with Lady Jeffreys, whose husband at the time was the highest ranking officer in the British Army and A.D.C. General to the King. It was he who rode at the head of the coronation procession. At noon, when George VI proceeded up the aisle to the throne, General Sir George Jeffreys dropped into the seat at the other side of his wife. She had pointed out to me how many of the lords and ladies below us had been bringing out sandwiches from beneath their robes. She also had come similarly prepared and shared hers with me.

When I inquired about the press, the several hundred newsmen who had come from all over the world, I was told they were far above us, in the tower, from where, with the aid of binoculars, they could get a glimpse of the ceremony. Webb Miller, of the United Press, my Chicago pal of prewar days, spotted me with a hand telescope. He was dumbfounded, and no wonder.

After the ceremony I did my broadcast to America from a BBC studio which I shared with poet laureate John Masefield.

Prosper, Truman Talley and I stayed up all night after the crowning of the new King, editing the film and recording the narration. Then we rushed the reels to a U.S.-bound steamer. Five days later, an airplane took off from New York, flew to the limit of its outbound range, where it found the ship steaming westward, and snatched the film off its deck with a hooked rope. And so in those primitive days before transatlantic air travel, Fox-Movietone had found a way to scoop its rivals.

Two days after our all-night session of cutting, editing and narrating the spectacular coronation films, we headed for home aboard the *Queen Mary*. A fortnight before, on the way over, I had met a lady who told me a refreshingly American story. When planning to sail to England for the coronation, she had seen a news item about the chauffeur of the former King. Having driven Mrs. Simpson to Cannes immediately after the abdication, he now found himself out of a job. Without delay, the good lady, who owned the Absorbine Jr. company, cabled him to meet her with a car at Southampton: she was engaging him for the coronation week. Now, homeward bound, I included in my shortwave broadcast from the ship how, for the coronation period, the ex-King's chauffeur had become the chauffeur for the queen of Absorbine Jr.

Well, if you will forgive the unavoidable pun, the little item riled some Royal blood—that of John Royal, head of NBC, and in his day the colossus of the radio world. John, as was true of many Americans, had long been an admirer of England's young King and had a much-prized signed photograph of Edward VIII on his Radio City office wall. When the Wally Simpson romance developed, General Sarnoff insisted he remove it lest he confuse the rank and file as to their first loyalty. So he had it in his coat closet and often brought it out to show to a visitor. Now my broadcast infuriated him, and he fired off a wire to me aboard ship to tell me I had used miserable judgment, worse taste and, on top of it all, had committed a flagrant violation of the so-called "dual sponsorship" rule by mentioning Absorbine Jr. on a program paid for by Sun Oil.

I thought it all over—for a few minutes. Then I went up to the radio room and wired back:

DEAR JOHN, IF YOU ARE REALLY IRRITATED
I SUGGEST YOU TRY ABSORBINE JUNIOR.
LOWELL

A week or so after my return, having heard that Royal was so mad he had threatened to fire everyone at NBC, I stopped by his office to make peace. "Look," I said to his glamorous blond receptionist, Miss O'Connor, "I'd like to have a talk with your boss."

Smiling sweetly, she replied: "I suggest you come back about a *year* from now!"

George Gershwin was also standing there waiting for an appointment. He went in. I didn't.

However, several years later John Royal and I were at a banquet where I was the speaker and I couldn't resist telling the story to the audience. Had he really been all that angry at me when he sent the radio message to the *Queen Mary?* I don't know. On this occasion his laugh was the heartiest, and we have remained friends down the years.

It would be a long time between laughs thereafter. When Europe marched inexorably on to war, on the evening of September 1, 1939, I broadcast the bleak news to America:

It's a heavyhearted thing tonight to begin the reciting of war bulletins. Today the German command announced an advance all along the line, drives into Poland on three sides, pushing on everywhere . . .

Warsaw was bombed several times.

London and Paris took simultaneous action. . . . If Nazi Germany doesn't draw back . . . Great Britain and France will intervene in the struggle. . . .

Every American is thinking—what about ourselves?

Then came the December Sunday in 1941 with the news of the Japanese attack on Pearl Harbor. So the wondering was over: we were in it, too.

None of us could be sure what the future held. The United States, wanting peace, prepared for a long and bitter war. Young Lowell, then an undergraduate at Dartmouth, tried at once to organize an aerial squadron patterned after the Lafayette Escadrille of World War I. As for me, I would soon be off to cover the war fronts. A golden age was over for all of us, for all Americans. And in the spring, it was poignantly underscored by a brief letter I received from President Roosevelt:

Dear Lowell, I am afraid Hitler has ended our ball games for the duration. . . . As ever yours, F.D.R.

AVON ◆ THE BEST IN
BESTSELLING ENTERTAINMENT!